A

BOOK

The Philip E. Lilienthal imprint
honors special books
in commemoration of a man whose work
at University of California Press from 1954 to 1979
was marked by dedication to young authors
and to high standards in the field of Asian Studies.
Friends, family, authors, and foundations have together
endowed the Lilienthal Fund, which enables UC Press
to publish under this imprint selected books
in a way that reflects the taste and judgment
of a great and beloved editor.

The Age of Irreverence

STUDIES OF THE WEATHERHEAD EAST ASIAN INSTITUTE,
COLUMBIA UNIVERSITY

The Studies of the Weatherhead East Asian Institute of Columbia University were inaugurated in 1962 to bring to a wider public the results of significant new research on modern and contemporary East Asia.

The Age of Irreverence

A New History of Laughter in China

新笑史

Christopher Rea

UNIVERSITY OF CALIFORNIA PRESS

The Publisher gratefully acknowledges the generous support of the Philip E. Lilienthal Asian Studies Endowment Fund of the University of California Press Foundation, which was established by a major gift from Sally Lilienthal.

University of California Press, one of the most distinguished university presses in the United States, enriches lives around the world by advancing scholarship in the humanities, social sciences, and natural sciences. Its activities are supported by the UC Press Foundation and by philanthropic contributions from individuals and institutions. For more information, visit www.ucpress.edu.

University of California Press
Oakland, California

© 2015 by The Regents of the University of California

All rights reserved.

First Paperback Printing 2025

Library of Congress Cataloging-in-Publication Data

Rea, Christopher G., author.
 The age of irreverence : a new history of laughter in China / Christopher Rea.
  pages cm
 Includes bibliographical references.
 ISBN 978-0-520-28384-8 (hardcover)—978-0-520-41927-8 (pbk) 1. Chinese wit and humor—History and criticism.
2. Popular culture—China—History—19th century. I. Title.
 PL2403.R43 2015
 895.17'4809—dc23   2015010050
 GPSR Authorized Representative: Easy Access System Europe, Mustamäe tee 50, 10621 Tallinn, Estonia, gpsr.requests@easproject.com

For Julie, Peregrin, and Permenia

The world today seems absolutely crackers
With nuclear bombs to blow us all sky high.
There's fools and idiots sitting on the trigger.
It's depressing and it's senseless and that's why . . .
—ERIC IDLE, "I LIKE CHINESE" (1980)

CONTENTS

Executive Preface   ix
Acknowledgments   xiii

1. Breaking into Laughter 失笑   1
2. Jokes 笑話百出   16
3. Play 游戲大觀   40
4. Mockery 罵人的藝術   78
5. Farce 滑稽魂   106
6. The Invention of Humor 幽默年   132
   Epilogue 笑死   159

Appendix 1: Selected Chinese Humor Collections, 1900–1937   167
Appendix 2: Which Classic? Editions and Paratexts   193
Abbreviations   199
Notes   201
Glossary   267
Bibliography   291
Index   319

EXECUTIVE PREFACE

Congratulations on buying the Executive Edition of this book. You have chosen wisely, and I value your discerning taste in deciding to pay the few extra cents for a product of real quality. Everything in this book has been designed to meet the exacting standards that you have naturally come to expect. The content has been quality graded to give you the finest in reading pleasure. The paper itself has been milled from the very finest British Columbian softwood. The text has been printed to fit exactly onto the pages of your book, or e-reader, with all the precision of finest Californian craftsmanship. There is little or no offending academic jargon apart from four metacritical interventions, two hermeneutical exegeses, and a paradigmatic (re)inscription. And as they only occur in this preface, you're past them now.

"An age of irreverence, happily exploding established rituals" is how historian Neil Harris has described the cultural atmosphere of pre–Civil War America.[1] The Jacksonian era witnessed a decline in the prestige of the expert. An American public distrustful of authorities now acclaimed the common man as the arbiter of fact versus humbug and delighted in exposing, satirizing, and mocking commonplaces and bogus knowledge. Yet this new cultural trend of go-getting skepticism had unexpected results. Among other things, it created opportunities for a new generation of entrepreneurs, not least such purveyors of humbug as the showman and hoaxster P. T. Barnum.

A similarly dubious attitude toward authority animated Chinese culture during the first decades of the twentieth century. The late Qing period, which began with several aborted reform efforts in the 1890s, and the Republican era ushered in by the 1911 revolution, were turbulent times. Life in dynastic China had long been replete with established rituals, both in court and among the populace. The Confucian classics were the basis of learning and political advancement. But in the wake of the Opium Wars and the Taiping Rebellion, social confidence plummeted. From the late nineteenth century and culminating with the iconoclastic May Fourth Movement of 1919, Chinese intellectuals, frustrated with what they saw as the backwardness of the empire and captivated by Japanese and Western models of modernization, attacked the established order and challenged cultural authorities of old. A seemingly endless succession of crises continued to erode moral certainties with bewildering speed, fueling anxieties about China's future. Revolutionaries overthrew the Manchus in 1911, but the republic that replaced China's last dynasty inspired little faith in new institutions or ways of thought.

Chinese writers and artists responded to these social and political convulsions with various forms of laughter. They caricatured their abusers. They told jokes to lighten, or at least commiserate about, the latest depressing news. They mocked old and new cultural habits alike. They envisioned futures for China both comedic and absurd. This mirth was not merely a side effect of modernization because it influenced some of the directions that modern Chinese culture was to take. Jokes, play, mockery, farce, and humor—the five cultural expressions of laughter I explore in this book—helped to shape the tone, the grammar, and the vocabulary of modern China. These different comedic sensibilities, each symbolized by a term popular during that era, became integral to the business of a burgeoning publishing industry and conspicuous features of a modern print culture that crossed national borders. In spirit and in form, they remain a part of Chinese literary expression today. Even the ways that people talk about what's funny owes much to the legacy of the early twentieth century.

This book surveys several Chinese cultures of comic amusement and shows how they changed in the modern age. It traces how writers, artists, entrepreneurs, and audiences helped to shape modern China through a broader culture of irreverence. It highlights the central role that print and other media played during this period in democratizing Chinese humor and broadcasting it farther than ever before. The diversity of comic sensibilities found here should confound any notion that Chinese people have a limited, monolithic or static sense of humor. But above all, this is a study of the poetics and rhetorics of laughter itself, one that explores from a new perspective a chapter in the history of the Chinese language.

Humor studies—a risible discipline if ever there was one—lives with helpful truisms like E. B. White's: "Humor can be dissected, as a frog can, but the thing dies in the process and the innards are discouraging to any but the pure scientific mind."[2] But if the law of diminishing returns works swiftly in this particular field of scholarly inquiry, I am unconvinced that it is summarily lethal. White's premise, to begin with, is questionable: at least in certain American high schools, the frog is dead before it even reaches the lab. As much as I might like to think of historians as sadistic conjurors, few of us would resurrect frogs only to kill them off again. As for pitting the scientist against the artist, it is not hard to think of confounding examples, such as Ding Xilin, the physicist and comic playwright who appears in chapter 6. Henri Bergson's *Le Rire* offers a simile that I find more apt for my own approach to the topic. Bergson likened the comic poet to a naturalist who enumerates and describes the main varieties of a species in order to define it. The same might be said of someone curious about how the frog interacts with other critters in its ecosystem—what it feeds on, how it reproduces, and where it exists on the food chain.

Scholars who follow the historiography promoted by the Chinese Communist Party tend to view the cultural milieu of late Qing and Republican China as akin to an alligator-infested swamp in which predators fought tooth and nail for survival and dominance. They rarely notice the frogs. Some, squinting through the opaque glasses of ideology at what the Party after 1949 dubbed the "Old Society," have even mistaken the frogs for leeches. This book—to flog the metaphor—tries to get at what all the croaking was about, to convey something of its various intonations, and to show what the comic cultures of this period spawned. Not all the frogs died off during the Anti-Japanese War or after the establishment of the People's Republic in 1949. Though the cultural ecosystem has changed dramatically several times since the early twentieth century, its timbre and pitch, at times, echo the earlier epoch discussed in these chapters.

Readers curious about the historical and theoretical issues that motivated this study may proceed directly to chapter 1. Those who suspect they might prefer other people's jokes to mine should consult chapter 2. Parody and humorous allegory sprawled widely across Chinese entertainment culture of the early twentieth century; chapter 3 offers a sampling. Gentle readers are advised to skip altogether the curses in chapter 4. If you caught a whiff of Python in the preamble, you might appreciate the discussion of plagiarism and hoaxes in chapter 5. Moralists will enjoy the polemics bandied about in chapter 6, which shows how creative writers, critics, and cultural institutions contributed to what I call the "invention of humor." The epilogue briefly discusses several legacies of late Qing and Republican China's cultures of laughter, including later cycles of death and rebirth. But first, please turn the page to meet the people who made this study possible.

ACKNOWLEDGMENTS

But he is worst, who (beggarly) doth chaw
Others' wits' fruits, and in his ravenous maw
Rankly digested, doth those things out-spew,
As his own things; and they are his own, 'tis true,
For if one eat my meat, though it be known
The meat was mine, th' excrement is his own.

—JOHN DONNE, CA. 1595[1]

I worked on this book, on and off, for the better part of a decade. Readers will decide for themselves whether or not the fruits of others' wits have come out well digested. What began as a literary study soon grew into a more omnivorous project of tracing comic ideas across genres and identifying conventions and outliers. Cartoons, joke books, films, biographies, scholarly studies, dictionaries, advertisements, and various print culture ephemera together, I've come to believe, offer a more comprehensive picture of early twentieth-century comedy than do literary works alone. This is particularly true in China, where periodical publishing enabled much of the proliferation of humor and shaped some of the forms it took. Note that, with the exception of a few diaries and letters, this study is mostly confined to what people put into print.

Research involved a fair amount of treasure hunting. I sought out original editions when possible, since these give a better and more accurate sense of context than later anthologies. I had a lot of help with research leads; these and other scholarly debts I credit in the notes. The notes are also the place to look for additional details on some of the stories behind this story, including the cut and thrust of ongoing scholarly debates. I hope that you, like me, enjoy a book that can be read in more than one way.

Here I would like to thank Monty Python, an inspiring companion since childhood, and an amusing muse to this day. One of the highlights of a year I spent at the Australian National University was an evening show at the Canberra Theatre featuring John Cleese. Eric Idle I thank for permission to use lyrics from his song (performed in the Pythons' 2014 reunion show) in the epigraph.

David Der-wei Wang first gave me the opportunity to pursue Chinese literature as a career and has been a generous mentor ever since. Eugenia Lean, Anne Prescott (who introduced me to Donne), Shang Wei, and the late Pei-yi Wu shaped this book's first incarnation as a doctoral dissertation at Columbia University. At Dartmouth, where I learned Chinese, I had an exceptional group of teachers, among them Sarah Allan, Susan Blader, Shelby Grantham, Lynn Higgins, Li Xueqin, Annabelle Melzer, the late Konrad von Moltke, Hua-yuan Li Mowry, and the late Peter Rushton.

Friends and colleagues made the process of writing this book a joy. Huzzah for Alexander Beels, Michael Berry, Sue Jean Cho, Eileen Cheng-yin Chow, Dong Xinyu (who introduced me to the work of Neil Harris), Linda Feng, Rivi Handler-Spitz, Michael Hill, Hui-Lin Hsu, Wilt Idema, Paize Keulemans, S. E. Kile, Liao Ping-hui, Hayes Moore, Thomas Mullaney, Shaw-yu Pan, Song Mingwei, Song Weijie, Nicolai Volland, Wang Pin, Wang Xiaojue, Joe Wicentowski, Ellen Widmer, Wong Nim Yan, You Jingxian, Zha Mingjian, and Zhang Enhua. Special thanks to Enhua, Hayes, Joe, Michael, Mingwei, Nico, Paize, and Tom for commenting on individual chapters, as well as to H. Tiffany Lee for generously sharing her research on early Chinese photography. Markuz Wernli created the composite images in chapters 2 and 3.

In Taiwan, Hu Siao-chen, Peng Hsiao-yen, and Yang Mu sponsored me on two occasions to spend a year doing research at the Institute of Chinese Literature and Philosophy of the Academia Sinica, first during graduate school and later during a faculty sabbatical. Mei Chia-ling and her students welcomed me into the academic community at National Taiwan University in 2004. Dr. Wu Jing-jyi, Julie Hu and the staff of the Fulbright Foundation in Taiwan were generous hosts. Jen-Peng Liu and Ho Li-hsing made it possible for me to teach an undergraduate class on modern Chinese comic literature in the Chinese Department at National Tsinghua University in 2005—an extraordinary opportunity for an American graduate student. More recently, Professor Hsiao Feng-Hsien invited me to give a series of talks adapted from this book at Buddhist Tzu Chi University; thanks to her and her colleagues and students for hosting me in Hualien in 2014.

In Suzhou, Fan Boqun introduced me to the works of Xu Zhuodai. Tang Zhesheng, who wrote the first book on *huaji* literature, shared books from his collection. "Dean" Ji Jin invited me to participate in multiple conferences at Suzhou University—the Deputy Dean salutes! I am grateful for the friendship and hospitality of Brenton, Jennie, Isabella, and Marguerite Smith, who hosted me during several research trips in Shanghai.

Library staff members at the University of British Columbia, the University of Washington, the Australian National University, Columbia University, Harvard University, the Academia Sinica, Fudan University, Suzhou University, the Shanghai Library, and the Suzhou Municipal Library went beyond the call of duty to help me access research materials. I would like to thank in particular Liu Jing at UBC's Asian Library, Ouyang Dipin at the National Library of Australia, and Zhang Chengzhi of the C.V. Starr East Asian Library at Columbia for their assistance.

Danke to Hans Harder and Barbara Mittler for including me in a workshop on *Punch* magazine at the University of Heidelberg in 2009 and to Barbara again for inviting me back to Heidelberg to give a seminar on early Republican satirical periodicals in 2011. Rudolf Wagner provided invaluable comments during both trips and in subsequent correspondence. I-Wei Wu shared rare late Qing and Republican periodicals and cartoons.

My research was generously funded by Columbia University's Graduate School of Arts and Sciences, Harvard University's Graduate School of Arts and Sciences, the Weatherhead East Asian Institute at Columbia University, the Chiang Ching-kuo Foundation for International Scholarly Exchange, the Fulbright Foundation, the Whiting Foundation, the Ministry of Education of the Republic of China, the US Department of Education (FLAS), the Peter Wall Institute for Advanced Studies at UBC, the Social Sciences and Humanities Research Council of Canada, and the Australian Centre on China in the World.

I have the great good fortune to work with fantastic colleagues at UBC. I would particularly like to thank Lonnie Chase, Timothy Cheek, Ross King, Christina Laffin, Joshua Mostow, Anne Murphy, Maija Norman, and the members of the UBC China Studies Group. I appreciate the research assistance of Michelle Cheng, Xenia Chiu, Si Nae Park, and Wu Meng.

I spent 2012 on a postdoctoral research fellowship at the Australian Centre on China in the World at the Australian National University. I am grateful to Geremie Barmé, Gloria Davies, Benjamin Penny and the other members of the CIW management group for affording me this opportunity. A conversation with Ben and Geremie inspired me to radically redesign (and—reader, take note—shorten) this book. Fellow postdocs David Brophy, Shih-Wen Chen, Johanna Hood, Elisa Nesossi, and Qian Ying were excellent companions. William Sima shared valuable research materials and ideas during our collaboration on a special issue of *China Heritage Quarterly* devoted to *The China Critic*. Jessica Milner Davis was the first to make my family welcome when we set foot on Australian soil. She also introduced me to the Australasian Humour Studies Network and invited me to speak at its symposium at the ANU. Equally welcoming was Jocelyn Chey, who hosted my family in Sydney. I've benefited greatly from Jessica and Jocelyn's research expertise, especially their two edited volumes on Chinese humor. Gerry Groot and Claire M. Roberts at University of Adelaide; Gloria Davies at Monash University; Debra Aarons and Yu Haiqing at the University of New South Wales; and Bonnie McDougall at University of Sydney made it possible for me to give talks related to this book project, and to meet Australian scholars who contributed to its development. While at the ANU, I also benefited from conversations with Duncan Campbell, John Makeham, Mark Strange, and Veronica Ye Zhengdao.

Parts of chapter 5 originally appeared as an article in the journal *Modern Chinese Literature and Culture*; thanks to Kirk Denton for permission to reproduce them. Thanks to Jim Cheng, Anatoly Detwyler, and Eugenia Lean for helping me to obtain the image that appears on this book's cover.

I am indebted to Linda Jaivin, who reviewed a draft of the manuscript and improved its style considerably. Perry Link and three anonymous reviewers at the University of California Press I thank for their invaluable suggestions during the refereeing process. Reed Malcolm, an inspired editor, has been enthusiastic about this project since we first met. Michael Bohrer-Clancy, Stacy Eisenstark, and Francisco Reinking ably saw the book through production. Looking for a good copyeditor? Her name is Robin O'Dell.

With love and affection, I thank my family: Pat, John, and Alexander Rea, Jin and Tsui-yen Wang, Emily Wang, Chris Crew, and Malcolm Wang. I dedicate this book to Julie Ming Wang, and to our children, Peregrin and Permenia, from whom I've learned that the age of irreverence is between two and six—no, seven . . .

1

Breaking into Laughter
失笑

In 1903, Wu Jianren, one of the most innovative and prolific Chinese writers of the early twentieth century, began serializing two works in the same issue of Yokohama's *New Fiction*, a leading literary journal of Chinese reformers in exile. The first, a novel, he entitled *A History of Pain*; the second, a series of jokes, he called *A New History of Laughter*.[1]

These two titles appeared at a moment when China's future was unclear. The Qing court was still reeling from an 1895 defeat in the Sino-Japanese War, an aborted reform movement in 1898, and, close on its heels, the Boxer Rebellion. Wu was among a group of educated men who might once have sought a position in the government bureaucracy but were now turning to literary and entrepreneurial pursuits for a living. In expressing their emotional state, these writers tended to put anguish front and center. *A History of Pain* appeared at the front of the journal and *A New History of Laughter* at the back. Then there is the novel *The Travels of Lao Can*, which Wu's contemporary, Liu E, started writing that same year, and which begins as follows: "When a baby is born, he weeps, *wa-wa*; and when a man is old and dying, his family forms a circle around him and wails, *hao-t'ao*. Thus weeping is certainly that with which a man starts and finishes his life. In the interval, the quality of a man is measured by how much or little he weeps, for weeping is the expression of a spiritual nature." "The passionate weeper," as Liu styles himself, invites readers to join him in weeping.[2]

Liu was invoking an age-old idea: that tears are a powerful vehicle of communion among humans, or even with the cosmos. In the legend of Meng Jiangnü, a northern peasant woman goes in search of her beloved husband, a corvée laborer on the Great Wall, only to discover that he has died and been buried within it, and her weeping causes the wall to collapse.³

Cultural revolutionaries of the modern era spoke of tears as a vehicle of social empowerment. One catalytic moment was the May Fourth Movement of 1919, when students and other citizens of the Republic of China, infuriated at its poor treatment under the Treaty of Versailles, demanded radical changes to Chinese culture. In 1921, activist Zheng Zhenduo called for writers to reject the traditional focus on beauty and replace it with a "literature of blood and tears" that would accurately represent the sufferings of the Chinese people.⁴

In 1924, a popular Shanghai writer named Cheng Zhanlu published a response to the current literary trend: "A Delightful Story of Blood and Tears." He noted, by way of introducing the piece: "People nowadays who write tragic stories [*aiqing xiaoshuo*] always like to sprinkle them with words like blood and tears. But whether or not a story is sad is *not*, in fact, determined by the literal meaning of the words themselves. Today I've written a joyous story [*xiqing xiaoshuo*] and mixed in the word 'blood' eight times and the word 'tears' ten times. Based on the words themselves, it should be excruciating. But actually, this is a tale of not pain, but delight." Sure enough, his story is awash with tears of joy. It begins: "The *blood*-like sun set slowly in the west. In an upstairs apartment two newlyweds were whispering sweet nothings to each other. Their *blood* cells were filled with a million of the deepest passions. As *blood* pulsed round and round in their veins, the husband said, 'My darling.'"⁵

Cheng's parody inverted an old cliché: if laughter is often a cover for tears, a writer can also use tears and blood to evoke laughter. "Selling tears," the scholar-writer Qian Zhongshu later remarked, has been no less useful to writers "than the courtesan's ploy of 'selling smiles.'" Even the famed "debt of tears" owed by Lin Daiyu, the tragic heroine of the canonical Qing dynasty novel *Dream of the Red Chamber*, he said, was something of a bribe, one that used pathos as currency in an emotional transaction.⁶

The tears–laughter pairing has remained a conspicuous part of modern Chinese culture since Wu Jianren's day, but it seems to have been a particular obsession during the early twentieth century. One of the best-selling novels of the 1930s, Zhang Henshui's *Fate in Tears and Laughter* (1931), invoked it as a metaphor for the vicissitudes of life. A decade later, Lin Yutang's polemical English-language book *Between Tears and Laughter* (1943, later translated into Chinese) used it as a symbol of intellectuals' anguished frustration. Left-leaning, politically progressive films of the 1930s, such as Sun Yu's *Daybreak* (1933), habitually represented the lives of the urban lower classes as tragicomic.

Modern Chinese writers have invoked blood and tears even when cracking jokes. One of the most prolific fiction writers of the Republican era went by the pen name Bao Tianxiao, or Embrace Heaven and Laugh. When he coauthored works with the writer Cold-Blooded, they combined their noms de plume into a Cold Laugh, or Sneer. The 1914 joke book *Laughing Through Tears* tells of a "man of conscience" who moves his audiences by weeping at the beginning of each speech; the stimulant turns out to be raw ginger hidden in his handkerchief. *The Travels of Lao Can*, plaintive preface notwithstanding, offers a zesty picaresque tale, and generations of readers have found it to be a very funny book.[7]

The Chinese Communist Party turned displays of tears into a political ritual during the civil war of the late 1940s, and again during the Mao era, by organizing meetings at which the people would "speak bitterness" (*suku*) about hardship under the Nationalists. But a few early promoters of realism for ideological purposes became aware that tragic catharsis has its limits. In 1924, the celebrated writer Lu Xun wrote "The New-Year's Sacrifice," a short story about a peasant woman who has suffered the death of two husbands, the loss of a job, and the shock of having her young son eaten by a wolf. Xianglin's wife goes around repeating her tale of woe to fellow villagers: "I was really stupid, really . . . I only knew that when it snows the wild beasts in the glen have nothing to eat and may come to the villages."[8] At first, her story draws genuine tears and sympathetic sighs from her audience. After several retellings, however, their sympathy turns to indifference and eventually contempt. They mimic her self-reproaches and mock her to her face. Her son's fate has not changed, but tragedy has collapsed under the weight of repetition.

Stories of trauma abound in contemporary scholarship on China. Michael Berry's study *A History of Pain*, which takes its title from Wu Jianren's novel, chronicles a litany of traumas that have buffeted modern China from without and within since the nineteenth century. David Der-wei Wang writes of a legacy of violence that has left modern Chinese literature haunted by "the monster that is history."[9] Wang Ban, drawing on the German literary critic Walter Benjamin, has likened modern Chinese history to an accumulation of wreckage. Official responses to historical trauma, which subscribe to a narrative of revolutionary modernization, "stare at the bloody image for a stunned moment, and then turn away to weave a narrative in a hurry, [striving] to shape nonmeaning into meaning, the absurd into the tragic, the stagnant into the progressive, the horrific into the triumphant." Writers who rejected this progressivist narrative, he continues, learned instead to "linger on such images a bit longer, collect more fragments from the wreckage, and archive them for criticism and reflection."[10]

Another way of regarding history, as we saw with Wu Jianren's *A New History of Laughter*, is as an accumulation of jokes. Suffering does not always preempt laughter; it may even call for it. At the end of Shakespeare's *Love's Labour's Lost*, Rosalind exhorts the glib-tongued nobleman Biron to use his wit not to court her but to cheer the sick and dying. Only this penance will convince her of his sincerity. He objects that "Mirth cannot move a soul in agony," but Rosalind reminds him that

> A jest's prosperity lies in the ear
> Of him that hears it, never in the tongue
> Of him that makes it.
> (5.2.2804–5)

Chinese writers of the early twentieth century did not need a lover's encouragement to seek humorous ways to minister to the citizens of a dying empire (or, later, a sickly republic). Many threw themselves into cheering everyone up with gusto, conceiving of uses for laughter besides the palliative. Jokes could inspire reform; playfulness could lead to new discoveries; mockery could shame the powerful into better behavior. Conversely, laughter could be a symptom of cultural illness. In one of Lu Xun's most famous stories, "Diary of a Madman" (1918), the narrator raves about seeing daggers in men's smiles in a China as hypocritical and murderous as Macbeth's Scotland. Writers spoke of laughter and tears not just as opposites but also as symbols of a complex spectrum of feeling. They did so within a literary market increasingly subdivided by genre. This may be one reason why Wu Jianren wrote separate histories of laughter and pain, rather than just consigning laughter to a supporting role in a grand drama of historical trauma.

I use the word "laughter" in this book to denote a broad spectrum of attitudes and behaviors ranging from amusement to buffoonery to derision. I am interested in when and why certain modes of laughter have become culturally endemic and, at times, propelled history in unexpected directions. Few would argue that China's modern experience has been primarily jolly. But its wits and wags have arrested attention and influenced public sentiment. "Humorists fatten on trouble," E. B. White noted, and in modern China there was plenty of that to go around.[11] Even poison, the pharmacologist Li Shizhen discovered in the sixteenth century, can induce laughter if prepared with the right recipe.[12] And modern Chinese writers and artists have been adept at comic alchemy, converting toxic politics into nourishment for cultures of mirth.

A HISTORY OF LOSS

Shixiao 失笑, the phrase appearing in this chapter's title, means to give an inadvertent laugh, or to break into laughter. The word *xiao* 笑 itself has multiple possible meanings, as a verb (to laugh, to smile, to mock), as a descriptor (laughable, ridiculous, derisive), and as a noun (laughter, smile, joke, jest). Chinese shares the semantic overlap of smile/laugh with Romance languages such as Latin, Italian, French, and Spanish, and with German (*lächeln*, to smile; *lachen*, to laugh), though not with English.[13] The graph 笑 is rooted in natural imagery. A love poem in the

Classic of Poetry, dating back more than twenty-six hundred years, likens a young woman's fetching smile to "peach flowers blossoming bewitchingly, shining with youthful radiance." The metaphor of the smile as a flower in bloom can be found in other languages too.[14]

Chinese characters, however, allow for unique forms of visual wordplay (more examples of which appear in chapter 3). During the Song dynasty (960–1279), the poet Su Shi once criticized the overly literal interpretations in fellow poet Wang Anshi's book *Chinese Characters Explained* with a riddle that alluded to an ancient form of the graph. "Why does using bamboo to beat a dog result in laughter?" (Put bamboo 竹 on a dog 犬 and you get laughter 笑.)[15] Zhu Zhanji, who ruled as Emperor Xuanzong of the Ming dynasty, used a similar graphic pun in his 1427 painting *A Laugh* (see figure 1.1).[16]

Shixiao, to adopt a literal reading, could mean not to lose oneself to laughter but to lose laughter itself. In Umberto Eco's novel *The Name of the Rose*, a murder mystery set in a medieval Italian monastery leads to a copy of Aristotle's lost book on comedy. The murderer, who sees mirth as a metaphysical threat to the Benedictine order, has poisoned its pages so that readers laugh themselves to death. Discovered, he burns the book (in the process setting the entire library ablaze) so that the source of laughter is lost forever.[17]

In "A History of Laughter," a short story by the May Fourth writer Zhu Ziqing published around the same time as Cheng Zhanlu's parody, a young woman tells how her childhood penchant for hearty laughter eroded away.[18] She marries, and her laughter is suppressed by in-laws who demand that she conform to standards of ladylike propriety. The family falls on hard times and, step by step, her hearty laughter gives way to muted laughter, then silence, tears, and finally a numb inability to laugh or cry. Reaching abject middle age, she comes to resent the laughter of others.

The story makes an implicit call for women's liberation typical of socially progressive fiction of the 1920s. Readers responded with expressions of "inexpressible sorrow" and sympathy for the protagonist, calling her the oppressed "sacrificial object" of China's patriarchy, even as some blamed her for being too weak to cast off her slave mentality.[19] In this story, laughter is a pathetic foil to a broader social tragedy, and Zhu's history of laughter turns out to be about its disappearance.

In the 1930s, Zhu's story was anthologized in the influential *Compendium of China's New Literature*, making laughter's disappearance part of the modern Chinese literary canon.[20] Nor has the loss of laughter been purely fictional or metaphorical. When it appeared in 1902, the political reformer Liang Qichao's futuristic novel *The Future of New China* (discussed in chapter 3) was accompanied by playful commentaries; most later anthologies left them out, in doing so hiding Liang's participation in the bantering side of Chinese literary culture.

FIGURE 1.1. "A Laugh" (1427), a hanging scroll painted by Emperor Xuanzong of the Ming dynasty. Image courtesy of the Nelson-Atkins Museum of Art, Kansas City, Missouri. Purchase: William Rockhill Nelson Trust, 45–39.

After the founding of the People's Republic of China (PRC) in 1949, every schoolchild learned that the Old Society was a time of bitter suffering; the only people who laughed in that era's propagandistic depictions of the Old Society were evil capitalists and landlords. Any other past laughter became something to explain away. At best, as symbolized by the Party-lauded satire of Lu Xun, it testified to the resilience of the Chinese people, their ability to "make merry amidst their bitter lives" (*kuzhong zuole*), to allow themselves a "bitter smile" (*kuxiao*), or to mock their tormentors.

Various local forms of comic performance, such as Beijing- and Tianjin-based *xiangsheng* ("face-and-voice," often rendered as "comic cross-talk") and Shanghainese farce (*huaji xi*), had long provided vibrant, bawdy, and often politically satirical entertainment in village marketplaces, city streets, teahouses, theaters, and, during the Republican era, on the radio as well. During the early days of the PRC, as part of the Party's rejection of elite culture in favor of popular folk traditions, scholars transcribed routines by old masters of Shanghainese farce. Yet they were compelled to "clean them up" for political correctness. As the editor of Jiang Xiaoxiao's "Ah Guan from Shaoxing Rides the Train" explained in 1958, the play had originally made fun of country bumpkins, but, as peasants were now a venerated social class, he "realigned the satirical barb" to point at the son of a rustic rich man.[21]

In a very real sense, then, China's modern literary history is one of lost laughter. Yet, as many historians have pointed out, history is experienced differently than how it is later reconstructed as a series of events (contextualized with the benefit of historical hindsight) or transformed into myths to serve present agendas.[22] Histories of events tend to focus on the traumatic and the dramatic, rather than on everyday moments of communal or private amusement. The Old Society was a time of tears and sorrow—this is the bedrock myth on which the Communist Party after 1949 built its narrative of socialist progress. This book is a "new" history in part because the laughter of the preceding era tells a different story.

Breaking into laughter is, after all, an involuntary act. Doctors of early imperial China diagnosed excessively frequent or hearty laughter as being a symptom of mental illness, demon possession, food poisoning, poor circulation of the *qi*, or illness of the viscera. (A common prescription: stop laughing.) The Ming dynasty *Systematic Materia Medica* records pathological cases of involuntary, excessive laughter, including one woman who laughed uncontrollably for six months.[23] In late Qing and Republican China, people laughed in spite of authoritative voices claiming either that they should not laugh or, after the fact, that they did not laugh. What a person does with the "uninvited snicker," E. B. White wrote, with hyperbole that his contemporary Lin Yutang, then hailed as China's "Master of Humor," would appreciate, "decides his destiny."[24] Not a few Chinese writers invited snickers by parroting injunctions to gravity. Zhang Tianyi introduced his 1931 novel *Ghostland Diary*: "I have refrained from putting anything amusing, funny, or irreverent in this diary. My attitude has been entirely serious, so I must request that you also—read it seriously."[25]

Wu Jianren called his joke series a *new* history of laughter to distinguish it from old histories. The *Records of the Grand Historian*, a monumental work dating back more than two thousand years to the Han dynasty, contains an entire chapter on the humorous sayings of court wits. Song and Ming writers compiled at least three separate collections entitled *A History of Humor* (*Xie shi*). A Qing editor retitled one Ming joke collection *A History of Laughter from Ancient to Modern*. At least two more *Histories of Laughter* appeared in the nineteenth century.[26]

Wu Jianren's title was not unique even in its own day. In the early twentieth century, Shanghai's newspaper of record, the *Shun Pao*, carried dozens of "histories of laughter" (*xiaoshi*), including news items about public figures who had made fools of themselves, as well as jokes appearing in its literary supplement.[27] One 1915 item in the local news pages related a "new history of laughter" about a mother and daughter who made their living defrauding men by arranging marriage contracts and then absconding with the dowry money.[28] A 1918 abridged translation of Charles Dickens's *The Pickwick Papers* was a *xiaoshi*. So was a 1920s novel called *The Ridiculous Miser*. So was a translated 1930s comic strip featuring American silent film comedian Harold Lloyd.[29]

Wu Jianren, in short, was borrowing a common trope, one that uses the word *history* loosely. The *Shun Pao* examples, to begin with, might be better called funny stories, absurd tales, or mock biographies rather than histories in the grand sense. *Xiaoshi* tended to emphasize the laughter rather than the history. If "history" refers to actual events, Wu Jianren's claim is spurious at best, as only a few of its jokes claim to be true stories, rather than fictional contrivances. His *New History of Laughter* is also fragmentary, an assemblage of short narratives tenuously connected by general headings. And not all of them are new: Wu admits to retelling others' jokes.

Literary historian Judith Zeitlin remarks of the various Chinese "histories" of the supernatural published between the sixteenth and eighteenth centuries that "the term 'history' in their titles seems only to indicate that these works are compilations on a specialized subject," and that "in certain contexts, [it] may approach the earliest Greek meaning of *historia*—an 'inquiry into' or 'an investigation of.'"[30] One preface to the late Ming collection *Expanded History of Humor* suggested that it could "expand not only humor, but also history; and not only history, but also the minds of those who read history."[31] In the publishing industry when Wu Jianren was writing, "histories" of laughter tended to be humor compilations rather than theoretical investigations, which appeared under other designations, from informal chats (*zatan*) to formal discourses (*lun*).

The proliferation of Chinese "histories of laughter"—enabled by an expanding modern press—reveals, in a material sense, the coexistence of many histories within History. Popular culture and print culture were shaped by an array of comedic impulses, from one-upping adversaries with humorous insults to playing with everyday objects and discovering fun in the mundane. While sometimes inspired by topical concerns, comic works of this period represent more than just sideways glances at recent traumas or the wreckage of history, since they also look ahead. In embracing, mocking, or making light of what is or what has been, comedy also invites expectation. The history of laughter is a history of, among other things, anticipation—of "wait till you hear this one" and "tell me another one."

THE AGE OF IRREVERENCE

China's Republican period was one of remarkable openness, a new climate of earnest searching and experimentation with roots in the exploratory culture of the late Qing.[32] Irreverence—meaning an insouciant attitude toward convention and authority—was one disposition driving the exploration. Breaking rules, disobeying authorities, making mischief, mocking intransigent behavior and thought, and pursuing fun all contributed to an atmosphere of cultural liberalization. Open contempt for the Manchu royal court fueled the 1911 revolution. Irreverence also helped to enable positivistic blue-sky thinking, as seen in a wave of futuristic science fantasy novels in the 1900s. Impudent humor, of course, is not the exclusive province of modernists or traditionalists, conservatives or radicals. Chinese writers and artists of the early twentieth century were equally irreverent in inveighing against the fads, excesses, and new sacred cows of the modern era.

The book outlines five of the most important comic trends of the early twentieth century, each identifiable by a key word or phrase: *xiaohua*, *youxi*, *maren*, *huaji*, and *youmo*. The English terms found in the chapter titles—jokes, play, mockery, farce, and humor—are not direct translations. They point in a general direction and give anchor to the individual chapters, which delve into the connotations of and often fluid interrelations between specific coordinates of the Chinese lexicon of the comic. With the exception of *maren*, which is always corrective or abusive, each of these words was used at one time to denote "comedy" or "humor" in the broad sense. Their meaning and currency changed during the twentieth century, sometimes profoundly. For a couple of decades, *youxi*, *huaji*, and *huixie* were the main terms for humor; in the 1930s, it was *huaji* and *youmo*. Each key word also had a narrower range of meanings, denoting a particular comedic form or intonation. *Huaji*, for example, had for hundreds of years meant simply humor or wit, but the Republican writer Xu Zhuodai cultivated a *huaji* persona that was primarily farcical. *Huaji*, in other words, cannot be conflated with farce, though they overlap considerably in that writer's work. Some terms accrued regional connotations, as *youxi* did in Shanghai. But in the publishing market of the day, all of them granted comic license. They denoted an intention to be funny, created an expectation of amusement, and gave permission to laugh.

During the first four decades of the twentieth century, playfulness, derision, frivolity, profanity, absurdity, and other expressions of humor abounded in China's public sphere. One driver of the proliferation of funny stories, cartoons, parodies, curses, and other expressions of mirth was a fast-growing transnational Chinese-language publishing market. In 1872, China's first modern broadsheet, *Shun Pao*, began publication in Shanghai; by 1876, it had sales centers in a dozen Chinese cities, including Hong Kong, and a daily circulation in the high thousands.[33] By the mid-1900s daily circulation was around 20,000, and by 1930 it had reached around 150,000. At the turn of the century, a wave of new urban tabloid or "small" newspapers emerged—between 1897 and 1911 more than forty were published in Shanghai alone—offering readers an alternative source of entertainment and political commentary to "big" (and often more conservative) papers like the *Shun Pao*.[34] Between 1876 and 1937, more than three hundred publishing houses and bookshops set up operations on Fuzhou Road in Shanghai, the center of Chinese publishing.[35] By 1929, the southern province of Guangdong had more than two hundred periodicals and Jiangsu Province (on the Yangtze River) more than three hundred; by 1935, Shanghai had almost four hundred.[36]

The result of this rapid growth was incessant demand for copy with immediate appeal. Shanghai readers could seek instant gratification from an endless stream of tabloids, which went by titles such as *Laughter Stage* (1918), *Absurd World* (1926–27), *Absurd Laughter* (1927), *Shooting the Breeze* (1927), *Addle-Brained* (1927–28), *New Forest of Laughs* (1928), *New Laughter* (1928), and *Nonsense* (1929). At least two different newspapers called themselves *Chaplin* (1926; 1930) and *Really Happy* (1927; 1928) and three invoked a *Happy World* (1914; 1926–27; 1927).[37] Major dailies started carrying jokes, humorous poems and essays, and comic strips. The 1930s ushered in the heyday of the cartoon magazine and also saw many of China's top writers contributing to a new magazine specializing in literary humor.

Jokes (*xiaohua*), anthologized by literati for centuries, assumed new functions during the late Qing publishing boom, becoming staples of the entertainment press. A new class of professional writers accrued celebrity as joke tellers. Laugh-inducing or smile-inducing talk, as *xiaohua* might be translated more literally, differs from the Anglophone idea of the joke in that the funny events or anecdotes they relate sometimes purport to be true. This ambiguous claim on truth took on new meaning in the late Qing when the journalistic genre of the "joke novel" helped to establish the joke as a symbol of the blurry lines between the real and the fake in an age when old hierarchies were no longer to be trusted.

The early Republican period saw jokes spread through the entertainment press as space fillers and appear as features in periodicals ranging from major newspapers to literary journals based at universities. In subsequent decades, joke books proliferated as stand-alone commodities. Chapter 2 examines the effects of jokes on modern media culture and vice versa. It also introduces an enduring presence in the Chinese history of laughter: voices warning of peril in an emerging culture that treated everything as mere grist for a new humor mill.

Around the turn of the century, writers and editors also began promoting an urban entertainment ethos of "play" (*youxi*) in magazines, tabloids, and humor columns. Writers wrote parodic verses and essays, whimsical commentaries, and fantastical novels that envisioned ideal futures for China. Artists invented new forms of visual wordplay, such as "comical characters" that contained hidden allegorical meanings, and wrote palindromic poems. Novelties such as zoetropes and peep shows competed for the attention and pocketbook of the man on the street. Around the turn of the century, one enterprising Frenchman set up a gramophone on a Shanghai street corner and charged listeners ten cents to listen to a record called "Laughing Foreigners," offering money back to any listener who managed to suppress his or her laughter. Apparently few could, because by 1908, he had earned enough to found China's first record company, Pathé Orient.[38] In the 1910s, amusement halls, called "playgrounds," sprang up in cities like Shanghai and Singapore, drawing in crowds with technological attractions like fun-house mirrors. Photography studios offered trick portraits and Chinese filmmakers began making slapstick shorts with such titles as *The Difficult Couple, The Romantic Monk, Bicycle Smash-Up, Blind Man Catches a Thief,* and *Punter Plays Dead*.[39] Chapter 3 surveys this panorama of play, which ranged from word games for the classically educated to popular entertainments accessible for a nominal price.

Reformists and revolutionaries sometimes adopted a derisive tone in their efforts to exorcise the specter of Confucianism and throw off the Manchu yoke. Chapter 4 shows how China's cultural and political future was contested through not just rational debate but also mudslinging battles and arguments shrill with sarcasm. Cursing was an ancient form of rhetoric, but the modern press broadcast private feuds to amuse a broad public audience. The political figure Wu Zhihui and the writer Lu Xun became famous for their use of invective and inspired imitators. In 1926, during China's "warlord period" when militarists carved much of China into personal fiefdoms, a professor of linguistics named Liu Fu, who was associated with the literary avant-garde, sparked controversy about the tone of public debate by republishing *Which Classic?*, a mid-Qing novel whose protagonists are all curse words, many using the character *gui* (ghost/devil). Through the story of this bizarre novel, its reception, and its celebrity promoters, chapter 4 traces how the politics of the humorous curse changed from the eve of the Opium Wars to the 1930s.

If being a modern writer was not all fun and games, neither did all of them hurl breathless invective. Even as many leading cultural critics were cutting one another down to size in the late 1920s and early 1930s, popular writers of a more entrepreneurial bent, particularly in Shanghai, were focusing on just being "funny" (*huaji*). They were preoccupied with the incidents of fraud that seemed to be part and parcel of modern urban life, and in particular scams and deceptions perpetrated in print media, such as plagiarism and bogus advertisements. Farce was particularly popular among writers like Xu Zhuodai who also worked as editors, actors, playwrights, filmmakers, radio broadcasters, and consumer product vendors. In their stories they celebrated practical jokes for fun and profit and often cast entrepreneurs like themselves as dynamic figures uniquely suited to navigating the pitfalls of modernity. Chapter 5 focuses on this cultural interest in everyday delusions, a world in which frauds, con women, and pranksters were not only welcome companions but even models of emulation.

Chapter 6 reveals how—possibly for the first time in Chinese history—humor itself became an object of reverence. *Youmo* (humor), a transliteration coined by the popular writer Lin Yutang, came to stand for a new comedic sensibility that sought to displace the irreverence of the early 1900s. In the 1930s, in his new Chinese-language humor magazine, *The Analects Fortnightly*, Lin popularized not only *youmo* but with it the notion that humor was a humanistic virtue that China (for all its preexisting comic traditions) lacked. The vogue for humor literature influenced scores of writers and continued for more than half a decade before being cut short by war. During that time, humor and laughter became the focus of unprecedented theorizing and polemical debate. What was humor? Did China need it? How could and should Chinese people laugh? (Or should they just smile?) Lin's campaign to promote *youmo* as a moral ideal that would refine the individual and civilize the body politic left a legacy that outlasted the 1930s heyday of humor. So did, as I discuss in the epilogue, the cultures of laughter that preceded it.

Some of these cultures coalesced around personalities. Writers like Xu Zhuodai, Wu Zhihui, and Lin Yutang might well have agreed with a comment by their seventeenth-century predecessor Li Yu: "Broadly speaking, everything I have written was intended to make people laugh."[40] They tended to be gregarious and socialize widely. The cultures they promoted were not just communities of the imagination, because participants were often friends, colleagues, and personal acquaintances. Their social lives, in turn, often influenced their comedic rhetoric, the languages and modes of expression that constitute the primary focus of this book. Biographies of figures like Lao She and Qian Zhongshu (whose major novel *Fortress Besieged* lies beyond its scope), to name just two writers famous for their humor, in chapter 6 cede center stage to humor itself.

Modern China's comic cultures were influenced by global trends. Chinese doctors at the turn of the twentieth century, responding to Western ideas about physiology, began suggesting that their patients laugh more, rather than less.[41] Comedic novels, jokes, and poems were translated in large volumes. Comic strips—a turn-of-the-century departure from the single-panel caricature popularized by

London's *Punch*—became increasingly prominent in print culture. Filmmakers drew on a global cinematic language and even packaged Chinese film comedies for foreign audiences. Vaudeville-style variety performance and amusement park machinery made its way to big cities. The phonograph record of "Laughing Foreigners" was being played on the streets of Shanghai around the same time that African American recording artist George W. Johnson's "The Laughing Song" became a hit in America and Europe. That the sound of recorded laughter "never failed to draw grimaces, smirks, and guffaws" around the world suggests a broader convergence of modern technology and comic amusement.[42]

These global currents inspired Chinese intellectuals to reappraise their traditions, and to measure foreign imports against domestic standards. Cultural trends circulated especially rapidly in cosmopolitan Shanghai, home to a lively foreign-language media. Between 1907 and 1913, translators introduced physiological interpretations of laughter from Denmark, America, and Japan; a Chinese version of Henri Bergson's *Le Rire* appeared in 1921.[43] More translations and discussion followed in the 1920s and 1930s. In 1936, one critic even claimed that Charlie Chaplin's performance style was quintessentially Chinese.

"Modern Chinese" humor of this period thus comprised a blend of influences—foreign and domestic, old and new. And China itself became an exporter of comedy. Chinese emigrants, foreign students, and exiles established Sinophone enterprises in Japan, Europe, North America, and Southeast Asia, particularly newspapers and other periodicals, which featured comedic works. Some of the most outlandish anti-Manchu vitriol of the 1900s was printed in Paris, a hotbed of anarchist thought. Chinese-language film comedies made in the production centers of Shanghai, Singapore, and Hong Kong circulated regionally beginning in the 1920s. Soon thereafter, Lin Yutang put Chinese humor on the global radar with his prodigious and highly popular writings in English.

The conspicuousness of laughter inspired heated debates about literary aesthetics, moral values, and China's broader cultural climate. Writers of the late Qing and Republican periods were highly ambivalent about laughter, celebrating its pleasures while deploring its social and political effects. They argued about how art ought to respond to suffering. They realized that non-verbal gestures could enable ambiguity and evasion. As the prominent essayist Zhou Zuoren observed, "it is not for nothing your wise man in chatting will only say, 'The weather today . . . ha ha ha,' without elaborating further"—often it was easier just to "pass things off with a laugh."[44] But they also appreciated the ways in which laughter created kinship and community rhetorically. It could put people in their place, but it could also amuse and endear.[45] A few critics insisted, to paraphrase Neil Postman's study of American television culture, that the Chinese were amusing themselves to death.[46] These polemics tell part of the story of how irreverence has shaped, for better or worse, modern Chinese culture. In them we also see the appearance of new theoretical concerns, notably quests to identify and define a "Chinese sense of humor."

The comic cultures of this historical period, I argue, were too heterogeneous to be reducible to a cozy sense of humor defined by ethnicity or nationality. They crossed barriers between high and low, Chinese and foreign, and between genres and modes of cultural production as well. This book tries to capture their different textures as expressed in literature, film, cartoons, photographs, memoirs, advertisements, and other parts of popular culture. Chapters 2 and 3 offer a broad survey of print and popular culture; chapters 4, 5, and 6 give more detailed accounts of individual events, artists, and trends. While a study of this sort is inherently comparative, this one concentrates on making Chinese voices audible. It falls short of an exhaustive or exhausting survey of all Chinese humorists and comic genres, but it does offer a few ways to read Chinese cultural history across the grain. When upper-class ladies speak in novels of the imperial period like *Dream of the Red Chamber* they always "say it with a smile" (*xiaodao*). The late Ming novel *Jin Ping Mei*, composed by the "Scoffing Scholar of Lanling," is a literary classic filled with jokes.[47] This book hopes to encourage further exploration of such antecedents, as well as of other key terms in the Chinese comic lexicon, such as *fengci* (satire), *huixie* (jocularity), *manhua* (cartoons and comics), and more recent neologisms. Extensive comparisons to other historical and cultural contexts also await future scholars.

While focusing on a period spanning about forty years, this book thus opens up genealogical threads that extend in multiple directions. It chronicles changes in how Chinese people laughed, what they laughed at, and how they talked about laughter, as well as what drove those changes. Instead of following a single or linear chronology, it highlights how multiple cultures of humor changed and influenced one another over time. It shares with Vic Gatrell's study of late eighteenth-century and early nineteenth-century London an interest in the diversity of "subjects that people think it appropriate to laugh at; what kinds of people laugh; how cruelly, mockingly, or sardonically they laugh (or how sympathetically and generously); [and] how far they permit others to laugh."[48] It is less concerned with extolling the virtues of Chinese comic traditions (and modern innovations) or defending them against their critics.

This new history of laughter contrasts with the usual portrait of late Qing and Republican China, focusing not on the angst, earnestness, drudgery, and political anger of that age, but on the wit, sarcasm, glee, and irreverence that made it bearable and even fun. It follows a new historical periodization, its turning points being not just the fall of the Qing dynasty or the clarion call of May Fourth's literary revolutionaries but also the rise of the tabloid press in the late nineteenth century and a 1930s campaign to civilize China with humor. Its protagonists are whimsical poets, vaudevillian entrepreneurs, renowned revilers, twee essayists, winking farceurs, and self-promoting jokesters. It is also a story about how leading cultural figures as diverse as Liang Qichao, Wu Jianren, Wu Zhihui, Lu Xun, Zhou Zuoren, Liang Shiqiu, Lao She, Lin Yutang, and even Mao Zedong affirmed the value of laughter to their various campaigns to transform China, even though they at times felt compelled to distance themselves from its commoditized forms. It approaches laughter on its own terms and on the terms imposed on it.

The early twentieth century changed the way Chinese people talked about what's funny. Yet despite the dominance that *youmo* established in the 1930s as the new humor standard, strains of the old laughter can still be heard in China today.

2

Jokes
笑話百出

> *I wasn't planning on telling jokes,*
> *But jokes keep forcing themselves upon me.*
> —LI YU, 1671[1]

Wu Jianren was one of the first prolific Chinese joke writers of the modern age. In the 1900s, hundreds of his jokes appeared in magazines under headings such as *The New Expanded Forest of Laughs*, *Funny Chats*, and *Wisecracks*, as well as *A New History of Laughter*.[2] In his 1906 preface to *Wisecracks*, he tells readers:

> I've always enjoyed a clever jest. Guests and host will be sitting together in a large gathering, and when I arrive they'll always welcome me with, "He's here!" When the conversation starts flowing, I might chime in with an occasional remark that never fails to leave everyone in stitches. Even I can't say why I'm so funny. After I've told a joke, I'll always jot it down to send to various dailies—I've contributed to virtually every paper that specializes in humor. Most of the papers in Canton, Hong Kong, and Southeast Asia carried my jokes, and even Shanghai tabloids picked them up. A few years ago I got tired of doing this, but recently when I've happened to read one of the newest tabloids I've often come across my old works.[3]

He goes on to complain that so many people have been plagiarizing and altering his jokes that it's been ruining his reputation. As such, he's decided to republish his favorites in his new journal, the *All-Story Monthly*. A sampling from Wu's various joke series hints at what made them so popular:

> "FOR RENT"
>
> There once was a scholar who was abysmally poor. His cooking fire was always going out, and he was wretched from exhaustion and hunger. One day he squatted by the roadside with a note pasted to his cheek that read: "This mouth for rent." A person asked him: "Why are you renting out your mouth?" He replied: "So someone will fill it!"[4]

"CALF AND FOAL"
It's common for people to refer to their children using the pejorative moniker "little dogs." The practice began with [the second- and third-century military commander] Cao Cao, who noted that Liu Jingsheng referred to his sons as "pigs" and "dogs." One man who called his children "calf" and "foal" was asked about this unique form of address, and he explained: *"After China is destroyed, all Chinese people will become beasts of burden. My children are still young, so of course I should call them calf and foal."*[5]

Wisecracks contains animal allegories like "Bestowed the Yellow Jacket," which mocks self-important imperial officials in their robes of office:

A white dog walked by a cesspit and, delighted by its stench, lowered its head and began eating. As it was happily stuffing its face, a mischievous boy snuck up from behind and kicked it into the pit. The dog frantically climbed out, covered in feces, and turned its head around to lick its back clean. Its front was covered in gold-colored filth, and, seeing this, it strutted into the marketplace wagging its tail. Everyone was repelled by its filth and kept their distance. The dog sighed to itself: "It's true—those of renown dazzle the low-born! Today, seeing me wearing the Yellow Jacket, these peasants are all intimidated."[6]

"A Pig Explains Nature's Law" notes that foreigners in China are meticulous about food preparation, as they have all their livestock examined for plague and instruct their butchers to slaughter only those fit for eating. To someone who observes the irony that diseased hogs live longer than the healthy ones do, a pig replies that this is Nature's Law—witness China's plague of officials. In another joke in the same vein, the Lord of Hell, out touring, comes across maggots squirming in a privy and decrees that they will return in the next life as humans. He then comes across maggots eating through a corpse and sentences them to eternal damnation. Why? Feces-eating maggots are humble enough to take others' leftovers, but the world already has plenty of government officials—no need for more flesh-eating maggots.[7]

Newspapers were awash with gallows humor in the years leading up to the 1911 Republican Revolution. Allegories about filthy, diseased animals testify to widespread animosity toward the Manchus, as well as toward government officials, who were routinely derided as curs and vermin. But no one knew what lay ahead for China, and Wu Jianren, a journalist and editor, as well as an author, like many of his peers, feared that revolution would only hasten China's demise.

Jokes had currency in a literal sense as well. Wu Jianren, who often discussed the changing writing profession, joked that he "sold smiles" for a living, a phrase typically associated with the prostitute's come-on.[8] For centuries writers had gleaned jokes from oral culture and anthologized them in collections for the literate minority. Now literacy had spread (by the late Qing, an estimated fifth to a quarter of the population could read[9]), and jokes became regular fare in newspapers, magazines, and tabloids, to be consumed alongside news articles, fiction, poems, and essays.

Reading a joke in the newspaper, of course, is not the same as hearing it in person, particularly in a time of crisis. The famous Ming essayist Zhang Dai wrote of one uncle who founded a "Laughter Club" with his friends in the capital to tell jokes during the waning years of that dynasty.[10] Late Qing writers like Wu Jianren tried to simulate the intimacy of a group of friends. Those with a background in journalism, especially, also tried to capture the excitement of live performances. Wu's contemporary, Li Boyuan, recounted how one Suzhou comedian packed theaters in Shanghai's Yu Gardens and foreign settlements, giving multiple performances a day in which he "rattled off jokes without repeating a single word."[11]

Scholars of jokes sometimes say that jokes are authorless because their origins are impossible to trace. As a type of folklore, they are "a geyser that spouts for anyone with a handy pail"—including competing joke tellers.[12] But the newspaper age changed Chinese joking practices by putting last night's witticisms down "in black ink on white paper," and under a byline. Writers of Wu Jianren's generation strove to claim ownership over their own jokes and, as editors, often credited authorship to others.[13] In China, as elsewhere, editors had long attributed jokes to famous wits, such as the Han Dynasty scholar-official Dongfang Shuo.[14] Familiar names drew readers. Wu, then in his most active period, clearly enjoyed his reputation as a master joke teller and felt threatened by hacks of an everexpanding popular press who stole his jokes with impunity and published them elsewhere.[15] So he did two things: he reasserted authorship over jokes already in diaspora—effectively taking credit for promoting (if somewhat inadvertently) a broader humor culture—and he published more jokes.

Jokes became a serious business among literati who had had their dreams of securing government employment dashed in 1905 when the Qing court abolished the centuries-old civil service examinations. The impoverished scholar featured prominently. Jokes also commented on a litany of political and cultural crises. The Qing government had lost sovereignty over Taiwan and suzerainty over Korea in 1895 following its defeat in the first Sino-Japanese War. An attempt by a progressive faction in the Qing court to push through a series of modernizing reforms in 1898 ended in failure, with some prominent intellectuals executed and others fleeing into exile. The empress dowager's support of the antiforeign Boxer Rebellion in 1900 led to a further weakening of the state as an eight-nation alliance of troops moved to relieve the Boxer siege of the Legation Quarter in Beijing and protect foreign interests in Shandong and Tianjin. Foreign troops afterward looted and pillaged as the emperor and his court fled the capital.

For writers like Wu (who never even attempted the civil service exams), the periodical press was at once a source of income, an outlet for literary creativity, and a vehicle for influencing national politics. Wu published some of his earliest jokes, as mentioned in chapter 1, in the magazine *New Fiction*, which Liang Qichao, a former member of a reformist faction of the Qing court, had founded in 1902 while in exile in the treaty port of Yokohama. Not all of Wu's jokes were explicitly political. He wrote jokes about Halley's comet, which became visible to the naked eye in April 1910 (and which some took as a portent of the dynasty's passing), and supplied a steady stream of groaner puns, hoping, for instance, that readers would not mistake *New [Xin] Fiction* as being published in the province of Xinjiang. Jokes in this and other periodicals reflect a mix of motivations to earn, educate, and entertain.

Wu felt compelled to explain why he wrote so many jokes, as well as how his differed from those in *The Expanded Forest of Laughs* (1761), a Qing dynasty collection that had become the most popular and influential joke book of his day. *The Expanded Forest of Laughs* became a touchstone—often negative—for modern writers discussing humor. As late as 1934, when Lu Xun wanted to warn the editor of a new humor magazine, the *Analects Fortnightly*, that its humor was becoming glib, pedestrian, and malicious, he put it like this: "It seems that Chinese people's so-called humor never strays from the style of *The Expanded Forest of Laughs*—it's a lost cause."[16]

And so, in 1904, after *New Fiction* moved its base to Shanghai, Wu opened *The New Expanded Forest of Laughs* with these prefatory remarks:

> Scholars in recent times have been profoundly alerted to the fact of fiction's capacity to reform society, so they have vied to speak of fiction. In my opinion, when it comes to influencing people through writing, humorous language works better than stern rhetoric. This is why I hold "joke stories" [*xiaohua xiaoshuo*] in such high esteem. While the genre is by no means new to China, books of this type are stale and derivative, lacking any particularly new consciousness or flavor. The one I would single out, *The Expanded Forest of Laughs*, is known to every woman and child. Unfortunately, its content is vulgar and base, consisting entirely of obscene jests of the lower orders. Not only does it hold no benefit for the reader, it might even lead him to slide into licentiousness. After mulling over the best way to reform that book, I wrote *The New Expanded Forest of Laughs*.[17]

By "vulgar" and "base," Wu might have had in mind jokes like "Promoted," the very first joke in *The Expanded Forest of Laughs*:

> An official got promoted and said to his wife: "I've got a bigger title than before."
> His wife replied, "Your title might have gotten bigger, but did that thing of yours get bigger too?"
> "Of course," he replied.
> The next time they did it his wife complained that it appeared to be as small as ever. The official told her: "It is much bigger, you just can't feel it."
> "And why is that?" she asked.

He replied: "Do you think that if the husband is promoted the wife would stay the same? Clearly, now that mine's bigger, yours is bigger too."[18]

This particular joke uses euphemisms like "that thing" (*ciwu*) and "did it" (*xingshi*), but *The Expanded Forest of Laughs* contains an entire section on body parts (many with genital punch lines), as well as jokes about adultery, farts, defecation, and incest. In the early twentieth century, it was so canonical that writers borrowed both its title and the pen name of its compiler, the Master of Play.[19] Wu's preface to *The New Expanded Forest of Laughs* made it clear that he would not go down its well-trodden path. He aimed to elevate the joke from mere entertainment product to vehicle of social reform by using buzzwords like *reform*, *consciousness*, and *flavor*.[20] In linking the joke to *xiaoshuo* (stories or fiction) he sought to tap into the new prestige of the fiction genre, which Liang Qichao had promoted two years earlier in the same journal. Liang argued that fiction unconsciously influenced readers' thinking by couching its moral lessons in entertainment; Wu thought that the moral would be most effective if it was funny. In using a familiar joke book title, Wu was putting new wine in an old bottle.[21]

Philosophical tracts of the Warring States period, the time of Confucius, were replete with jokes, usually in the form of parables. The "man of the state of Song" (elsewhere, the "man of Lu") appears in both the *Mencius* and the Legalist tract *Hanfeizi* as a stock archetype of stupidity, like Polish people or blondes in formulaic American jokes of yore. Parables in the *Mencius* include that of the man who saw a rabbit break its neck running into a stump and abandoned working in the fields in the false hope of a repeat windfall, and the farmer who, trying to make his crops grow faster, tugged at the shoots. Each story entered the language as an idiom for wrongheaded behavior.

Riddles, another ancient form of joke, appear in the "Biographies of Court Wits" chapter of the *Records of the Grand Historian*, as well as imperially commissioned histories like the *History of the Former Han*. Late imperial novels such as *The Plum in the Golden Vase*, *Mirage*, *Flowers in the Mirror*, and *Dream of the Red Chamber* contain scenes of parties at which the protagonists tell jokes as a forfeit in a drinking game or as a contest of wits.[22] During a crab-eating party in *Dream of the Red Chamber*, for example, Jia Baoyu composes a poem about the main course, which contains a couplet alluding to the creature's associations with imperial officials: both have an unfriendly demeanor, are heartless, are given to drink (wine being an obligatory pairing for the delicacy), and "walk sideways," meaning that they break the rules with their transverse movements:

> Old Grim-chops wants wine, though he's got no inside,
> And he never walks forwards, but all to one side.[23]

Novelists also used jokes to pace their narratives. In the Qing dynasty satirical classic *The Scholars*, Mr. Yan has for three days been too weak to speak and lingering on the brink of death. An oil lamp is lit on his table, and relatives crowd around. His death rattle is audible but the old man refuses to die, holding out two fingers from under the covers. His relatives speculate about his meaning in vain. Then Mrs. Yan steps forward: "They're all wide of the mark. I'm the only one who knows what you mean." Chapter 5 ends on that cliff-hanger. At the beginning of chapter 6 she reveals: "You're worried because there are two wicks in the lamp—that's a waste of oil." Sure enough, as soon as she removed a wick, the miser breathes his last.[24]

China's earliest-known collection of jokes, *Forest of Laughs*, dates to the Three Kingdoms period (ca. third century CE).[25] Over the centuries, collecting jokes and compiling them in books became a hobby as well as a commercial enterprise for literati—so the motivations of "earn, educate, and entertain" were hardly unique to the twentieth century. The late Ming was a high point in Chinese joke publishing, as humor collections were rapidly reprinted and added to. They featured one-line witticisms and setup–punch line jokes, as well as humorous poems, puns, and other word games. Editors divided them into sections by subject. Feng Menglong's late-Ming collection *Treasury of Laughs* (1620), which also became popular in Japan, for example, contains sections on "Age-Old Envy (The Rich and Powerful)"; "Rotten Scholars"; "The Untouchable"; "Occultism and Medicine"; "Monks, Priests, and Miscellaneous Occupations"; "Extraordinary Faculties"; "Petty Sport (Whoring and Gambling)"; "Vulgarity"; "Sexually Sophisticated Women"; "Body Parts"; "Funny Mistakes"; "Daily Necessities"; and "Intercalary Words (Miscellany)."[26] Errors of judgment, frustrated desires, and slippery language are favorite themes that come together in jokes like "Peace and Quiet":

> A man who preferred peace and quiet had the misfortune to live between two blacksmiths. Day and night their racket pummeled his ears, leaving him miserable. He was often heard to remark, "If those two were to move someday, I'd happily pay them in thanks." One day, the blacksmiths came to him together and said, "We're both ready to move and have come to take you up on your offer of compensation." He asked what date they planned to move, and they said: "Tomorrow." Delighted, he promptly paid them a handsome sum. After treating them to a drink, he asked, "And where will you two be moving to?" They replied: "He's moving to my place, and I'm moving to his."[27]

Scholars also included jokes in imperially commissioned literary anthologies and encyclopedias (*leishu*). *Forest of Laughs* is no longer extant, but some of its jokes were preserved in the Song dynasty (960–1279) *Taiping guangji* and other anthologies. They usually appear near the middle or at the back of such collections, indicating the low status they shared with *xiaoshuo* (which encompassed other "minor" writings, including fictional stories). Literati generally considered both to be subliterary vestiges of oral culture.

Joking, the philosopher Ted Cohen points out, is a "'two-stage' art" because a joke's inventor and teller need not be the same person.[28] Wu Jianren may have chafed at others retelling his jokes, but he should not have been surprised, since jokes had been handed down from one teller to the next for centuries. Scholars have established that China's premodern joke canon was fluid (as jokes could be added or deleted without materially affecting a collection), while favorite jokes were repeatedly anthologized. Wang Liqi, the editor of an important 1956 anthology, observed that most collections since the Yuan and Ming dynasties repeat earlier jokes.[29] Editors as early as the Ming dynasty were continually improving upon their predecessors with "sequels" to and "expansions" of their favorite collections.[30] Many joke collections from the imperial period include "Forest of Laughs" (*xiaolin*) in their title, and *The Expanded Forest of Laughs* (which Wu made a "new" version of) was itself a compilation of at least three earlier joke books, including *Treasury of Laughs, Bowled Over with Laughter,* and *A Good Laugh*.[31]

AMUSING ANECDOTES OF AN EXPIRING EMPIRE

Studies of Chinese jokes typically halt at the end of the nineteenth century, before jokes supposedly began to be influenced by foreign culture. This misses a joke boom that started in the late Qing period and accelerated in the republic, and that changed the Chinese rhetoric of joking by popularizing the word *xiaohua*. *Xiao* and *hua* may be interpreted as nouns (laughter/smiles and speech), verbs (to laugh/smile and to talk), or modifier and noun (laugh- or smile-producing speech). Before the twentieth century, the term *xiaohua* often appears in the captions of jokes themselves but rarely in the titles of collections.[32] Some imperial collections refer to *xiaotan* (laughing, or humorous conversation) or *xiaoyan* (laughing speech), but many more pair the character *xiao* (laughter, smiles, jokes) with a metaphor of volume, such as forest, ocean, waves, history, treasury, records, notes, or anthology.[33] Other collections promise that their readers will experience a physiological response to their contents, cracking a smile (*jieyan, qiyan, jieyi, jie'e, qi'e*), for example, clapping (*fuzhang*), clutching the belly (*pengfu*), falling over (*xiaodao*), laughing loudly (*xiexue*), spitting rice (*penfan*), or snapping the chin strap of one's hat (*jueying*).[34]

Dozens of humor collections of the early twentieth century drew on these metaphors, but in the 1910s they also began advertising their contents as *xiaohua*. This was new. One factor contributing to the change was a broader transition from a classical language based on one-character words to a modern vernacular featuring two-character words, or binomes. *Xiao* became *xiaohua*. Yet it is possible that *xiaohua* was a return loan word from the Japanese *showa*, which uses the same Chinese characters and means "amusing story."[35]

For the first decades of the twentieth century, the joke was part of a broad print market for literary humor that emphasized variety, and joke books can be hard to distinguish from other humor anthologies based on title alone. Joke books, comic novels, and essay collections alike, for example, were entitled "A History of Laughter."[36] Works like Jiang Hangong's *Funny World* (1919), a two-volume compendium of comic amusements grouped into thirty-seven categories, is virtually indistinguishable from contemporary collections of "games" (*youxi*), discussed in chapter 3.[37] It was in the 1930s that publishers began to distinguish fictional punch line jokes from other forms of humor more categorically by branding them as *xiaohua*.

The Chinese term *xiaohua* and the English word *joke* differ in one key respect: their truth-claim. Christie Davies, a leading scholar of jokes, notes that "jokes are known to be fictions, even when told with a straight face."[38] Ted Cohen distinguishes two "particular kinds of contrivance": "a very short story—fictional" and jokes that are "more obviously formulaic."[39] In both of Cohen's cases, the scenario is understood to be made up. Thus, even the joke in the form of a short story confirms not the fact of a specific event, but rather a general principle or fundamental pattern that applies to language (for example: words can have multiple meanings), to a category of people (used car salesmen lie), to humans generally (people always want what they can't have), or to the cosmos (shit happens). The takeaway "truth," of course, is better described as a prejudice or a commonplace. Jokes tend to validate shared assumptions—this is what Cohen means when he speaks of the "insinuating quality" of jokes.[40]

Xiaohua, in contrast, denotes a funny short narrative, either a made-up story or a true, humorous anecdote. This means that *xiaohua* make a type of claim on truth that a joke generally does not. In common parlance, *joke* and *xiaohua* may both be used as a pejorative metaphor to dub a real situation a sham, farce, or absurdity. But a person who says, "Let me tell you a *xiaohua*" is just as likely to relate an actual experience he or she found to be funny or outrageous as to share a canned or formulaic joke.[41]

Distinguishing the two types of *xiaohua*—funny anecdotes and fictional contrivances—poses little problem in normal conversation. In the journalistic literary culture of the late Qing dynasty, however, gossip, rumor, and hearsay were often mixed in with fact. Journalist-litterateurs, as Wu Jianren and his class of professionals are sometimes called, wrote in a way that muddied the waters. Novels exposing carpetbagging officials of a failing government, which were ostensibly fictional narratives, might incorporate *xiaohua* about purportedly real events their authors had read about in the newspaper. *Shun Pao*, as mentioned earlier, carried *xiaohua* that were often personal anecdotes about political, literary, or courtesan celebrities. A rhapsody introducing the new Shanghai tabloid *Laughter* in 1897 promised

> jokes [*xiaohua*] and news items as thick as hedgehog quills
> and funny stories [*xiaotan*] and witty remarks as continual as cicadas' song.[42]

Wu Jianren was so famous for his entertaining anecdotes that a book of *Anecdotes about Contemporary Celebrities* (1923) was spuriously attributed to him thirteen years after his death.⁴³

Wu's 1907 short story "Smooth Path to the Peak of Officialdom" concerns an ignorant acquaintance who has made a shrine in his home for a gift he received from his superior—a foreign bedpan. The story was advertised as "joke fodder" (*xiaobing*).⁴⁴ *Illustrated Amusing Stories [xiaohua] from New-Style Schools; or, An Exposé of New-Style Schools* (1910), a twenty-five-chapter comedic novel in two volumes, relates curious happenings in the educational field following the abolishment of the civil service examination.⁴⁵ In the 1900s, during a theatrical production that students at Shanghai's Minli Middle School staged in honor of Confucius's birthday, a male student playing a female role had the misfortune to have his pants drop to the floor; decades later, Xu Zhuodai remembered it as a *xiaohua*. These purportedly true events were *xiaohua* because they were funny. But Xu remembered this one as having had serious consequences, as provincial authorities used the incident to prohibit future productions on moral grounds.⁴⁶

What Wu Jianren called "joke stories" was a vague category that included the humorous anecdotes in his joke collections, jokes, and novels made up of jokes and humorous anecdotes. The practice of writing novels by stringing together *xiaohua*, according to literary scholar Chen Pingyuan, represented a major change in Chinese fictional narrative.⁴⁷ Ming-Qing vernacular novels, as mentioned earlier, had built isolated scenes around jokes, such as joke-telling parties. During the late Qing, entire novels became vehicles for retelling funny stories.

Wu's primary contribution to the new joke-story genre was *Strange Events Eyewitnessed over Twenty Years* (serialized, 1903–10), often considered to be one of the four great novels of the era. Its first-person narrator is a naive young man who mixes with corrupt officials and records his "eyewitness accounts" of their behaviors. Some he observes, while others he hears about from others, especially his friend and employer, Wu Jizhi, a metropolitan-level degree holder and veteran of Qing officialdom. Though the central conceit of the novel is that its events had been eyewitnessed (*mudu*), Wu is known to have derived much of his material from news reports and political gossip. But regardless of whence it drew its raw material, this new genre of novel purported to show readers what others had seen— and seen through. It would rip away the facade of society and politics to reveal the rotten reality underneath.

One episode from chapter 6 of *Strange Events* illustrates how the novel uses *xiaohua* to convey a sense of penetrating or transparent vision. Jizhi is talking to the narrator about ethnic Manchus, China's rulers under the Qing dynasty whom, like many Han Chinese, he resented and despised: "Those Manchus are always putting on airs . . . I'll tell you a funny story [*xiaohua*] I heard from one of my servants; once you've heard it [the *xiaohua*] you'll understand."⁴⁸

Jizhi goes on to relate an anecdote about a Manchu bannerman (banners being a Qing administrative and military organization) whom his servant once saw in a Beijing teahouse. Despite having lost his government stipend and fallen into poverty, the bannerman is desperate to keep up appearances. A waiter remarks that the jasmine tea leaves the customer has brought with him (so that he would only have to pay for hot water) are too few for a proper cup of tea, and the Manchu mocks him for failing to recognize them as a special variety imported from France. Jizhi's servant, who overhears this exchange, observes that they are nothing of the sort. The Manchu spends over an hour nursing his cup of weak tea and nibbling on a *shaobing* (a type of baked flatbread sprinkled with sesame seeds), and then licks his finger and appears to be writing Chinese characters on the table. Upon closer inspection, the servant discovers that he is in fact picking up the sesame seeds that have fallen off his flatbread. At one point he stops, as if deep in thought, and smacks the table in a sudden epiphany. In fact, the servant realizes, the Manchu merely wanted to dislodge the sesame seeds that had fallen between the table cracks.

The joke continues. The Manchu's young son arrives and urges his father to hurry back home because mom has to go out and dad is wearing the single pair of pants they share—a common trope for extreme poverty. Mortified, the bannerman loudly chastises his son for feigning poverty when there is no one around who might otherwise attempt to borrow money from them. As he tries to leave without paying, the waiter confronts him. He claims to have been flustered by his son. Penniless and pressed for security, he gives over the only thing he has, a dirty handkerchief, which the waiter ruefully observes he can at least use for wiping down tables. The story finished, Jizhi asks his friend: "Is this not proof that the Manchus put on airs?"[49]

The framing of this anecdote is strikingly similar to a convention of premodern Chinese fiction. In classical vernacular novels such as *The Water Margin*, the storyteller will occasionally interrupt the narrative to recite a poem that testifies to a general moral truth, prefacing it with the phrase: "A poem stands in evidence" (*you shi wei zheng*). In Wu Jianren's novel, a *xiaohua* stands in evidence of the truism that Manchus are poor but proud—a commonplace rather than an objective fact. But whereas some modern readers have found that poems in premodern novels impede narrative flow,[50] the joke in the joke-novel is the main source of reading pleasure.

At the time Wu was writing, the Manchus were experiencing the shattering of what historian Mark Elliott has called "the iron rice bowl of banner privilege," which included a government stipend and other preferential treatment.[51] Wu's sources for jokes like these included tabloids like *The Fable*, an imitator of Li Boyuan's *Play*, which carried a column of "jokes about officials."[52] In this and other scenes in the novel, a fictional joke teller puts the real reader (us) in the position of an intimate listener who participates in the conspiracy of laughing at another social group.

Whether or not jokes are true stories is a running theme of the novel. In chapter 12, Jizhi tells the narrator about a drug smuggler who retaliated against a customs agent who had confiscated his opium by tricking him into seizing a can, which, when the agent presented it to his superior, turned out to contain feces swarming with grasshoppers. "I've heard that one before too," the narrator responds. "It's probably just a joke." In chapter 24, the two swap stories about the common practice of high-ranking officials using their prestige to solicit cash bribes in the form of "gifts." Jizhi tells of one member of the imperial Hanlin Academy who committed a faux pas while making the rounds in the jurisdiction of his relative, a viceroy, and cried all night after the viceroy forced him to return all the money he had received. "The incident must be real, but some of the details were likely distorted somewhat," the narrator says, reasoning that no one would have known about the nighttime crying. (Jizhi insists that a servant overheard him sobbing.)[53]

Strange Events was a key instigator of public discourse about the bizarreness of life in contemporary China. It popularized a method of writing fiction that recycled news, gossip, and hearsay. (The joke about the bannerman, for one, had made the rounds in Beijing.)[54] Ironically, the "journalistic immediacy" of these novels, as literary scholar David Wang has noted, resulted in depiction of social phenomena that was not more realistic, but more distorted and grotesque. In their pursuit of ever more outrageous stories, the narrators of novels like *Strange Events* and Li Boyuan's best-selling *Officialdom Unmasked* (serialized, 1903–6) adopted a cynical attitude that viewed "the bizarre as routine."[55]

Wu's novel simulates a social environment of friendly and competitive amusement. In chapter 66, the narrator, Jizhi, and two friends play a riddle game, in which the riddle-teller has to tell a joke if someone guesses the riddle correctly. Losers drink a forfeit. In this game, jokes are "an accompaniment to wine," but the players specifically exclude two types: old jokes and vulgar jokes in the style of *The Expanded Forest of Laughs*. Come the narrator's turn to tell a joke, he promises "a guaranteed laugh," but Wu Jianren, like the author of *The Scholars* before him, makes his reader wait until the next chapter.[56]

Novelists now used jokes to compete in the fiction market. One joke about an ailing military governor whose subordinate suggests that his wife give the governor a "massage" to cure him appeared in novels by Wu Jianren, Li Boyuan, and at least one of their contemporaries.[57] In the mid-1910s, novels exposing officialdom were followed by a new genre that drew heavily on sensationalistic news reports about urban vice. These purported to reveal what lay behind the "black curtain" of Shanghai's social scene, even as they blurred the line between muckraking re-

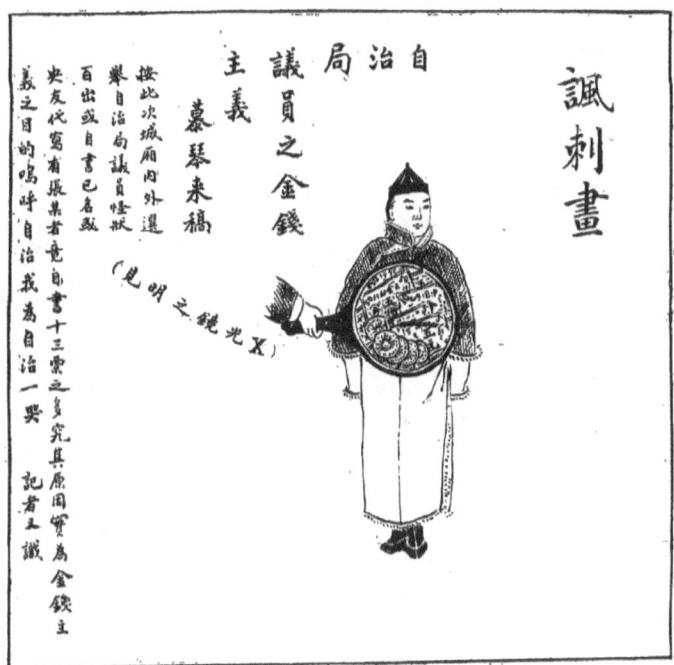

FIGURE 2.1. Machinations of late Qing politicians as a transparent joke: "Self-Governance Bureau Representative's Money-ism," in *Illustration Daily* 162 (ca. January 1910).

portage and fiction. *Xiaohua* leavened the moral castigation, which became even more strident during the warlord politics of the 1920s. They encouraged readers to see reality not just as absurd but also amusing.

They also show how literal-minded late Qing political critique could be. A *xiaohua* in chapter 86 of Wu's novel tells of a terrified peasant who is dragged before the magistrate for some minor offense. Suddenly, a gust of wind blows away his fear of the official's imposing demeanor: the curtain before the bench lifts enough for him to see that the man has one boot off and is scratching between his toes. A satirical drawing from 1910 combines the rhetoric of exposure with modern technology (see figure 2.1). Picking up on a recent news story, it shows a man in official garb and explains that the "money-ism" at his core is "clearly visible through an X-ray glass." The inset text even uses Wu Jianren's term—"strange events"—to refer to the irregularities surrounding recent municipal Self-Governance Bureau elections.[58] The X-ray, a new pseudoscientific metaphor, flatters the reader for having literally seen through the facade to the truth inside—in other words, for already knowing the joke.

A REPUBLIC OF JOKES

Within a few years of the republic's founding in 1911 (and Wu's death in 1910), China's periodical press was bursting with jokes. Columns in a wide variety of magazines and newspapers carried headings such as "Forest of Laughs," "Western Jokes," and "History of Laughter."[59] Jokes appeared in "miscellany" sections at the backs of magazines and served as handy space fillers (*bubai*) throughout. Newspapers like Shanghai's *Forest of Laughs* even named themselves after joke books.[60] Print capitalism vastly increased the volume of published literary comedy in China, just as it lifted other genres. Demand for short, modular content is one of the likely factors that helped the joke displace the anecdote as the predominant *xiaohua* of the day.

By a conservative count, more than one hundred Chinese humor collections were published between 1900 and 1937, a volume that compares favorably with the number of known joke books from the preceding two thousand years.[61] Titles include *Fresh Jokes and Remarkable Stories* (1911), *A Collection of Cold Laughs* (1913), *Political Jokes about Yuan Shikai* (1913), *World of Jokes* (1917), *Side-Splitters* (1917), *The Comic Spirit* (1919), *Priceless Laughs* (1920), *Shooting the Breeze* (1922), *Ha! Ha!* (1923), *One Thousand Jokes* (1923), *Panorama of Jokes* (1927), *Instant Laughs* (1931), *Laughs for the Masses* (1932), *Smile-Raisers* (1933), *Absolutely Bizarre and Hilarious Modern Jokes* (1935), *New Jokes* (1935), *Humorous Jokes* (1935), *Fount of Laughter* (1935), *A Crate of Fresh Jokes* (1936), *Ocean of Laughs* (1937), and *King of Fresh Jokes* (1937). It was not necessarily the case that more jokes were now being told per capita, but many more were certainly appearing in print.

Shanghai, the center of modern China's publishing industry through the 1940s, also appears to have been its center of joke writing. Joke writers came from across the literary spectrum, from Wang Dungen, the editor of the best-selling *Saturday* magazine, to the renowned scholar and essayist Zhou Zuoren. Zhou observed that most premodern joke books were compiled by southerners, and, in fact, little had changed, for the most prominent compilers of jokes in the twentieth century similarly hailed from Zhejiang, Jiangsu, Shanghai, and Guangdong.[62] Li Dingyi, a prolific novelist and magazine editor, compiled at least five collections of jokes, including *Expanded Forest of Laughs* (1917), *Collection of Humorous Writings, by Genre* (1917), *Bizarre Tales* (1919), *The Comic Spirit* (1919), and *Jokes and Bizarre Sights* (ca. 1920s). Xu Zhuodai, a multifaceted cultural personality and writer whose jokes regularly appeared in the *Shun Pao* and other periodicals, had at least six joke books to his credit, including *Laugh-Getters* (1924), *New Forest of Laughs* (1924), *A New History of Laughter* (1924), *Three Thousand Jokes* (1935), *Illustrated Jokes* (1937), and a short collection for children entitled simply *Jokes* (1935).

Many collections were a team effort. At least five names are credited, for example, in *Laughing Through Tears* (1914). Li Jingzhong (Li Duo, n.d.) first collected jokes and classified them into six sections; Shen Ganruo (n.d.) then edited and revised them, adding a seventh section. Xu Zhenya, Hu Jichen, and Li Dingyi, all well-known writers who had each published his own humor collections, contributed prefaces. Hu Jichen and Xu Zhenya write of a turbid age reeking of immorality, but *Laughing Through Tears*, Li Dingyi says, will be a "broom to sweep away worries." Two years earlier, several of these writers had contributed to *Civil Rights* (1912–14), a newspaper affiliated with the fledgling Liberal Party. *Civil Rights* was harshly critical of the corruption, cronyism, and ineffectualness of the administration of Yuan Shikai, a Qing dynasty military commander who had strong-armed his way into the first presidency of the Republic of China. *Civil Rights* operated in Shanghai's foreign settlements, outside Chinese jurisdiction, so Yuan ordered the postal service not to distribute it. Unable to survive as a daily, *Civil Rights* closed after two years, but its founder quickly replaced it with Civil Rights Press, which published *Laughing Through Tears* that same year. Many of the book's jokes take revenge against Yuan and his cronies. The chortling militarist who appears on its cover (and the cover of this book), wearing riding spurs, coattails, and medals bearing the five-colored flag of the republic, also bears some resemblance to the bald president.[63]

Besides political satire, jokes were packaged for market segments including readers interested in modern education, the sexes, classical literature, as well as those simply seeking childlike glee. Popular collections were quickly reprinted: *Side-Splitting Chats* (1913), compiled by Hu Jichen from materials previously published in the major newspaper the *National Herald Daily*, where he was an editor, and Qinshi Shanren's *Worth a Laugh* (1918) reportedly were each reprinted at least ten times.[64] Magazine editor Zhao Tiaokuang compiled *Funny Stories from the Ladies' Chambers*, which by 1927 had gone into its seventh printing.[65] Covers touted their editors as the Artisan of Laughter, King of Comedy, and Master of Humor, and anthologies boasted of being comprehensive, new, fresh, and modern. The marketing climate is perhaps best represented by Shanghai's New-New Bookstore, which in 1923 released *Mr. Chuckling at the Mortal World's Enlarged and Expanded Forest of Laughs, Featuring One Thousand New Elegant Jokes from Collections Ancient and Modern*.[66]

Such showy pitches notwithstanding, these same anthologies drew from contemporary periodicals, which, like *Punch* and other predecessors, solicited jokes from readers. Such crowdsourcing naturally made it difficult to separate what was original from what was recycled.[67] In his 1923 story, "Plagiarist in Western Dress" (discussed in chapter 5), Xu Zhuodai accused fellow writers of borrowing stale jokes from *The Expanded Forest of Laughs*, reclothing them in suit and tie, and passing them off as new Western jokes.[68]

In the late Qing, as we saw, journalist-litterateurs monitored society and officialdom and then converted the results of their surveillance into *xiaohua*. Writers of the Republican period also had their eyes out for absurd and disingenuous behavior. In 1925 the broadsheet *China Camera News* noted that when Xiong Xiling, who had served briefly as premier and minister of finance in Yuan Shikai's cabinet, told a joke at a banquet, *Shun Pao*'s editors reported it but failed to recognize that Xiong had cribbed it from a magazine. "Clearly," the writer concluded, "when it comes to jokes it doesn't matter whether you made it up yourself or ripped it off; your listeners' willingness to flatter you is all that matters."[69]

Jokes themselves ran the gamut from parables for children to scatological humor, sexual humor, tendentious social satire, puns, humorous verse, arcane literary allusions, and situational jokes, as well as language-based jokes that drew on classical Chinese, regional dialects, modern vernacular, and foreign languages. No selection could be truly representative of their diversity, much less of some sort of essential Chineseness. Consider, for example, "The Heroic Boar-Slayer," from the 1935 Shanghai collection *Fount of Laughter*:

> A man who called himself a hero without equal told his friend, Mr. Wu: "Mr. Wu, you should congratulate me for what I did yesterday."
> "What was that?" Wu asked.
> "Yesterday I went up the mountain to hunt boars and came across one as big as a calf. It was as vicious as a hungry tiger and had a look that would frighten anyone to death. I, however, took out my knife and sliced off its tail."
> "Hey, if you're such a hero," Wu replied, "why didn't you cut off its head?"
> "Ay—don't bring it up! Some bastard did that days ago."[70]

The joke has little distinctively Chinese in it other than the surname Wu and the tiger—the consummate ferocious beast of Chinese legend. The main thing that makes it modern is that it was written in the vernacular. The theme of the braggart hunter is as old as hunting itself.

Prefaces to joke collections sometimes mislead about the tone of their contents. Mr. Foolish strikes a lyrical, if parodic, note of literati contemplation in his preface to *One Thousand Jokes*, speaking of sitting in his courtyard watching the falling autumn leaves and "scouring old volumes to dispel my recent melancholy." The results of his search include jokes with titles such as "A Sore Anus," "Penis on Head," "Shit on Lips," "Fouler Than a Dog Fart," and "Ghost Gets Raped." By 1923, *One Thousand Jokes* was in its fifth printing.[71]

The Republican period was a turning point in which type of *xiaohua* held sway in the publishing market. In the late Qing, funny anecdotes predominated; in the republic, the proportion of formulaic jokes in circulation increased dramatically. A similar qualitative transition in joking styles had occurred in the late Ming when joke books began to include more jokes about social types rather than funny anecdotes about famous people, which had dominated Chinese joke books in the past.[72] But the publishing market was now bigger and more international.

Indeed, China's early twentieth-century joke boom was part of a global phenomenon. Henry Jenkins writes that turn-of-the-century America saw

> a massive proliferation of comic materials, a large-scale commodification of the joke. According to one study, the number of joke books in the United States grew from 11 in 1890 to 104 in 1907 and continued to expand throughout the first two decades of the twentieth century. More than thirty-five humor magazines, many of them weeklies, were added to the market in the years 1883–1920. . . . For the first time, it was possible to make a good living just writing jokes, and advice for would-be joke writers can be found in the pages of many of the day's leading literary journals.[73]

Compared to in the United States, the print market of the early twentieth century reached a smaller percentage of China's population owing to lower literacy and per capita income, but it still had writers like "Space-Filler King" Zheng Yimei, who specialized in providing jokes, anecdotes, gossip, and other short items for various newspapers and magazines.[74] Chinese publishers had also exchanged jokes with their foreign counterparts since the mid-nineteenth century, when British expatriates established humor periodicals in Asian colonies and treaty ports modeled on London's humor weekly *Punch*. Those in East Asia included Yokohama's *Japan Punch* (1862–87), Hong Kong's *China Punch* (1867–68, 1872–76), and Shanghai's *Puck, or the Shanghai Charivari* (1871–72) and *The Rattle* (1896–1903).[75]

The circulation of these magazines was mostly regional. News of *Puck, or the Shanghai Charivari*, however, spread as far as England and North America within a few years of its Shanghai debut. An 1877 study of *Caricature and Other Comic Art in All Times and Many Lands*, published in New York, devotes much of its chapter on China to an anecdote from the British press in 1874 that mentions *Puck*. It relates a story about the alleged awe felt by Thomas Francis Wade, the British ambassador to China, upon meeting the Chinese emperor. Parton discusses the revelations of a reporter for the London literary magazine *Athenaeum*: "It now turns out that the imaginary narrative first appeared in the columns of *Puck*, a comic paper (in English), published in Shanghai; that it was translated into Chinese by some native wag, who palmed it off on his countrymen as a truthful account of the behaviour of the English barbarian on this occasion; and that some inquiring foreigner, ignorant of the source from whence it came, retranslated it into English, and held it up as another instance of the way in which the Chinese pamphleteers were attempting to undermine our influence in China by covering our minister with contempt!"[76] Whether or not the particulars are true, the account (which Wu Jianren would have called a *xiaohua*) confirms that *Puck*, a magazine by and for Western expatriates in Shanghai, reached a Chinese audience as well as readers abroad.

In 1906, Wu Jianren related a conversation with a publishing colleague whom he observed reading a book written in a Western language. "I asked him what kind of book it was and he replied 'It's a book of jokes, much like China's *Expanded Forest of Laughs*.' 'Why don't you choose a couple and translate them?' I said. 'Make me laugh.' Zhangzi thereupon translated a few, but none of them were funny. Zhangzi said, 'Westerners have a different sensibility from us; any Westerner who read these would be rolling on the floor. I've often contemplated translating this book but been reluctant to do so for fear I'd make a hash of it.'"[77] Wu's story (which is really about inadequate Chinese translation practices) confirms that foreign jokes were being translated into Chinese at the turn of the century. In subsequent years, French, Japanese, and other languages also became sources for Chinese joke writers. Chinese-language periodicals of the 1910s regularly featured bilingual puns, such as this one in the Shanghai magazine *Relaxation*: "The English are a generation behind the Chinese. Why? Because an English 'son' is like a Chinese *sun* (grandson)."[78] A few books brought together jokes by celebrity humorists like Mark Twain,[79] and George Bernard Shaw's bon mots appeared regularly in magazines in the 1930s.

Chinese foreign students and other travelers also brought foreign humor styles back to China. The *Chinese Students' Monthly*, an English-language periodical run by Chinese students studying in the United States, in 1914 carried a column of "Wit and Humor," which included jokes like C. P. Wang's "Who Was ahead in Ancient Civilization?": "Two missionaries, one returning from Egypt and the other from China, met in New York. 'Talking about ancient civilization, why, the ancient Egyptians knew all about electricity centuries ago. Just the other day a piece of copper wire was discovered in one of the pyramids,' explained the Egyptian enthusiast. 'That is nothing,' grinned the missionary from China. 'The Chinese had long dispensed with wires. They have been using the wireless for we don't know how many centuries.'"[80]

Numerous jokes alluded to the race to modernity. But not all topical jokes were freighted with nationalistic anxieties. The *China Critic*, an English-language weekly based in Shanghai that played a key role in promoting humor in China in the 1930s (see chapter 6) regularly featured on its front page a joke alluding to international headlines, such as this one that appeared on 15 August 1935:

80 WIVES

Konstantin Manea, aged 28, has been arrested at Belgrade for having married and deserted 80 wives in 5 years. After marriages in haste, he may now repent at leisure.[81]

The joke in the next issue cut closer to home:

ANNEXATION
Rengo [the Japanese Trade Union Confederation] reports General Tada as disclaiming any intention on Japan's part to annex North China. One wonders why such a disclaimer was even necessary.[82]

Japan had in fact annexed Manchuria in 1931, when it set up the puppet state of Manchukuo; following further conflicts, China would declare war in 1937.

Chinese-language jokes circulated overseas between the 1900s and the 1930s thanks to a global Sinophone print culture that encompassed Hong Kong, Japan, Southeast Asia, Australia, North America, and Europe. In Singapore—then a part of British Malaya—*Chinese Daily News* (*Thien Nam Sin Pao*, 1898–1905) in 1904 began regularly featuring "Miscellaneous Morsels of Humor" (*zazu huixie*) on its last page. Later tabloids like the *Comical Weekly* (1927–28), the *Happy Times* (1929), and *A Laugh* (1930) featured jokes and satirical content alongside doggerel, cartoons, photos, and gossip, with the *Comical Weekly* promising "to publish only humorous writings and not touch on politics."[83]

During the early twentieth century, Japanese anthropologists and folklore specialists collected jokes in Chinese, Taiwanese, and other languages as part of a project to understand cultures affected by Japan's imperialist expansion. In 1915, twenty years into Japan's colonization of Taiwan, Japanese scholar Kawai Sanenaga compiled a bilingual *Collection of Taiwanese Jokes*, some of which had come to Taiwan via classical Chinese joke books. "Nothing to Deliver," in which a candidate for the civil service examination tells his wife that childbirth is easier than producing an essay because she at least has something in her belly, for example, appears in several Chinese joke books from the dynastic period.[84]

The early twentieth century was important in the history of Chinese jokes not only because of the sheer volume of production but also because many rare classical jokes were anthologized, punctuated, annotated, and published. In 1909, Wang Guowei, a scholar better known for his work on tragedy, compiled a collection of *Sayings of Jesters* from various classical sources. Folklorists and philologists became interested in jokes as an academic pursuit—part of the nostalgia and root seeking inspired by a time of uncertainty. In an influential 1918 essay in the May Fourth journal *La Jeunesse*, Zhou Zuoren included "books of low-grade humor (such as *The Expanded Forest of Laughs*)" among ten categories of "humane literature," which he considered to be in short supply in the Chinese tradition. Though finding them morally objectionable and of only occasional literary merit, Zhou believed that they were valuable for their insight into the psychology of a people.[85]

A decade and a half later, Zhou seems to have had a change of heart. In 1933, he compiled *Selected Jokes from the Bitter Tea Studio* (the name of Zhou's Beiping study), his goal being "restore jokes to some modicum of status in the spheres of literature and folklore studies." His sources included late Ming and early Qing collections *Treasury of Laughs, Bowled Over with Laughter,* and *A Good Laugh,* as well as *Stories of Xu Wenchang,* a collection of folk anecdotes about an eccentric Ming scholar.[86] His foreword outlines the joke's rising and falling fortunes throughout the dynasties—down in the Song, up in the late Ming, down again in the early Qing. He makes a spirited defense of the joke against the habitual snobbery of the literati, deploring their preference for moralistic jokes and enumerating jokes' virtues as persuasive allegories, social entertainment, comic narratives of literary value, and registers of popular sentiment.[87] Jokes revealed enduring truths, which could check modern man's self-superiority. As Zhou put it: "The whip was cracked at others, but you feel its lash on your own spine."[88] He cited as an example a joke about the traditional Confucian filial ideal of the son who cuts flesh from his thigh to nourish an ailing parent: in the Qing dynasty version, the son cut flesh from someone *else's* thigh. After Japan invaded in 1931, Zhou noted, there were plenty of such filial sons about.

These modern editions of old joke collections hint at how Chinese joking conventions had changed. Each joke in *In Praise of Jokes* is followed by an admiring commentary. When that Ming dynasty collection was rediscovered and published in 1932, its modern editor remarked that the "praise" (*zan*) was superfluous and detracted from the humor.[89] In 1933, during what came to be called the Year of Humor (on which, see chapter 6), T. K. Chuan translated a selection for the *China Critic*, including the following: "A hen-pecked husband who was being beaten by his wife tried to hide himself under the bed. The wife said: 'Come out, quick!' The man said: 'When a great man says No, he means it!'"[90] Chuan cut the commentary that had appeared in the Ming edition: "Every time a hen-pecked husband sees his wife he completely falls to pieces, like a snake going limp when it hears the crane's call. This man, however, is brave enough to dive under the bed and refuse to come out. If he's not a great man, who is?"

In 1934 and 1935, two different Shanghai publishers issued their own editions of *Laugh upon Laugh,* a Qing dynasty joke compilation by the Happily Retired Cave-Dwelling Hermit. The Hermit says he collected amusing stories to "dispel melancholy and boredom" he had suffered owing to chronic illness, which had twice flared up and kept him in bed for more than half a year. Jokes, he writes, proved a better tonic than more academic diversions. His 1879 preface mentions that he spent more than thirty years collecting them, a period covering both the Taiping Rebellion (1850–64) and the Second Opium War (1856–58). His sources include not only works of fiction but also Shanghai newspapers such as *Shun Pao*.[91] Market demand for comic literature during the republic thus helped to ensure the survival of a humor compilation that crossed multiple historical epochs.

FIGURE 2.2. In Republican China, jokes typically appeared first in periodicals and were later repackaged in books, sold by both large and small publishing houses. The examples pictured here were published in Shanghai. Clockwise from top left: The covers of *Free Magazine* (issue 2, 1913), distributed by the publisher of the major daily *Shun Pao*; the *Happy World* magazine (issue 2, 1914), published by the independent Happy World Press; *New Funny Stories* (1920), released by Xinhua Books (no relation to today's state-run Xinhua); and *New Jokes about Men and Women* (seventh ed., 1922), issued by one of Republican Shanghai's four biggest publishers, World Books.

FIGURE 2.3. An early Chinese joke adapted in Ye Qianyu's comic strip *Mr. Wang*. Image source: Ye, *Wang xiansheng xinji*, 3:225–26.
Panel 1: Mr. Wang: "Just look at these stupid rustics. How is a bamboo pole supposed to fit through sideways?"
Little Chen: "Let's wait here and see if he'll be able to make it into the city."
Panel 2: Peasant A: "It won't go in sideways or standing up. I'll just have to go home."
Peasant B: "If you saw it into shorter pieces you can get it through!"

Jokes were important not only to writers but also to professionals in the performing arts, cartooning, and cinema. Hou Baolin, a comedian specializing in the northern performing art of *xiangsheng*, began collecting jokes in the 1940s both for his personal pleasure and to enrich his professional repertoire. In one instance, he is said to have sold his overcoat to buy a Ming dynasty edition of *In Praise of Jokes*.[92] Lin Buqing, a performer famous in Suzhou and Shanghai for his dialect mimicry and parodic ballads, recorded multiple phonograph records of his routines in the 1910s. Hundreds of his jokes were later transcribed into books such as *New Jokes about Men and Women* (1920), which was reprinted seven times by 1922 (see figure 2.2).[93] Despite its title, only a minority of jokes in that collection are about the sexes, and, not surprisingly, not all of them are new. "A Brilliant Trick," for example, adapts a joke that appeared in several premodern collections:

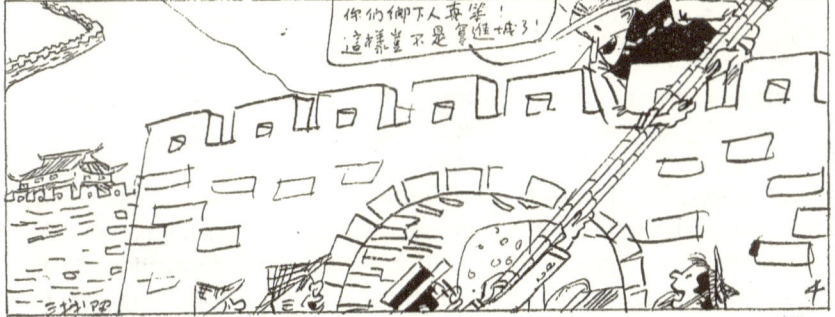

FIGURE 2.3. *(continued)*
Panel 3: Mr. Wang: "Hey! Let me help you figure it out!"
Panel 4: Mr. Wang: "You rustics are so stupid! This is the way to do it!"

There once was a man who made his living as a swindler, and his son followed in his trade. The father, concerned about this, asked his son: "What technique do you plan to use to trick people?" The son replied: "Depends on the situation; the possibilities are numerous." Incensed by his arrogance, the father, who was upstairs at the time, asked: "Do you have the guts to try tricking me? If you can trick me into going downstairs I promise I'll allow you to continue in this trade." The son replied: "That's too hard. But if you were downstairs I could trick you into going upstairs." The father went downstairs to see how his son would do it and the son smiled: "But see—now you've come downstairs." The father burst into laughter.[94]

Like many of its competitors, *Jokes about Men and Women* was printed on rough paper and crudely bound. These cheap volumes, meant to be enjoyed quickly and replaced with new ones, were as ephemeral as Hou Baolin's performances. But they aided professionals in other entertainment industries as well. Cartoonists like Ye Qianyu drew on joke books for material to meet their daily deadlines. In one comic strip featuring his famous cartoon heroes "Mr. Wang" and "Little

Chen" (see figure 2.3), Ye adapts a two-thousand-year-old joke from *Forest of Laughs*:

> A man of Lu carrying a bamboo pole was trying to enter the city gates. He first tried to carry it in vertically but failed; he then tried horizontally but failed again. He was at a loss when, a short while later there arrived an old man who said to him: "I'm no sage, but I've been around a bit. Why don't you cut the pole in half and bring it in that way?" And so he did. Of all the stupidity in the world, nothing tops this.[95]

THE SECRET OF BEING A JOKER

In 1671, the dramatist and author Li Yu spoke from years of experience directing opera troupes when he wrote that comic relief should be natural and spontaneous. The best jokes were not rehearsed in advance but inspired by the moment—they forced themselves upon the performer. In the early twentieth century, funny goings-on forced themselves to the attention of writers, readers, and performers, who reworked them for the public. But China's internal turmoil only partly explains the proliferation of jokes, not all of which were topical or tendentious. Population growth, urbanization, and the engine of print capitalism also fueled their production. The result was not only that Chinese people were besieged by an "avalanche of absurdities" (*xiaohua baichu*), but also that—to take literally the Chinese idiom appearing in this chapter's title—jokes were appearing everywhere.

A new class of cultural professional was drawn to the virtues of humor. Wu Jianren was one of the first Chinese modern writers to propose that "to influence people through writing, humorous language works better than stern rhetoric." Many writers of the republic followed his lead, even as others were drawn to the metaphorical possibilities of the *xiaohua*. Xu Xu, a writer affiliated with Lin Yutang's magazines of the 1930s, likened one type of bad writing to a child cracking up before he gets to the joke he's supposed to be telling—all the self-congratulatory noise obscures the point.[96]

In 1924, a decade and a half after Wu Jianren, Lin Yutang made his first pitch for conducting serious debates in a jocular rather than ponderous tone. Lin believed that the Chinese language circumscribed how Chinese people could talk about talk itself. They were trapped into treating "serious talk" (*zhengjinghua*) and "laugh-producing talk" (*xiaohua*) as being mutually opposed. China needed some other category of talk, which he called *youmo* (humor).

The neologism represented a radical attempt to change the language game, a process whose unexpected results are discussed in chapter 6. It did not, however, readily displace the tendency to interpret all humorous speech or behavior as a form of joking. Lu Xun, for one, saw grave risks in mode of speech concerned only with amusement. In "The Secret of Being a Joker," a 1933 essay critiquing the recent humor movement, he illustrated the danger of telling *xiaohua* by paraphrasing the Danish philosopher Søren Kierkegaard: "Fire breaks out in a theater. A clown takes the stage and informs the audience. Everyone takes it to be one of the clown's jokes [*xiaohua*] and applauds. The clown repeats his message that the place is on fire, but the audience only laughs and applauds more uproariously. The way I see it, the world will come to an end thanks to these jolly people who treat everything as a joke [*xiaohua*]."[97]

Lu Xun's comments bring to mind a famous line from the Daoist classic the *Dao De Jing*, also known as *The Way and Its Virtue*, in which the laughter of the ignorant helps the wise man to recognize the Truth: "When the inferior man hears the Dao he laughs uproariously—if he didn't, it wouldn't be the Dao." They also recall a basic distinction that the philosopher Harry G. Frankfurt has made between the bullshitter and the liar. The liar knows the truth but conceals it; the bullshitter, in contrast, is concerned only with getting away with impressing the audience. The bullshitter may or may not know the truth and may or may not speak it (including inadvertently), but ultimately one who speaks "unconstrained by a concern with truth" is its greater enemy.[98]

Promoters and opponents of joking were equally concerned about laughter on a societal scale, whether manifested in the communal laughter of the crowd or broadcast through the press. Some proponents of joking in the early twentieth century spoke of it as a progressive force, a handmaiden to reform. Jokes that covered the Manchus with contempt might indeed have strengthened the resolve of some revolutionaries to take up arms against them, confident that public opinion was on their side. But most readers, no doubt, simply sought diversion. Talk needed not be entirely accurate if, like gossip, it evoked laughter or amusement. To critics with a social agenda, joking encouraged a culture of blithe irreverence that was more concerned with the funny than the true. In one of his most famous metaphors for China's predicament, and a decade before he wrote of the clown in the burning theater, Lu Xun had portrayed the Chinese people as being asleep in an iron house and on the point of suffocating in their sleep. Now, he wrote, they were awake and alert but distracted from taking any action to quench the encroaching flames of their own destruction.

3

Play
游戲大觀

Go to the zoo and watch a pair of monkeys picking each other's ears, and there you have the promise of an Isaac Newton or an Albert Einstein.
—LIN YUTANG, 1937[1]

Lu Xun wrote about jokes and jokesters as if their proliferation were an omen that the end was nigh: everyone would ultimately be consumed by their bullshit. But to many of his contemporaries, adopting a playful attitude toward modern changes was a way to find China's future. In the 1890s, when Lu Xun was still a teenage Zhou Shuren, the very word *play* (*youxi*) came to stand for a culture of amusement involving experimentation with literary form and modern devices. Play remained a prominent symbol of fun for about thirty years, until around a decade and a half after the 1911 revolution. Newspapers and magazines offered readers a steady diet of parodic essays, humorous poems and stories, puzzles, cartoons, caricatures, and novelty photographs. New "playthings" (*wanyi*) were also appearing: cameras, lenses, spectacles, scopes, mirrors, and other gadgets and machines.

Youxi, translated here as "play" or "game," became a buzzword in print media in the late 1890s and spread to other parts of popular and visual culture. In the 1900s and 1910s, *youxi* was an umbrella category for humor somewhat interchangeable with *huaji* (funny or comical, and the subject of chapter 5). But it encompassed a broader range of amusements. *Panorama of Play* (*Youxi daguan*, 1919), a six-volume compendium of word games, puns, lantern riddles, tangrams, jokes, drinking songs, athletic activities, operatic arias, and magic tricks, is emblematic of the term's breadth.[2] Writers and illustrators of the era played with familiar genres and ideas using parody, allegory, and various sorts of word games; moving pictures and other technologies of viewing and projection, meanwhile, were becoming conspicuous toys of modern mass culture, enabling new types of play.

The *you* of *youxi* can mean to play or to wander. These dual meanings converge in the picaresque playfulness of China's greatest comic novel, the sixteenth-century *Journey to the West* (*Xiyou ji*), which parodies Buddhist practices (such as the religious pilgrimage) as it follows the roamings of a mischievous monkey.³ Crazy Ji, a picaresque and comical figure of popular religious lore, was a wandering Daoist whose signature move was to somersault and expose his privates.⁴ Leisure papers of the late Qing referred to armchair travel as travel of the mind or heart (*xinyou*) or of the easy chair or bed (*woyou*, literally reclined travel).⁵ *Xi* can mean to play or jest but also refers to a play in the sense of the theater or opera, carrying associations such as costume, makeup, masks, performance, singing, artificiality, and ephemerality. *Youxi* can mean amusement, recreation, games, sports, playing, frolicking, or having fun. The phrase *youxi renjian* may refer to taking a jaded or cynical view of life or to indulging in worldly pleasures with the aloofness of an immortal. In Buddhism, *youxi sanmei* refers to the attainment of a state of spiritual purity and calm; its lay usage can connote the opposite: hedonism.

The literary category of "playful writings" (*youxi wenzhang* or *youxi wenzi*) encompasses prose compositions done in jest or for fun, including parodies, jokes, riddles, and ghost stories. (Ludic poems, a vast category, also went by other names.)⁶ A famous example from the Tang dynasty is Han Yu's "Address to the Crocodiles," which he wrote while prefect of Chaozhou, a post then on the southern fringes of empire, in what is now Guangdong province. In it, Han admonishes the reptiles plaguing the local waterways and issues an ultimatum: "I now hold the crocodiles to the following covenant: within three days they must lead their foul ilk southward to the sea, thereby quitting the presence of the Son of Heaven's appointed representative. If they leave not within three days, I shall grant them five; if they leave not within five days I shall grant them seven. But if they leave not within seven days, this means that they will never be willing to move; this means that they will neither acknowledge the Prefect nor heed his words. Or it may mean that crocodiles are stupid and insensitive." In any event, if they stay, they will be killed. Some of Han's biographers, missing the parody, claimed that the obstinate beasts heeded his words.⁷

The concept of play was central to the business interests and lifestyle of men who ran Shanghai's tabloids (known as *xiaobao*, or small newspapers) between the 1890s and 1910s. They encouraged their readers to view the metropolis as "China's biggest playground" by offering in their pages, in historian Catherine Vance Yeh's words, a "daily peep-show of articles featuring the city's entertainment life and its celebrities," particularly opera stars and courtesans.⁸ Juan Wang has argued that "tabloid literati made the pursuit of fun and play a cultural fetish" by promoting an escapist ethos in papers such as *Have Fun While You Can*.⁹ And, indeed, they often spoke of "having fun with the era" (*wanshi*) to signal their ironic detachment from the troubles of the world.

Li Boyuan founded one of the most influential of these small newspapers, *Play*, in June of 1897.[10] He wrote as the Master of Play, a pen name that had been used by the editor of the eighteenth-century joke book *The Expanded Forest of Laughs*, mentioned in chapter 2, and that also recalls the Shanghai Masters of Play, authors of an 1895 guide to Shanghai courtesan houses.[11] This playful self-image, to Yeh, symbolizes the late Qing literati's coming to terms with their diminished cultural authority in the modern era—no longer viewed as moral paragons, they could at least entertain.[12]

And entertain they did. The most popular tabloids reached tens of thousands of readers per issue; their circulation was comparable to the big dailies. Their interests were social as well as literary, and the demimonde, where courtesans and their patrons and handlers engaged in ritual role play, was of special interest. *Play* brought that rarefied sphere into the public domain by sponsoring reader elections of a Queen of the Flowers and publishing photographs of contestants.[13] It also engaged readers by hosting debates about the merits of various opera stars while listing performances around town.

Play offered "playful pieces written in a humorous style" on a wide range of topics, and contributors offered style points to aspiring writers.[14] The goal, Li said, was to make people smile through indirect means such as satire and allegorical exhortation, while never expressing something directly, and thereby leaving no room for maneuver. Its overnight success inspired imitators such as *Laughter* (est. 1897), *Leisure Pursuits* (est. 1897), and *Forest of Laughs* (est. 1901).[15] *World of Play* (est. 1907), a magazine based in Hangzhou, offered a different model that emphasized sundry literary amusements, such as parodic verse, stories, lantern riddles, jokes, and book reviews, which was to become even more popular in the early Republic.[16] On *Play*'s two-month anniversary, Li described the paper's "fundamental significance" as using allegories to show the masses that worldly affairs were "really but a game." News items, though humorous, strived for accuracy and the trust of readers. The editor's "playful detachment" (*youxi sanmei*) expressed an attitude of nonchalance (*wanshi*) that, he clarified three months later, was really a strategy for moralizing (*xingshi*).[17] For Li Boyuan, then, play was at once a literary aesthetic, lifestyle, statement of values, marketing strategy, and political manifesto.

Play's title, Li wrote in 1897, "was copied from the West."[18] Though he did not name a specific source, inspiration might have come from foreign periodicals circulating in China or from China's foreign-language entertainment press. One contemporary was *The Rattle* (1896–1903) (see figure 3.1), an illustrated humor magazine issued irregularly in the Shanghai International Settlement by Kelly and Walsh. *The Rattle* was an encore to *Puck, or the Shanghai Charivari* (1871–72),

FIGURE 3.1. The cover of the first issue of the Shanghai-based expatriate humor magazine *The Rattle* (May 1896). Image courtesy of Widener Library, Harvard University.

an illustrated humor magazine from a quarter century earlier, and it closely followed *Puck*'s style and format, offering caricatures, verse, essays, news commentary, gossip, letters, and other short pieces. In the late 1890s, *The Rattle* stopped publishing for a couple years after having "absolutely drained Shanghai of humour," but it revived in November 1900 when the Boxer Rebellion—which threatened Shanghai—provided new material.[19]

Its humor, often at the expense of the Chinese for the benefit of expatriate westerners, was aimed at the easily amused—those "pleased with a rattle, tickled with a straw," a line from Alexander Pope's "Essay on Man" (1734). The passage alluded to begins in infancy and ends:

> Some livelier plaything gives his youth delight,
> A little louder, but as empty quite:
> Scarfs, garters, gold, amuse his riper stage,
> And beads and prayer-books are the toys of age:
> Pleased with this bauble still, as that before,
> Till tir'd he sleeps, and life's poor play is o'er.[20]

The Rattle's innocuous title thus hints at a grimmer message that life is but a series of self-distractions with empty playthings. Despite their linguistic and cultural differences, British Shanghailanders turned to play and whimsy for reasons similar to Chinese contemporaries like Li Boyuan. National affairs were one motivator; others were boredom and money. The ending of one submission to *The Rattle* captures their shared tendency to apologize for their own frivolity:

> I earn my living with my pen
> Upon a wooden stool,
> And my companions, soulless men,
> Consider me a fool.
> "Listen to that eccentric coon,"
> Says Jerry, Dick, or Tom,
> "He's adding figures to the tune
> "Pom-Pom, Pom-Pom, Pom-Pom!"[21]

ENTERTAINING POSSIBILITIES

Playfulness also enlivened literature with a forward-looking political agenda, most of which was not marketed as *youxi*. One of the most famous turn-of-the-century novels is Liang Qichao's *The Future of New China*, which he serialized in his magazine *New Fiction* in 1902. Liang was in exile in Japan after an attempt by the emperor to introduce political and economic reforms in 1898 ended when the empress dowager put the emperor under house arrest and rounded up the intellectuals who had advised him, executing a number of them; the price on Liang's head was 100,000 taels of silver.[22] While overseas, Liang advocated a program of gradual reform that would preserve the monarchy, even as he criticized the Manchus. During five years living on and off in Yokohama, he founded several reformist magazines, camouflaging his involvement with pen names and misleading credits.[23] These periodicals contained novels (many translated) of science fiction, romance, and other genres, as well as essays on political topics and news commentary.

The year 1902 marked the peak of both Liang Qichao's political radicalism and his popularity as a writer,[24] and *The Future of New China* would have had a wide readership. The novel is set upon the sixtieth anniversary of a fictional New China's Reforms. China is hosting heads of state from around the world—England, Japan, Russia, the Philippines, Hungary—for a Shanghai Expo and the ratification of a world peace treaty. The keynote speaker of a series of educational lectures about Chinese history, held concurrently in the envisioned capital of Nanjing, is a descendent of Confucius. Just as the fictional Shanghai Expo anticipates the actual one held in 2010, the character Kong Juemin, or "Confucius, the Awakener of the People," anticipates by over twenty years Lin Yutang's reinterpretation of the Sage as a humorous philosopher (discussed in chapter 6).[25] Most of the novel is the transcript of Mr. Kong's speech, "The History of China's Past Sixty Years."

China, in Liang's vision, is no longer a bullied and backward nation. It has regained its status as the Middle Kingdom and is sharing its culture with an admiring world, as represented by the foreign dignitaries. Mr. Kong evaluates New China's recent political progress and reviews in detail the policies that served as the political foundation for its growth and development. This set piece of ventriloquism let readers hear what a leading reformist thinker wanted to see in his government, including a constitution and stable party politics.[26]

The novel contains a second text that is not reprinted in most later editions.[27] From page 1, a commentator sustains a running dialogue with the story's narrator. The commentary is attributed to the Master of the Pavilion of Equality, a pen name of Di Baoxian, a fellow protégé of the reformist courtier Kang Youwei's and reformer-in-exile. Di's commentary appears in two places on the page: in interlinear comments (*jiawen*) printed in half-size font within the vertical columns of main text, and in "eyebrow" comments (*meipi*) on the top margin of the page. The "Wedge" (*xiezi*), which precedes chapter 1, begins: "The story goes that 2,513 years after the birth of Confucius [2,453 years after today], being the year 2062 by the Western calendar [today being the year 2002], in the *renyin* year of the 60-year cycle, the first of January was the day the Chinese people held a nationwide celebration marking Sixty Years of Reform." The asides (indicated here in square brackets) open up a gap between the narrator, who inhabits the future, and the commentator who inhabits the present. But a calculation error reveals Liang's haste (or that of a typesetter) in making his vision public: later plot details confirm that Liang meant to set his novel not in 2062 but in 1962—sixty years ahead of the year in which he was writing.

As Kong Juemin prepares to give his address, the narrator anticipates a question from readers: how will foreigners understand a speech delivered in Chinese? The answer: China's academic reforms have inspired foreigners to study Chinese. More than thirty thousand are enrolled in Chinese schools and more than twelve hundred have already graduated. China is now a global intellectual magnet and an exporter of knowledge. The commentator is incredulous: "I never imagined they'd all be studying Chinese now!" The narrator notes that the entire speech is being telegraphed to Yokohama, where it will be published in *New Fiction*, prompting the commentator to exclaim, "That would be one expensive telegram!" Mr. Kong quips that he'll keep his speech short because he doesn't want the transcript to put *New Fiction* readers to sleep, causing his audience to burst out laughing.

Banter punctuates the work. The narrator mentions that Old Mr. Kong is now seventy-six years old. The *jiawen* adds: "That means the gentleman is 16 years old today." The narrator calls Kong's learning "unsurpassed"; the commentator—sixty years behind—replies, "Unsurpassed indeed!" The audience falls quiet and "waits respectfully" to hear Mr. Kong's wisdom; the commentator remarks: "I've been waiting sixty years!"

Mr. Kong begins his speech: "My dearest ladies and gentlemen, I have no doubt that today we all participate in this conference in a spirit of sincere patriotism. Yet sixty years ago, no one could have imagined a day like today. [Today being what day?] No one would have even dared hope for a day like today. [What day is today?]" The date calculation error, noted above, makes Di's questions especially ironic. Kong reviews the stages China has gone through in the past sixty years: the Preparatory Period ("From the Eight-Power Allied Army's invasion of Beijing [1900] up to Guangdong's self-governance"), the Divided Governance Period, the Unification Period, the Period of Colonial-Capitalism, the Period of Foreign Competition, and finally the Soaring Period. The eyebrow-margin commentary reads: "These are the six stages that China must venture through. The reader is invited to play carefully with each of them (*xiwan zhi*)." Playing politics here takes on a hypothetical dimension: Di's suggestion seems to be that readers entertain themselves by entertaining the possibility of this future history.

The Future of New China is in a mode that literary historian Michael Gibbs Hill calls the "future perfect—what *will have been* achieved when a program for reform is implemented."[28] Its commentary makes the futurism interactive, highlighting the gaps between the future perfect of Mr. Kong and the present of the commentator and the reader.

Di Baoxian's persona, by turns wisecracking and naive, treats the text not with reverence, as with classical commentaries, but with the bantering style of one half of a comedy duo. Scholars have often characterized the fiction of this period, with its amalgam of traditional and modern sensibilities, as schizophrenic.[29] Di's commentary creates a dialogue that is more akin to a conversation between friends than neurotic self-interrogation. This provides a comfortable basis for a fantasy of national role-playing, which has China trying on possible future identities.

Also notable is that the commentary is the product not just of humans but of machines. Around the turn of the century, Chinese periodicals began to use precision machine-age printing to reproduce the style of marginal and interlinear comments and punctuation marks that commentators used to write with brush and ink. Top margins took up a quarter to a third of the page, and this excess blank space largely disappeared from magazines by the 1920s. The brief interval before the "eyebrow commentator" was squeezed out by economic concerns enabled a type of packaged spontaneity: the reader is treated to a literary game that has been first played, and then typeset.

Liang abruptly ended *The Future of New China* after four chapters, leaving it unfinished, but it inspired other writers to adopt the jocular commentarial style.[30] (Di himself went on to become the publisher of the influential daily newspaper *Eastern Times*, to which he added a comic supplement.)[31] The following year, in 1903, Liang's popularity dropped when he began supporting constitutional monarchism even as popular opinion moved in the opposite direction. Liang's visions of China's future, to many, had begun looking too much like its past.[32]

Futuristic fantasy nevertheless remained popular through the 1900s, as authors continued to toy with various possibilities of national reinvention. One of the most famous examples is Wu Jianren's 1905 novel *New Story of the Stone*, which begins with an apologia.[33] *Story of the Stone*, an eighteenth-century novel better known as *Dream of the Red Chamber*, had inspired many dreadful sequels. Am I, Wu asks rhetorically, making the same mistake of "adding legs to the painting of a snake?"

The story then sets off at a clip, abandoning the tragic heroine, Lin Daiyu, and following the adventures of her erstwhile love interest and kindred spirit, the young scion Jia Baoyu, who concludes generations of Buddhist self-cultivation to find himself in the year 1901. Teahouse patrons mock him for being delusional when he tells them he is Jia Baoyu trying to find Rong Mansion, his home. While making his way to Shanghai by steamer, he is stunned when a fellow passenger tells him that Lin Daiyu is now the city's most famous prostitute. It turns out to be a case of mistaken identity. As Baoyu discovers, role-playing is the fashion among late Qing courtesans, who—in real life as well, as readers of Li Boyuan's *Play* would know—often called themselves after characters in romantic novels.

In Shanghai, Baoyu witnesses inequalities between foreigners and Chinese that prompt him to devote his energies to strengthening China. There he also encounters his dissolute cousin Xue Pan (another time traveler), who sells books and enjoys a modern playboy lifestyle. Baoyu finds himself drawn to the social, political, and technological reform ideas he reads about in Liang Qichao's newspapers.

The effete Baoyu of *Dream of the Red Chamber* is transformed into a tireless seeker of new scientific, geographical, technological, and political knowledge. Halfway through the novel, having traveled around China, he passes through a portal into the Civilized Realm. (Wu explains this turn to fantasy as having been inspired by a Mr. Mirror of the Self [Jingwo], who offered to write a commentary on his manuscript.) Baoyu's guide through this futuristic realm is Old Youth,[34] who introduces him to technological marvels such as the Character Examination

Lens (*ceyan xingzhi jing*), which screens new arrivals for barbarism; an anthropomorphic talking clock; chemically altered seasonal weather; and health drinks that substitute for food. Baoyu goes hunting in a flying car (helping to bring down a roc in Africa) and a flexible glass submarine, encountering sea monsters and merpeople. They eventually reach the South Pole and pursue a sea loach through a tunnel to Australia. Presided over by a man named Oriental Civilization, the Realm surpasses the West in every respect, including as a departure point for adventure.

Wu's picaresque fantasy draws on works of Victorian science fiction, such as Edward Bellamy's *Looking Backward: 2000–1887* (1887) and Jules Verne's *Vingt mille lieues sous les mers* (1870).[35] The search for solutions is consistent with the mainstream hope of late Qing intellectuals that imported technologies and ideas could be used to strengthen China. So is its undercurrent of anxiety. Baoyu complains bitterly about China's situation and embarks on his quest with zeal bordering on desperation. Near the end of his journey, he witnesses an international peace conference held in an idealized China (the Civilized Realm) akin to the one in *The Future of New China*, but, unlike in Liang Qichao's novel, it turns out to be only a passing dream. Literary scholar David Wang calls Baoyu "a lonely, puzzled adventurer outside of history," unhappy to find himself "a late spectator of what 'will already have' happened."[36]

Yet Baoyu does not dwell on his own anachronism; he adapts to the times. Nor is all of Wu Jianren's humor, as the Lin Daiyu joke reveals, venting of nationalistic anxiety. There is much situational comedy: Baoyu trips over his personal servant, Beiming, and gets cursed for being a "blind bastard." He is puzzled by a newspaper and frightened when a match ignites. Baoyu becomes a plaything of the author, a figure of slapstick and country bumpkin humor, his "naiveté and provincialism" akin to Granny Liu of *Dream of the Red Chamber*, who is bedazzled by the opulence of the Rong Mansion's Grand View Garden.[37]

Modern objects inspire not just anxiety but amazement. These include everyday items as well as novelty machines that are both technological marvels and spectacular curiosities. Baoyu's exploratory attitude toward steamers, the gramophone, Morse code, a pocket watch, a flashlight, an iron-smelting factory, firearms, and the other things he encounters convey what Neil Harris in his study of the nineteenth-century American showman P. T. Barnum calls an "operational aesthetic," namely, a fascination with machines and the way thing work.[38]

This enlightenment disposition is motivated by the social imperative that citizens be scientifically literate and cultured. One of its expressions, Harris notes, is a cultural interest in frauds, hoaxes, practical jokes, and methods of differentiating the real from the bogus. (I discuss hoaxes in chapter 5.) Another is autodidacticism, which requires being open to new ideas. In Wu's novel, Baoyu's obsessive reading and traveling and his eagerness to learn English represent an operational aesthetic caught up in late Qing evolutionary nationalism, which stressed strengthening the empire and the race over pursuing personal gain. Baoyu's response to the conundrum of how Chinese technology might catch up with and surpass the West is (like that of his interlocutor Wu Bohui, or Capable of Anything) relentlessly optimistic and exploratory.

Technical marvels possess value as more than just symbols of China's lagging scientific knowledge—they astonish and delight by virtue of their own properties. In *The Future of New China*, the focus is on the way things *will* work in China's future perfect. *New Story of the Stone* is a tale of dream-work involving geographical and technological escapade. Neither Wu's heavy-handed ending (itself a genre convention of the age) nor Liang's lack of an ending negates the games that precede it. Notwithstanding their concern for China's current national plight,[39] both novels have fun with futuristic conceits.

IDLE AMUSEMENTS

The revolution of 1911 meant to propel China into the future as a modern nation-state. In the short term, it ushered in ennui. In December of 1913, the editor of *Newest Humor Assortment*, a certain Mr. Tottering in the Clouds (*Yunjian diangong*), reflected on the first anniversary of the founding of the Republic of China. "The five peoples have been united!" was on everybody's lips, he wrote.[40] But what did the coming together of the Han, Manchus, Tibetans, Mongols, and Muslims mean to a middle-aged idler like himself who cared only for good food and amusing literary works? This new publication, he hoped, would provide that rarest of treasures—laughter. For, as the sage-poets Du Mu and Su Dongpo attested, "In life, one so rarely has occasion to laugh," and "a contented smile is so rare a thing."[41]

Mr. Tottering relates an incident from his trip to Shanghai to find a printer for his humor anthology, which included items gleaned from periodicals as well as works by him and his friends. En route he was drawn into a restaurant by a sign promising "A Complete Republican Banquet featuring Specialties of the Five Peoples." As the dishes arrived one by one, his expectations were disappointed. He elaborates with a series of puns. The first, eel, prompted him to reflect that nowadays one has to go to a Japanese joint for "fried" ***MAN[CHURIAN]***li, since the Japanese are "stronger" on that dish. The dish of soy-sauce-braised *zang* (Tibet) innards has had all its original flavor "stolen away" by all of the ham hocks (*yingtui*) (English) mistakenly added by the cook. The le***MON[GOL]***ade (*ningmengguo*) reeks of goose (*e*, i.e., Russian) fat; the Muslim (Hui) chicken is too tough to swallow; and the pr[*H*]*AwNS* in the house's best-known dish are "overheated." When the bill came, Mr. Tottering was taken aback by the exorbitant price.

The Republican Banquet turns out to be an unpalatable travesty. It is a picture of disunion, in which each individual dish is so unsatisfactory that the meal as a whole collapses. Several dishes allude to specific territorial threats to China. Japan, following its victory in the Russo-Japanese War of 1904–5, had expanded its interests in the northeast area then known as Manchuria. British soldiers had been making incursions into Tibet since 1904.[42] The area now known as Mongolia had been part of the Qing Empire since the seventeenth century, but it declared independence in 1911 and soon fell under growing Russian influence.

Allegories of national consumption circulated widely in the late nineteenth and early twentieth centuries. Cartoonists around the world depicted foreign and domestic powers carving up China and other threatened territories, particularly in eastern Europe, like a cake, a pig, a sausage, or a melon. China's internal contests for power they routinely represented as a cannibalistic struggle that would result in the country's eventual consumption by foreign onlookers.[43]

Carve up like a melon (*guafen*) in Chinese carries a hint of emasculation; a similar phrase, "break the melon" (*pogua*) means to take a woman's virginity.[44] China was being violated. Chinese cartoonists also created visual symbols based on indigenous motifs. "Insects in a Fresh Moon Cake" (see figure 3.2), an illustration that appeared in the new newspaper *Civil Rights* a little more than a year before Mr. Tottering's banquet, depicts a Chinese pastry associated with the annual mid-autumn festival. Newly made by the Five Peoples, whose names surround the flag of the Republic, it is being nibbled away by vermin: "England," "Russia," and "Japan."

Mr. Tottering's version twists the cliché: instead of foreigners or power-hungry Chinese leaders consuming the nation, it is a citizen sampling the flavors of the age. The tone, furthermore, is exploratory rather than indignant—that of a gastronome trying something new and finding that it does not suit his tastes.

Mr. Tottering in the Clouds was a pen name of Lei Jin (1871–1941), a second-level graduate of the Qing civil service examinations who now ran a venerable Suzhou publishing house that had been forced to move to Shanghai during the Taiping Rebellion. The Mountain Lodge of Swept Leaves was one of a number of presses in the early Republic specializing in affordable editions, from ancient classics to modern fiction. Comedy was one of its specialties.[45] Lei had been a critic of the old regime, writing an exposé of the "myriad oddities of Qing officialdom" in the style of Li Boyuan.[46] His pen name alludes to Shanghai using an image of literati reclusion inspired by a late-Ming group from the region known as the Cloud Poets (Yunjian pai). It also recalls the Daoist eccentric Ji Gong, a comic folk hero also known as Crazy Ji (Ji Dian). Given Lei's interest in parody, it further suggests the serene aloofness of a man who inverts (*dian*) things from on high—a Mr. Lofty Inversions. And Lei came up with the pen name when the Manchu regime itself was already tottering (*dianwei*) on an insubstantial foundation.

Radicals derided intellectuals like Lei as *yilao*—relics or old leftovers—of the Qing dynasty. They attacked them for dilettantism and triviality, as well as for

FIGURE 3.2. "Insects in a Fresh Mooncake," in a pictorial supplement to *Civil Rights* 182 (25 September 1912).

writing for the market. The ideology of amusement and self-amusement they found offensive in part because it was popular. Lei and his fellow writer-editors knew that parody and allegory resonated with their readers, and they encouraged them to face unpleasant realities with a playful attitude.

SERIAL PARODISTS

Around the time of the Republican Revolution, playful writings spread to major newspapers. In 1911, *Shun Pao* inaugurated a special section that specialized in them. "Free Talk" picked up where Liang Qichao, Li Boyuan, and Wu Jianren left off in couching polemics in a jocular style.[47] It became a major forum for public discourse, attracting intellectuals of all political stripes into the 1930s. Two years after its launch, its editor capitalized on the column's popularity by repackaging some of its best playful writings with new works in *Free Magazine*. A

"Congratulatory Poem" appearing in the inaugural issue of October 1913 closed with this stanza:

文章笑罵罵文章	Writers mutually mock and lambaste,
滋味酸鹹試細嘗	Sour counteracts savory—have a taste;
欲把詼諧當藥石	Should you seek humor as the antidote,
故翻格調學東方	Change your style and learn from the East.[48]

Ridicule had been a central feature in the late Qing Shanghai tabloids, and Republican editors welcomed witty disparagement as part of the game.[49] Salty language and the well-placed literary allusion both added flavor to the Republican Banquet that Lei Jin found so insipid. (In the last line, *Dongfang*, or the East, may allude to the famous Han dynasty court wit Dongfang Shuo.) *Free Magazine* soon changed its name to *Youxi zazhi*, or *Playful Magazine*, advertising the style of writing "Free Talk" was best known for.[50]

Writers in this entertainment market parodied anything and everything—from individual works to familiar styles, forms, and genres. Novelists wrote picaresque sequels to such vernacular classics as *Investiture of the Gods*, *Journey to the West*, and *Flowers in the Mirror*, filling them with humorous anachronisms and incongruities resulting from encounters between tradition and modernity.[51] Poets and essayists parodied selections from canonical works such as the *Book of Change*, the epic poem *Li Sao*, the *Four Books*, and the *Five Classics*. Short parodies often used formulaic title prefixes like "A play on . . ." (*xi*), "In imitation of . . ." (*ni*), "In playful imitation of . . ." (*xini*), and "Mimicking . . ." (*fang*).[52]

Du Fu's "Meeting Li Guinian in the South," for example, would be immediately recognizable to any schoolchild familiar with *Three Hundred Tang Poems*:

岐王宅裡尋常見	In King Qi's Manor I often saw you,
崔九堂前幾度聞	In Cui the Ninth's Hall I frequently heard you sing;
正是江南好風景	Now amidst the lovely scenery of the south,
落花時節又逢君	In the season of falling blossoms we meet again.

The poem expresses Du Fu's surprise and regret at finding a talented court musician singing for his supper in exile, having been driven south by an eighth-century rebellion. In 1918, a contributor to the cartoon monthly *Shanghai Puck* "mimicked" (*fang*) the Poet-Immortal's verse as follows:

野雞	"Streetwalker"
貴州路口尋常見	On the corner of Guizhou Road we often met,
樓外樓頭幾度聞	In Fantasy Mansion I frequently heard your voice;
馬路排班怕巡捕	Your street pimp fears the policeman on the beat,
青蓮閣下又逢君	At Green Lotus Pavilion we meet again.[53]

Parodists renewed a comedic form dating back to the Tang dynasty by writing short mock-biographies of Rice Moth, Layabout, Crab with a Human Face (rapacious officials, like crabs, "walk sideways," or run amuck), Mr. Yes-Man, Mr. Cuckold, Miss Pockmarked, and Kowtowing Parasite.[54] They composed rhapsodies (*fu*) to opium addicts, streetwalkers, magistrates, beards, revolution, fake coeds, and the streets of the foreign concessions, as well as celebrations (*he*) and encomia (*zan*) of things like fires and poverty.[55] They parodied speeches, advertisements, confessions, petitions, orders, handbills, notices, policies, regulations, resolutions, discourses, explications, sutras, memorials to the throne, and conference minutes. We have an exchange of letters between the Queue and the Beard and Eyebrows. We have a eulogy for a chamber pot. We have "Research on Why Men Have Beards and Women Don't," "A Telegram from the Thunder God to His Mother Resigning His Post," and "A Public Notice from the King of Whoring Prohibiting Playboys from Skipping Debts." One "travelogue" consists of a head louse and a foot louse discussing the perils they experienced journeying over the landscape of a body.[56] Another records a trip to sleep.

Enterprising editors resold parodies (as they did jokes) by packaging them in compendia. Li Dingyi's *The Comic Spirit* (1919), for example, collects work by more than four dozen authors (some, like Li, the Pacifier of the Barbarians, are identifiable by their pen names),[57] sorting them into six categories: essays, poems and lyrics, practical advice, fiction, stories, and news. Poems and lyrics include topical verse making fun of runts, beanpoles, fatties, the pockmarked, mutes, blind men, hunchbacks, the deaf, the paralyzed, old relics of the Qing, wearers of Western suits, fiction writers, bureaucrats, compradors, and journalists.

Essays include discourses (*lun* or *shuo*) that use systematic logic to develop a preposterous proposition. "The Opium Addict as Master of the Sciences,"[58] for example, ticks off reasons why the consummate Sick Man of Asia is an expert in all fields of modern learning. Commerce: he sends money overseas. Phonics: listen to him take drags and exhale smoke. Chemistry: he processes raw opium into a smokable paste. Gymnastics: his bowed posture can be measured with his straight pipe. Philosophy: he lies peacefully and lets his mind wander. Ethics: the scene of his wife, concubines, and children chatting nonchalantly as he lies passed out on the couch is one of domestic harmony. And so on through optics, medicine, hygiene, electrical engineering, and metaphysics. The piece is one of innumerable humorous literary testimonials to China's failure to modernize. Other discourses follow a similar pattern of reinterpreting a modern imperative—science, education, constitutional democracy, equality of the sexes—through an indigenous trope.

Funny practical advice includes parodies of a familiar advertising genre: the cure for the common ailment. "Cure for Toothache" reads: "A toothache can make eating and drinking extremely inconvenient. It can even make it difficult to sleep at night. Try putting three live poisonous centipedes in your mouth and keeping them there for an hour. The pain will stop immediately. Should centipedes not be available you can achieve similar results by applying a bottle of high-grade morphine to the affected area."[59] Other prescriptions follow the same formula: an expression of sympathy followed by the precise dosage of a lethal cure. Child with runny nose? Pour molten tin into nostrils and when it sets the snot will stop. Scabies? Dunk head in boiling oil to kill the bugs and eradicate the illness. Stutterer? Sew mouth shut. Sore throat? Cut out windpipe. Unsightly cripple? Cut off legs at knees, attach steel poles, put on wheels, and hire assistant to push. Every remedy is touted as simple, new, scientific, and efficacious.

These parodies bring the reader up short by flagrantly violating ethical taboos. They also obliquely reveal the democratization and commercialization of knowledge that newspapers were then facilitating in areas like medicine. Pharmaceutical companies were aggressive advertisers; self-medication advice columns were common in newspapers like *Shun Pao*; and Western medicines threatened the livelihoods of Chinese herbalists and pharmacologists.[60] These parodists' attitude toward new words (like *mafei* for morphine), ideas, and categories of knowledge tended to be facetious and skeptical, though rarely expressing the outright hostility leveled at new politicians by China's cartoonists.

THE PLAYFUL BRUSH

The spread of lithographic and photographic technology in the late nineteenth century enabled newspapers to produce pictorial supplements, notably *Shun Pao*'s pioneering *Dianshizhai Pictorial* (1884–98), which featured illustrations news stories, strange tales, and fantastical machines. Some of these supplements spun off into independent pictorials.[61] In the early 1910s, illustrations were increasingly joined by photographs and cartoons.

The *National Herald*, a major daily newspaper founded in 1907, issued a twice-weekly pictorial supplement where many talented Chinese cartoonists cut their teeth, among them Shen Bochen, who went on to found the bilingual humor magazine *Shanghai Puck*.[62] Cartoons relied heavily on allegory, visual punning, and wordplay. "Damming the River" (see figure 3.3), which Ma Xingchi "painted in jest" (*xibi*)—or with a "playful brush"—depicts two Qing officials trying in vain to stop the torrent of public opinion from a pair of anthropomorphic mountain springs.[63] The power of public opinion was a modern concept that spread alongside print journalism. Flood control was a traditional duty of officials. This association, which harkens back to the Great Yu, the mythic tamer of the floods, was renewed in the 1900s in *The Travels of Lao Can*, whose hero attempts to help local

FIGURE 3.3. Qing officials trying in vain to stop the flow of public opinion. From *National Herald Illustrated* (10 August 1909).

officials ward off natural disaster with an innovative river-dredging plan. In Liu E's novel, official interference prevents those plans from being implemented, a symbol of the corruption and chaos of the age. The cartoon takes the side of the rhetorical force of nature that will submerge the old order.[64]

Ma Xingchi, a native of Shandong province, had moved to Shanghai in 1893 at age twenty to earn a living from painting but in 1894 relocated to Guangzhou to join the Revolutionary Party. Qing government suppression forced him into exile that year, and he spent ten years abroad with Sun Yat-sen and founded an art magazine in Paris before returning to Shanghai around 1904. When the *Herald* was founded in 1907, he served as its main artist and in 1910 became the editor of its illustrated supplement. In 1912, Ma began producing cartoons for Shanghai's largest-circulation newspaper, *Sin Wan Pao*, becoming editor of its graphics section in 1918. He also drew for the *True Record*, a thrice-monthly Shanghai magazine that charged itself with overseeing the governance of the new republic, monitoring the people's welfare, and providing new information from around the world. It promised "literature and images both serious and comic,"[65] and packaged polemical essays with humorous illustrations.

In a two-page cartoon appearing in the *True Record*'s second issue, Ma Xingchi adapts an old motif to depict the artist's enlightenment role (see figure 3.4). The "mysterious bottle gourd" (*men hulu*) refers to a puzzling situation, alluding to the dubious potions peddled by itinerant medicine men. To be "trapped in a gourd" is to live in, or have been put into, a state of ignorance. Using his brush, the cartoonist "breaks open the bottle gourd" to allow a free flow of knowledge to two audiences. One is the New-Style Person on the outside who has "knowledge of the world" but is ignorant of the "contents of [Chinese] society." The other is the Old-Style Person trapped in that society who is ignorant of the outside world. Below the central panel's image of rupture is an inscription that suggests continuity. On June of the First Year of the Republic (1912), Ma Xingchi wrote that he was "painting the same old gourd"—a figure of speech for mechanically following routine. The conflicting allegorical messages are typical of the era's print radicalism: we have new power, but nothing is changing.

Ma also did comics with bilingual captions, such as "The Unwholesome Fruit (A Metaphor)," which represents nation building as the careful cultivation of a fruit tree—a new life being nibbled away from the inside by snakes and grubs.[66] The same issue presented evidence implicating President Yuan Shikai in a political assassination, and the *True Record* was promptly shut down. The pictorial nevertheless marked a turning point in Chinese print culture. Periodicals now courted foreign readers with bilingual content. Narrative comic strips were joining single-panel illustrations like "Insects in a Fresh Mooncake," resulting in more lively page layouts. In the 1900s and 1910s Chinese cartoonists experimented with

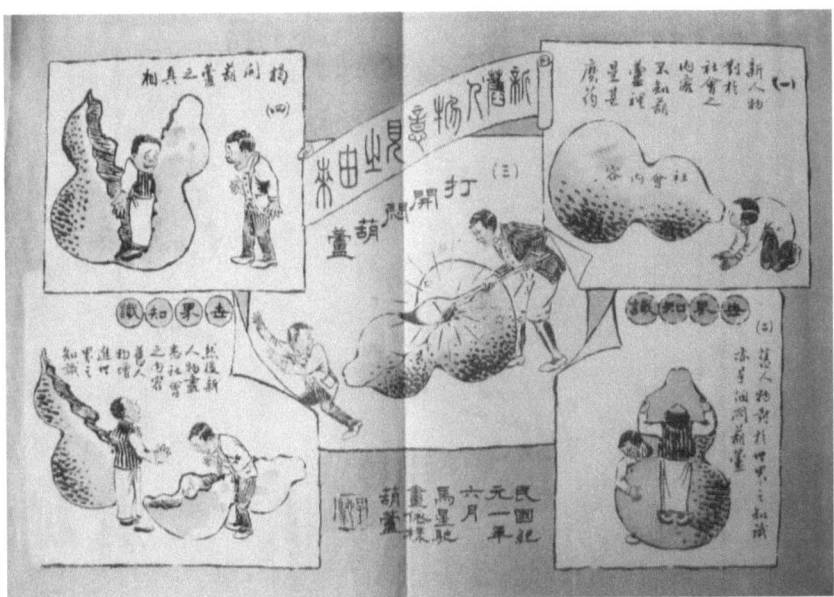

FIGURE 3.4. Ma Xingchi's cartoon "The Source of New- and Old-Style People's Thinking," which reads vertically, right to left, shows the cartoonist's contribution to "Knowledge of the World" (the words in circles). From the *True Record* 17 (1 March 1913).

copying and translating American comic strips, such as Rudolf Dirks's *The Katzenjammer Kids* (est. 1897) and Bud Fisher's *Mutt and Jeff* (est. 1908), but single-panel cartoons still predominated. Only in the late 1920s did comic strips become a regular feature in Chinese periodicals.[67]

Political cartoons often involved visual puns, wordplay, and cryptic puzzles. Some of the most radical experiments could be found in *Civil Rights* (mentioned in chapter 2), a daily newspaper founded in Shanghai shortly after Yuan Shikai's accession to the presidency.[68] Its illustrators often represented Yuan as a monkey, playing on the fact that his surname, Yuan 袁, was a homophone of, and also visually resembled, the word for ape: *yuan* 猿. "Weaving the Cabinet" depicts a simian in a Western suit sitting at a loom and weaving his cabinet with a shuttle of "intimates" (see figure 3.5). The "ape" appears in other images manipulating puppets, wearing a mask, and dreaming of himself as emperor.[69]

The Chinese script itself was a site of allegorical wordplay. In 1903, the *Chinese Times*, a revolutionary newspaper based in Melbourne, signaled its wish to overthrow the empress dowager 西太后 and the Qing 清 dynasty by printing their names upside down as 呈太西 and 淸 (*dao* meaning both to topple and to

FIGURE 3.5. President Yuan Shikai as an ape "Weaving the Cabinet" of the Republic of China with a shuttle of "intimates" as a dog looks on, in *Civil Rights* 97 (14 August 1912).

invert).⁷⁰ In the 1900s and 1910s cartoonists also developed a genre called "funny words" (huaji zi), a type of visual puzzle that uses the structure of Chinese characters. Compositions alter the meaning of an expression or phrase by erasing parts of component characters to comment on politics and society.

Japan's 1905 victory in the Russo-Japanese War, for example, impressed Chinese observers not just as a yellow nation's triumph over a white one, but also of a constitutional system over an autocratic one, and that year saw a spike in essays parodying, speculating about, and criticizing efforts to establish a Chinese constitution. In 1906 the Qing court announced that a constitution would be drafted, but it soon became clear that the court had no interest in relinquishing authority.⁷¹ In January of 1908, a cartoonist for the Herald darkened select brushstrokes in the phrase "but an empty dream," which, put together, form xian 憲, or Constitution (see figure 3.6). In 1912, two months after Yuan Shikai took over the presidency, a cartoonist for Civil Rights removed one and a half strokes from the top of Yuan Shikai's surname, Yuan 袁, to predict that Yuan would "end" in ai 哀, or "sorrow."⁷²

Such wordplay resembles glyphomancy (chaizi), a divination practice that involves breaking the characters that compose a person's name into parts in order to reveal hidden meanings about their inner nature or to tell their future.⁷³ Funny words diagnosed and prognosticated. They decoded front-page issues to reveal their true implications. Many were accompanied by an explanatory caption.

Sinographic puzzles were a long-standing visual genre in both China and Japan.⁷⁴ One modern variant was the bilingual composition, such as the English word "hand" covering the Chinese character for "mouth" 口 (see figure 3.7) in a graphic allegory for the power imbalance between foreign and Chinese discourse.⁷⁵

The anthropomorphic character was another popular genre. One political cartoon shows the character for Asia (ya) in two human guises (see figure 3.8). The top version with heavy eyelids and a closed mouth is labeled "mute with a mouth (elected representatives)." The lower version, "evil with a heart (traitors)," sports an aggressive visage and clenched fists. Each refers to how the meaning of the character ya alters with the addition of a new component, or radical: by adding a mouth 口, ya 亞 turns to ya 啞 (mute); the addition of a heart 心 changes 亞 to e 惡, or evil. The word game suggests that those who have a duty to speak are silent and that politicians are conscientious only in betraying the people to benefit themselves.⁷⁶

Some games were participatory. Civil Rights held several competitions that rewarded winners with publication of his or her brush-drawn and captioned illustration and a product, such as a piece of pottery or a pair of socks. The goal appears to have been less to identify and reward talent than to obtain cheap copy: the magazine held no fewer than five such competitions and published as many as one hundred reader submissions to each. In one contest, each entry was to

FIGURE 3.6. A Chinese Constitution 憲 as "but an empty dream," in Shanghai's *National Herald* 279 (6 January 1908).

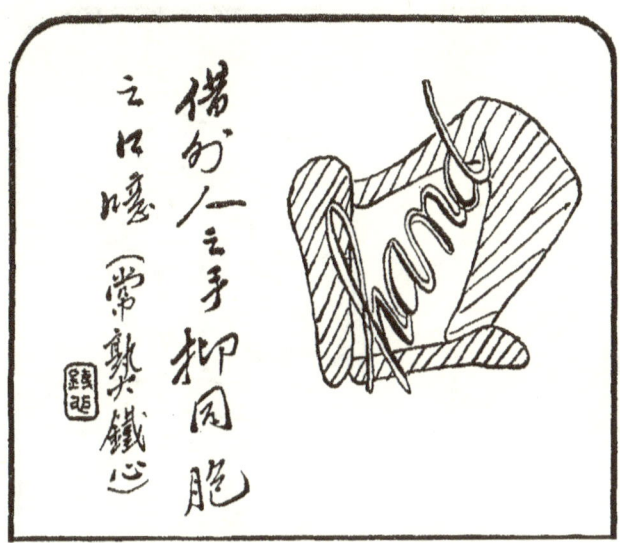

FIGURE 3.7. A Western hand over a Chinese mouth. The caption states: "Using outsiders' hands to silence our compatriots' mouths. Alas!," presumably referring to Chinese politicians using Westerners to aid their power struggles. From *Civil Rights* 102 (18 August 1912).

incorporate an image of a running man holding a stick behind his back, as if chasing someone he wants to beat (see figure 3.9).[77] The man is always in the same pose, but his target varies. In one image, he has misinterpreted the common expression "go chicken hunting" (*da yeji*), or patronize streetwalking prostitutes, as meaning not to hit on them but literally to hit them. In another, a nutcase in a temple attacks the Laughing Buddha, whom he thinks is laughing at him. The cumulative effect is an artistic game of incremental innovation.

Variations-on-a-theme games featured in other parts of print culture. For its 1922 Chinese New Year's issue, the editors of the *Recreation World* commissioned more than twenty "New X" pieces, like *New Journey to the West*. The inaugural issue of the *Merry Magazine* (*Kuaihuo*, 1922) contained the following contents, each by a different author: Merry Manifesto, Merry Old Man, Merry Monarch, Merry True Meanings, Merry Couple, Merry Groom, Merry-ism, Merry Monk, Merry World, Merry Mandarin Ducks, Merry Fortune, Merry Marriage, Merry Martial Artist, Merry Meeting, Merry Night, Merry Miss, Merry Dream, and Merry Flower.[78] Even as writers and print artists were experimenting with mechanical aesthetics, physical machines were transforming the landscape of urban popular entertainment.

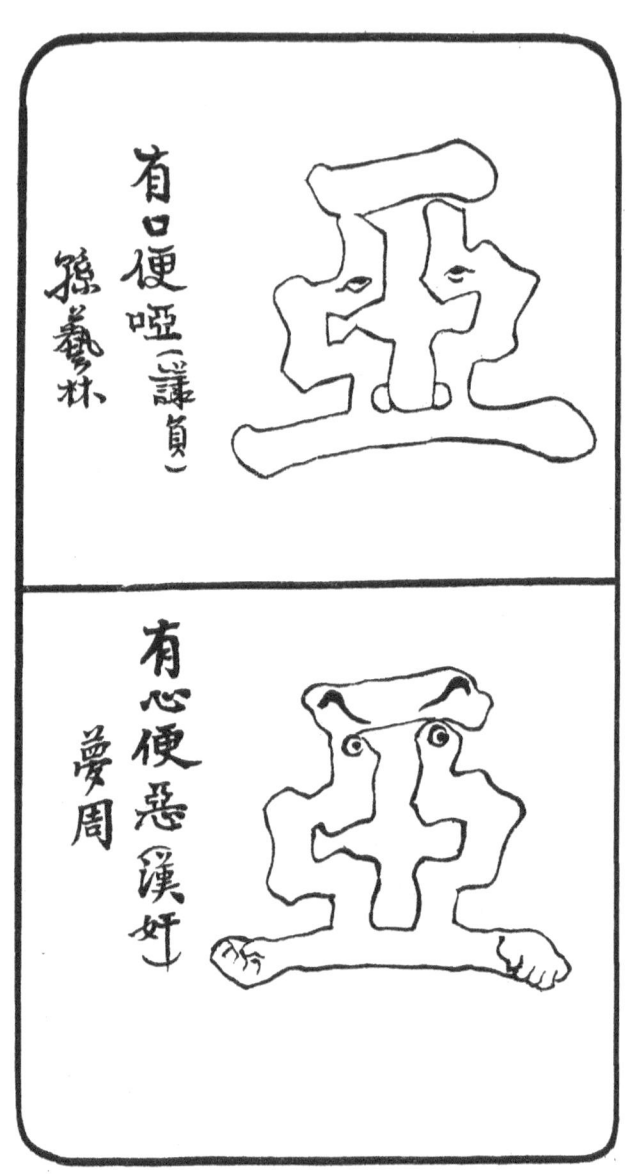

FIGURE 3.8. Political word games: Asia (*ya*) turns mute (*ya*) and evil (*e*) with the addition of a mouth and a heart, respectively. From *Civil Rights* 109 (26 August 1912).

FIGURE 3.9. Four examples from hundreds of reader submissions to an illustration contest sponsored by *Civil Rights*, ca. 1912–14.

PLAYGROUNDS

A front-page article in a July 1890 issue of *Shun Pao* describes a new summer entertainment venue founded by a foreign merchant called Flying Dragon Island. Ten cents gained admission to the premises, which featured a teahouse, bar, and a roller-coaster-style ride on a "self-propelled vehicle" (*zixingche*, same characters as the current word for "bicycle," suggesting that it was pedaled). The contraption could seat ten people and followed a track that wound and undulated, one visitor reported, like a dragon or the Yellow River.[79] The novelty machine is said to have been manufactured in America in 1885 and traveled to Europe and Japan before reaching China. Neighbors complained about "the racket from the pedaling, which continues incessantly from eight or nine until midnight."[80]

In the 1910s Chinese entrepreneurs began building indoor amusement halls on a large scale. The New World, established in Shanghai in December 1916, was one of the first. It was soon joined by the Great World (est. July 1917), the Small World (est. 1918), whose names drew on a motif from global print culture. Like Canada's the *Globe* (est. 1844, later the *Globe and Mail*), the New York *World* (1860–1931), and the *Boston Globe* (est. 1872), they promised a "world" of information and entertainment accessible to all for a nominal price.[81]

"Play venues" (*youxi chang*), as they were most often identified, were also known as *youyi chang* (performing arts venues) and *youle chang* (amusement venues). They became major attractions for both locals and out-of-towners of modest means, offering a wide variety of amusements to suit various tastes of an overwhelmingly male clientele.[82] In 1919, daily admissions at the New World during the week of Chinese New Year topped thirty thousand.[83] Sincere Paradise (est. August 1918), located at the intersection of Nanjing Road and Zhejiang Road, in 1919 advertised itself as "China's only large amusement hall." An encore to the Sincere Paradise built in Hong Kong in 1917, the Shanghai building boasted an elevator and other mechanized rides, and a "star-touching spire" on levels eight and nine. Admission was a dime, and, like many Chinese amusement halls, between 1918 and 1927 it published a daily newspaper advertising its attractions. The Bazaar (est. October 1917), located in the section of Shanghai under Chinese jurisdiction, used a name popular with other entertainment venues, including one that opened in Tianjin in 1928. At least two amusement halls successively used a space on the corner of Fuzhou Road and Hubei Road in the foreign concessions. Embroidered Cloud Heaven lasted only a few years before closing around 1918. The building remained dormant for months before someone used the space for Flower World, which opened on Chinese New Year's Day of 1919. The place was so decrepit, one journalist remarked, that it had likely been opened just to cash in on the New Year's rush and was unlikely to last long.[84]

China never had as many amusement halls or parks as, for example, the United States, which by 1912 had as many as two thousand.[85] But like American venues they featured a mixture of live performance and mechanized spectacle (including rides, films, kinetoscopes, and the like) in one place. This centralized model of urban entertainment also inspired amusement parks in Hong Kong and Southeast Asia. Singapore alone had a New World (est. 1923), a Great World (est. 1932), and a Happy World (est. 1936, renamed Gay World in 1966), set on sprawling campuses rather than in high-rises. In the mid-1930s, the Tiger Balm King Aw Boon Haw and his brother Aw Boon Par invested large sums to build a pair China-themed Tiger Balm Garden amusement parks in Hong Kong (1935) and Singapore (1937) to promote their most famous product.[86] The monumental architecture of these complexes changed the face of cities. Shanghai's Great World, which added a multilevel spire in 1928, remains a landmark to this day.

The different levels of the New World featured acrobats, musicians, storytellers, and comedians, as well as other novelty acts. The program for 15 September

1917, for example, included Little Treasure spinning plates and bowls, three performers of the eight-cornered drum, variety acts, and clapper-ballad (a rhyming story performed with clappers), a comedian, a player of the three-string banjo, a drama troupe composed entirely of women, a shadow play, a troupe from Tianjin performing drum songs, *shuanghuang*, skits, and singers of Suzhou chantefables and other opera styles.[87]

One foreign sojourner remembered The Great World as being "a department store of entertainments... to which the crowds flocked daily in the thousands."[88] Mechanized rides requiring a ticket included an elevator and a mechanized carousel. Live performing arts, such as Shaoxing drama and Suzhou chantefables, which had previously been performed primarily in teahouses and story houses, also drew crowds.[89] Professional storytellers who could mimic a range of dialects ensured that the visitor to The Great World "was always sure of a laugh in his hometown idiom." But amusement halls also became symbols of phony humor, places full of, as essayist Liang Yuchun wrote in 1927, "dull faces whose laughter is of the skin but not the body, or of the body but not the soul."[90]

The founder of the Great World, pharmaceutical entrepreneur Huang Chujiu, used the venue to advertise his medicines and cross-sell other products, such as banking services.[91] After Huang's death in 1931, a mob boss conspired to take control of the Great World, and the institution soon gained a reputation for seediness. The writer Eileen Chang remembered the Great World of the 1940s as "the first place country people wanted to see when they came to town... the slum tenement of entertainment where magicians, comedians, Peking opera, Soochow opera, Shanghai opera and girlie shows were piled on top of each other, floor after floor, beginning with the Ha Ha Mirror at the entrance that distorted patrons into lanky freaks or fat dwarfs."[92]

DOUBLE YOUR FUN

The ha-ha mirror (*haha jing*), or funhouse mirror, which debuted in Shanghai in 1915, was emblematic of the new machines and technologies of modernized "play." The Great World imported several dozen from Holland and set them up flanking its entrance.[93] They were a hit with young and old alike. Yang Huasheng, a performer of Shanghainese farce who as a child visited the Great World regularly with family members in the 1920s, called the experience of seeing oneself terrifically distorted "unforgettable."[94] The ha-ha mirror offered patrons, who experienced it individually and in groups, the sensation of "a new self placed within [a] new world."[95] Its Chinese name (possibly from the Dutch *lach spiegel*, or laughing mirror) suggests that this new world was in its very essence comedic. The popularity

FIGURE 3.10. Ha-ha mirrors in Republican print culture: One fictional autobiography appearing in the popular magazine *The Story World* used images of the ha-ha mirror to represent twelve stages of his life (right to left, top to bottom). This composite image, created by Markuz Wernli, brings together a dozen illustrations from *Xiaoshuo shijie* 1, no. 9 (2 March 1924). Material courtesy of the Library of the Institute of Chinese Literature and Philosophy, Academia Sinica.

A decade later, cartoonist Huang Yao had his popular character Ox-Nose looking into a phalanx of mirrors and wondering, "How did I get this way?" The cartoon appeared in the major Shanghai daily newspaper, the *News* (9 February 1935) and was signed "W. Buffoon." Image courtesy of the Huang Yao Foundation.

of the ha-ha mirror outlasted that of the peep shows, kinetoscopes, and many other novel visual technologies. Its motif of multiple self-reflection was readily adopted in print culture, inspiring writers and cartoonists alike (see figure 3.10). It also entered the vocabulary of political satire: one 1921 cartoon in *Shun Pao* shows militarists looking into "A New Ha-Ha Mirror" and seeing a tiger.[96]

The funny multiplying effect of the ha-ha mirror resonates with other changing parts of visual culture, such as photography. Western entrepreneurs had begun setting up photography studios in China in the 1850s, and in 1873 a Chinese-language book on photography spurred interest in the technology and its applications.[97] Studios took portraits of families and bridal couples, graduating classes, and gatherings of various associations and societies, as well as creating publicity photographs for stage performers and a wide variety of other professionals engaged in their trade.

As in the other parts of the world, around the turn of the twentieth century, role-play (the staging of costume vignettes) and the application of special effects became popular in Chinese photographic portraiture. Courtesans, prostitutes, and opera stars posed for magazines in fantasy settings. Throughout the 1920s and 1930s, entertainment magazines regularly featured studio photographs of celebrities, Chinese opera performers in costume, and subjects dressed up as foreign film stars, such as Charlie Chaplin.[98]

Photography studios offered clients the possibility of portraying themselves as Daoist immortals, peddlers, or in various Western fashions, as well as in settings such as airplanes, castles, gardens, and the seaside.[99] The appeal of dress-up photos reached to the top of the social hierarchy. Between 1903 and 1905, the empress dowager Cixi had her foreign-trained court photographer take a series of portraits of her in the Forbidden City. Some of these images were meant to project imperial authority at home and abroad, a recent fashion among sovereigns such as Queen Victoria. Other compositions were more elaborately theatrical, with Cixi appearing in costume as the Bodhisattva of Mercy attended to by immortals, one played by her chief eunuch. These photographs circulated in the press and photography studios sold them to the public as postcards.[100] Their didacticism aside (Cixi as divine paragon), the costume photographs reveal that even the seventy-year-old regent appreciated photography as a medium for developing and projecting a double image of the self.

One genre of photographic portraiture that became popular during the late Qing, the "split-self image" (*fenshen xiang*), represented two or more versions of the subject within a single frame. The trick image could be created either through taking two photographs and then combining them into a photomontage or through double (or multiple) exposure. The result was the illusion of a subject interacting with his or her double: standing and sitting, pouring tea, playing chess, holding hands, chauffeuring oneself and family members in an automobile, holding one's own head or body on a platter, or admiring one's selves from multiple angles. In the 1920s, magazines like *Leisure Monthly* referred to split-self photos and dress-up photos alike as "playful pics" (*youxi zhao*) (see figure 3.11).[101]

Multiple exposure techniques date back at least to the 1850s and are discussed in Chinese photography manuals as early as 1907.[102] Photomontages and other composite photographs had been popular in both Japan and Europe since at least the late nineteenth century (see figure 3.12); many of the techniques and poses used in China are described in a popular trick photography how-to book first published in New York in 1896.[103] In the early twentieth century such photo shoots could be purchased from studios not only in major metropolises but also in smaller cities, such as nearby Hangzhou's famous Two-Mes Studio (Erwo xuan); the Real-Me Photo Studio (Zhenwu zhaoxiangguan) in Lishui, located about 270 miles southwest of Shanghai; and in the town of Lukang in Japanese-occupied Taiwan.[104]

Writing in 1925 about split-self photographs in his hometown of Shaoxing (also in Zhejiang Province, about halfway between Lishui and Shanghai), Lu Xun dated the practice to the 1890s: "Some of the more popular involved first having two shots taken of oneself in different garb, say as guest and host or master and servant, and then joining them together into one print, which was called the 'two

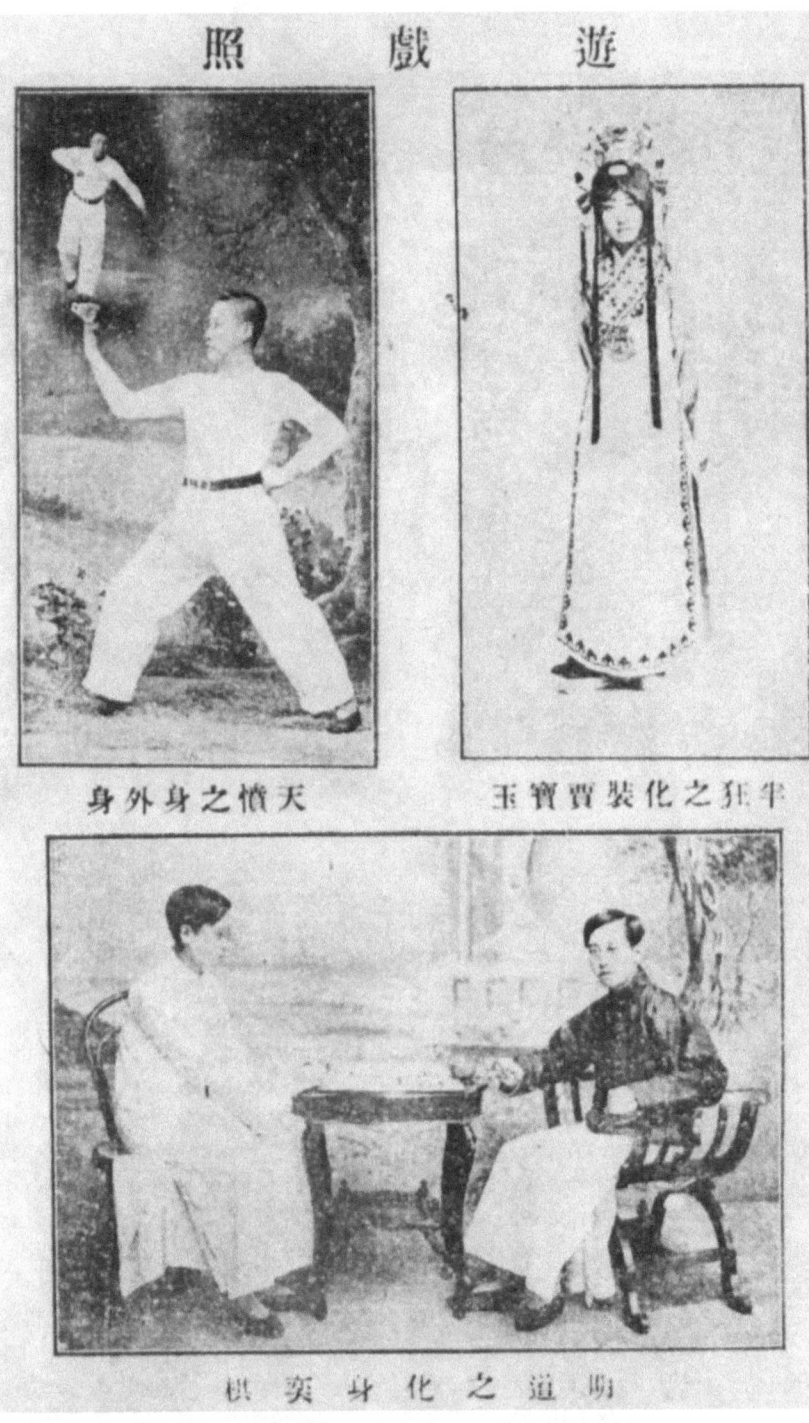

FIGURE 3.11. "Playful pics" of writer-contributors to Shanghai's *Leisure Monthly*, ca. 1921: two split-self photos—one of Yu Tianfen (1881–1937) as a strongman holding up a miniature version of himself, another of Gu Mingdao (1897–1944) and his double playing chess—and a dress-up photo of You Bankuang (fl. 1910s–20s) in costume as Jia Baoyu, the male protagonist of the novel *Dream of the Red Chamber*.

FIGURE 3.12. French painter Henri de Toulouse-Lautrec (1864–1901) posed for this trick photograph of himself as both painter and subject around 1890. Toulouse-Lautrec also did costume sittings as a clown and a cross-eyed samurai. Image courtesy of the Philadelphia Museum of Art/Art Resource, New York.

me's photo' (*erwo tu*)."[105] Lu Xun noted that the developed print was invariably inscribed with a caption or poetry before being hung on the wall of the study for display. He also identified a subgenre: "if one of the two selves was depicted sitting in a haughty pose while the other kneeled before the sitter in a lowly and pitiable pose, it also went by a second name: the 'self-beseeching photo (*qiuji tu*).'"[106] An example of the latter depicts a woman dressed as peasant begging for money from herself as an upper-class lady against the backdrop of an opulent interior (see figure 3.13).[107]

The name for this type of imagery draws from a Confucian injunction to self-reliance: "it is better to ask of oneself than to ask of others" (*qiuren buru qiuji*), a moral message that appears twice the *Analects*.[108] In painting, the self-beseeching image has antecedents dating back at least to the Song dynasty. One scroll paint-

FIGURE 3.13. Postcard of a "self-beseeching photograph" (*qiuji tu*) taken in a Chinese photography studio against a painted backdrop, ca. 1910s–30s. Image courtesy of Siu Yung Wong.

ing attributed to the eighteenth-century painter Jin Nong has a disciple bowing before himself dressed as a robed monkish master. The inscription says that the "Self-Beseeching Picture" (*qiuji tu*) was "inked in jest" (*ximo*), indicating an ironic intention.[109] The phrase gained new currency during the late Qing era, when "self-strengthening" was the watchword. Xu Yongchang, who later became one of the Republic of China's leading generals, named his study the Ask of Oneself Studio (*Qiuji zhai*). And, to be sure, asking citizens to ask of themselves had obvious appeal for a weak government. In 1910, a cartoonist and poet offered an ironic take on what had become a "popular expression" among China's poor (see figure 3.14).[110]

Like the costume photo, the split-self image was an alternative to decades of staid portraiture. It was a popular amusement with women, whereas literary "play" was, by the numbers at least, more of a men's game. It appealed to middle and upper classes alike. Even Aisin-Gioro "Henry" Puyi, the deposed last emperor of the Qing, had a split-self photograph taken of himself as a teenager sitting on a bench in the Forbidden City in the 1920s.[111]

Split-self photographs suggest a shift in attitudes toward photography, as well as toward the self. Besides offering stark proof that the camera can and does lie,

FIGURE 3.14. "Better to ask of oneself than to ask of others," a cartoon appearing in the series "Common Expressions" in Shanghai's *Illustration Daily* in 1910, about a year before the Republican revolution. The accompanying doggerel, which recounts the indignities the poor suffer in begging from the rich, concludes: "My two hands make any job a snap / My two legs will run me there and back. / Why suffer cold shoulders or beg and scrap? / Enough! / Relations galore, all out of reach / It's myself I should beseech."

they were novelty tokens that Chinese consumers used to amuse themselves, their friends, and the general public. They circulated in periodicals and on postcards. Whether used for professional promotion (for example, by actors or photography studios) or whimsically by ordinary consumers, photographic manipulation was *fun*. The camera was no soul-stealing machine, and the uncanny illusion of multiple phantom selves appealed more for being seamless than for being ghostly (though ghosts could be amusing, too, as we'll see in the next chapter).[112] Republican critics saw the genre as expressive of subjects' "split personalities," echoing interpretations of composite and double exposure photographs common in the West since the nineteenth century.¹¹³ But the reception of such photos in China was in some ways unique, most obviously in the tongue-in-cheek moralizing of the self-beseeching photos, which interpreted this novel technology via an indigenous proverb. Though by the 1930s, some critics spoke of the split-self photo as a quaint relic of a bygone era, photography studios continued to sell them for decades.¹¹⁴

CIVILIZING PLAY

The fun that Chinese consumers found in split-self photographs represents a pattern also found in contemporaneous narratives involving mirrors, X-rays, binoculars, kinetoscopes, and telescopes. Similar allegorical motifs appear as imaginary devices like Wu Jianren's Character Examination Lens and as fictional characters like Mr. Mirror of the Self.¹¹⁵ Like the "funny word," which must be read in two ways, the split-self photograph encouraged one to see double.

This visual culture of remarkable optical devices and multiple vision fed into the trick cinematography common in early cinema, which in China was first received as a form "shadow play" (*yingxi*), a term derived from shadow puppetry.¹¹⁶ In the silent short *Laborer's Love* (1922), the earliest extant Chinese film, Fruit Seller Zheng, a former carpenter, courts the daughter of the quack Doctor Zhu. He earns her father's blessing by boosting his business, for example, by turning a staircase into a slide that brings a crowd of rowdy nightclub-goers down in a heap. Fast-forward cinematography turns the slide's construction into speedy mechanical labor and transforms injured patients receiving treatment at Doctor Zhu's office into products in a jerky assembly line. The film blurs the line between play and work, treating every tool as a toy, every object as a plaything. Split-screen cinematography at one point even creates a "two me's image" of the fruit seller thinking of himself with his lady love. This parody of romance and social climbing also contains allegorical motifs, such as the cutting of a melon as a symbol of romantic or sexual desire. Bilingual intertitles and Zheng's characterization as a returnee from Southeast Asia indicate that the film was to be projected to a global audience.¹¹⁷

Play held the promise of being a civilizing force. Lin Yutang devoted one chapter of his bestseller *The Importance of Living* to "On Playful Curiosity: The Rise of Human Civilization," cited in the epigraph to this chapter. He would have agreed with his Dutch contemporary Johan Huizinga's expansive and influential claim that "civilization arises and unfolds in and as play."¹¹⁸ The producers and actors of *Laborer's Love* were themselves veterans of the "civilized play" (*wenming xi*), a dramatic form of the 1900s and 1910s, which sought to civilize China through socially progressive theater. This broader culture of play, which crossed the 1911 political divide, as we've seen, could be escapist, aspirational, nihilistic, realistic, or futuristic. It used comic license to reimagine the individual's place in China and China's place in the world. It even inspired fundamental reconsiderations of what constitutes art. In 1906, aesthetic theorist Wang Guowei argued that literature itself was a "playful enterprise" (*youxi de shiye*), properly understood as neither a means of livelihood (as it was for Li Boyuan) nor one of improving the body politic (as it was for Liang Qichao), but as a vehicle for expressing fundamental truths.[119] Wang's was nevertheless a minority voice, and others readily embraced the notion that play was fundamental to progress, propelling experimentation, discovery, and the acquisition of new knowledge—and fair game for earning a living.

In subsequent decades, leading writers continued to write literary parodies just for fun. In 1924 Lu Xun, using a different pen name, submitted to Beijing's *Morning Post* a love poem entitled "My Lost Love," which begins "Alas! Alack! I shall die!" The chief editor apparently took offense at this travesty and cut it, leading the editor of the literary supplement, Sun Fuyuan (who went on to found the journal *Threads of Discourse*, discussed in the next chapter), to resign in protest.[120]

They also deployed parody to deflate civilizational fantasies. Shen Congwen's 1928 novel *Alice's Adventures in China* drew from both Lewis Carroll and Jonathan Swift's "Modest Proposal" to indict a wide range of social ills. The hero of Zhang Tianyi's 1933 novel *The Pidgin Warrior* believes himself to have walked out of a martial arts novel into modern Shanghai, whose con men are all too ready to sell this would-be hero a Thermos to Save the Nation from the Japanese invaders in the frigid northeast.[121] Lu Xun's 1936 collection *Old Tales Retold* dragged heroes and heroines from the founding myths of Chinese civilization down to the level of the mundane.[122] In this post-heroic world, the goddess Nü Wa creates mankind out of boredom and giant turtles save humans from the flood only by accident. Hou Yi, the hero who shot down nine of the ten suns, experiences diminishing returns on hunting trips, prompting his wife, Chang'e, to gripe about "Noodles with crow sauce again!" (The future Lady of the Moon herself is cast as a grumbling housewife who plays mah-jongg.) The deeds of the Great Yu, tamer of the floods, cede center stage to squabbling courtiers. Lao Tzu's lectures on the Dao put his audience to sleep. For all of the topical satire in these stories, one gets the sense that Lu Xun's main enemy, like that of Lei Jin before him, was boredom.

Government and commercial interests promoted a more utilitarian conception of play. Science and language-learning games made their way from publications for adult readers like the late Qing *Illustration Daily*, which carried a section called "fun with science," into Republican school textbooks aimed at children.[123] The Nationalist government promoted athletic games in the modern schools to encourage a stronger, healthier population—symbolic of a stronger, healthier body politic—a policy inspired by similar programs in Meiji Japan and the West.

Editors sought to ennoble entertainment publications by aligning them with this trend. Zhou Shoujuan introduced the *Recreation World* (*Youxi shijie*) in 1921 by arguing for the "civilizing effects" of play and citing both Chinese and Western authorities. The *youxi* (game) of the title was a composite of Confucius's advice to "explore widely (*you*) in your cultivation of the arts" and the *Classic of Poetry*'s praise of a man who was "skillful at teasing (*xi*) and joking / without malice."[124] Zhou also cites unnamed "major Western philosophers" who have, he writes, recognized play as "an outpouring of the spirit" and "an inheritance from our ancestors" that "exercises one's capabilities." Games benefit both mind and body, Zhou said, and his magazine sought to exercise readers' minds through a mix of facetiousness, erudition, cynicism, and fun.[125]

Play, toys, and playthings remained dominant metaphors of social criticism and political allegory. First translated into Chinese in 1918, Henrik Ibsen's 1879 play *A Doll's House*, in which a woman leaves her self-centered husband and the comfort of her middle-class home in order to find herself, electrified progressives eager to liberate women from China's patriarchal social structure.[126] Pictorial satirists regularly employed motifs of toys, gadgets, and games. A 1918 cartoon in *Shanghai Puck* depicts a bureaucrat thumbing his nose at new morals as he sends them flying off a seesaw (see figure 3.15).[127] The bag of money suggests that he is not playing by the rules. Cartoonists of the 1930s portrayed modern women as puppets of old rich men and young men as the playthings of women, while lifestyle publications like the *Young Companion* used Western-inspired trick photography to indict social vices, such as by placing a high-heeled young woman in a champagne glass next to another flapper dwarfed by a wine bottle, playing cards, and money.[128]

Leftist filmmakers invoked the pathos of the abandoned toy. In Sun Yu's classic silent film *Playthings* (1933), handcrafted toys (and actress Ruan Lingyu, who plays a master artisan) represent traditional community, innocence, and fun, all of which is being destroyed by modern foreign industry and invasion.[129] The artist Feng Zikai, expressing a similar sentiment, remembered his favorite childhood pastime as being making objects out of clay, "the main attraction of the modeling kit [being] that it allowed him to produce objects according to whim rather than having to content himself with manufactured toys of a fixed and immutable shape."[130] Cai Chusheng's 1934 film *New Women* uses the motif of the self-uprighting doll as an ironic symbol of feminine resilience in the face of modern pressures. (The heroine, a single mother, kills herself.) Both Sun and Cai anticipated Chaplin's message in *Modern Times* (1936), in which the Little Tramp, working on the assembly line, gets drawn into and then spit out of the cranks and gears of a massive machine: individuals had become playthings of larger modern forces.

But forces of modernity (as in the case of photography) also helped to revive old games, such as palindromic poems, which appeared in entertainment

FIGURE 3.15. A cartoon from the December 1918 issue of *Shanghai Puck*. The Chinese caption reads: "New morals and old officials are incompatible, and current social circumstances tend to favor the old officials. This is why China remains in the doldrums." The seesaw is labeled "Contemporary Society."

magazines. Palindromic poems, like genre parodies, display the author's virtuosic mastery of formal constraints. Besides according to conventions of meter, rhyme, and thematic continuity, a palindromic poem must be readable in reverse. Professional punctuators, hired for the republication of classical texts, which were traditionally unpunctuated, best appreciated the virtues of the old language, in particular the fluid syntax that made such play possible. Many were drawn to a form that confounded their profession and anthologized palindromic poems into collections.[131]

For Feng Zikai, copying out palindrome poems in calligraphy was, in his understated way, a polemical statement. Punctuation marks compelled one reading at the expense of others, as did the grammatical particles that cluttered up the

FIGURE 3.16. A five-character circular palindrome poem, in the hand of Feng Zikai (1898–1975).

modern vernacular. At a fundamental, if increasingly subliminal, level both represented the tyranny of modern rationality. Palindromic poems, which literally makes sense backward and forward (and, in the circular poem in figure 3.16, from any starting point), now became monuments to the classical language's hyper-intelligibility. The modern age of machines, which enabled new types of play, also inspired new appreciation of the old.

4

Mockery
罵人的藝術

Why have Chinese writers been unable to produce good literature? "Elegance" is truly the chief culprit!
—HUANG TIANSHI, 1928[1]

Three years ago, just as the shit was really beginning to stink, who appeared but that scourge of the Chinese race, Thief Liang, Bandit Liang, Cuckold Liang, Swine Liang, Doggie Liang, Beast Liang. The so-called Liang Qichao, in baselessly promoting the endless continuation of the imperial Manchu line, in washing his asshole clean to get cock-fucked and then clucking on like a hen about bullshit such as "political revolution" and "responsible government," is only deceiving himself in his attempt to deceive others.
—"INFLAMED," 1909[2]

Liang Qichao, as we've seen, occasionally expressed his prescriptions for political reform in a jocular manner. Even a former official in exile, with a price on his head, could participate in the fun side of late Qing "play" culture. Others played by mocking. Writers ridiculed each other and were ridiculed in turn, some going to extremes in escalating competitions to deride intellectual rivals. Liang himself inspired the pseudonymous Inflamed and other proponents of radical change to profanity when his views on monarchy turned conservative in the late 1900s.

From the late Qing era onward, Chinese civil discourse on culture and politics has frequently degenerated into vitriol.[3] Mockery and invective moved into the mainstream with anti-Manchuism in the late Qing; again with national outrage at a foreigner-instigated massacre of protestors in Shanghai on 30 May 1925; with the anti-Japanese rhetoric that followed the declaration of war against Japan in 1937; and with the lambasting of collaborationist "traitors" following Japan's defeat in 1945. Mockery has, more than once, shifted the course of Chinese cultural history, but scholars have tended to downplay the "tittle-tattle of name-calling."[4] Though as a rhetorical mode it is easily dismissed as petty, trivial, and immoral, mockery draws attention to how the boundaries of the culturally permissible are drawn, tested, and policed.

LAUGH TO SCORN

"The True Story of Ah Q," a 1921 novella by Lu Xun, offers one example of how in early twentieth-century China parody and wordplay could slide into mocking laughter. Written during the ferment of the May Fourth period and set around the time of the 1911 revolution, "Ah Q" created a searing negative archetype of Chineseness; a protagonist both cowardly and bullying, petty and opportunistic, with a self-regard founded on arrogance and ignorance and a penchant for comforting himself with "spiritual victories" in the face of real-world defeats.

Ah Q is to this day the most famous indictment of the Chinese national character.[5] Less well known is that Ah Q owes his existence in part to market demand for the type of wordplay and facetious biographies discussed in chapter 3. Invited to contribute a piece to the "Happy Talk" column of Beijing's *Morning Post*, Lu Xun wrote a first installment that mimicked the pedantic formulas of traditional biographers. In it, his authorial alter ego recounts his struggle to begin writing about the deceased Ah Q. Mindful of the Confucian dictum that "if the name is not correct, the words will not ring true," he tries but fails to fit Ah Q into various ready-made genres of biography: unofficial biography, unauthorized biography, autobiography, and so on. He dismisses them mechanically, one by one, before settling on the "true story." The problem is one of fuzzy lineage: was Ah Q's surname Zhao? People used to call him "Ah Quei" but which Chinese character did that "Quei" (which appears in English) stand for? At least the character "Ah," he reassures himself, is "absolutely correct."

He appeals to "disciples of Dr. Hu Shi, who are so perversely fond of philological research," to help him investigate Ah Q's origins. The allusion was to a practice of textual authentication popular among the new crop of Chinese literary historians and thought to be a scientific, and thus modern, method of determining the origins of texts. In naming Hu Shi, the leading figure of the New Culture Movement of the late 1910s, Lu Xun insinuated that his methodology was merely a latter-day incarnation of the stuffy traditions it sought to displace.

Ah Q's lack of identifiable origins is crucial to his symbolic power. Though he is poor, his anonymity and social isolation make him less a stand-in for a single social class than a representative of and mirror to the Chinese body politic, his psyche perverted by an intense obsession with origins and "face." The town scapegoat, he consoles himself with fantasies of grand lineage that excuse his cruel and opportunistic behavior in the present. He dies as just another anonymous political martyr, and onlookers regret only that he was not executed in more spectacular fashion.

After the first chapter, the *Morning Post* editor deemed the story's tone to be insufficiently "happy" and shifted the rest of the novella to a different column. And only after the story became popular did Lu Xun, who had written it under the pen name Baren, claim paternity. He included it in his first story collection, *A Call to Arms* (1923), where it confirmed his reputation as a master of mockery and satire. Yet in 1926, in an account of how he had come to write the story, Lu Xun claimed that the playful tone of the first chapter had been forced upon him.[6] Indeed, though begun as parody, "Ah Q" entered the language as a curse.

Xiao, as we saw in chapter 1, can mean to laugh or smile, or refer to a joke or a jest. This chapter is concerned with yet another meaning of *xiao*: to mock, as in the expression *xiaoma*, "mock and scold," or "laugh to scorn." The phrase chimes with the longstanding western philosophical notion of derision as being a primal motivator of laughter. One influential theory, extending back to Plato and Aristotle, describes laughter as an expression of delight in discovering one's superiority over one's fellow man, a sensation of schadenfreude that Thomas Hobbes dubbed "sudden glory."[7] Later evolutionists attributed the impulse to mock to a survival instinct, with laughter expressing real or imagined triumph in competition. The association between mirth and cruelty is acknowledged in one of the most oft-cited Chinese prescriptions for humor, derived from a line in the *Book of Poetry* that praised the gentleman "skilled at teasing and bantering without malice." Mockery is also anathema to modern notions of rational argument and civil discussion. Yet that form of charged rhetoric, so closely associated with shame and humiliation, has been a powerful coercive force in modern Chinese cultural politics.

THE FINE ART OF REVILING

By 1924, the New Culture Movement, which Lu Xun had been a part of, appeared to have achieved many of its goals. Then, on 12 March 1925, Sun Yat-sen, widely revered as the Father of the Revolution, died, and with him hopes of a quick end to fighting between warlords in the north. Just two months later, foreign-commanded police massacred striking workers and their sympathizers in Shanghai's foreign concessions. The event, later known as the May 30th Movement, inflamed public indignation at China's perceived impotence in the face of foreign aggression. In March of 1926 Beiyang government troops shot hundreds of protesting students in Beijing; further threats against intellectuals who spoke out against this outrage, including Lu Xun and Lin Yutang, resulted in a mass exodus to the south. It would be several months before the Nationalists' successful Northern Expedition (1926–28) against China's warlords boosted public confidence in the nation's future stability.[8]

Some intellectuals, like the humanist Liang Shiqiu, called for fellow critics to abandon the "romanticism" and "infantilism" of the May Fourth period and face reality.[9] Disagreements were now settled with sharper language. Abusive criticism, as literary scholar Michel Hockx has observed, became a "pervasive custom" in literary journals of the 1920s and 1930s, and however much "critics deplored factionalism and abuse, they never shied away from practicing it themselves."[10] Their mockery was personal, belittling, and aggressive. In Hockx's words, "the object of *ma* [abuse] . . . is invariably a person (a writer or another critic), not a text," and ad hominem stung because of the long-standing Chinese truism that the writing and the writer are one in the same.[11] Yet mockery could also be categorical, with fictional figures like Ah Q indicting an entire nation.

Social progressives appreciated the democracy of cursing as a rhetorical antidote to elitism. It was how the lower classes "really talked" and thus popular with fiction writers striving for realism. At the same time, derisive laughter provoked profound ambivalence. To writers of this era, Hockx points out, ad hominem cursing was as objectionable as flattery (*peng*), for being both gratuitous and contaminated by ulterior motives. The class element, too, cut both ways. Cursing was the idiom of loudmouthed women haranguing each other in the street (*pofu majie*), and to curse was to make a spectacle of oneself. "The gentleman talks with his mouth, not his fists" (*junzi dong kou budong shou*), the saying has it, but even in speech the gentleman was supposed to exercise restraint. In the leftist writer Zhang Tianyi's satirical stories of the 1930s, old-fashioned moralists reveal their hypocrisy when they lose their solemn demeanor and spout oaths. And, as Wu Jianren noted in one joke, the line between mockery and self-mockery could be a fine one: when parents scold their children by calling them "beasts," what does that make the parents—or their ancestors?[12] Cursing was a potentially self-degrading enterprise.

In July 1925 Lu Xun extolled the "genius" of what he called China's "national oath." "His mother's!" was an epithet that could be used by and directed at anyone. It deflated pompous types by bringing their ancestry into question but could also be sprinkled into casual conversation. This type of tongue-in-cheek humor helped *Threads of Discourse* (*Yusi*), the journal in which it appeared, gain a readership in the tens of thousands during its run from 1924 to 1930.[13] In other essays in *Threads of Discourse* Lu Xun honed his own pugnacious style, one often characterized as "freezing ridicule and burning satire" and "playful mockery and furious invective."[14] Admiring peers and later scholars ennobled his derision by calling it "satire."

In December 1925 Lin Yutang wrote that one goal of the journal was to "smash the 'face' of 'scholarly dignity' " by cursing those who deserved to be cursed without regard to how it affected one's own status. H. G. Wells, Bernard Shaw, Friedrich Nietzsche, Mark Twain, and Lu Xun all had this courage and independence of spirit. The main thing was to curse "skillfully and artistically," to encourage a type of "healthy belligerency." As such, Lin seconded Lu Xun's brother Zhou Zuoren, who advocated a British ethic of "fair play." Lin enjoined his fellow writers not to "beat a dog that has just fallen in the water," referring to a Chinese expression for pouring further abuse on an unscrupulous person who has fallen from power. Lu Xun responded with a parodic rebuttal in the form of an eight-legged essay, in which he enumerated the reasons why "a dog in the water may—or rather should— be beaten."[15] So long as Chinese are engaged in a fight to the death with "dogs that bite men," one should not pull punches, no matter whether one's opponent is a powerful villain like Yuan Shikai, or merely his lapdog. China needed fair play, but not just yet.

In March 1926 the Beiyang government massacred protesting students from the Teachers College for Women, where Lin Yutang and Lu Xun were working. They and other writers for *Threads of Discourse* lashed out at the rival Beijing journal *Contemporary Review* for its progovernment stance. In April, invading warlords shot two Beijing journalists. But the press itself was corrupt and scurrilous; blackmail, bribery, and rumor-mongering were the norm.[16] As far as editors were concerned, "wars of words" (*bizhan*) made great copy, and the more sarcastic or personal the attacks the better. Underscoring the commercial appeal of mockery, one Shanghai celebrity gossip tabloid of the day, *Xiaobao sanrikan* (1926–31, literally *Laughter*), gave itself the English title the *Ridicule Press* (see figure 4.1).

In 1927, Liang Shiqiu published an ironic how-to guide to mastering the rhetoric of the day. *The Fine Art of Reviling* began by observing that reviling was an "extremely moral" activity and a "profound field of learning." It then proffered Ten Commandments:

1. Know thyself and know thy man
2. Revile not thy inferiors
3. Revile to the appropriate degree and no more
4. Attack by innuendo
5. Remain composed
6. Use refined language
7. Feign retreat in order to advance
8. Entrap thy adversary
9. Magnify petty faults
10. Isolate thy opponent[17]

In pithy and elegant prose, *The Fine Art* advised readers to "mock only those more powerful than you" and to "launch surprise attacks." The wise reviler maintains control of any exchange by projecting indifference and refraining from foul language, as the more you play the gentleman, the more your opponent will become agitated and desperate. Belittle yourself so as to take the wind out of your adversary's sails. Wait until he's exhausted himself and then toss off a comeback to make him erupt again. In picking faults, make mountains out of molehills.

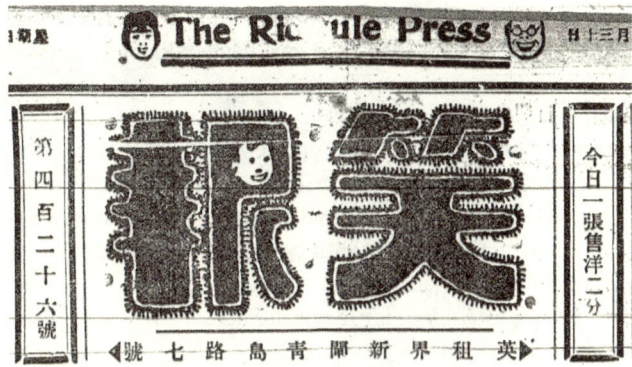

FIGURE 4.1. The masthead of *The Ridicule Press* (1926–31), a Shanghai tabloid.

Connoisseurship of the humorous insult was a literati tradition. The fifth-century collection *A New Account of Tales of the World*, for example, devotes an entire chapter to examples of "Taunting and Teasing."[18] *Fine Art*'s focus on rhetoric bears some passing resemblance to Cicero's *On the Orator*, a 55 BCE guide to persuasive speaking and besting one's opponents in verbal sparring. Liang's tongue-in-cheek piece is also akin to some of the parodies discussed in chapter three: a paradoxical encomium that extols undeserving behavior in a playful spirit. And despite being written in classical Chinese, the essay is doubly modern as a contribution to the self-help genre and a style manifesto imitative of Hu Shi's reformulated "eight don'ts" for writers from 1918 (Don't write without substance; Don't moan without illness; Don't be ungrammatical; Don't imitate the ancients; Don't use clichés; Don't use allusions; Don't emphasize parallelism; Don't avoid common expressions). The essay responded directly to the fractious intellectual climate of the late 1920s. Liang's *xiaoma* "laughed at the mockers" by taking their rhetorical style more seriously and systematically than they did themselves.

In 1933, Liang himself came under attack. A writer signing himself "Overabundance," writing in *Shun Pao*'s "Free Talk" section, called Liang a "number-two clown," referring to the role of the upper-class sycophant in East Zhejiang opera. In doing so, he implied that Liang was dependent on the Nationalist government but feigned independence by criticizing it.[19] The author turned out to be Zhou Shuren, who used over one hundred other pen names in his attack essays of the 1930s, after authorities banned as a political threat his most famous nom de plume, "Lu Xun." Though not enamored of Liang, Lu Xun nevertheless used some of his tactics; when on the attack, he habitually derided himself as useless, selfish, and biased. Both writers were on record as saying that cursing was a matter of style as well as morality. In 1932, Lu Xun cautioned editors of the left-leaning *Literature Monthly* not to mistake fiction with curse-inflected dialogue for authentic proletarian literature, and to avoid imitating Ah Q by cursing someone's parents and walking away feeling victorious.[20]

The feeling of being hemmed in by cursing inspired critics to be more adventurous in analyzing it. In 1935, a contributor to the journal the *Aurora* blamed cursing for the recent decline in the quality of critical discourse. Criticism (*piping*) was being routinely conflated with cursing (*ma*), leaving the critic always at fault. If it failed to differentiate between a "wanton broadside" (*manma*) and "taking someone to task" (*tongma*) for his or her actual shortcomings, China's critical sphere would never achieve greatness.[21]

WHO'S YOUR DADDY?

The appeal of cursing to modern Chinese writers is evident from a literary controversy that broke out in the 1920s over a dirty old book. Scholars of China's comic literature often trace a direct line from the eighteenth-century novel *The Scholars* to modern satirists of the communist literary canon such as Lu Xun and Zhang Tianyi. Lu Xun's pioneering study, *A Brief History of Chinese Fiction*, completed in the mid-1920s, elevated the satire of *The Scholars* above the castigatory novels of the late Qing, discussed in chapter 2, whose mockery he considered too blunt. Lu Xun's survey concludes just before his own era, that of "New Literature"; literary historians have generally followed his cue and identified him as the inheritor of the relatively restrained style of *The Scholars*.[22] To his targets and many observers, however, Lu Xun was less the doyen of satire (*fengci*) than of cursing and scolding (*maren*), a master of name-calling and character assassination.

One missing link in the history of Chinese literary comedy is *Which Classic?* (*He Dian*) (see figure 4.2). A relatively obscure novel written in the mid-Qing dynasty, *Which Classic?* began as a private amusement and circulated for some seventy years in manuscript form. In mocking Confucian deference to authority and the rapacious officials empowered by the Confucian order, it was far ahead of its time. Later, its ribald poetics played an unexpected role in the modern literary revolution and its denunciations of tradition.

The novel is divided into ten chapters of comparable length, each preceded by a lyric and followed by a short commentary. The opening lyric set the tone with a final line that stuck in the minds of generations of readers:

> I'm no glib-tongued raconteur, / No pedantic wordsmith;
> As others spout stinking maggots / I confound men with my devilry.
> Bullshit! Bullshit!—a true absurdity!
> (To the tune *As in a Dream*)

FIGURE 4.2. Cover of a 1928 Guangzhou edition of *Which Classic?* Image courtesy of the Library of the Institute of Chinese Literature and Philosophy, Academia Sinica.

Literary scholar David Wang summarizes the plot of the novel as follows:

> This novel deals with the tragicomedy of the family of a ghost called Devil Incarnate. Devil Incarnate and his wife, She-Devil, are rich devils. Their fortune, however, has become the target of both local dark forces and officials. The local magistrate, named Greedy Devil, has Devil Incarnate arrested on a false charge, and will not

release him until all his fortune has been squeezed away. Devil Incarnate soon dies in anger and despair. His wife, She-Devil, despite a vow to remain a chaste widow, soon remarries. The storyline then follows the adventures of Devil Incarnate's son, Living Dead, highlighting his expulsion from his uncle's household, his rescue by an immortal, Crab Shell, and his romance with a girl devil called Miss Stinky Flower, daughter of Stinky Devil. After he learns all the magical skills of Master of Devil's Gulch, Living Dead volunteers to lead a crackdown on a riot led by two big-headed ghosts, Green Fatty and Pitch Black. He succeeds, and the novel ends with his extracting vengeance for his father's death and marrying Miss Stinky Flower.[23]

The narrative follows the standard two-episode-per-chapter framework of a traditional vernacular novel, its style loose and picaresque. In the first chapter, for example, Devil Incarnate (*Huo gui*) and his brother-in-law Handsome Devil (*Xingrong gui*) travel to the Temple of the Five Organs to pray for a son. Sailing along the Nai River, which separates the mortal world from hell, they come to a bridge, at which point the narrative suddenly detours to play with several figures of speech:

> Watching as they neared the bridge, they saw an old devil. Around his neck he wore a string of beads and around his waist was tied a yellow sash. He cupped his testicles in his hands and walked slowly across the bridge with large strides.
> Devil Incarnate laughed and said, "Look, that old devil isn't holding on to the railing of the bridge. Instead, he's holding his boner in both hands—is he afraid someone's going to bite it?"
> The crewman said, "You gentlemen may not know, but an Obsequious Pixie has recently appeared under the Nai River Bridge, and he likes to blow men's penises like a bamboo flute. If he sees a man crossing the bridge with his penis dangling, he'll suddenly drill out through the bridge from below and chomp his penis. And once he bites it, he doesn't let go. Many people have had theirs bitten off! Even if you carry your privates safely like that fellow, he'll bite your bladder if he can't reach your penis. That's why men who cross the Nai River Bridge all carry their privates that way."[24]

In these episodes, storytelling becomes a vehicle for joke telling. Here, the curse "Obsequious Pixie," derived from Shanghai slang, is personified as a character who literally carries out the stereotypical behavior of an effeminate or homosexual flatterer. To hold one's penis while crossing a bridge, meanwhile, means to exercise the type of undue caution that peasants saw in scholars hitching up their gowns in the countryside to keep them clean.[25] (The old devil is a Buddhist monk, identifiable by his robe and prayer beads.)

Within the novel's "collage of standard sayings and clichés,"[26] we find a debased Confucian Rectification of Names (*zhengming*) in which every Devil lives up to his or her identifying epithet. Sex Fiend is an attempted rapist; Greedy Devil is an avaricious official; Heedless Devil is quick to quarrel; She-Devil betrays her husband and after his death remarries Devil-Beater Liu, who turns out to be an abusive husband. Living Dead disembowels Pitch Black, turning him literally into a Heartless Devil. The ghost pantheon also includes little devils, old devils, wandering ghosts, Pushy Devil, Ghost Whelp, Ghost Burier, and Nosy Devil, each of whose name encapsulates his or her behavior.[27]

In this hell, everyone speaks in curses. Non-devil curse words also have cameos. In chapter 6, for example, Living Ghost has run away from his aunt's home and is passing through Mean Dog Village when he is set upon by a pack of dogs, including Sour-Mouthed Pup, Watchdog, Hasty Hound, Grinning Ankle-Biter, Buff Mutt, Pissy Bitch, Four-Eyed Dog, Bitch Slap, Glutton Mutt, Coattail Chaser, Guard Dog, Lap Dog, Petty Pooch, Dumb Dog, Local Bitch, Running Dog, and Big Tail-Wagger—all slang insults, here rendered loosely.[28] This persistent and universal degradation led literary scholars Wilt Idema and Lloyd Haft to classify the work as a "reductionistic" novel, "in which the author limits himself to describing a single aspect of reality, or to using a single register of language" to display literary virtuosity or for satire and caricature.[29]

Besides abusing types of people, the book also reviles moral precepts and the writing system that perpetuates them. The Chinese script consists of "bitch-cunt characters," literary compositions are "empty words on the page" and "writings not worth a fart," and the Four Books (*sishu*) of the Confucian canon are "dead books" (*sishu*).[30] Such colorful language was common in dynastic joke books. In one joke from a Ming collection, the King of Hell rewards a dead scholar with an extra decade of life for an impromptu ditty, "In Praise of Farts," he composed after passing wind in the King's presence.[31] But vulgarity sets *Which Classic?* apart from a long history of doctrinal mockery. *Mocking the Dao* (*Xiao Dao lun*), a tract presented at the Northern Zhou court in 570 CE, for example, used scornful argumentation to inveigh against Daoism for being inferior to Buddhism and Confucianism as a guide to governance.[32] *Which Classic?* differed less in the targets of its ridicule—corrupt officials, the Confucian belief system, and the literary practices it had evolved—than in its indiscriminate name-calling. As one admiring twentieth-century commentator put it, "This book views everything as miniscule. No matter whether it is the Son of Heaven himself or a tortoise [cuckold] louse, the author treats them alike as a worthless devil of a thing."[33]

The underworld setting is also a pretext for constructing paradoxes based on inversions of the mortal and ghost realms, similar to the type of literati play we saw in chapter 3. When Devil Incarnate celebrates his deathspan (*yin shou*) rather than lifespan (*yang shou*), partygoers eat short-life noodles (*duanmian*) instead of long-life noodles (*shoumian*). But since death is eternal, what is the cause for celebration? Literary scholar Roland Altenburger notes, "While, on the one hand, the text pretends to create an internal logic for its fictional ghost world, on the other hand, it derives part of its irony from negating the assumed inversions of its artificial world."[34] Thus, Devil Incarnate, who as a ghost is already dead, can die again to become a "ghost of a ghost." The phrase, which implies that Devil Incarnate is more devilish than other devils, is characteristic of the novel's "play with infinity."[35]

The hell conceit is a pretext for exuberant play in multiple linguistic registers. The book overflows with obscenities, comically altered idioms, and expressions in the vernaculars of the Suzhou and Shanghai region, collectively known as Wu dialect.[36] In addition to being one of the earliest extant novels to make extensive use of Wu dialect, the text is sprinkled with hundreds of classical expressions and set phrases, many of which are modified or used in a playful and unconventional fashion.[37] The novel has links to a genre of late imperial novels that use ghosts as a vehicle for social or political satire but otherwise defies classification.[38] David Wang, observing the book's "grotesque pastiche" of at least half a dozen literary genres, has interpreted its title to mean not "Which Classic?" but "What Sort of Book is This?"[39] The novel also differs from its peers in its use of language, and in particular the rhetoric of "ghosts," "devils," "demons," and "fairies"—captured by a constellation of Chinese terms including *gui*, *yao*, and *jing*.

Like the English word ghost, *gui* refers to the spirit (or spirits) of the deceased, which may assume various forms and be malicious or benign. Chinese ghosts haunt the human realm because of some unresolved grievance, withdrawing to the netherworld (or being elevated to heaven) only after they find justice. Like ghosts in other folklores, they inhabit a liminal space in both existential and psychological-emotional senses. As paranormal beings, ghosts are simultaneously present and absent; as symbols, they represent human memory and longing.[40]

Encounters between ghosts and humans is the subject of a vast literature of the fantastic, including the famous Qing dynasty literati story collections *Strange Tales from the Liao Studio* (ca. late seventeenth to the early eighteenth century) and *What Confucius Didn't Talk About* (1788).[41] In these stories, ghosts appear in various guises, from seductive and vitality-sucking fox fairies to vengeful wraiths and bumbling dupes. Though supernatural and often frightening, *gui* are as fallible as human beings and, being bereft of life, ultimately more pitiable. *What Confucius Didn't Talk About*, compiled by the poet and scholar-official Yuan Mei, takes its title from the Confucian injunction against concerning oneself with anything but the social, ethical, and moral problems of the mortal realm: "Respect ghosts and divinities, but keep them at a distance."[42]

Gui also has a long history as a popular curse. A first century CE dictionary notes that *gui* has a *yin* (female) aura that is "harmful and goes against the public good." While it has signified that which is foreign or distant, literary historian Judith Zeitlin observes that "over the centuries it acquired an array of extended meanings, including 'cunning' (in the sense of both crafty and well crafted); 'covert,' 'stealthy'; 'unfathomable,' 'mysterious'; and 'nonsensical.'"[43]

The 1800s saw the beginning of a cultural shift from interest in ghosts as supernatural phenomena to their usefulness as a political symbol. When *Which Classic?* was written at the turn of the nineteenth century, *gui* was already in widespread use both in China and abroad to brand people as "non-Chinese," marking them as people of unfamiliar cultural practices, if not 'beyond the pale' of civilization."⁴⁴ A few decades later, China was dealt a crushing blow to its self-esteem by the "foreign devils" (*yang guizi*) who routed Qing forces during the Opium Wars of 1839–42 and 1856–60. The foreign trade in opium led to the appearance of the "opium fiend" (*yangui*), an object of lament, revilement, and fascination in literary and pictorial representations of China. By the 1870s, when *Which Classic?* was first published, Chinese society also had "fake foreign devils" (*jia yangguizi*)—Chinese seen to be mimicking foreigners in their dress, speech, and behavior. By 1921, Lu Xun mocked the widespread and indiscriminate use of the curse "fake foreign devil" by putting it in the mouth of Ah Q.

When referring to an actual ghost, *gui* usually denotes an Other, a deceased stranger rather than deceased kin. As an epithet, however, *gui* implies familiarity. Just as parents might affectionately refer to their children as "little devils" (*xiao gui*), people who apply the term *gui* to others (be they Chinese or non-Chinese) peg them to what historian Adam McKeown calls a "habitual stereotype."⁴⁵ A "little devil" is persistently mischievous, a "foreign devil" is always culturally distant, a "drunk devil" is perpetually alcoholic, and a "wretched devil" is forever impoverished. Whether used as a term of revilement or endearment, *gui* denotes a way of being or set of behaviors that is predictable.

Which Classic? was first published in an unpunctuated edition by the Shun Pao Publishing House, a commercial enterprise founded in Shanghai in 1872.⁴⁶ An advertisement gives hints as to what features the publisher thought would appeal to readers:

> *Which Classic?*, ten chapters. This book was compiled and edited by Passerby. Messers Tangle and Between-the-Lines wrote the commentary and Taiping Traveler wrote the preface. The characters in the book include Devil Incarnate, Wretched Devil, Living Dead, Miss Stinky Flower, and Kept Woman. It makes readers laugh so hard they spit out their rice. Moreover, as you will read, everything the book records is in the vulgar language of a three-family village, created out of thin air, leisure snatched from a busy life. Its characters talk devil talk and have devil names, and their affairs consist of harboring hellish intentions, making devil faces, summoning hellfire,⁴⁷ raising hell, and putting on shows of devilry. The *Analects* ask: "Which classic did this come from?" Henceforth, one author who writes in the vernacular can immediately respond: "From *Which Classic?!*"⁴⁸

Vulgar and rootless language, devil puns (which connote various types of social misbehavior), anti-Confucian humor, and iconoclastic commentaries—these are the selling points that will make readers "spit out their rice." The novel is comprised of "devil talk," or malicious nonsense, yet everything springs from its pages. The *Analects* quotation invites the reader to launch a wild goose chase in search of *Which Classic?*'s own referents, while boasting—with winning disingenuousness—that it is a sui generis work of art.

Which Classic?'s irreverence toward genealogy is evident in the jokes and curses that punctuate its meandering narrative, its refusal to play any one genre "straight," and its penchant for paradox. Its underlying joke, furthermore, was not that it had uprooted itself from its origins, but that the book itself was the wellspring of all knowledge. Besides mocking the age-old literary practice of anchoring all new creation in the established canon, the book begs a more subversive set of questions about the importance of naming, pedigree, and precedent that were of crucial importance to cultural modernizers of the new republic.

For one thing, authors of the book's paratexts—highlighted in the ad—cloaked their identities in pseudonyms.[49] This was a typical practice, even a game, for writers in literary genres such as tales of the strange, courtesan novels, and pornography.[50] The Shun Pao edition contains prefaces by Taiping Traveler and Passerby, a postscript by The Shanghai Traveler Who Dines on Rosy Clouds, and chapter-end commentaries by Mr. Tangle & Mr. Between-the-Lines.[51] Several pseudonyms are picaresque. Taiping Traveler connotes a worldly, experienced person, his knowledge being about ghost lore. Taiping Traveler appeals to a variety of classical sources on the question of whether or not ghosts exist—precisely the type of behavior that the novel mocks.[52] Mr. Tangle & Mr. Between-the-Lines, the author of the chapter-end commentaries, is a joke name alluding to how commentators wrote between lines and thus got tangled up with the text.[53] Though these commentaries do not sustain the same type of banter with the main text that we saw with Di Baoxian's commentaries on *The Future of New China* (see chapter 3), the pseudonym is consistent with the novel's parody of literati habits.

Passerby suggests an old hand, someone steeped in the linguistic milieu of the novel. It is likely the pen name of the author, whose familiarity with various dialects suggests he was well traveled in the Wu region.[54] The itinerant pseudonym reinforces the theme of rootlessness. It is also an ironic name for the implied narrator of a novel set in the underworld, since no mortal can "pass by" hell. Passerby's 1878 preface, on which the Shun Pao advertisement draws, reads:

> I have created something out of nothing, collecting together strange tales from overseas. I have snatched a moment of leisure from amidst life's hustle and bustle to build castles in the sky. Relying solely on off-hand jests and quips, I have no need for "Confucius says . . ." or "The *Book of Poetry* reads . . ." Why bother munching prose and chewing words, or pedantically showing off my mastery of the classical language?[55] I'm just playing along on the occasion and spouting nonsense. Why not get riled up when the chance arises and play pointless tricks? I just snatch at things

as I go along, as if to make a matching pair of cattail sandals. I write as if combing my beard for lice, or, better yet, making cakes out of the morning dew. I have a sharp tongue but I never mean it, so I don't put myself in others' shoes. As my book is a mere trifle, I don't refrain from indulging in unverifiable prattle. At every turn I play a new trick, using stale sayings to hold together this old chamber pot. I take everything for granted and indulge in wishful thinking. I shoot the breeze and not a word makes sense. I make people laugh till they bust a gut in delight. Just let me gape my maw and flash a row of yellowed teeth while making irrelevant comments. "Heaven in a nutshell and the ocean under wraps"—the more I talk the less sense I make. I come and go like a phantom, leaving everything muddy in my wake. Could it be that I am making mischief by spreading rumors? Sometimes my words are entirely baseless. Go ahead: pick up a tome and do your research. Only then can you be sure they came from *Which Classic?*

In this tour de force, Passerby musters every set phrase and idiom at his disposal to emphasize the fictional nature of his work and mock literary composition via quotation and allusion. His nonsense and buffoonery contrast with the staid, predictable language of the Confucian canon, and he teases the reader to trace the origins of his baseless words in a circle.

Two more editions of the book appeared in Shanghai in 1894 (see appendix 2), one of which changed the book's title to *The Eleventh Book of Genius: A Pack of Lies*.[56] This conceit followed the lead of the seventeenth-century commentator Jin Shengtan, who compiled a list of Ten Books of Genius, including *Jin Ping Mei* and *The Water Margin*. The label was later recycled by another Shanghai publisher who printed a two-volume illustrated edition of the book in the early years of the republic.

RESURRECTING DEVILS

This putative work of genius found an enthusiastic audience after it was rediscovered, punctuated, annotated, and republished in May 1926 by Dr. Liu Fu. Liu Fu was a linguist, poet, amateur folklorist, and photography enthusiast. He had returned to warlord-controlled Beijing in 1925 after six years of study in England and Paris with a doctorate in phonology and was embarking on a promising new career. Appointed chairman of the Chinese Department of the Université Franco-Chinoise, he was soon recruited to join the Chinese Department of Peking University.

Liu was an active figure in the New Culture Movement of the mid-1910s and the 1919 May Fourth Movement, which called for radical changes to Chinese culture and politics. Nowadays he is remembered primarily for his participation in early campaigns to promote a New Literature written in vernacular Chinese, or *baihua*, albeit in a supporting role to Hu Shi, Peking University president Cai Yuanpei, and Lu Xun. In addition to being a noted poet, Liu made a lasting mark on modern Chinese by inventing the gendered pronouns used throughout the Chinese-speaking world today.[57]

Liu had gotten his literary start in Shanghai, writing stories for middlebrow publications such as *Chinese Fiction World*, and doing translations for a two-penny amusement hall newspaper.[58] Inspired by Beijing intellectuals' call to literary revolution, he reinvented himself and his literary style, dropping classically inflected language in favor of the Westernized grammar and vocabulary of *baihua*. He even modified his courtesy name from the Shanghainese-style Bannong 半儂 ("half of you") to the self-deprecating Bannong 半農 ("half-peasant"). He also publicly dismissed what he saw as the sentimentalism of the Shanghai writers he used to work with, branding them the "Mandarin Duck and Butterfly School." Though tame to the ear, this pejorative epithet of Liu's coining, which gained wide currency, relegated a wide swath of the Chinese literary field to decades of disrepute and obscurity. In 1919, Liu's new Peking University colleague, Qian Xuantong, spoke of this category of fiction in the same breath as scandal fiction and pornography.[59]

When he moved to Beijing in the mid-1910s, Liu began contributing to the new literary monthly *La Jeunesse* (est. 1915). It's said that it was one of these essays that impressed Cai Yuanpei enough to offer Liu a position on the Peking University faculty in 1917. Liu's subsequent step of pursuing doctoral studies abroad completed his self-remolding into a pedigreed modern man of culture.

Even before that move, Liu and fellow activists in Beijing had viewed literary culture as a key battleground on which the future of the Chinese nation would be decided. To them, the field had ossified, primarily because of its stubborn adherence to a canon of literary works written in an arcane, outmoded language. Whereas radicals like Qian Xuantong advocated the wholesale substitution of Chinese characters with Esperanto, Hu Shi and others promoted *baihua* as the centerpiece of language reform and pushed to shift the literary canon toward low or popular vernacular literatures, including works written in dialect.

Which Classic? was a prime candidate for inclusion in this new canon, thanks to its use of dialect and its impious tone. Its central theme also dovetailed with one of Hu Shi's eight prescriptions for literary reform from 1917: "Do not use allusions."[60] Echoing this theme in a preface to Liu's 1926 edition, Lu Xun wrote that this book's creative use of idioms "make its language particularly lively" in contrast to the "dead ancient allusions" found in traditional literature.[61] A novel enmeshed in a web of pseudonyms also anticipated the rhetorical stance of modern literary revolutionaries that the entire Chinese literary tradition was ghostwritten, embodying a set of dead worldviews that should be buried once and for all in favor of a universal humanism.

These humanists nevertheless became captivated by the novel's mocking and dehumanizing rhetoric. By the 1920s, simply denouncing Confucianism was already passé. But vulgarity was an antidote to one of Chinese literature's ills. As the Cantonese journalist Huang Tianshi saw it, Chinese writers had followed an elitist precept into the grave: "Why have Chinese writers been unable to produce good literature?," he wrote in a preface to a 1928 edition of *Which Classic?*, "'Elegance' (*ya*) is truly the chief culprit!"[62] Scatological literature was not without risks to its elite promoters. Indeed, Professor Liu's experience with *Which Classic?* was virtually the inverse of the Shanghainese saying, "The more you piss [a homophone of "put out books"], the earlier you'll make professor,"[63] as after he republished the book he found his position under attack.

Chinese scholars traditionally disdained the pursuit of financial gain through writing, and the New Literature vanguard publicly derided profit-minded "commercial" writers.[64] But in the 1920s the Beiyang government was often months late in paying professors' salaries, and many depended on publishing books, stories, and articles for regular income.[65] Perhaps for this reason, *Which Classic?* was launched with an aggressive marketing campaign. Teaser advertisements in the journal *Threads of Discourse*, to which Liu Fu was a regular contributor, featured the book's catchphrase, in large type:

BULLSHIT! BULLSHIT! A TRUE ABSURDITY!
Whatever does this mean? All will be revealed in the next chapter.
Yours respectfully, Head of Beixin Books.[66]

Two issues later, Liu formally announced the book's release on the journal's front page. The front matter of the book included the forty-seven-year-old *Shun Pao* advertisement for *Which Classic?*, a page of cartoon ghost faces sketched by Liu himself, and then this announcement:

AN APOLOGY TO THE READER:
When this book was to be re-published, we had arranged for Mr. Doubt-the-Ancients [Qian] Xuantong to write a preface. The advertisement was ready to go, and there was no doubt that it would happen. But before Mr. Doubt-the-Ancients was able to pick up his pen, Mrs. Doubt-the-Ancients unexpectedly became severely ill. Her illness became worse and worse, until publication time arrived and we received this letter:

... My wife is on the brink of death and may breathe her last at any moment. At present, my mind is in turmoil, my grief beyond words. In any case, it will be impossible for me to submit a preface to *Which Classic?* in the immediate future. Given the circumstances, I will be unable to manage it, and I hope you can forgive me ...

On the one hand, we hope that Mrs. Doubt-the-Ancients will quickly recover from her illness; on the other hand, we have to publish this book soon to avoid trying our readers' patience. Once the preface is eventually written and printed, the supplement will be distributed to vendors, and an announcement will appear in *Threads of Discourse*. At that time, *please tear off this sheet and redeem it at the place where you originally purchased the book.* This is truly the only way out of an intractable situation, and we beg our readers' forgiveness.
Respectfully submitted,

Head of Beixin Books[67]

Qian Xuantong was Liu Fu's friend and colleague from *La Jeunesse*, and himself something of a literary celebrity. But the use of his jocular pen name, "Doubt-the-Ancients," to refer to his dying wife is puzzling, and the gravity of the situation incongruous with the "Bullshit!" marketing campaign. Readers appear to have taken the apology at face value, and, indeed, the offer appears sincere, since the page on which it was printed was perforated for easy tearing. In a reprint of *Which Classic?* later that year, a second apology assured readers that Mrs. Doubt-the-Ancients had recovered and claimed that her husband's preface was still forthcoming. But it appears that he never got around to writing it.[68]

Liu Fu and Qian Xuantong had a history of manufacturing sensationalism. Eight years earlier, in the March 1918 issue of *La Jeunesse*, Qian fabricated a letter to the editor attacking the magazine for its revolutionary agenda. Written in classical Chinese under the name Wang Jingxuan, the letter derided the new literature as absurd and upheld the translator Lin Shu, a noted stylist in classical prose, as a paragon of China's literary morals.[69] Liu Fu's response was more than three times its length and consisted of a witheringly sarcastic critique of the author, of Lin Shu, and of the cultural values they supposedly represented. Liu ended his counterattack by pointedly disdaining to respond to Wang's "curses" (*maren hua*) and then mocking him for having dated his letter by the traditional lunar calendar—if he was so behind the times, why didn't he just say "Tenth year of the [deposed] Xuantong Emperor's reign"?[70]

The incident, intended to stir up a response to the magazine's calls for literary revolution, made Liu Fu famous. Later accounts praised him for having systematically rebutted Wang until he was "utterly eviscerated" and left advocates of old-style literature "so resoundingly cursed out that they were completely vanquished."[71] Lu Xun joined the fight two months later, sending *La Jeunesse* the short story "Diary of a Madman." Lu Xun later praised Liu for having "cursed Wang Jingxuan to his knees" and immortalized the episode in an obituary.[72]

In any event, the advertisement for the phantom 1926 preface would have had readers purchasing *Which Classic?* and reading *Threads of Discourse* religiously for updates. The reader was also well compensated with no fewer than three other prefaces, including by Liu Fu and Lu Xun. Lu Xun praised the author for his innovative use of "new allusions just like classical allusions" and for "turning a somersault" in front of Confucius, a courageous gesture of impudence in a less tolerant age. Lu Xun's interest in a book that mocks officials may have also been partly motivated by personal circumstances. Up to 1925 he had been nominally employed at the Beiyang government's Ministry of Education but was relieved of his post in 1925 for his public support of a student protest. Though reinstated in January 1926, he fled the city later that year after his continued outspokenness led to a warrant for his arrest. He eventually took up a teaching post in Fujian Province at Amoy University, which was headed, to his annoyance, by a neo-Confucian chancellor.[73]

Lu Xun's preface was likely an even greater selling point than the allegedly missing one.[74] Professor Liu Fu, however, came under attack for crass commercialism, likely prompted by the flashy ads in *Threads of Discourse*, and on 25 May 1926 Lu Xun jumped in again to dismiss the suggestion that a professor selling books posed any threat to academia.[75] By the time Lu Xun's second essay was appended to a revised 1933 edition, Liu Fu's book had already gone through at least four reprintings, and by 1935 at least five competing editions had appeared in Shanghai and Guangzhou.

Liu Fu also found himself accused of shoddy scholarship. Dialect, as mentioned earlier, was one of the novel's particular attractions for Liu, who, along with Hu Shi, was promoting dialect literature with the aim of rejuvenating Chinese literature in general.[76] Yet Wu dialect proved challenging even to readers from that region, including Liu, who was from Jiangsu province. The birthday dishes served at the celebration of Devil Incarnate's deathspan, for example, include "blood-drenched pig's head; a fight-addled chicken; pickled shrunken bitch's eggs; a crab with no hole to crouch in; eel slow-cooked in the shaft of a writing brush; and a duck unkilled by throttling." These terms of abuse refer to, respectively, someone who blushes easily from embarrassment or drinking; someone prone to fly off the handle; someone easily dispirited by setbacks; someone feeling mortified; a nosy trouble seeker; and someone who is not easily dissuaded.[77] Lists of dialect curses are a significant feature of the book's linguistic comedy, giving the work a Rabelaisian quality of exuberant accumulation.[78] Some of the jokes and insults, however, did not resonate with the new readership. Zhou Zuoren confessed that he did not understand some parts of the book, and publisher Zhao Jingshen later attested that even native speakers of Wu dialect would be unsure about some expressions.[79]

In June 1926, less than a month after the book's release, the poet and scholar Liu Dabai published an essay on the front page of the journal the *Aurora* criticizing the quality of Liu Fu's annotations and listing dozens of errors and omissions.[80] He begins by expressing his regret that he had not bought a copy of the 1878 Shun Pao edition, which originally cost fifteen cents, instead waiting for Liu Fu's edition, which cost fifty. Praising the author's ingenious "use of the novel form to compile a dictionary of rustic slang idioms," he gives several comparative examples of humorous slang rhymes drawn from *Poems of Hangzhou Idioms*. He identifies literary ancestors such as *History of Roaches*, *Spring and Autumn Pharmacopeia*, and poems composed entirely of names of things from a certain category, such as stars or medicines. Liu Fu, he charged, had failed to mark all slang expressions, inaccurately speculated about the meaning of expressions he did not understand, and marked some common dialectic expressions as inexplicable.

A few days later in *Threads of Discourse* Liu defended some of his interpretations and conceded on others. Liu Dabai then published another open letter in which he listed more philological disagreements and questioned Liu Fu's expertise. The two debated for two months, with the tone of the exchange growing increasingly sarcastic, each using language from the novel to attack the other. When Liu Fu's friend Lin Shouzhuang wrote a letter to *Threads of Discourse* offering "a few reliable corrections" that contradicted Liu Dabai's points, Liu Fu could not resist adding a note at the bottom sarcastically assuring "my dear Mr. Liu Dabai" that Shouzhuang's reference to people "munching prose and chewing words" and "getting gored by the horns of the bull" when their analyses proved incorrect did not refer to him.[81] Liu Fu eventually tried to put a stop to it all with a letter entitled "No More Bickering with Mr. Liu Dabai," but Dabai claimed the last word.[82]

Liu Fu was also criticized for having censored the book. He hadn't been troubled by its numerous scatological episodes. Chapter 1, for example, concludes with a protracted description of Devil Incarnate releasing a bout of diarrhea into an open grave at the Temple of the Five Organs that the monks have converted into a latrine. To "pray at the Temple of the Five Organs" means to fill one's belly at a lavish feast—the natural result of excessive eating being excessive shitting.[83] The wooden seat is covered with rats eating excrement and the pit swarms with maggots. After relieving himself, Devil Incarnate discovers a dog mired in the shit and proceeds to beat it ("dog in the privy" referring to a vile character who has fallen from power).

Sex appears to have been Liu Fu's main hang-up. Genitalia abound in the novel, which also turns sexually explicit expressions into plot elements. In chapter 4, after Devil Incarnate's death, for example, the newly widowed She-Devil discovers that she has "cunt-biting bugs"—an affliction of the oversexed female—that can only be exterminated by the "jumping pubic hair lice" of a "cunt-shy monk," who is only too happy to oblige. The episode, which reinforces longstanding Chinese stereotypes that every widow is merry and every monk lascivious,[84] proved so objectionable to Liu Fu that he replaced offending words with empty squares. Lu Xun chided Liu for his "literati arrogance," an opinion that Liu Dabai and others seconded. Following the backlash, Liu Fu complained in an open letter that "I've suffered plenty of abuse from my seniors for having used empty squares in *Which Classic?* Some have scolded me to my face, while even more have written letters roundly cursing me. Were I to compile them, I could even ask [my publisher] Boss Li to publish a volume of *Libelous Letters!*"[85]

The year 1926 was an eventful one in public discourse about sex. In May, just one month before it issued *Which Classic?*, Beixin Books released *Sex Histories*, a collection of case histories of contemporary Chinese sexual behavior with extensive pseudoscientific commentary by Zhang Jingsheng.[86] *Sex Histories* became a best seller but was banned almost immediately, spawning numerous pirated editions and bogus sequels published under Zhang's name.[87] It also earned Zhang instant notoriety as "Dr. Sex" (*Xing boshi*), a label that haunted him for the rest of his long career.

Zhang, like Liu, had earned a PhD in France and was a professor at Peking University. Like Liu, Zhang advocated a more scientific approach to the study of language and culture. But many of Zhang's erstwhile supporters turned against him after the publication of *Sex Histories*, charging, among other things, that his mix of scientism and aestheticism had regressed toward pornography.[88]

At the same time that Zhang was being attacked for licentiousness (including in *Threads of Discourse*), Liu Fu was being criticized simultaneously for degrading the prestige of a university professor and for being a prude. These mutually contradictory pressures must have been particularly acute for a former Mandarin Duck writer whose conversion to the literary revolution would later be hailed as "the most glorious chapter in his life."[89] In a new 1933 edition Liu restored the full text.

Cursing, a strong thread in *Which Classic?*'s reception history, was intimately tied to question of literary origins, which, the literary historian Marston Anderson notes, "generally dominated critical polemics in the 1920s."[90] Almost without exception, Republican era champions of *Which Classic?* felt compelled to explain how they became involved with this bizarre novel. They invariably described their discovery of the novel as accidental or fortuitous, as if the book had thrust itself upon them. Some, like Lu Xun, had heard of its title but not been able to find it, or, like Liu Dabai, had seen it advertised long before they purchased a copy; others, like former *La Jeunesse* editor Yuan Zhenying, who wrote a preface to a 1928 edition, claimed to have never heard of the book. Upon reading the novel, however, all seem to have immediately thought of one man: Wu Zhihui.

Wu Zhihui (see figure 4.3), a native of Jiangsu province, was one of the most prominent and unconventional political figures of his day: an anarchist thinker, a founding father of the Chinese Nationalist Party (KMT), and later a virulent anti-Communist. As a young man Wu had become acquainted with Sun Yat-sen, and their friendship contributed to his reputation, after Sun's death, as an elder statesman of the KMT. Yet throughout his life Wu maintained his independence, shunning official appointment and speaking truth to power in colorful polemical essays. Wu's radical rejection of Confucianism and advocacy of language reform

FIGURE 4.3. Wu Zhihui (aka Wu Jingheng, Tsin-Hang Woo, 1865–1953), a prominent intellectual and founding member of the Chinese Nationalist Party. Image courtesy of the Kuomintang Archives, Taipei.

made him a hero to many May Fourth progressives, who joined him in a "friendship of sarcasm" against the old order.[91] He was an early contributor to *La Jeunesse*. In the issue featuring the Wang Jingxuan hoax, Qian Xuantong introduced this "old man" as having "the newest mind of the twentieth century." Hu Shi, in an early critique of Chinese cultural history, took cues from Wu, "a hero who single-handedly demolished the shop peddling Confucianism."[92] As a promoter of Esperanto, Wu was party to the most radical proposal for dealing with the challenges of the Chinese script—abolishing it altogether. Though he had experienced success in the civil service examinations of the Qing dynasty, Wu denounced the entire system, quipping that he'd duped the examiner with an illegible essay written in beautiful calligraphy.[93]

Yet Wu was more than just a political figure whose outlook chimed with that of the restless younger generation. He was also a storied eccentric and a literary style-maker. A "renowned reviler" (*mingma*) since the 1900s, when anti-Manchu rhetoric reached a fevered pitch, Wu was democratic in his abuse. He had derided the Manchus as a "dog-fucked" race, the Empress Dowager Cixi as a "withered old hag" and a "whore," the royal court as comprising a "thief emperor and his dog ministers." Upon the deaths of the Guangxu Emperor and the empress dowager in 1908, he complained of the "vixen empress and vermin emperor" that their "lingering stench makes me vomit."[94] The northern warlord Cao Kun, who in 1923 bribed his way into the third presidency of the Republic of China, he called the "sperm president." Wu reportedly explained this epithet as follows: if a man could turn each of his sperm into a human in one go, Cao could have just had his millions of descendants elect him and saved all the money he'd spent on bribes.[95] When Zhang Shizhao, a political and literary reformer and former friend, took a conservative turn, Wu branded him a reactionary haunted by the ghost of the old Qing court.[96]

In 1903, Wu fled from China to Europe to avoid retaliation for an obscene tirade against the empress dowager that had appeared in a Shanghai newspaper edited by one of his former students.[97] In Paris, his writing became even more outrageous. "The Whore Revealed," written in the voice of the empress dowager, is representative of misogynistic vitriol that Han Chinese directed at Cixi at the end of her reign. It has Cixi defending her old-age licentiousness while comparing the Revolutionary Party unfavorably to her head eunuch, saying that "their three thousand Mausers couldn't stand up to half of our old Li Lianying's shriveled dick."[98] This and "Chinese Swine and Sons of Bitches," the 1909 essay excerpted at the beginning of this chapter, are two of many similar pieces Wu wrote pseudonymously for *La Novaj Tempoj* (*Xin shiji*, 1907–10), a weekly newspaper he had founded while in exile in Paris. *La Novaj Tempoj*'s Esperanto title symbolized its anarchist bent, and its contributors called for throwing out the Chinese script along with the Manchus.

Wu's professed hostility to the Chinese language is belied by the glee with which he wielded it. Wu had met the pro-reform intellectual Liang Qichao in 1897 in Tianjin and been in Japan at the same time as Liang between 1901 and 1902, but as Liang became more conservative Wu grew more radical. In "Chinese Swine," Wu rails that China was plunging headlong into darkness thanks to monarchists like Liang.[99] Signing himself "Inflamed," he indicts lead writers for "dog newspapers" who give positive press to the boy Emperor Puyi with articles he dubs "pure farting" and "foul as rotten dog shit"—clarifying that whereas their farting is sonorous and pungent, their shit is so fetid it makes one dizzy.[100] The essay's frenzied tone is extreme even by the standards of late-Qing revolutionary nationalism, which scholars have often viewed as "little more than racial antagonism to the Manchus."[101] Yet Wu clearly was not just expressing outrage; he was also playing for laughs.

"Devil Farts" (1907) is one of several essays appearing in *La Novaj Tempoj* in which Wu alludes to *Which Classic?* The essay begins: "The Chinese are a people who talk devil talk [*guihua*, i.e., malicious nonsense], and consequently they have handed down a devil talk ethos. Since they so clearly speak for devils, naturally they let out strings of devil farts at will."[102] Wu opines that the nation was suffering from a slave mentality and blames prominent political figures such as General Yuan Shikai and Grand Council member Zhang Zhidong (1837–1909) for deceiving the people and creating civil strife across the country.

Wu's quick ascent to national political prominence following his return to China in 1912, combined with his penchant for cursing, made him catnip to the tabloids. Admiring anecdotes about "Old Wu's" latest quip regularly appeared in the pages of the *Ridicule Press* during the 1920s and in Civil War-era tabloids of the late 1940s, such as the *Merry Voice*.[103] Liberals hailed his outspokenness as a free speech ideal that they hoped would eventually extend to all Chinese. Lin Yutang, writing in the 1930s, called him "the only living Chinese who writes exactly as he talks without any fear of being vulgar, and yet who always succeeds in fascinating his readers."[104]

Not everyone took a sanguine view of Wu's antics. In Zhou Zuoren's view, Wu was not a hero but a menace who pandered to his countrymen's worst instincts. Zhou called Wu's willingness to "defile corpses"—not just after the deaths of the empress dowager and the Guangxu Emperor, but again after the Kuomintang's purge of communists in 1927—symptomatic of a "vicious and base streak in the Chinese character."[105] Wu was proof that China was still a barbaric nation. Lu Xun questioned Wu's bravery as a young radical hurling much of his anti-Manchu invective from overseas and beyond the reach of the Qing court. He further objected that Wu's style was self-aggrandizing and counterproductive. In the 1930s he recalled witnessing Wu give a speech in Japan in the 1900s that undermined his admiration for this dashing revolutionist:

> But when he got to the point where he proclaimed, "As sure as I, Wu Zhihui, stand here before you now cussin' that old hag, she must be back there cussin' me too . . ." and the whole audience broke into hysterical laughter, I could bear it no longer. Such frivolity seemed incongruous with study abroad.
>
> Of course, by "that old hag," he was referring to our empress dowager. Now there was no doubt in my mind that Mr. Wu Zhihui had stood before us at a meeting in Tokyo "cussin'" the empress dowager, but I felt it highly unlikely that a similar meeting was being convened simultaneously in Peking by an elderly empress bent on hurling invective at Mr. Wu. I'm not against perking up a dry speech with a bit

of humor, but that type of pointless asininity can serve no purpose at all and may, in fact, prove deleterious [to a cause].[106]

A widely repeated story has it that when Wu first came across *Which Classic?* in 1895, at age 31, he was so delighted that above the title he inscribed the phrase "Wu Zhihui's writing teacher."[107] Indeed, Wu's fondness for the expletive "Bullshit!" (*fangpi*, literally, "to fart"), which appears in *Which Classic?*'s memorable opening lyric, is apparent throughout his essays, which Wu said followed the principle of "if you have something to say, then spit it out; if you have to fart, then let it out."[108] The editor of a 1929 collection of Wu's letters echoed the common view that he "loved nothing more than reading Wu Zhihui's *Which Classic?*-style writings."[109] Lu Xun himself was later to follow Wu's example in borrowing the "bullshit" phrase from *Which Classic?* and using it extensively in his own satirical writing.[110] Subsequent commentators agreed that *Which Classic?*'s language and tone resembled Wu's vulgar, reckless style—but that Wu's writing was superior.

This was the man who would teach citizens of the new China how to speak. When the Ministry of Education convened the Conference to Unify Pronunciation in 1913, it named Wu Zhihui chairman. The conference was marred by acrimonious feuds between proponents of Beijing and southern-based standards. Wu's later editorship of a Ministry-commissioned *Character Dictionary of National Pronunciation*, published by the Commercial Press in 1919, earned him much scorn; he called a competing proposed phonetic alphabet based on Beijing pronunciation "utterly worthless dogshit."[111]

Liu Fu's 1926 preface introducing *Which Classic?* relates how Wu had told Qian Xuantong about a book with the title *How Absurd!* (*Qi you ci li*), sending Qian on a five- to six-year wild-goose chase.[112] Eventually, Qian realized that Wu had gotten the title wrong—what he had remembered was a line from the book's opening lyric. Liu himself was first drawn to read the book when a friend told him that it was written in "Old Wu's style."

Prefaces to a 1928 edition published in Guangzhou stressed Wu's anti-communism. The previous year, in the midst of the Northern Expedition against the northern warlords, the Nationalists under Chiang Kai-shek had conducted a violent purge of communists and suspected sympathizers in Shanghai, an event later known as the April 12th Incident. Three of the four Guangzhou preface writers mention the anti-communist campaign and express conflicting attitudes about Wu himself. Yuan Zhenying's preface notes that the book is in "Wu Zhihui's bizarre literary style" and follows with a lengthy rant about how the world today is a "living hell" full of hypocrites and China a "country of devils."

> Chapter Two describes a foolish husband and wife who put on a play to repay the spirits and end up getting persecuted by corrupt officials who stop at no evil. No

surprise that nowadays the rampaging Communist Party also shouts the slogan "Down with corrupt officials!" In fact, the Communist Party came into being due to corrupt officials. Do those corrupt officials have any right to go around saying "Down with the Communist Party!"? "He who tied the bell on the tiger should be the one who takes it off." Corrupt officials generally ignore the Principle of the People's Livelihood, but instead force the people to become robbers, bandits, and communists![113]

Zheng Tianjian said that the same chapter reminded him of a friend whom a KMT official falsely accused of being a communist. In his preface he wondered aloud: "Oh, [KMT] comrades who would topple corrupt officials, where are you hiding?"[114]

The style of the Guangzhou commentators' style is generally livelier than their Beijing counterparts' and closer to that of the novel. The Southern Society poet and newspaperman Zheng Tianjian notes that the book was in line with Wu's anti-Confucianism since it directly violated the *Analects*'s admonition that "The Master didn't speak of oddities, feats of strength, chaos, or spirits."[115] Yuan Zhenying elaborates on *Which Classic?*'s facetious banter about rootlessness by linking its language and ghost tropes—often ingeniously—to a broad array of texts. He notes the resemblance between the title of Tolstoy's play *The Living Corpse* (ca. 1900) and the names of *Which Classic?*'s characters Devil Incarnate and Living Dead. He also compares the work to Ibsen's play *Ghosts* (1881). As for *Which Classic?*'s alleged lack origin or issue, he endorses Edmund's apologia for bastards in *King Lear* and Hu Shi's claim that "Sages have no successors." Confucius and Jesus, he notes, were both "illegitimate children" (*sishengzi*).[116] *Which Classic?*, by implication, was a product of immaculate conception.

A few critics did attempt to place *Which Classic?* within a literary classification, such as "the comical novel."[117] Liu Dabai's and Yuan Zhenying's nominations of domestic and international antecedents represent a more flexible approach that avoided "forc[ing] it into some ready-made category."[118] But Wu Zhihui was everyone's touchstone. The cover of a 1946 edition of *Which Classic?* touted "the immortal masterpiece recommended by Mr. Wu Zhihui" and a sixth Beixin edition, dated 1949—the same year the Nationalists (Wu included) retreated to Taiwan—included the cover advertisement: "Recommended by Wu Zhihui."[119] Zhang Nanzhuang's identity was a mystery and his literary influences were obscure, but a celebrity reviler gave modern readers a frame of reference. Even advocates of New Literature, it appears, were unable to shake off the age-old concern with literary precedent which the novel so thoroughly mocked—what might be called an anxiety of *no* influence. And publishers were happy to capitalize on that.

THE RIDICULE PRESS

The history of *Which Classic?* reveals a cultural gap between the unabashedly ribald and parodic ethos of the mid-Qing era and the cultural insecurity of the late 1920s. Zhang Nanzhuang's extreme rhetorical tactics suggest an impulse to vent heavy cultural pressure. Yet Qing era commentators treated billingsgate, scatology, and sexual obscenity as part of a game of toying with language and taboo. Editors in the 1870s did not omit obscene characters, free from the sort of Victorian sensibility that was later to trouble Liu Fu. This playfulness, as we saw in chapter 3, remained a strong current in literary culture well into the 1910s.

Engagé writers of the Republican period seem to have been primarily interested in the novel's utilitarian possibilities as a tool of derision. Its mockery obscured some of its other complexities, the laughter in its *xiaoma* becoming the victim of its scorn. The novel's role in a modern culture of mocking people in print was enhanced by its putative affiliation with the "bullshit!" artist Wu Zhihui, whose celebrity—more than Lu Xun's or Liu Bannong's—helped it to reach a wide readership.[120] One might say that if Lu Xun was the father of modern Chinese cursing, Wu Zhihui was the granddaddy. The book shaped public memory of "Old Wu" as something of a potty-mouthed caricature. But it also helped to canonize a model he pioneered: the radical public intellectual who engages in politics while keeping politicians at spitting distance.

What had changed since Zhang Nanzhuang's day was not just the popularization of curse words like "foreign devil" but the advent of a popular press fed by ridicule. Private feuds became public as never before, and the writer with the wittiest, most outrageous, or hilarious curses had the upper hand. Publishers were so keen on a ribald old novel because cursing sold. The controversies it generated also fed into a wide variety of ideological campaigns in a modern era that had produced new ghosts and devils.[121]

In scholarly circles it has already become something of a cliché to say that modern Chinese literature is haunted. But Lu Xun's most famous literary creation is a living ghost in multiple senses. Ah Q is an inhabitant of the Tutelary God Temple, the abode of spirits, and his appellation *Quei* is a homonym for *gui*. A dead man walking, Ah Q stands for buried cultural norms. As a fictional creation, he possesses zombielike immortality as a specter that haunts those who would seek to vanquish Ah Q-ism once and for all.

Lu Xun's involvement with *Which Classic?* anticipates his turn to mockery as his favored literary mode into the Nanjing era (1928–37), which also saw his protégés urging Chinese to "break out of ghost pagoda" and satirizing the contemporary political arena as a "ghostland."[122] These works' overtones of indignation and despair resonate with the backdrop of increasingly brutal party politics against which *Which Classic?*, a more playful work, gained popularity.

The case of *Which Classic?* shows that cursing can be banalized in such a way as to lead to reflexive habits of reading, speaking, and thinking. Passerby's description of his novel as something created out of nothing (*wuzhong shengyou*) also contradicts the notion, pervasive in modern China, that art must reflect reality. To treat insults as a game appears to have been difficult for New Literature advocates, who tended to take them personally.[123] But some segments of the literary market used insults as a come-on. *Social News Monthly*, a 1934 spin-off of a popular Shanghai tabloid, introduced itself to readers by asking: "As the saying goes, 'Actors are loonies, and audience members are idiots.' We admit we're loonies. But are you willing to be idiots and listen to our ravings?"[124] The cursing culture of the 1920s helped to pave the way for the 1930s humor movement, which generally avoided extreme language and confrontation in favor of droll self-scrutiny. High on the list of prohibitions for contributors to Lin Yutang's magazine the *Analects Fortnightly*, founded in 1932, was an injunction against gratuitous cursing.[125]

This shift toward self-deprecation was partly prudence. Like Liu Fu in 1926, Lin Yutang in 1929 found himself caught up in controversy when a stage production of his "one-act tragicomedy" *Confucius Saw Nancy* was shut down in Confucius's hometown. Lin was sued by the Sage's descendants who found his treatment of their ancestor blasphemous. The case made national headlines and prompted Lu Xun once again to come to a colleague's rescue.[126]

Another reason was the revelation that cursing did not always shame the powerful into changing their ways. In a 1933 speech, Lin Yutang summarized the Chinese official's cynical view of freedom of speech as being encapsulated by the saying,

> Let them laugh and scold who want to laugh and scold.
> A good official am I, a good official am I.

Officials have thick skins, but, as Lin argued, "only when people's laughter and scorn do not hurt do they have that freedom. When they hurt, the 'good official' may shoot them."[127]

The politics of *xiaoma*—the relationship between laughter and scorn—brings into question just what type of impulse really held sway in the lineage of Chinese *xiaohua* collections. The character *xiao*, as we've seen, can mean not only to smile, laugh, or joke, but also to mock. As the compiler of the late-Qing joke book *Xiaolin guangji* (*Expanded Forest of Laughs*) wrote in his 1900 preface: "It is those who take my writings to consist of 'playful mockery and furious invective' [*xixiao numa*] who know me best."[128] Perhaps he was expanding not a *Forest of Laughs* but a *Forest of Mockery*.

Lin Yutang set in motion a fundamental shift in the way Chinese people talked about laughter, as we'll see in chapter 6. But Lin and his peers also used another pre-existing type of comic discourse as a foil in defining humor. At the same time that Liu Fu and Lu Xun were debating *Which Classic?*, Liu's erstwhile peers in Shanghai were pushing the traditional aesthetic of *huaji*, or "funny" laughter in new directions. At once writers, educators, dramatists, businessmen, filmmakers, and participants in other professions, these cultural entrepreneurs shared a commercial ethos of comedic invention, novelty, resourcefulness, and adaptability. Working in a topsy-turvy urban world of plagiarists and con artists, they favored a particular mechanism for enlightening people about modern life: the hoax.

5

Farce
滑稽魂

China is being ruined by our farcical view of life, by our ruthless realism and humour, by our tendency to turn everything and anything into a joke, by our inability to take anything seriously, not even when it concerns the salvation of our country.
—LIN YUTANG, 1930[1]

Jili geluo, jili gulu, bili buluo.
—XU ZHUODAI, 1923[2]

In early 1928, Shanghai became entranced by a mysterious woman named Qiu Suwen. Her poems and essays were a sensation in the popular press, as were her paintings at art exhibitions. But she had never been seen, and the public was burning with curiosity about what she looked like. Then one day, a notice appeared in the newspaper announcing that Miss Qiu was seeking a husband. One thousand two hundred thirty-four men responded to the ad, and she replied to each with a letter on which was imprinted a small photograph of a beautiful young woman. In the letter, she asked the man to meet her in a public park wearing a red flower, saying that she would wear green. The appointed time found 1,234 beflowered men milling about the park, but no lady in green.

The next day, each man received an angry letter from Qiu accusing him of orchestrating a hoax and requesting that he "sever relations." He could only mail back a bewildered apology. Miss Qiu relented and set another rendezvous at a cinema. That evening, the movie played to a full house, but few of the men in the audience actually saw it because they were too busy looking around for their absent date. The next day, a notice appeared in the newspaper saying that Miss Qiu had been in a car accident the previous evening and was now in hospital with minor injuries. In fact, Qiu Suwen had rented out the theater and made four hundred dollars off her suitors, which she used to take her girlfriends to Hangzhou. When she returned to Shanghai she found her post office box stuffed with letters inquiring about her condition and asking for her home address. She responded by giving the 1,234 men each other's addresses. Only then was her true identity revealed: Qiu Suwen was a fifty-six-year-old widow with a grandson in university, and the young woman in the photo was her recently deceased granddaughter.

Miss Qiu is the heroine of "Woman's Playthings," a short story by Xu Zhuodai, one of Republican Shanghai's most prolific writers, and an influential promoter of a comedic style known as *huaji*.[3] *Huaji* in the early twentieth century was a generic term for humor and comedy, including the types of parody, allegory, and other comic amusements discussed in chapter 3. When Lu Xun remarked in 1926 that he had added some gratuitous *huaji* content to the first chapter of "The True Story of Ah Q" to satisfy his editor,[4] he was chiding himself for having participated in this culture of commercialized humor, which had flourished since the last decades of the Qing dynasty.

In the 1920s, *youxi* (play) largely shed its comedic associations, leaving *huaji* as the most common general term for humor. Other common words for humor circulating at the time included *huixie* (jocular, humorous), *fengshi* (later *fengci*, satirical), and *xiaohua* (joke, humorous anecdote).[5] The title of one 1919 humor anthology suggests the capaciousness of the term *huaji*: poems, stories, anecdotes, facetious advice, and amusing news items were all expressions of *The Comic Spirit (Huaji hun)* (see figure 5.1).[6] Nowadays, *huaji* is more often used to denote the silly, ridiculous, or farcical. This narrowing of meaning is attributable in part to the popularization in the 1930s of a new term for humor, *youmo*, as we will see in chapter 6, but likely also to the rise in the 1920s of a farcical sensibility rooted in the urban milieu of Shanghai.

Shanghai's swelling urban population, its hunger for variety entertainment, and the proliferation of mass media outlets gave rise to all manner of comedic sensibilities. Farce was one of them. The publishing boom of the 1910s, as we saw in chapters 2 and 3, helped to expand the urban readership of periodicals beyond classically trained literati. Newspapers and magazines increasingly catered to the tastes of "petty urbanites" with modest levels of literacy and disposable income.[7] By the 1920s the Chinese market for mass entertainment was diverse, sometimes bewilderingly so. In literature, pictorial art, stage performances, radio broadcasts, gramophone records, and films alike Chinese audiences could find humorous commentary about the pitfalls of modern life, not least the misunderstandings, delusions and outright deceptions enabled by an increasingly chaotic media environment.

Funny Shanghai, as this culture might be called, had the communal aspect of "play" culture but was more upbeat. It offered an alternative to the abusive tone that pervaded both tabloids and highbrow literary journals. Its air of buffoonery nevertheless drew criticism for being cynical and defeatist. Lin Yutang, quoted above, saw China as being a nation of farceurs and expressed exasperation at their

FIGURE 5.1. *The Comic Spirit* (1919), an early Republican era humor anthology edited by Li Dingyi. The grinning man in a Western suit holds a copy of *Forest of Laughs*, China's first-known joke book, upside down. Its inversion (*dao* 倒) means that humor has arrived (*dao* 到).

inclination to treat everything as a grand joke. Lin also saw China as being a farcical place in the sense that it provided nonstop displays of unconscious humor—his countrymen, he said, had a knack for unwittingly making fools of themselves.[8] Funny Shanghai, however, was a world that many could relate to: one in which one had to stay on guard against being tricked, and in which it was common to see other city-dwellers fall prey to hoaxes.

FUNNY BUSINESS

Huaji (archaic: *guji*), translated here loosely as "funny," for most of Chinese history meant comical or humorous. Its connotations have varied over time to include slippery, greasy, unreliable, opportunistic, smooth talking, witty, and devious. It can also refer to funny people. The Han dynasty *Records of the Grand Historian* contains a chapter on "Biographies of Court Wits" ("Guji liezhuan") who remonstrated with wayward sovereigns cleverly and indirectly. When the King of Qi sent a paltry gift to the State of Zhao along with his request for aid to forestall an invasion, his jester Baldy Chunyu told him about a peasant he had just seen squatting by the roadside offering a pig's trotter and a cup of wine to the gods in return for an abundant harvest. The king promptly increased his gift ten-fold and saved his kingdom.[9] Dongfang Shuo, an eccentric known for being boastful and slovenly, nevertheless could best any courtier in verbal sparring and won the favor of Emperor Wu for his outspokenness on critical matters of state. Witty speech flowed from their lips like wine from a jug—*guji* also referring to an ancient type of pouring vessel.[10] Later critics saw moral hazard in their facetiousness: in confusing right and wrong they violated the Confucian tenet of the Rectification of Names, which held that the names of things should match their inherent properties.[11] Such linguistic transgressions could be excused only if they helped the kingdom.

In the early twentieth century, *huaji* retained associations with performance, artifice, and (sometimes) moral purpose. Preface writers endorsed collections of comic literature by favorably comparing the wit of their writers to that of the virtuous Baldy Chunyu and his peers.[12] Punch lines in Wu Jianren's 1910 joke series *Funny Chats* are often delivered by a wag known as "the one who is *huaji*" (*huaji zhe*). The term also accrued additional meanings in relation to new genres, modern technologies, and foreign languages. Wang Guowei in his 1907 retranslation of a Danish scholar's *Outlines of Psychology*, rendered "the sense of the ridiculous" as "the *huaji* sensibility."[13] Xu Zhuodai and Zhou Zuoren, among others who studied in Japan in the 1900s, compared Chinese *huaji* with literary and dramatic forms of *kōkkei* (written with the same characters), and would have been familiar with the popular Osaka satirical pictorial *Kōkkei shimbun* (Comical News, est. 1901).[14] When Charlie Chaplin's films took China by storm in the 1920s, he was acknowledged as the King of Huaji.[15]

The literary market paved the way for Chaplin's reception. Around the turn of the twentieth century, magazine editors began subdividing fiction according to subject matter (such as politics, society, family), didactic purpose (satire, allegory, and so on), and affective mode (such as tragedy or comedy). This marketing strategy gave readers a convenient guide for shopping and reading based on their own individual tastes, or *quwei*.[16] Wu Jianren coined the term *huaji xiaoshuo* (comic fiction) in 1906 to advertise his serialized novel *New Investiture of the Gods*. In 1907, translators Lin Shu and Wei Yi rendered *Nicholas Nickleby* as *Huaji waishi* (loosely, *The Unofficial Biography of a Slippery Character*) and embellished Dickens's droll prose with their own comedic flourishes.[17] Numerous compendia of jokes and humorous writings used the term *huaji* in their titles.[18] There were also *huaji* cartoons (*hua*), essays (*wen*), poems (*shihua*), anecdotes (*yishi*), and words (*zi*). Major newspapers and magazines of the 1910s and 1920s featured *huaji* columns and issued special *huaji* supplements to entice readers.[19] *Civil Rights*, the early Republican newspaper discussed in chapters 2 and 3, carried a regular Funny Chronicle (*huaji pu*) of jokes and anecdotes. A note on the cover of *A Crate of Fresh Jokes* (1911) specified that the book contained *funny/huaji* jokes.[20]

Writers specializing in the *huaji* style include Cheng Zhanlu (mentioned in chapter 1, and the author of such works as "The Female Poet's Toilet"), Zheng Yimei, Gong Shaoqin, Wu Shuangre (a former editor at *Civil Rights*), and Geng Xiaodi. At the same time, according to literary historian Fan Boqun, "virtually every single author of modern popular literature wrote *huaji* works, the only question being of volume."[21] *Huaji* was so prevalent in the late-Qing entertainment press that some literary historians have viewed the term as a virtual stand-in for "fiction."[22] Would-be Huaji Masters (*huaji dashi*) nevertheless competed for that title on the single criterion of funniness.

THE ARTISAN OF LAUGHTER

Xu Zhuodai (1880–1958)[23] was known as a Huaji Master. A native of Suzhou, in 1902 he traveled to Japan, one of the first Chinese students there to major in physical education. He also translated Japanese short stories and plays, read Western fiction in Japanese translation, and learned ballroom dancing. In 1905 he returned to Shanghai, where he authored textbooks on gymnastics and sport physiology and, along with his wife, Tang Jianwo, founded the city's first sports academies.[24] In the late 1900s he was drawn to modern theater, later becoming a playwright, actor, troupe leader, and drama historian. He gained wide popularity in the 1920s for his humorous stories, which were reprinted in numerous collections. He also recorded comic skits for radio, cofounded and produced slapstick films for two film companies, and authored several how-to books on filmmaking, radio broadcasting, and judo.[25]

As part of a literary career lasting half a century, Xu Zhuodai edited newspapers like the *China Times* and the *Shanghai Morning Post* and magazines such as *Illustrated Laughter* and *New Shanghai*.[26] His stories, plays, essays, memoirs, advice columns, editorials, jokes, and photographs appeared in no fewer than three dozen periodicals, from major newspapers to special interest monthlies and tabloids.[27] Thousands of his jokes were anthologized in collections, and other writings appeared under such titles as *An Absurd Diary* (1923), *The Unintelligible Collection* (1923), and *Drunk and Sniffing Apple Blossoms* (1929). In *Three Thousand Jokes* (1935), Xu parodies authorial puffery with a preface composed entirely of grammatical particles.[28]

Hu Jichen, a fellow author and joke anthologist, noted in 1923 that although Xu wrote in many genres, he was famous only for comedy. Reading his comic stories was like watching a Chaplin film. Zhao Tiaokuang, another editor-colleague, said that Xu's comic fiction stood out from the run of the mill for its philosophical insight. Yet another collaborator praised him for being, like Molière, a conscientious satirist of his times.[29]

Xu was reputed to be as funny as his writing. His contemporaries liked to say that "at age 43, he actually looked only 33, wrote stories which seemed written by a 23-year-old, joked with the lightheartedness of someone 13, and, if he really tried, could make himself up and effectively imitate the speech and laughter of a 3-year-old."[30] Much of Xu's farce embraced an ethos of childishness, symbolized by the figure of the juvenile mischief maker.

Like the American entertainment impresario P. T. Barnum or Li Yu, one of the great personalities and comic writers of the early Qing dynasty, Xu Zhuodai was a tireless and inventive self-promoter. His reputation as an Artisan of Laughter (*xiaojiang*) fits both his industriousness and his devotion to craftsmanship. Xu created alter egos for his various occupations, most based on linguistic puns or double meanings. His given name, Fulin, sounds like "slow-witted" (*fuling* 勿靈) in Wu dialect, which inspired him to adopt the pen name Zhuodai. *Zhúo* 卓, meaning outstanding or exceptional, is a homophone of clumsy (*zhúo* 拙), while *dai* 呆 means stupid. Taken together, the name Zhuodai was at once self-deprecating and self-inflating, intimating that this blockhead was "above the common herd" (*zhuo er buqun*).[31] In his theatrical work he went by Banmei 半梅 ("half plum"), a visual pun based on a classical variant of the character for "plum" (*mei* 梅), which was originally written as two *dai* characters (*mei* 槑). He also gave himself the name Zhuo Fuling, "Clumsy and Slow-witted," which punned on Charlie Chaplin's Chinese name, Zhuo Bielin. Other self-administered titles included Master of the Broken Chamber Pot Studio and Half-Old Grandpa Xu, a male version of a common expression for an aging beauty who still retains her charm (*banlao Xuniang*). In the 1940s he and his second wife, Hua Duancen, set up a factory that produced artificial soy sauce, and he adopted the pen names Soy Sauce Seller and Old Man Soy Sauce.[32]

Literary historians often group Xu Zhuodai with the Mandarin Ducks and Butterflies school of commercial fiction writers, but the breadth of his cultural activities and social circle defies such reductive classification. His work in education, drama, literature, publishing, radio, cinema, and other fields brought him into contact with a broad cross section of the Shanghai cultural field. While promoting physical education in the 1900s, for example, he collaborated in establishing a gymnastics society with Huo Yuanjia, a now-legendary figure in the history of Chinese martial arts (played by Jet Li in the 2006 film *Fearless*).[33] In the 1910s, Xu was also employed by Huang Chujiu, the pharmaceutical entrepreneur and proprietor of The Great World amusement hall, who hired Xu to write advertising copy for his medicines.[34]

FROM KNOCKABOUT NEW DRAMA TO SLAPSTICK CINEMA

Xu was a central figure in early twentieth-century China's drama reform movement, joining and founding several theater troupes, and forging a longtime collaboration with modern theater and cinema pioneer Zheng Zhengqiu. In 1911 he started a regular column in the newspaper *Eastern Times* advocating a style of New Drama (*xinju*) inspired by Japanese *shimpa-geki*. Magazine publicity photos of Xu in costume from the 1910s indicate his versatility as a stage performer (see figure 5.2); as mentioned above, he was just as versatile socially.[35] It was during this decade that the Shanghai stage saw a new genre of farce, known as *huaji xi*.[36] Like the Beijing and Tianjin comic performing art known as *xiangsheng*, Shanghainese farce often features a dialogue between a storyteller and a listener-interlocutor. But it combined repartee (often in dialect) with slapstick elements. The form drew inspiration from, among other sources, the calls and ditties of street vendors, one-man plays (*dujiao xi*), and the Civilized Play (*wenming xi*), a type of Westernized spoken drama that the Spring Willow Society theatrical troupe introduced to China from Japan in 1907. Performers like Laughing Jiang, Boisterous Bao, Wimpy Wang, and Liu Chunshan supplemented the money they earned from stage, radio, and film appearances with the sale of phonographs and booklets of their routines, which were part of the daily offerings of amusement halls like the New World.[37] Though the dramatic form is closely tied to Shanghai and the neighboring provinces of Zhejiang and Jiangsu, *huaji xi* also came to be used as a general derisive term for a farcical situation or travesty.[38]

Xu Zhuodai, who made his stage debut in Shanghai in 1910, wrote some thirty short comic plays, reportedly more than any other playwright of the period.[39] One of the happiest periods in his professional life was his involvement in the 1920s with the Laughter Stage, a nonhierarchical troupe of seven members that specialized in new drama and advertised its stage productions with idiosyncratic tag lines. For *Hamlet*, it was: "A woman is wont to marry as the rain is wont to fall," referring to the remarriage of Queen Gertrude.[40] The troupe's tastes extended from Shakespeare to Japanese *shimpa*, adaptations of Beijing opera, experimentalist works like Hong Shen's *Yama Zhao* (1922), and Xu Zhuodai's own farces.[41]

FIGURE 5.2. Xu, identified by his stage name, Banmei, in costume as an old man, a laborer, a western lady, and a Chinese lady. This photo feature appeared in the second issue of *Amusements* (September 1914), an entertainment magazine affiliated with the Shanghai major newspaper *Eastern Times*, for which Xu wrote articles on drama. The girl in the middle is identified as "the little New Drama actress Jade." Image courtesy of the Menzies Library of the Australian National University.

Xu's plays featured characters from the lower social classes, reflecting his anti-elitist attitude toward literature and entertainment. Decades later, he would write:

> There was a segment of society that dubbed new drama "civilized drama." They believed that since weddings without pipes and drums were called "civilized weddings," naturally plays without pipes and drums should be called "civilized drama." Around the time of the 1911 Revolution, every new social phenomenon was invariably labeled "civilized" or "reform." Walking sticks, for example, were called "civilized canes," and women's coiled bangs were called "civilized hairdos." . . . At the time, the word "civilized" was extremely trendy—everyone used it. . . . Nevertheless, I've always found the term inappropriate. After all, wouldn't it mean that plays with pipes and drums were "uncivilized drama"?[42]

One of Xu's stage successes was "The Devil Messenger" (1923). A poor man named Ah Ba welcomes the God of Fortune each New Year only to find himself even poorer at year's end, so he changes tactics and prays to the God of Misfortune. A friend who overhears him, Wang Jinhu, dresses up as a devil sent by the Lord of the Underworld and tells Ah Ba that he will die at midnight. Terrified but resigned to his fate, Ah Ba decides to make the most of his remaining hours. He borrows money from his landlord and orders on credit a banquet, a set of funereal clothes, and a coffin. He gets drunk, dons the funeral garb, climbs into the coffin and falls asleep, snoring loudly. The next morning when his creditors come calling, Ah Ba, surprised to discover that he is not dead yet, jumps out of the coffin pretending to be a ghost and addresses them:

> Old Mr. Qiu [his landlord], you still owe me a condolence gift: five silver dollars and a set of new clothes will do it. Noodle-shop owner, whip me up two plates of chicken chow mein and one foreign dollar. You, from the Wan Jia Xiang Restaurant, bring me a plate of curry chicken over rice and one foreign dollar. Wineshopkeeper—three and a half gallons of Shaoxing wine and one foreign dollar. You, from the Zhengyuan restaurant—a bowl of braised meatballs and one foreign dollar. You, from the Canton snack shop—a plate of stir-fried beef with onions and one foreign dollar. You, from the Longevity Funereal Shop—a pair of new shoes and two foreign dollars. I only need all this stuff for tonight; tomorrow you can take it all back. If you refuse me, don't be surprised if your entire family dies, young and old.[43]

The hoarding calls to mind the ghost meals in *Which Classic?* Here, though, Xu piles up not slang terms but evidence of Ah Ba's greed. The shopkeepers comply, and, sure enough, Ah Ba begins to enjoy prosperity thanks to the God of Misfortune. As he is getting sloshed, the "devil" returns and demands a bribe not to take Ah Ba to the underworld. Ah Ba gives him half the money and invites him to share the meal. As they drink together, the devil betrays his true identity as Wang Jinhu. Ah Ba wants to thump Wang, but the latter points out that it is he who is to be thanked for the windfall. So reconciled, they carouse until the creditors return again, discover the hoax, and trick the panicked pair into hiding together in the coffin, which they nail shut and trundle off.

"The Devil Messenger" is a typical reversal farce, in which "the tables are turned on the original rebel or joker, allowing the victim retaliation in return."[44] All is noise, fast-paced movement, and surprises, with constant exits and entrances. Ah Ba himself is repeatedly climbing in and out of the coffin—putting in a mattress and food, peeking out to count the dishes arriving for him, smoking and drinking, then hiding again. Characters think aloud in a stagey, expository fashion for the audience's benefit. We have inversions, such as Ah Ba's disappointment that he has not died by morning. We have excesses, with all the imbibing, gorging, lying, evasion, and deception. The atmosphere of continual surprise may be one reason why the play was performed at least five times by two troupes between 1923 and 1927.[45]

Other works incorporate burlesque, as with "Two Couples" (1923), a travesty of modern, upper-class free courtship.[46] A young man, Bu Xiaolian (Shameless), and a young woman, Ma Yingwu (Parrot) meet on a park bench, hold hands, declare their mutual affection, and, having assured the other that father will consent to the match, agree to marry, and go off to lunch. This exchange is witnessed by the driver Lucky (Ah Fu) and the maid Happy (Xiao Xi), who spy on them from behind trees. When their masters leave, the servants come out from their hiding places determined to secure a mate in the same fashion. They return bizarrely dressed and reenact the earlier courtship scene. Both courtships, presented here side by side, begin with the man showing off his worldliness by reading aloud from a foreign book:

UPPER-CLASS COURTSHIP	WORKING-CLASS COURTSHIP
Shameless: "A man and a fan."[47] That's the ticket. So, it says that the price of rice in China is high now. This foreign magazine's reporting is really detailed! There's more: "A pen and a fan." It says that 13,293 people died in an earthquake in Italy.	*Lucky*: "Jili geluo, jili gulu, bili buluo." This foreign book says that rice in China is too expensive, so drivers have to eat flatbread. "Jiela ban jisi, huotui jia tusi, yao er san si."[48] So, seventy-four and a half people died in an earthquake in Italy.

Whereas Shameless's mistranslation of meaningless English marks him as a charlatan, his servant's mimicry combines a line of baby babble (*jili geluo*) with a second line of seeming gobbledygook that is actually a rhyming list of foods ("Mustard pepper mixed with chicken strips, toasted ham sandwich, one two three four").[49] Each man then asks his lady love's age and makes a vow:

UPPER-CLASS COURTSHIP	WORKING-CLASS COURTSHIP
Shameless: So, you're nineteen and I'm twenty-four. Subtract the two and we're only five years apart. What a jade-like pair . . .	*Lucky*: You're nineteen, and I'm twenty-four. Together we are forty-three—what a perfect couple we are!
Shameless: . . . So happy! Now we can swear a solemn lover's pledge: the sea may go dry and the mountains collapse, but our love will never change.	*Happy*: Like a pair of mandarin ducks.
	Lucky: Our intertwined heart is deeper than a cesspool . . .
Parrot: With all my heart.	

Shameless tells Parrot that young love is like "being in heat" (*fa qing*), a violent desire that society should not repress. Lucky tells Happy: "When I held hands with you, I felt for a moment that each and every one of the 36,000 pores on my body had opened." Lucky also speaks of courtship in terms of a trinity of defecation (their "cesspool-deep" love), sex (his local temple god, he explains, permits whoring), and eating. Modern love is mere physical reaction.

Lucky and Happy go to a Chinese restaurant, where Lucky insists on ordering German food "the way they do it in Germany"—by having the waiter read them the menu. The couple learn to use knife and fork by imitating another diner, who misleads them by drawing circles in the air with the knife, bopping himself on the head with the fork, and so on—a country-bumpkin-in-the-city routine. The pair flees when Shameless and Parrot arrive at the restaurant. In the third and final scene, at Shameless and Parrot's wedding, the proceedings are interrupted by Lucky, who rushes in and, mistaking Parrot for Happy, berates her for marrying another man. He is followed shortly by Happy, who misrecognizes Shameless as Lucky and accuses him of betraying her. Upon spotting each other, Happy and Lucky express relief at having found the "real" Shameless and Parrot. They hold hands, and the wedding party welcomes "another conjugal pair."

The servants enact an imagined social ascent, assuming the trappings of master and mistress to play the love game. Like in "The Devil Messenger," members of the lower class enjoy a temporary respite, here via romantic escapade. Lucky gets to "fool around for a while with a co-ed" (his word for an available female); that is, to flirt, court, and otherwise experiment with newfangled social behaviors. And the carnival does not end: their superiors tolerate the escapade and approve the love match. Instead of putting Happy and Lucky back in their place, the ensemble allows them to remain in their deluded world.

Scholars of popular literature have criticized Xu's plays for being "long on *huaji*, short on thought," "bland and uninteresting," and offering merely "petty domestic humor."[50] These dismissals measure farce by standards typically applied to ethical dramas or comedies of manners, which emphasize verbal wit. Xu's plays, in contrast, are driven by schemes, hoaxes, deceptions, reversals, impersonation, and other devices that pair ingenuity with delusion—farcical elements that also appear in Xu's stories and films.

Xu was one of a number of Chinese theater veterans who became film pioneers. (In early American cinema, too, many actors came from the vaudeville stage.)[51] In 1924, the year that Lin Yutang coined the term *youmo* (humor), Xu and fellow dramatist Wang Zhongxian cofounded the Happy Film Company (see figure 5.3), which specialized in comic shorts. That same year, Xu wrote China's first book on film studies, *The Science of Shadowplay* (1924); he later wrote two other books on film production and film projection. The Happy Film Company was a budget operation—Xu dubbed its frugal business practices "cigarette butt-pickup-ism"— that drew acting talent from the Laughter Stage.[52] It also had competition from major corporations, such as the Commercial Press, which were getting into the film business in the mid-1920s, producing slapstick shorts like *Big Dummy Catches a Thief* (1923).[53] Wang and Xu acted in such films as *Cupid's Fertilizer* (1925) and *Strange Doctor* (1925), in which Xu's wife also appeared.

These films made heavy use of trick cinematography. Though none of the films survive, discussions of some techniques appear in company-issued fanzines, reviews, and Xu's books on filmmaking. Film historian Zhang Zhen notes that in *The Science of Shadowplay* Xu's "fascination with *tuolike* [trick] technique ... resonates with a peculiar cultural perception of the body and objective reality, beyond simple toying with the camera."[54] It is also consistent with the operational aesthetic of early global cinema (discussed in chapter 3), which was obsessed with gadgets, machines, and the modern comedy of figuring out the way things work.[55]

The timing of Xu's filmmaking enterprise would seem propitious, as a market for film comedy was well established. Harold Lloyd and Charlie Chaplin had even spawned local imitators, such as Zhang Shichuan's *The King of Comedy's Shanghai Sojourn* (*Huaji dawang you Hu ji*, 1922), which featured a British resident of Shanghai as the Little Tramp. Xu and Wang, popularly known at the time as the Laughter Artisan of the Page (*wentan xiaojiang*) and the Laughter Artisan of the Stage (*wutai xiaojiang*), respectively, acted in all of their two-dozen-plus films. But their foray into slapstick film coincided with a general shift in audience tastes away from the gag-driven cinema of attractions and toward longer dramas. In Xu's own account, the company folded because of poor reviews and the low market price of *huaji* shorts relative to feature films. A second joint effort, the Candle Film Company, met a similar demise.[56] Though his own filmmaking enterprises were

FIGURE 5.3. Xu Zhuodai (left) and Wang Youyou (right) performing in *Temporary Mansion* (1925), produced by their Happy Film Co. "Your wife tricked me! She left her sewing on the bench and told me to sit anywhere—ouch, my bum!" The still appeared in *The Half-Moon Journal* 4, no. 24 (30 November 1925). Image courtesy of the East Asia Library of the University of Washington, Seattle.

short-lived, Xu remained in demand as a screenwriter as late as 1940, when he was contracted to write a series of screenplays based on one of his hit fictional characters, the ingenious problem solver Li Ah Mao.

TRICKSTER TRIUMPHS

Xu continued writing and translating plays well into his sixties, but his hopes that New Drama could "broaden the minds of the people" diminished in the 1920s, and he turned his attention to fiction. In a 1922 essay he claimed that the traditional linked-chapter novel was ill suited to modern reading habits, and that the goal of fiction was to represent realistic slices of life. The short story, he believed, was best suited to this purpose. He pointedly condemned the general tendency of traditional Chinese novelists to bend over backward to please their readers by contriving happy "grand finales."[57] To remedy these perceived inadequacies, Xu experimented with a wide variety of modes and forms. Yet his own literary fame came not from realism but from a style that conveyed truths through practical jokes, confidence tricks, and hoaxes.

In his stories, the targets of these ruses are often fictional readers. "Opening Day Advertisement" (1924), for example, begins by introducing Zhang Yuehen, a talented but down-on-his-luck New Drama actor who tends to choke onstage at the crucial moment.[58] Now a friend has found him a good gig and he is determined to prove himself.

The night before his new play opens at the Weiguang Theater Zhang checks into the neighboring Pacific Hotel. There he is assisted by the bellhop Jiang Jinbao, who is an avid reader of detective novels and hopes someday to become a detective himself. Having helped Zhang to his room, Jiang goes back to reading a novel, but he is soon interrupted by a summons to the front desk. A young woman, Yu Dezhu, is looking for Zhang. She claims to be Zhang's recently divorced wife and says that she has come to see her ex-husband one last time at his request. She then makes a request of her own: Zhang, she tells Jiang and the front-desk cashier, has a terrible temper. Could one of them wait outside of Zhang's room while she's meeting with him? If she yells, or if she fails to emerge within half an hour, she'll need to be rescued.

Jiang and the cashier take up their posts, but thirty minutes pass with no word from Yu, so they summon the concierge and the manager. Upon entering the room they find Zhang, but no Miss Yu. Believing the cashier's eyewitness testimony that Yu did enter the room, the manager notifies the police, and word spreads that there's been a murder at the Pacific Hotel. The police and a reporter arrive, and they burst into the room only to discover sitting inside a smiling Miss Yu. After a few minutes of their flustered questioning, she removes her wig and reveals herself to be Zhang Yuehen in drag. The manager and policeman are unamused, but the reporter exclaims, "Marvelous! Wonderful! What talent!" Zhang explains that he put on the show to get the public to acknowledge his skill at impersonation, and then fields their questions about how he pulled off the scheme. The story concludes:

> As he finished speaking, Zhang Yuehen wore an expression of uncontainable delight. The young journalist who had been focusing on writing everything down stopped and remarked cheerfully, "This is no crime. In fact, this news item is even more remarkable than a crime. I've finally gotten some great material; the title will be 'The Bizarre Incident at the Pacific Hotel.'" Outside the door of the Pacific Hotel, Zhang Yuehen's friend Qian Yinghan distributed a handbill, on which was written:

This is no crime. It's Zhang Yuehen's signature performance. Please go to Weiguang Theater tomorrow night to see the second act.

The story reminds Shanghai readers not to believe what they see, read, or hear, and certainly not to be as gullible as Jiang, who imagined he was living in a detective novel. But the dramatist in Xu also wants us to appreciate the publicity stunt—just enjoy the show!

The deceptive advertisement was a common artistic trope in a city awash in ads.[59] Xu's innovation in stories like "Woman's Playthings," summarized at the beginning of this chapter, was to highlight the agency of a newly conspicuous figure in cities like Shanghai: the cultural entrepreneur.[60] Xu's heroine Qiu Suwen, for example, earns money by crafting her image via a variety of media. She fuels the public's desire by creating an abstract image of a modern woman of culture through her writings, paintings, and letters.[61] She also employs a different type of trick photography: the bait-and-switch. Having fashioned herself into an abstract ideal, she then uses an advertisement to lure readers into a written exchange and finally into a real place in which they make a spectacle of themselves.[62] In this cycle of interaction, the trickster-writer controls the relationship, duping readers, who become the main show for Xu's readers.

"Woman's Playthings" also offered a twist on familiar stories about the "modern woman" and the "new woman," a fashionable genre in the 1920s and 1930s, in which (mostly) male writers often depicted women in roles then thought of as male.[63] The story points to male anxieties about women's new visibility and social power, the theme of innumerable contemporary stories and cartoons (see figure 5.4).[64] Yet Xu celebrates rather than condemns the manipulation that allows her to score a symbolic victory in the battle of the sexes. Qiu is not a realistic character (how could she write more than a thousand letters a day?) or an object of satire but the stuff of myth: a trickster.

The one-way practical joking in "Woman's Playthings" marks it as a humiliation or deception farce, in which the victim "is exposed to [his] fate, without opportunity for retaliation," and which requires "special justifications for the pleasure taken in the sufferings of others."[65] While the story makes fun of men's gullibility, the revelation about the deceased granddaughter injects a note of pathos, shifting attention from the dupes to the hoaxster. By circulating the photograph to a group of strangers, Qiu preserves and broadcasts the memory of a loved one.

In the 1930s, Xu developed his most famous trickster figure, Dr. Li Ah Mao (Li Amao boshi), as an alter ego for a newspaper advice column. Ah Mao is the sort of common, lower-class name that appeared in newspaper reports of court cases involving domestic servants, chauffeurs, rickshaw pullers, and other menial laborers. Xu wrote different Ah Mao columns for a range of Shanghai newspapers, sometimes using the unlikely honorific, well into the 1940s.[66]

FIGURE 5.4. A two-faced woman leads men to their doom on a front cover of the *Sunday* 48 (28 January 1923), a popular fiction periodical for which Xu Zhuodai wrote. Note foot of drowned man at bottom. Image courtesy of the Harvard-Yenching Library, Harvard University.

The persona proved so popular that in the late 1930s the Guohua Film Company proposed a series of Li Ah Mao movies. At least three films were made: *Li Ah Mao and Miss Tang* (1939) (which paired Li with a female counterpart of Xu's invention), *Li Ah Mao and the Zombie* (1940), and *Li Ah Mao and Dongfang Shuo* (1940), which paired Li with a classical comic icon. Each film was written by Xu and directed either separately or jointly by Zhang Shichuan and Zheng Xiaoqiu (son of Zheng Zhengqiu). These films did better at the box office than Xu's own Happy Film Co. productions, perhaps because they were family fare. As one reviewer said: "every little kid knows the three words 'Li Ah Mao.'"[67]

In 1941 and 1942, during the Japanese occupation of Shanghai, Xu wrote a series of twelve stories under the title, *The Unofficial Story of Li Ah Mao*.[68] "April Fool's Day," the first in the series, is in the form of a play, with dialogue, parenthetical mood cues, stage directions, and sparse narration.[69] Li Ah Mao arrives at the home of a husband and wife feuding over the man's love affair. Claiming to be the prior occupant, he asks them for a moment alone to pay homage to the wife he drove to suicide in this very house several years ago. The couple returns to the living room to discover that he has robbed them blind, but Ah Mao has distracted the woman from her suicide threats. The wife looks at the calendar and sees that the robber has left a calling card with the name Li Ah Mao next to the date: April 1st.

In "Please Exit through the Back Door," Ah Mao is approached by two recently unemployed friends, who ask him to save them from imminent poverty.[70] Ah Yang is a florist, but people can barely afford rice, and business is so bad that he has been forced to close up shop. Ah Ping's barbershop, which shares a back door with Ah Ying's shop, is in similar difficulty. Ah Mao takes out two advertisements in the newspaper, one saying that Ah Yang shop stocks a "fast-acting miracle hair-growth tonic" and another saying that Ah Ping's barbershop has the secret to a "new, super-economical head-shaving method." Customers throng their front doors, above which hangs a sign advertising the respective product.

> Strange to say! Passersby on the street could all see for themselves that the men going in Brother Ah Yang's door were all bald. Clearly, they were going to buy hair tonic. Before long, each emerged one by one with a thick head of hair and holding in his hand a paper packet—this was, of course, the so-called miracle tonic. Amazingly, among the customers coming out of the shop not a single bald person could be found. The news passed by word of mouth from one person to ten and from ten to a hundred. Soon, everyone was telling their bald friends and family members to go and buy tonic.
>
> Across the street from Quick Blade Barber Shop at Number 71 Zhenjiang Road there happened to be a teahouse. On that day, patrons on both floors saw above the door to the barbershop a cloth banner that read "Super-economical head-shaving method." As they watched, groups of men went in, one after another, each with wild and unkempt hair; a moment later, each man emerged clean-shaven. Naturally,

many people were astounded by this miracle. Word spread, and everyone went to find out about this super-economical head-shaving method themselves.[71]

In fact, the narrator tells us, the explanation is "not worth a laugh." After each customer makes his purchase, a sign on the wall directs him: "Due to the large number of customers, please exit through the back door" . . . into the other shop. Head-shaving customers return home and find the following instructions when they open the packet containing the secret formula: "Before bed, mix flour and glue together and mix into your hair. As you sleep, rats will come and eat your hair down to the nub during the night." Hair-growth tonic customers return home to read: "Grass will grow if this powder is applied to soil, but not to stone. If you find it doesn't work for you, your honorable head must be made of rock. In that case, drill a few small holes in your head and reapply. If that doesn't work, transplant fine rattan fibers onto your head, and that'll look pretty too."

This situation comedy draws on the Chinese comic aesthetic of raising hell (*da nao*) in a public space. (The most famous hell-raiser in this tradition would be Sun Wukong, the Monkey King who steals peaches of immortality in *Journey to the West*.) Xu's readership would have been well familiar with the advertisements for "miracle cures" (*qiyao*) that had appeared in newspaper pharmaceutical advertisements since the late Qing.[72] Parodists, as we saw in chapter 3, had long lampooned claims of immediate results. In Xu's story, the advertisement is not an object of parody but a prop in an urban performance, in which storefronts become stages for a public audience of passersby and teahouse patrons.

Hoaxes feature so frequently in Xu's works that they beg the question of why he thought they mattered in a modern, cosmopolitan metropolis. Scholars of popular literature have interpreted Li Ah Mao's hoaxes as symbols of resistance against economic oppression and material scarcity during the Japanese occupation—a strong theme in Xu's wartime writings.[73] Though ambivalent about Li Ah Mao's methods, they find redemption in Xu's expression of a popular spirit of stoicism and resourcefulness under foreign occupation. This interpretation chimes with French theorist Michel de Certeau's explanation of how marginalized individuals respond to a social reality over which they have little control. The method available to them is the "tactic," a practice for creating space for oneself within a larger structure of power. "Strategies" are the methods by which the powerful build those larger structures and establish their authority. Whereas strategies require significant investments of resources that render them relatively inflexible, tactics, driven by expediency, are fluid and adaptable. The "guileful ruse" of trickster, in Certeau's words, is "the art of the weak that enables them to exploit their understanding of the rules of the system, and to turn it into an advantage." Though lacking the power to overthrow the overarching social and political order, these acts of subversion indicate "a refusal to be subjugated."[74]

In stories like "Please Exit through the Back Door," Li Ah Mao does act as something of a Robin Hood in scheming to enrich his downtrodden friends. But the resistance interpretation does not explain the hoaxes in "Opening Day Advertisement" or in "Woman's Playthings," whose protagonist is no weak subaltern. It reinforces a refrain common to much mainland Chinese historiography since the Mao era: namely, that the only literary works of value written before the 1949 national "Liberation" are those marked by a spirit of resistance against feudal oppression, the Nationalist government, or the Japanese.

The stories of Qiu Suwen, Li Ah Mao, and Zhang Yuehen reveal that the economy of the hoax is partly aesthetic. In addition to earning money and filling bellies, they invest mundane experiences with comic potential, and, in doing so, turn daily living into art. As Lewis Hyde observes in a comparative study of tricksters around the world, "The trickster myth derives creative intelligence from appetite."[75] A figure like Li Ah Mao transcends the adverse circumstances that have forced him into his role as Mr. Fix-It.[76] His is can-do charisma, mixing the hustle of the petty entrepreneur and the observational genius of Sherlock Holmes. Indeed, *huaji* and *zhentan* (detective) fiction of the era share close generic affinity, hoaxes and murder investigations alike leading the reader on a journey from puzzlement to revelation and delight. This narrative arc appears in the symmetry of "Please Exit through the Back Door" and in the light comic justice that Qiu Suwen metes out to her correspondents. Through hoaxes, Li Ah Mao and Qiu Suwen reveal a Shanghai not of drudgery, but of possibility.

BEWARE THE PLAGIARIST!

Xu Zhuodai and his peers were not content with writing stories about fictional hoaxes. They also played practical jokes on readers. In Xu's 1921 story "The Fiction Material Wholesaler," Lit-Man Deng (Deng Wengong, literally, Literature Worker) is proprietor of a prosperous shop that sells story ideas under the slogan "Advocating Art & Literature, Promoting Domestic Goods."[77]

Tainted Fei (Fei Chunren), the first of Lit-Man's seven customers, declares that he detests fiction but wants to submit a piece to a certain magazine's fiction competition, explaining: "I'm hard up for ten dollars, so I want to write a story. Thieving or fiction-writing—it's one or the other if I'm going to put ten bucks in my pocket." Handsome Xiao (Xiao Bolian), whose name puns on both "pretty boy" (*xiao bailian*) and Bernard Shaw (*Xiao Bona*), is pretending to be a novelist to impress a prostitute. He assures Lit-Man: "I guarantee, once the story is finished, getting three or four lovers will be a piece of cake. What with royalties and allowances from my lovers—being a fiction writer is the best business! A story is more effective than any aphrodisiac." Floozy Yang, a college student, wants a tale of "pure love" but is offended by Lit-Man's story about a girl who has an affair with a classmate and falls into dire straits, since it mirrors her own situation. The scion of a wealthy family declares that he wants to write to improve society, but since he distains merchants he insists on publishing it himself. Another customer turns out to be looking for material for a phonograph record.

Lit-Man's business prospers so much that he considers opening branches in other cities. As each customer tries to haggle with him on price, Lit-Man repeatedly insists that he only sells "first-class goods." In fact, his plot summaries are derivative and cliché, populated with stock figures, such as talented lads and beautiful young ladies, maids, adulterous butchers, and prostitutes, or pandering to middling tastes for sentimental wartime romance and exposés of student sexual mores.

As Lit-Man is relating a story to a man named Swallowtail (Yan Weisheng), his seventh customer suddenly interrupts him and completes the story. "Lit-Man paled in amazement. 'You know it already?' 'Of course I do!' Swallowtail replied. 'How could you offer me this kind of material? This was published previously in *Short Story Monthly*.' Lit-Man became flustered. 'I had no idea. It must be a coincidence.' 'A coincidence?' Swallowtail asked. 'You're a fiction writer. How could you not know Wofoshanren's [Wu Jianren's] *Doctor's Intuition*?'"

This last detail would seem to corroborate, ten years after his death, Wu Jianren's 1909 claim (see chapter 2) that he was a victim of plagiarism. At this point in the story, Lit-Man's other customers burst in and rail at him for selling them plagiarized material, recounting the humiliation they experienced when they were exposed as having been ripped off *Strange Tales from the Liao Studio* or popular fiction magazines. Swallowtail condemns Lit-Man's "crime" but chides the customers for being ignorant readers. Together, they force Lit-Man to close shop and, in tears, he defends himself:

> Gentlemen... things having come to this pass, there's not much I can do. But my profession is providing materials wholesale, not manufacturing them myself. Selling other people's ready-made goods is all wholesalers ever do. It's entirely up to the buyer to determine whether or not they're used goods. If you like what you see, you buy it. As for plagiarizing, these days everybody is copying each other's works and rushing them to press. Why pick on me? And anyway, I promote Chinese goods. I never use foreign goods! Aren't those people who translate foreign fiction just plagiarizing? Why let them plagiarize and not me? Let's face it: fiction writers these days are a thick-skinned bunch. Compared to what they do, copying old works is a trifle. Some of them even have the audacity to lift a passage here and a section there and piece them together into a funny [*huaji*] story to trick readers. Isn't that even more absurd?

At this point, "Zhuodai comments: Uh oh! This Lit-Man Deng is on a tirade and might get around to cursing me. I dare not write another line, so it's time I lay down my pen." The implication, of course, is that Xu himself has been plagiarizing and that the reader has been the target of a literary hoax.

At one level, the story is a sweeping satire of the rampant plagiarism in Shanghai's bloated and hypercompetitive publishing industry, the commercialization of literature, contemporary social mores, and the Buy "Made in China" movement.[78] Lit-Man is a self-professed promoter of literary quality whose wholesaling further commodifies literature. Yet central to Xu's farce is the question of what constitutes literary creation: ethical considerations aside, how do translation, plagiarism, or other refashionings of existing writings differ qualitatively from original literary creation? Lit-Man's story ideas may not be original, but neither are they word-for-word reproductions. And, as he points out, a wholesaler's job is merely to sell "ready-made goods."

"Plagiarist in Western Dress," a story which appeared in *The Scarlet Magazine* in 1923, begins with Xu recounting the trouble his editor, Shi Jiqun (1896–1946), has had trying to spot plagiarized manuscripts.[79] He is amused by the thought that Shi trusts him and asserts: "I have a special plagiarizing method that can pull the wool over the eyes of editors and readers. . . . Fortunately, this special plagiarizing method of mine is extremely clever. I've just invented it, so no one will be able to detect it. Knowing this makes me so bold and thick-skinned that I might as well come out and announce to my editor and readers that this story of mine was plagiarized. . . . Having explained this to everyone up front, I'm going to skip the niceties, put pen to paper, and get plagiarizing."

The story that follows tells of a young foreigner named George who is enamored of one of his black slave girls, Melina. While George is away, Mrs. John goes to his room and finds that the black slave girls have been playing Ping-Pong and poker, and that the floor is covered with cigarette butts. She reprimands them for their misbehavior and then drinks a glass of brandy she finds out on the table. When the slave girls tell her that the brandy was being saved for Melina, Mrs. John leaves in a huff. George returns to discover that someone has drank Melina's brandy; Melina tells him that brandy gives her an upset stomach anyway and that she'd rather eat chocolate candy. She then distresses George with the news that her mother and brother have expressed a wish to buy her out of servitude. Following a long discussion of her fate, during which George becomes increasingly despondent, Melina reveals that she has actually already convinced her mom and brother to let her stay. George responds with tearful euphoria.

The story proper is followed by a note from Shi Jiqun, who exclaims, "So my old buddy is a plagiarist. I never knew!" He admits, however, that he can't detect any signs of plagiarism and concludes that the story is a translation. He mentions in passing, "Some places in the story are underlined in black. These are foreign names, which we specially marked to prevent reader confusion." Xu, he says, should come clean.

"Exposing Plagiarism" appeared in the next issue.[80] Jichun, Xu admits, has seen through him. The work was indeed plagiarized—not translated—and from a hugely famous novel that every reader knows but none will be able to identify. Xu appends "A Small Dictionary for Exposure of Plagiarists," which contains a list of key words for unlocking his plagiarizing technique and identifying the source text. These include:

ping pong	go
play poker	play "racing go" and "dice and dominoes"
cigarette butts	melon seed shells
chocolate candy	dried chestnuts
black slave girls	maids
brandy	koumiss [fermented mare's milk]
Mrs. John	Nanny Li
Melina	Aroma
George	Baoyu

The story, it turns out, comes from the most famous novel in the history of Chinese literature: *Dream of the Red Chamber*.[81] Having revealed his trick, Xu congratulates himself and continues to taunt the reader: "Dear readers, take this dictionary and see for yourselves just how formidable my plagiarizing method is.... I've insured myself with a Western insurance company, hired a Western lawyer on retainer, and hung up a Western shop sign—am I going to be afraid of anyone exposing me? I might as well give it to you straight: this plagiarizing method of dressing up in Western clothing wasn't even my invention. I plagiarized that too." His inspiration, he goes on, was all the jokes appearing in magazines nowadays, most of which are ripped off from *The Expanded Forest of Laughs*. While flattering his own plagiarizing techniques as "extremely clever," "novel," and "formidable," he pins the blame on the unnamed predecessors he learned them from.

Xu employs a number of stock storyteller conventions, such as posing and answering rhetorical questions, simulating dialogue with the reader, and misleading the reader with the disingenuous testimony of an accomplice. He flatters readers' smug self-assurance that they're onto the ruse while stimulating curiosity about how the scheme will play out. The transparent hoax also subordinates the drama of the main text to that of the paratexts—namely, the preface, commentary, and dictionary. Throughout, he keeps the focus squarely on the creative process itself.

THE NEW LITERARY ORDER

Literary critic Mike Lee Davis, discussing Mark Twain's "esophagus hoax," characterizes the literary practical joke as a sort of conspiracy targeted at the reader.[82] In his 1902 novella *A Double Barreled Detective Story*, Twain inserted a paragraph of lyrical but meaningless scenic description featuring a flying esophagus. Few readers noticed, he later claimed, and none who did detected a hoax. In that open letter, Twain chided his readers and gloated over the fun he'd had at their expense. Twain's hoax, Davis asserts, sought to burst the bubble of smug self-regard fostered by America's "national fetishization of [its own] innocence."[83]

Shanghai had been stereotyped for decades as anything but innocent—popular prejudice held that it was a realm of cheats and scammers. Beginning in 1914, the popular fiction magazine the *Saturday* regularly included a "Notice to Plagiarists" threatening to publish the real names and addresses of the "thieving vermin" who attempted to "swindle" its editors by submitting stories plagiarized from friends or the ancients.[84] In 1920, the year before "The Fiction Material Wholesaler" appeared, Lu Xun accused Li Dingyi, the popular writer and joke anthologizer, of plagiarizing a translation from his and Zhou Zuoren's collection *Stories from Abroad* (1909). The allegation was unfounded, if plausible.[85] Plagiarism was also part and parcel to a broader discourse of urban deception, one symbolized by the title of Lei Jin's illustrated book, *Shanghai's World of Swindlers* (1914).[86]

While building on longstanding stereotypes about double-dealing Shanghainese, the trope of the heroic cultural entrepreneur extended the stereotype into a new media and social context. Xu Zhuodai's farces emphasize the proximity of the reader; his tricksters are not high officials but people like you and me. His *Funny Shanghai* affirmed the common person's ability to survive, thrive, and even have fun in an adverse environment.

Xu's colleagues borrowed his ideas readily, in a kind of winking plagiarism. Four issues after the last installment of Xu's parodic series "Newest Prohibition and Exorcism Methods" appeared in the *Scarlet Magazine*, a colleague wrote a "supplement." Hu Jichen's "The Opposite Side of Mr. Xu's Stories" riffed on two of Xu's earlier works. "Exposing Plagiarism" was soon followed by two short pieces by other authors on the plagiarism theme.[87] Xu also inspired journalists, who in one case reported that Dr. Li Ah Mao, aka Xu Zhuodai, had made a fool of himself by canceling a date with his wife in order to go out with a dancer only to have the dancer stand him up for another man—but just in his role in his latest movie![88]

The spirit of the prankster is emblematic of a modern literary culture that appreciated practical jokes for fun and profit.[89] Early issues of the *Scarlet Magazine* regularly featured cover illustrations of naughty children playing practical jokes on each other and on grown-ups (see figure 5.5). The forty-three-year-old Xu's imitation of a three-year-old further indicates the appeal of figures who embod-

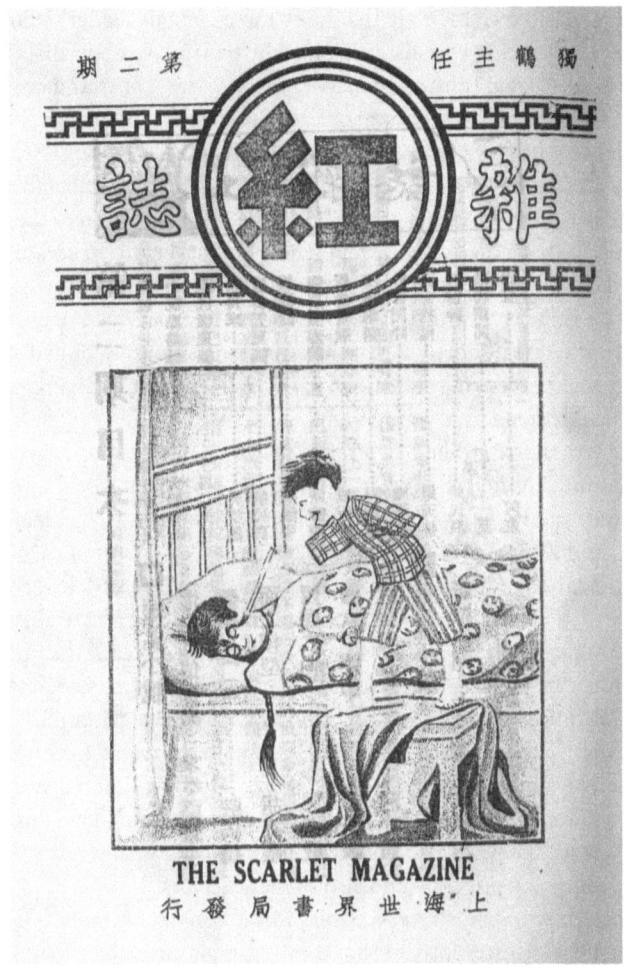

FIGURE 5.5. Childish pranks on the cover of the second issue of the *Scarlet Magazine* (August 1922). Image courtesy of the Library of the Institute of Chinese Literature and Philosophy, Academia Sinica.

ied childlike mischief. At the end of his 1918 short story "Diary of a Madman," Lu Xun had famously called upon readers to "save the children." Xu Zhuodai encouraged his to *be* the children.

Nor was this ethos restricted to a single segment of the literary market. Inside joking and tomfoolery in the popular press had long "helped fuel interest [in contemporary fiction] by giving readers a sense of participation." One male writer posed as a female so convincingly that he attracted a male reader's marriage proposal.[90] Literary hoaxing was also practiced by bourgeois modernists and members of the avant-garde. In the late 1920s, Sinmay Zau, a poet and cosmopolitan playboy, pulled a literary seduction trick on Zeng Pu, a famous novelist and editor of the Francophile Shanghai journal *Truth, Goodness, Beauty* (*Zhenshanmei*, 1927–31), by posing as a Catholic schoolgirl. Zau later remembered that "such hijinks were considered a creative exercise in the Shanghai salon of the late 1920s" and involved both Chinese and foreigners.[91] Beijing-based writers of the 1910s and 1920s like Liu Fu, as we saw in chapter 4, also used hoaxes to garner publicity for their own literary ventures. As it happens, Liu had been a protégé of Xu Zhuodai's in the 1910s, shortly before he and Qian Xuantong pulled their Wang Jingxuan stunt. Xu, then, may be said to have contributed to a "Shanghai modern" whose influence extended beyond Shanghai itself.[92]

Whereas writers from Liu E to Zheng Zhenduo had held up tears as expressions of genuine emotion, hoaxsters envisioned a modern world of guile. They played the fool and invited others to play along with them. In its playfulness, inclusiveness, and reversals, *huaji* farce evokes Bakhtin's notion of carnival laughter as "the social consciousness of all the people," with the trickster-writer as a Lord of Misrule.[93] As an inventor of fictional tricksters and as a trickster himself, Xu Zhuodai approximates what literary scholar Edith Kern calls the "quintessence of the absolute comic" who "by turning the world playfully upside down" "transports us into worlds where imagination and make-believe triumph."[94] For some New Literature writers, literature had to represent social reality faithfully through mimesis. Satire was acceptable only because its exaggerations and distortions measured the distance between what reality was and what it should be. But for others, practical jokes were a way to change reality, beginning with a reprieve from the drudgery of churning out copy and sifting manuscripts.[95]

Xu Zhuodai's protagonists are unusual in the context of modern Chinese fiction, and even in trickster lore, in that they triumph more than they suffer. Like Xu himself, they are prime movers in a Shanghai of their own making, orchestrating ethically ambivalent spectacles and inviting readers to join in the fun. Tricksters like Qiu Suwen are rarely punished with comic justice; more often, the reader becomes the scapegoat. On both levels, then, Funny Shanghai was a comic *cosmos*, a new reality. Its touchstone was the figure of the trickster who reorders the world and the relationships of people within it, employing tools of the cultural entrepreneur.

Like the late Qing literati discussed in chapter 3, Xu and his peers treated Shanghai like a playground. The self-aggrandizing deceptions perpetrated by corrupt officials in Li Boyuan's *Officialdom Unmasked* (which was later adapted into a Shanghai-style farce)[96] and Wu Jianren's *Strange Events Eyewitnessed over the Past Twenty Years* share with the shenanigans of Li Ah Mao and his friends a common theme of trickery for profit. Yet Xu's farce differs from the cynical jokes of his predecessors. His works feature neither abject pessimism about China nor the sense of forced gaiety found in many fin de siècle works. Like many May Fourth writers, Xu was a foreign-educated intellectual; unlike them, he made little pretense of castigating the ethically dubious behavior he portrayed. Everyday deceptions were a reliable source of amusement, something to look forward to.

Indeed, the fantasy triumphs that Xu allows his readers to vicariously experience through his protagonists seem to condone the sort of "psychological victory" that Lu Xun mocked and lamented in "The True Story of Ah Q." For Lu Xun, self-indulgent laughter was a pernicious and debilitating social habit that exacerbated national problems. China needed laughter that would attack social, political, and spiritual problems head-on. Xu Zhuodai and his fellow farceurs asked: What's the harm in enjoying the occasional psychological victory? Why not play jokes on each other if no one gets hurt? And why not part fools from their money when friends' welfare is at stake? Ah Q suffered horribly for his fantasies and his opportunistic behavior; Ah Mao's scheming marked him as a successful man of his times.

The sustained popularity of Xu's brand of humor, from his plays and stories of the 1920s up to the Li Ah Mao phenomenon of the 1930s and 1940s, indicates that hoax-driven farce was no fad.[97] Burlesque, too, had friends in high places—including the supposedly straight-faced "father" of modern Chinese literature himself. Lu Xun's *Old Tales Retold* feature an aloof literatus named Butt of Laughter (*Xiaobing jun*) and scholars who utter the same mix of pidgin (*hao tu you tu*=how do you do?) and gibberish (*gu lu ji li*) as does Ah Fu in Xu Zhuodai's "Two Couples."[98] Since at least the 1910s, farce, cursing, and buffoonery had provoked objections ranging from distaste to contempt, anxiety, and fear. In the 1930s, this opposition coalesced into a concerted campaign to change the tone of public discourse. The result might be called the invention of humor.

6

The Invention of Humor
幽默年

This New Humor . . . is the Old Humor writ small.
—QIAN ZHONGSHU, 1934[1]

On 13 May 1933, Chen Zizhan said he had a "stupid question" for readers of his column in the *Shun Pao*: What year is this? It was a question that any smart citizen of the republic could answer. For politicians, it was the Year of Constitutional Reform; for military officers, it was the Year of Bandit Eradication (i.e., wiping out communists). For industrialists and businessmen it was Buy "Made in China" Year, and for economists and agriculturalists it was Rural Revival Year. For thinkers it was Attack Hu Shi Year; for professional authors, it was Publish Your Autobiography Year; and for the rest of the literati it was the Year of Humor (*youmo nian*).[2]

Humor exploded onto China's literary scene on 16 September 1932 with the arrival of the *Analects Fortnightly*, a new Shanghai magazine edited by Lin Yutang.[3] Lin had coined a new term for humor, *youmo*, and the *Analects* broadcast his transliteration to a broad audience, along with a new philosophy of how to think, speak, and live. Within weeks of the magazine's first issue, Chinese critics were using new phrases and concepts such as a "sense of humor" (*youmogan*), "humor literature" (*youmo wenxue*), and the "humorous sketch" (*youmo xiaopin*). Pundits like Chen Zizhan (who also wrote for the *Analects*) filled the popular press with their opinions about the ethos behind—and implications of—a new literary movement that had, in a few short months, become a nationwide phenomenon.

In February 1933, Nobel laureate George Bernard Shaw visited Shanghai. In the less than twenty-four hours Shaw spent in town, he was photographed with Lin Yutang, Lu Xun (a contributor to the *Analects*), Soong Ching-ling (Sun Yat-sen's widow), and other notables. The *Analects* promptly brought out a special number on "Shaw in China" and for months the press was filled with Shaw anecdotes, bons mots, and discussions of his character and writings. A few months later, Maurice

Dekobra, a popular French novelist, arrived in Shanghai. Dekobra had recently compiled an anthology of definitions of humor by famous Western writers (including Shaw) to which Chinese critics referred for expert opinion on the subject.[4] His visit was less successful. Some observers considered the Frenchman's admiring comments about Chinese women to be sarcastic, and the press flayed him.[5]

Both celebrity visits drew even more attention to humor and to the *Analects*, which had entered a competitive market. More periodicals were published in China in 1933 than in any previous year; 1934 was duly dubbed the "Year of the Magazine."[6] The idea for a magazine dedicated to humor had emerged from a Shanghai literary salon hosted by Sinmay Zau, who became its publisher.[7] Like *Shun Pao*'s "Free Talk," founded thirty-one years earlier, the *Analects* was to be an open forum in which fun could coexist with serious criticism. Its liberal, independent spirit also echoed the founding mandate of *Threads of Discourse*, from which the *Analects* drew contributors such as Zhou Zuoren, Lu Xun, Liu Bannong, Yu Pingbo, Sun Fuyuan, and Lin Yutang. No -isms, positions, platforms, "fair play" (which Zhou and Lin had called for in *Threads of Discourse* in 1925), or political backers—just honest self-expression.

Yet it was humor and not these other ideals that set the *Analects* apart.[8] Competitors soon appeared, including the humor fortnightlies *Golden Mean* (1933) and *Breezy Chats* (1936–37), as well as encores like Lin Yutang's *This Human World* (est. 1934) and *Cosmic Wind* (est. 1935). *Modern Sketch* (est. 1934), which Zau also published, invited *Analects* readers to experience for themselves "the shooting comet of satire and humor magazines; the final authority among cartoon journals."[9] "Humorists" (*youmojia*) sprung up across China, beginning with Lin, whom the Chinese press hailed as the Master of Humor (*youmo dashi*). Even as Chinese communities overseas began picking up the new word *youmo*, Lin's prolific writings in English made him internationally famous as a Chinese humorist.[10]

HUMORISTS BEFORE HUMOR

Lin Yutang first used the word *youmo* in May 1924 in an essay for Beijing's *Morning Post*. He was then just returned from several years of graduate study at Harvard and Leipzig and was teaching English at Peking University, where he was a regular contributor to *Threads of Discourse*, the journal that had fueled 1920s debates about civility and cursing (see chapter 4). In 1926, he was among a group of intellectuals whose public statements antagonized a northern warlord, and he fled south, ending up in Shanghai the following year.

His 1924 essay identifies humor as a "major imperfection" in the history of Chinese literature. Chinese people had a sense of humor but had forgotten how to cultivate it, resulting in a stifling intellectual scene. Writers had an ingrained didactic streak and found it hard to be natural. In the West, even academic books contained off-hand jokes, he pointed out. But these jokes were "of a different sort" than Chinese jokes, he added more vaguely, "they were 'humor.'" What China needed was for Zhou Shuren to tell jokes not just as the literary celebrity Lu Xun but as the famous Professor Zhou. Then everyone would see that being humorous did not result in a loss of face.[11]

Lin's neologism gained only modest traction in the next eight years, even though by 1924, Chinese readers had already had decades of exposure to Euro-American humor.[12] Magazines like *Punch* and *Puck* had circulated in China since the nineteenth century, inspiring local imitators in multiple languages.[13] Dickens, Shaw, Twain, and Wilde had been available in translation since the early twentieth century.

Several new Chinese writers had also introduced their own versions of urbane British-style humor to China. Ding Xilin began writing one-act comedies of manners in 1923 while teaching at Peking University, shortly after returning from the United Kingdom, where he had studied in mathematics and physics and, in his spare time, read Shaw, Ibsen, and Wilde. *A Wasp* (1923), Ding's first play, stars Mr. Ji, a young man in his late twenties, who navigates China's fast-changing social norms, walking a tightrope between the elder generation's expectations and his own desires.[14] His mother complains about modern girls who disparage the traditional model of "virtuous wife and good mother," and Mr. Ji responds: "You have to forgive them. They haven't spoken for several thousand years. Now that they're finally able to pick up a pen and write they can't help rattling on and on and on. Even they don't know what they're saying." He quips that modern girls are new-style vernacular poems—without substance, rhyme, or reason—while traditional girls are eight-legged essays, the dry, formulaic examination compositions penned by imperial civil service candidates.

Mr. Ji's opportunity for self-realization appears in the form of Miss Yu, whom his mother has set up to marry his cousin. Mr. Ji has to think fast to reconcile his equivocal (and unconsciously sexist) statements about young women with this opportunity for romance. He advises Miss Yu that marriage dulls "the most precious thing a person has—his aesthetic sensibility," and then takes her hands and proposes that she "keep me company in not marrying." When she agrees to this unusual proposition, he exults that they're a "heaven-matched pair of prevaricators" and hugs her, causing her to yelp in surprise. Ji's mother and a servant burst in, and Yu covers her face.

> Ji: (*Coming over and taking her hands down*) Where? Did it sting you?
> Mrs. Ji: What? What is it?
> Yu: (*With a deep sigh of relief*) Oh, a wasp! (*Casts Ji a look of thanks*)

The pair of prevaricators thus manages to avoid arranged marriage, please Mr. Ji's mother (who secretly thought Miss Yu a good match for her own son), and preserve their youthful "aesthetic sensibilities."

Oppression (1926), widely regarded as Ding's masterpiece, features another quick-witted young pair.[15] A man has put down a deposit on an apartment but the landlady, upon discovering that he is a bachelor, refuses to rent out of concern for her daughter, who lives in the building. He refuses either to take back his deposit, or to lie, as the sympathetic maid recommends, that he has a family coming. As in *A Wasp*, the solution arrives in the form of a young woman. While the landlady is fetching a policeman to throw him out, a female prospective tenant arrives, and the young man allows her to believe that he is the landlord. But when he reveals his predicament, she surprises him by offering to pose as his wife long enough to help him get even with the landlady. They pretend to be a bickering couple, allowing the landlady, policeman, and maid to draw their own erroneous conclusions, even if they never explicitly claim to be married. When the policeman asks the man for the woman's name, he responds, truthfully: "I don't know. Ask her yourself." When the landlady asks the woman, "So, he's your husband?"' she responds: "I don't know. Ask him. See if he admits it."

While its title ostensibly refers to "oppression" perpetrated by the landed class and the elder generation, *Oppression* is also about talking one's way out of an impossible situation and thereby avoiding the oppression of language itself.

Ding's comedies were a breath of fresh air: a good-natured battle of the sexes and the generations featuring witty banter, unconventional approaches to social issues, and clever situational comedy. Their heroes established a new comic archetype of enlightened youth who resort to various sorts of subterfuge to realize their individualistic, modern ideals while placating or outmaneuvering their traditional-minded elders.

The best-known humorist to emerge from the 1920s was Shu Qingchun, who, while teaching Chinese at the University of London in his twenties in the late 1920s, published a trio of novels in China under the pen name Lao She. *The Philosophy of Old Zhang* (1926) reveals its title secret in its first line: Old Zhang believes in a Holy Trilogy of Money.[16] He embraces three religions (Muslim, Christian, Buddhist), has three professions (soldier, scholar, merchant), and speaks three languages (Mandarin, Fengtian dialect, and Shandong dialect). And, all told, he will bathe only thrice: at birth, before his wedding night, and on the day his corpse is washed for burial. His religion is dictated by the market: he is Muslim when lamb is cheaper than pork, Buddhist when both lamb and pork are expensive, and Christian when he has guests, since it's cheaper to treat them to tea, as the British do, than to a full meal. The novel follows Old Zhang's exploits as a schoolmaster (reminiscent of Wackford Squeers of *Nicholas Nickleby*) making life miserable for his charges in a village outside Beijing. Lao She's next two novels followed a similar formula of an ironic, familiar narrative voice, colorful characters, and picaresque plotline. *The Two Mas* (1929) observes British prejudices and misconceptions about China through a father and son living in London. Drawing on Lao

She's own experiences, the novel chronicles their misadventures with missionaries who serve them rice pudding (since Chinese eat rice) and British ladies who, having likely read too many Fu Manchu novels, worry that the Mas eat rats and will poison their tea. Mr. Ma Senior once writes out the Chinese character "beautiful" 美 for his landlady's daughter and has a rare laugh when she sews the pattern into her hat upside down as 羙 so that it resembles a distorted form of the phrase "big cuckold" 㐅王八.[17]

Lao She returned to China in 1930. In September 1931, the Japanese invaded China's northeast, Manchuria, and placed Puyi, the dethroned emperor of the Qing dynasty, on the throne of a new puppet state. Lao She, an ethnic Manchu, saw Manchukuo as a farce, but he was also infuriated by the lackluster response of his government and his countrymen. Then, on 28 January 1932, the Japanese bombed civilian neighborhoods in northern Shanghai (Xu Zhuodai's wife, Tang Jianwo, was among those killed), setting off a month-long battle. In August of 1932, while living in Shandong province, Lao She began serializing *City of Cats* in the modernist literary journal *Les Contemporains*. An allegorical fantasy set in a feline-inhabited Mars, the novel castigates Chinese apathy, factionalism, and incompetence in the face of crisis. A few years later, Lao She declared it an artistic failure and attributed its bitter tone to momentary despair over China's "nightmare."[18]

The *Analects*'s appearance in September of 1932 was fortuitous for Lao She, and its editorial philosophy inspired him to change course. He brought back his previous ironic and familiar style in a variety of short pieces. In 1934, Sinmay Zau's Modern Press collected some of these in the anthology *Humorous Poems and Prose by Lao She*, which it promoted heavily in the *Analects* and its sister publications. Four more of Lao She's novels appeared in these journals in the next three years, including his masterpiece *Camel Xiangzi* (1937).

As soon as he began contributing to it, the *Analects* transformed Lao She's reputation. *Les Contemporains* began calling him a "humorist," and other periodicals soon followed suit.[19] Lao She's domestic fame as a humorist soon surpassed even that of Lin Yutang, thanks to his storytelling talent, mastery of folk idioms, and ear for the vernacular. He nevertheless was highly ambivalent about his putative status as an authority on humor. In 1934 he remarked that he had heard various theories about what humor was that all sounded "reasonable," but he himself preferred being considered "muddled," as it saved a lot of explaining.[20]

"Reasonable" was one of Lin Yutang's favorite words. Like the nineteenth-century novelist George Meredith, Lin believed that humor was the ultimate expression of a reasonable spirit, and he leavened this message with his own wit and hyperbole. In 1935, he endorsed the American nudist movement by saying that "I have been a nudist all my life without knowing it," just a *reasonable* nudist who was "all for nudism at certain hours and in certain circumstances, in the bath-tub, for instance."[21] In 1937, with war brewing in Europe and Asia, he suggested: send "five or six of the world's best humorists to an international conference, and give them the plenipotentiary powers of autocrats, and the world will be saved." As humor represents "the highest form of human intelligence," all war plans would collapse as each delegate vies to deplore his own country's folly.[22] Self-deprecating humor would spread across the globe, changing the character of human thought, and leading to a Reasonable Age in which good sense and a "peaceable temper" reigned supreme.

THE REVOLUTION IS TRANSLATED

T. K. Chuan, a fellow bilingual writer and publishing colleague of Lin's, was more skeptical about cross-cultural humor. He wrote in 1931: "Laugh, and the world does not usually laugh with you, because the world generally fails to see just what there is to laugh about."[23] But the burgeoning humor movement in China was thoroughly multilingual in its sources, vocabulary, and audience.

Youmo, Lin acknowledged, was a rather arbitrary transliteration of *humor*. In his 1924 essay he had even included an alternative transliteration, *huimo*, made up of the characters for "humorous" and "copy" or "imitate." Colleagues and readers nominated other alternatives such as *yumiao* ("witty speech"), *youmiao* ("abstruse and wonderful"), and *youma* ("superior cursing"). In one Lao She story, two boys overhear their father exclaiming "How humorous!" as he reads the *Analects* and mistake the word *youmo* for a synonym meaning "apply paint." Wags talked about *you ta yi mo*, turning *youmo* into a transitive verb akin to "pull his leg." None ever mentioned *oumuya*, a transliteration of "humor" that literary theorist Wang Guowei had coined as early as 1906.[24]

The *Analects* carried a vast array of foreign humor, including cartoons reprinted from *Punch*, the *New Yorker*, *Collier's*, and the *Humorist*, often with bilingual captions. Early issues featured sketches by the Mexican cartoonist José Miguel Covarrubias (1904–57). Sapajou, the nom de plume of a white Russian resident of Shanghai, created cartoons for the *Analects* as well as for his regular employer, the *North-China Daily News*.[25] "Flowers in the Rain," which featured jokes, and "Western Humor," another regular column, carried translations of works by Bertrand Russell, Plato, Cardinals of the Vatican, Herman Bahr, A. Boukhov, and Arkady Avertohenko. Articles discussed the humor of Will Rogers and Charlie Chaplin, as well as the ubiquitous Bernard Shaw. A 1935 "Special Issue on Western Humor" featured translations and analyses of Shakespeare, Nietzsche, Twain, Boccaccio, Huxley, A. P. Herbert, Baudelaire, Heywood Broun, Chekov, Chaucer, Axel Munthe, André Maurois, Peter Fleming, O. Henry, and Hamilton Wright Mabie. Even the essay that came to be regarded as Lin's seminal treatise on the subject, "On Humor," was preceded immediately by a translation of a two-part essay of the same title by the Spanish writer Ramón Gómez de la Serna.[26]

The magazine's launch in September 1932 attracted the attention of China's foreign-language press. The 8 December issue of the *China Critic* carried a cover feature "Introducing 'The Analects,'" by T. K. Chuan, who translated article excerpts from its first issues, as well as its full decalogue:

1. We will not be counter-revolutionary.
2. We will not pass any judgment upon those who are not worth our criticism, (Our column "Ye Antique Shoppe" 古香齋 takes care of those) but we will criticize those whom we cherish, such as Our Country, the militarists, the promising writers, and the not-unpromising revolutionaries.
3. We will not resort to oaths and filthy epithets (Humor and good humor are one in the same; to honor the traitors as our parents would not do, but neither must we call them d—d fools—Chinese 王八蛋).
4. We will not want any outside financial help; we will not be anybody's mouth-piece (we do not propagandize for money; but we may propagandize or even counter-propagandize for love).
5. We will not play satellites to the élite, the powerful, or the rich (we do not "press-agent" for dramatic stars, cinema stars, social stars, intellectual stars, political stars, et al.).
6. We will not be a group of mutual admirers; we are against "Flesh-creepy-ism" 肉麻主義. (We will avoid using such terms as: "The famous Scholar," "the famous poet," and so on; and we are determined not to use the expression: "My good friend, Hu Shih.")
7. We will not publish any cheaply sentimental and romantic poetry.
8. We will not advocate justice; we make known only our honest prejudices.
9. We will not swear off anything (e.g., smoking, tea-drinking, late-rising).
10. We will not admit that our writings are poor and in bad taste.[27]

These disclaimers notwithstanding, the *Analects* did not shy from derision and scatology. Responding to a news report about Guangdong collecting a "special levy on feces and urine," it featured calligraphy of the couplet:

自古未聞糞有稅　Since antiquity, no one has ever imposed a tax on shit,
而今只許屁無捐　But now, the only thing exempt from levies is farts.[28]

Other features included jokes, bons mots, doggerel verse, parodies,[29] folktales, and ludicrous news items. In October 1932, it commented on the story of Liang Zuoyou, a shop clerk who had come to possess a $30 million check belonging to the government that had been on the person of "Dogmeat General" Zhang Zongchang, a notorious warlord who had recently been assassinated. Liang was given a first-class train ticket (which he exchanged for a third-class ticket, pocketing the difference) to return it to the treasury in Nanjing. Finance Minister T. V. Soong received Liang in person only to discover that Liang had misread the amount on

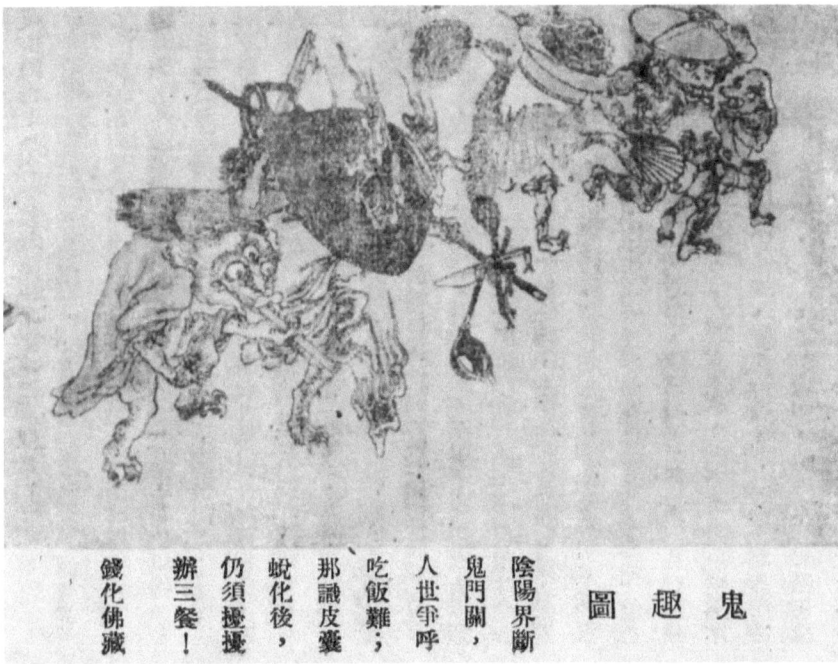

FIGURE 6.1. *Curious Ghosts*, one of several paintings in the collection of Qian Huafo (1884–1964), which appeared in the first of two special issues of the *Analects Fortnightly* devoted to ghost stories. *Lunyu* 91 (1 July 1936), 892. Image courtesy of the Library of the Institute of Chinese Literature and Philosophy, Academia Sinica.

the check, which was actually $300,000. Liang had enjoyed the VIP treatment for a pittance.[30]

The magazine also solicited content from readers. In 1936 it experienced an overwhelming response to its call for submissions on the topic of ghost stories and ended up doing two special issues. The first reprinted several ghost paintings from the collection of renowned painter Qian Huafo, including one accompanied by the verse (see figure 6.1):

> Between earth and hell lies Devil's Gate,
> Mortals' wail of hunger hard to sate.
> Little knowing that their baggy form, once sloughed,
> Will appear thrice daily on a devil's plate![31]

A two-page cartoon by Huang Yao in the same issue satirized the "devils" of contemporary society using a number the epithets found in *Which Classic?* (see figure 6.2).[32] Other special issues focused on topics such as experts, eating, and

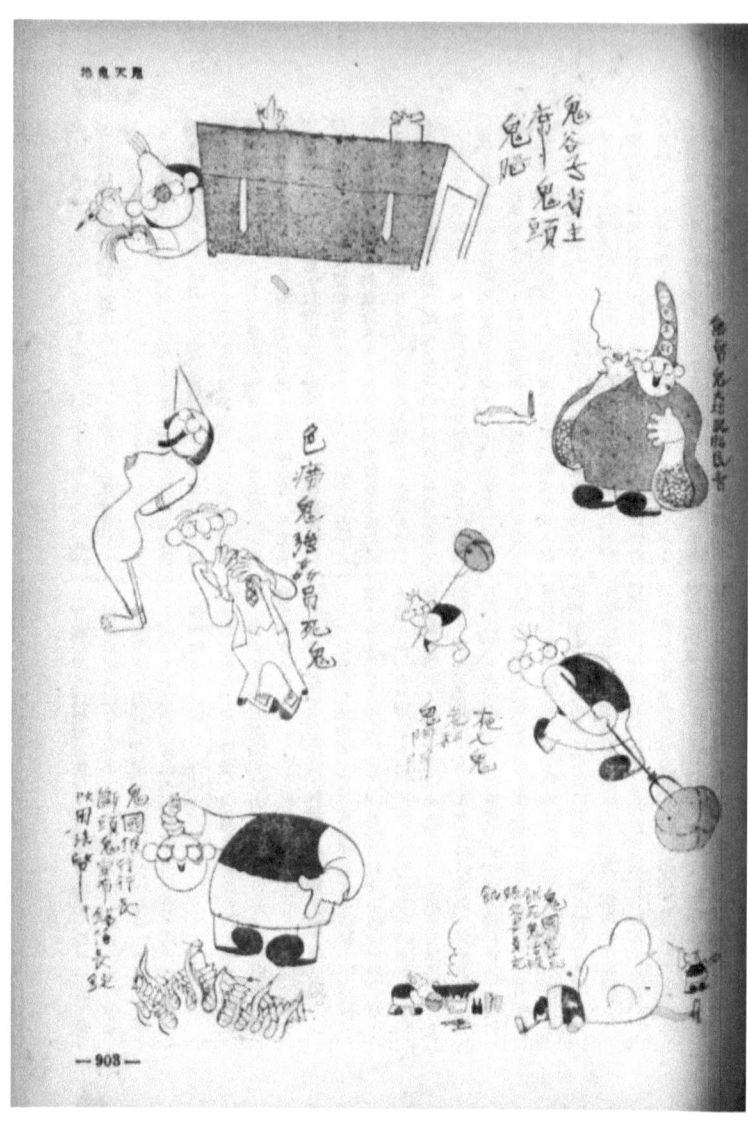

FIGURE 6.2. "A Land of Devils," by Huang Yao (signed "W. Buffoon"), featuring his character Ox-Nose, appeared in the first of two *Analects Fortnightly* issues focusing on ghost stories. *Lunyu* 91 (1 July 1936), 902–3. Image courtesy of the Huang Yao Foundation. Clockwise from top: The Stealthy Governor of Devil's Gulch, Opportunist Devil Scraping away the Fat of the Land, Yakshā Smuggling across the Styx, Starved Devil Who Perished in National Famine Appeases Hunger by Eating Relief Committee Member Alive, Decapitated Devil Chairman of National Devil Bank Announces Spirit Money as the New Legal Tender, Sex Fiend Rapes Hanged She-Devil.

Clockwise from top: The Great Commander Sleeping-on-the-Job Devil, Opium Fiend-cum-National Salvation Soldier, Small-Brained Traitor Devil Presenting a Map, Short-Lived Devil Committing Suicide over Lost Love, River Devil Transforming into Demon Seductress Mermaid.

sleeping. In fact, for all its declarations, the *Analects* was not all that different from some of its immediate predecessors in its liberality and eclecticism.

The *China Critic*, the English-language weekly in which T. K. Chuan's translation of the *Analects*'s decalogue appeared, was handmaiden to the humor trend. Founded in 1928, it became an important forum for broadcasting Chinese opinion on national and international affairs during the decade in which the Nationalist government was based in the southern city of Nanjing. For much of the 1930s it shared contributors and translated articles back and forth with Lin Yutang's various Chinese-language magazines, especially the *Analects*.[33] Many of Lin's extended essays commenting on the tone of public discourse appeared first in the *Critic*'s pages.

One of these was the transcript of a speech Lin gave in Shanghai on 14 January 1930 to the World's Chinese Students Federation deploring China's dearth of critical thinkers. China was the "greatest nation" not in literature but in "the art of saying perhaps awful things in the nicest and most sophisticated manner."[34] Writers excelled at "composing," but not thinking. They could arrange adages of the sages of old into marvelous confections, but this dependence prevented them from solving problems on their own and criticizing the sages of today. This was symptomatic of a graver problem: "A nation whose 'free play of the mind' has been denied and where thinking has become impossible, is bound to turn its whole energy to composing belles-lettres . . . and find therein a satisfying substitute for real thinking." China's literary sphere had followers of Li Boyuan "whose principal business seems to be to detail their often ludicrous attempts in the art of courtship and whose only Muse and inspiration is the Courtesan, and at the same time we have a crop of young poets who sing invariably of suicide, fire and brimstone, Marxism and the proletariat." Lin's verdict: "Chinese civilization today resembles very much a frivolous man of letters who has not yet attained to any depth of thought." The Chinese critical ethos, he implied, could benefit from more irreverence. Not the contrarianism toward traditional culture of earlier radicals, but rather intellectual independence and skepticism. A writer should neither be a slave to authority nor turn hedonist or solipsist, becoming a slave to the self.

The call for reason, logic and relevance in public discussion was by no means new; what distinguished Lin was the ease with which he blended jocular and expository modes of criticism, as well as his cosmopolitanism. The critical culture he espoused belonged "to the modern world as a whole."

But the modern world had not yet embraced China. Later that year, China lost out on a seat in the League of Nations to Uruguay. Lin attributed the failure, only semi-facetiously, to the Chinese people's self-defeating combination of humor and realism. In an irony-laced lecture to the Shanghai YMCA Men's Club that September, he claimed that what was ruining the nation "is nothing else than the Chinese imperturbable sense of humour, a humour that laughs at all ideals and smiles at sin as an essential part of human life." In every Chinese lurked an old rogue who "turns all political reforms into a farce and treats all human institutions as mere jokes." The Chinese were "the most ruthless realists and the greatest humorists on earth" who laughed off rather than rectified atrocities and political farces.[35] Chinese culture boiled down to three things: a "serious desire to lie," "the ability to lie like a gentleman; and ... the mental calm then shown by taking both your own lies and those of your fellow-men with a sense of humour, and being not overly serious about anything on earth."[36] The very way Chinese people talked trapped them in a perpetual cycle of cynical thinking and behavior.

By then, Cai Yuanpei had appointed Lin as editor in chief of English publications at the newly established government research institution Academia Sinica, and this position provided Lin not only with economic stability but also close ties to the Ministry of Education, which endorsed a series of his English language textbooks, published in 1929. The windfall from their commercial success gave Lin the wherewithal to launch an ambitious series of cultural projects aimed at encouraging his countrymen to think and speak as individuals.[37]

One of the first was "The Little Critic" column for the *China Critic*, which debuted in July 1930. The Little Critic was personable and familiar, a friend who confided his own feelings, opinions, and criticisms in an easy and humorous style. His essays offered idiosyncratic takes on social manners, common sense, everyday life, and politics, often with a veneer of leisurely nonchalance. "On Shaking Hands" begins: "One great difference between oriental and occidental civilizations is that the westerners shake each other's hand, while we shake our own," before going on to object to the Western custom on hygienic and other grounds.[38] "How I Bought A Tooth-Brush" navigates a bewildering consumer landscape of social pressure, industry advertising, and expert advice to conclude with an epiphanic meeting with a dentist: "We shook hands warmly, but desolately, like two souls who, between themselves, shared the secret of the universe."[39] "I Moved Into a Flat" tells of how Lin was driven from his Shanghai apartment by a neighbor's incessant racket. An Englishman, he says, would have confronted the offender; a Chinese would have ignored the existence of his own nerves; but "being an English educated Chinese I could do neither." Apartment living makes him feel cramped, and he rails against "the mutilation of the modern home" that is the convertible sofa bed. He ends up, happily, in a flat overlooking a small patch of greenery. The birds perched nearby move him to lyricism, but his poem ends with the sentiments of a writer muzzled by government censorship on the first anniversary of Japan's invasion of Manchuria: "But I still look on / While I am thinking of the one gone away."[40]

These essays added intimacy and idiosyncrasy to traditional literati genres such as the Discourse or Treatise (*lun*), normally ponderous in tone, by injecting personal views on an array of social, political, and cultural topics, both light and weighty. Essays appearing in both English and Chinese included "On Political Sickness" 論政治病, "On Chinese and Foreign Dress" 論西裝, "Confessions of a Nudist" 論裸體運動, "On Crying at Movies" 論看電影流淚, and "On Shaking Hands" 論握手.[41] Lin's self-translations could be markedly different. His Chinese version of "Confessions of a Nudist" (literally "On the Nudist Movement"), begins not with a focus on a persona, Lin Yutang the Accidental Nudist, but rather a rhetorical device: the familiar idiom "upon reaching an extreme, things always reverse" (wuji bifan). The Chinese version maintains a similar humorous personal tone to the English, but Lin "broaches the topic" (poti) of nudity as if writing an eight-legged essay for the old civil service examination, reframing the piece in a distinctively Chinese genre context and style of argumentation. Two collections of Lin's English-language Little Critic essays, published in 1935, drew foreign attention thanks in part to the enthusiastic endorsement of Lin's friend Pearl Buck, who in 1932 had won the Pulitzer Prize for her bestselling novel, *The Good Earth*.[42]

Liang Shiqiu observed in 1932 that "there is no 'humor form' [youmo ti]," since humor was not a genre but a style or a mode.[43] In the short term, however, *youmo* became most closely associated with the type of relaxed, informal, intimate, and idiosyncratic sketch at which Lin excelled. Practitioners called them *xiaopinwen* (literally, "little-taste essays"), linking them to a genre of the same name that was popular during the Ming dynasty. In modernizing the form, Lin and his peers introduced a bilingual idiom inflected with a healthy dose of *Punch*-style sarcasm and whimsy. They spoke of little-taste essays as vehicles for conveying individual thoughts, feelings, and predilections, as well as reflections of one's moral values, consumption habits, and outlook on society. Even as other sectors of the Chinese intellectual and literary world were busy aligning with either the right (the Nationalists) or the left (the Communists), for Lin and his group, the self was as much a concern as nation or race. They shared distaste both for top-down government censorship (which Lin partly credited for spurring the humor trend) and for social respectability, which, Lin wrote, "always wears a dog-collar." One should speak always for oneself, ideally in "un-buttoned moods."[44]

Lin's fame has overshadowed the contributions to Chinese humor writing of other Anglophones, such as Wen Yüan-ning (also known as Oon Guan Neng), an ethnic Hakka Chinese who was born in Indonesia and studied in Singapore and London before taking a degree in law at Cambridge. Arriving in China in the 1920s, Wen moved in high academic and government circles, first in Beijing and then in Shanghai and Nanjing. He wrote for the *China Critic* between 1933 and 1935, when he became editor in chief of *T'ien Hsia Monthly*, a new English-language journal focused on Chinese humanities and sponsored by the Nationalist government. Soon thereafter, he was appointed to the legislature.[45]

In early 1934, in the *Critic*, Wen inaugurated a series of "Unedited Biographies" of contemporary Chinese celebrities. The column, later retitled "Intimate Portraits," included Wen's own essays as well as contributions by other writers, fifty-one in total. In 1935, seventeen of Wen's were republished in the book *Imperfect Understanding*. Its title was likely inspired by two sources: Charles Lamb's essay "Imperfect Sympathies," and *Perfect Understanding*, a 1933 British film comedy starring Gloria Swanson and Laurence Olivier.[46] The contents of the *Critic* column live up to the *Pride and Prejudice* epigraph Wen chose for the book: "For what do we live but to make sport for our neighbours and laugh at them in our turn?"

The first "Intimate Portrait" to appear in the *Critic* featured Lim Boon Keng, one of the most prominent figures in colonial Singapore. The essay begins:

> By profession, Dr. Lim Boon Keng is a doctor; by inclination, a scholar; by reputation, a business man; and by accident, an educationalist. In reality, he is neither a doctor, a scholar, a business man, nor an educationalist: his real profession is to be a celebrity. He would like—just to be well known. If he can be well known as a theologian, well and good; if as a doctor, well and good also: but the great thing with him is to be well known: everything else is ancillary to that. Nothing he does, but is a peg for him to hang up his name upon. Nothing he writes, but is a sort of advertisement for himself. "And when he open his mouth, let no dogs bark!"[47]

The author (possibly Wen himself) credits Lim with "an *hors d'oeuvres* sort of mind—a smattering of everything: a hotch, composed of a bewildering variety of things. Ask Dr. Lim about Confucius, and he could hold forth for the length of an hour-glass, trotting out all the choice commonplaces he has culled from [translator of the Chinese classics James] Legge; but after he has done so, we may be comfortably sure, he has said all—and perhaps, more than he knows upon the subject."

He also finds Lim wanting when measured against Lord Brougham's maxim that a man ought to know everything of something and something of everything. He finishes by alluding to the career move that had brought Lim to the attention of mainland Chinese in the first place. In 1921, while still in his prime, Lim gave up lucrative business interests and moved to China to take up the presidency of the new Amoy (now Xiamen) University, a position he held until the outbreak of war in 1937. In the 1920s, Lim succeeded in recruiting several star professors, including Lin Yutang, Lu Xun, and Gu Jiegang, but his pomposity, insistence on speaking English, and avowed Confucianism at a time when many Chinese intellectuals were rebelling against the Sage soon led to equally high-profile departures.[48] If Lim had sought a bigger stage than Singapore, the writer puts him on a different one entirely:

> It is a misfortune for which Dr. Lim is not responsible that he should have been made President of Amoy University. I hear he is not appreciated there. I know there are places in Shanghai which would suit him perfectly: I refer to the cabarets. With his dapper little figure, his restless eyes, and his fine beard which hides a multitude of

sins, Dr. Lim's thin voice, discoursing on philosophy and God and Mammon, would not be unwelcome, coming in between the rattle of the wine-glasses, the inane talk of the dancing-girls, and the syncopation of the orchestra.

In the following issue Wen printed a long rejoinder from an incensed reader;[49] such writing was bound to touch a nerve. But the sketches were popular for capturing with flair the literary and political personalities of the day. Hu Shi, a standard-bearer of modern China's cultural Renaissance, was "not one of those who keep and hide their talents underground.... There is no mystery in him; all is sunshine, and no shadow." The Harvard-educated philosophy professor and romantic poet Wu Mi, while "one of nature's great gentlemen," had "a head shaped like a bomb, and [was] just as suggestively explosive." Zhou Zuoren possessed "the rare knack of transmuting the precious nothings of a man's life into golden chitchat," his essays "resembl[ing] nothing so much as gossiping carried to a fine art." Wu Zhihui was, like Dr. Johnson, remarkable "in the sense of being uncouth and yet that very uncouthness has become an attraction in itself." The deposed Qing emperor Puyi, on the eve of his installation as sovereign of the Japanese puppet state of Manchukuo, had the rare distinction of having been "made emperor three times without knowing why and apparently without relishing it." Hopefully Puyi would "outlive his usefulness."[50]

Wen's column also included unsparing yet sometimes touching obituaries, including one of the modernist poet Xu Zhimo ("a child"), and one of Wen's former students, the essayist Liang Yuchun, who died of illness at age twenty-six. Wen remembered Liang's unobtrusive modesty, his endearing stammer, the "odd fancies and humors" in his writings, and his puzzled look, which flattered a speaker's sense of superiority when in reality "Yu'chun takes in everything at once."[51] Wen's profiles, though popular at the time, were forgotten when he turned from writing to politics.[52] But *Imperfect Understanding* reflects core characteristics of the humor movement, not least its keen interest in personalities, its erudition, and its irreverence.

THE SEARCH FOR "CLASSICAL BEAUTIES"

Writers of old liked to quote the Classics ("Confucius says..."), Chen Zizhan observed in 1933; now it was all "Sun Yat-sen says...," "Marx says...," "Plekhanov [the Marxist author of *Art and Social Life*] says."[53] But since *youmo* was a foreign loan word, he added, Chinese humor theorists invariably felt compelled to root the concept in a domestic antecedent like Confucius or Zhuangzi.

Youmo became part of a broader fundamental reappraisal of Chinese culture that intellectuals had been engaged in since the late nineteenth century.[54] Lin Yutang believed that Neo-Confucianists of the Song dynasty had mislead generations of Chinese by distorting Confucius into a solemn patriarch when his teachings were essentially about how people, rulers included, ought to live their lives. In 1928 Lin wrote *Zijian nanzi*, a "tragicomedy" based on an episode in the Confucian *Analects* in which the Master has an audience with a queen of questionable morals, upsetting one of his disciples, Zilu. In the play, which Lin later translated as *Confucius Saw Nancy*, Confucius and Zilu misspeak, curry favor, embarrass themselves in public, are ignored by others, and otherwise behave like normal human beings. When the play was produced in Confucius's hometown in Shandong Province, his descendants filed a lawsuit objecting to this lighthearted and naturalistic presentation of their revered ancestor. Lin was briefly threatened with imprisonment, and the notoriety helped to propel him into the national limelight. Lin later often insisted that the "true" Confucius was a flawed human being, but one who always retained "personal charm and a good sense of humor" and was able to "laugh at a joke at his own expense."[55]

Lin was also enamored of the poets Tao Qian and Su Dongpo and the Daoist philosopher Zhuangzi, whose works he translated. Lin considered Zhuangzi, who routinely made fun of Confucius, to be a paragon of the unrestrained, absurdist strand in Chinese humor. The title of Lin Yutang's *This Human World* (*Renjian shi*), an encore to the *Analects Fortnightly*, came from one of the *Zhuangzi*'s chapters. Tao Qian, who turned his back on court life to tend his farm, was, to Lin, one of several classical exemplars of a humorous lifestyle and worldview. Su Dongpo was a "gay genius" of marvelous wit and human insight.[56] All offered wisdom on how to live life.

The *Analects Fortnightly* itself took its name from the Confucian *Analects*, a fragmentary assortment of "ordered sayings" and anecdotes about the Sage and his associates, and perhaps the single most influential text in the Chinese tradition. "Humor Selections" a regular section of the magazine, carried an eclectic mix; classical Chinese materials included jokes from Ming dynasty collections, essays by Qing scholar-official Gong Zizhen, and anecdotes about Confucius and his disciples. Another section, "What Confucius Didn't Talk About," took its name from an eighteenth-century collection of humorous ghost stories. In February 1935, following on its issue on Western humor, the *Analects* released a "Special Issue on Chinese Humor," which included selections from *Zhuangzi* (whose namesake Lin now dubbed "the father of Chinese humor") and other sources from antiquity to the Qing dynasty, and an installment of Lao She's new novel *Heavensent*.[57]

This collective archival work on Chinese humor complemented efforts to promote what Lin, who crafted a public image as a modern inheritor of China's humorous traditions, called a humorous way of life. Chinese scholars have traditionally named their studies: Lin called his the Some Things Left Undone Studio. This, he said, was only being realistic. A Shanghai publishing house calling itself The Mountain Lodge of Swept Leaves (the employer of Lei Jin, the Mr. Tottering in the Clouds of chapter 3), in contrast, was like a brothel calling itself Chastity and Virtue.[58]

Scholars also dug up those who laughed in other keys. In 1937, Zhou Zuoren held up a different ancient sage, Mencius, as "China's #1 celebrity reviler" for his habit of using derision to shame others into moral behavior. But Mencius's favorite curses, like "calamitous creatures" and "birds and beasts," Zhou said, had little effect on those content with an animal existence, including former sailors like himself.[59] Chen Zizhan wrote that contemporary writers' habit of insulting each other revived a late Ming practice, the spike in mockery being an unintended effect of humorists promoting self-expression.[60] At least humor offered a new antidote. Young men were fond of reviling cultural celebrities as being "running dogs," but those same celebrities could now channel Confucius, who once likened his never-ending search for patronage to the wanderings of "a homeless dog."[61] On the other hand, cartoonists readily used lines from the Confucian *Analects* to castigate what they saw as despicable social behaviors (see figure 6.3).

The *Analects* proved that there was a market for humor, and this inspired scholars and editors to compile and annotate collections of humorous folk songs, jokes, poems, and stories for a variety of market segments. The year 1933, for example, saw the appearance of Zhou Zuoren's *Selected Jokes from the Bitter Tea Studio*, whose jokes derived from Ming and Qing sources; a book of translated jokes and humor shorts from the language-learning magazine *Chung Hwa English Weekly* entitled *Smiles*; Beiping's *Laughs for the Masses*; and a collection of comic genre stories published in Tianjin. The publication of humor collections appears to have peaked in 1935, which saw the appearance of over a dozen (see appendix 1).

Even editors hostile to what they saw as a fad rebranded a wide variety of literary comedy as *youmo*. *Humorous Jottings* (1935), compiled by Hu Shanyuan, an editor at the major publishing house World Books, reprinted short pieces from the Tang, Song, and Yuan dynasties. Hu claims in his preface to be a curmudgeon who never reads popular humor magazines for fear of getting a headache. When a friend chided him for preferring old thread-bound books, he says he replied, "Don't panic. Just because it's not a 'modern girl' with a perm doesn't necessarily mean that it's a bound-foot crone in wedding finery." Upon reading a few selections from Hu's manuscript, his friend (he writes) declared it to be a "classical beauty," flung his humor magazines to the floor, stomped on them, and derided "foreign-spittle-slurping, gold-ring wearers who pretend to be so refined and fashionable." In the tradition of the serious scholar, Hu characterizes his work on humor as a pastime. But *youmo* has put him on the defensive: he wasn't trying to steal the livelihood of those who "eat out of the humor bowl" or to "raise a revolution in the kingdom of humor."[62]

In 1932, Lu Xun's friend Masuda Wataru invited him to nominate specimens of Chinese humor for an *Anthology of Humor Literature from around the World*. He responded that "China has no humor writers; at best, it has writers of satire."[63]

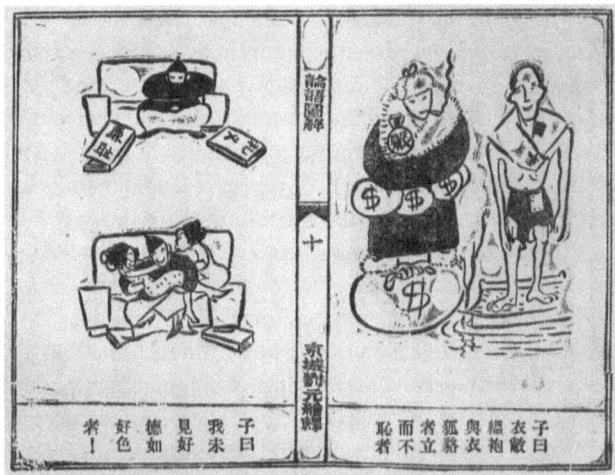

FIGURE 6.3. Part ten of Beijing cartoonist Liu Yuan's (1914–99) *Confucian Analects Illustrated*, which appeared in the *Analects Fortnightly*. Right caption: "The Master said: A man dressed in tattered clothes stands next to a man in furs and yet is not ashamed." Left caption: "The Master said: I have yet to meet a man who loves virtue as much as he loves sex (*se*)!" In the original *Analects*, *se* refers to female beauty more generally. *Lunyu* 81 (1 February 1936), 434. Image courtesy of the Library of the Institute of Chinese Literature and Philosophy, Academia Sinica.

He nevertheless selected eight specimens of Chinese humor writing dating back to the Han dynasty, including excerpts from the classic novels *The Water Margin*, *Flowers in the Mirror*, and *The Scholars*; as well as the complete novels *Which Classic?* and *The Travels of Lao Can*, and two contemporary short stories: Yu Dafu's "Two Poets" and Zhang Tianyi's "Little Peter."[64]

In his private letters from that period, Lu Xun opines that "humor is not a Chinese thing to begin with," that "Shanghai's 'humor' magazine, actually isn't humorous," and that his own fiction, which had been solicited for the *Anthology*, has nothing to do with humor.[65] He even nitpicks his own selections, nominating the late Ming collection *Remarkable Sights New and Old* (*Jingu qiguan*) with the qualification: "I can't remember if I saw any 'humor' in here." "Currently," he concludes, "laughter has been lost in China."[66] In March 1933, Lu Xun wrote to another Japanese friend that the translation of Chinese humor into Japanese "seems to have failed" because the *Anthology* sold only two thousand copies. Still, despite Lu Xun's characteristic pessimism, a year later found him signing off letters to Lin Yutang by wishing him "happy humoring."[67]

T. K. Chuan wrote in the *Critic* in January 1933 that "Whoever says that the Chinese have no sense of humor is either ignorant or lacks a sense of humor himself."[68] But naysayers abounded. Han Shiheng, a translator and member of the League of Left-Wing Writers, called the Chinese "a barbaric people completely unable to understand humor." They lacked a compatible philosophy, going through life with long faces, capable only of selfish, arrogant laughter and joking or cursing about sex. Despite occasional works of humor since the May Fourth Movement, China still had no great humorists to rival Lamb, Chesterton, Twain, or Chekov. Only Lao She, Han claimed, avoided the "silly guffaw" of *huaji* and the stinging chill of mockery to evoke a sweet, understanding smile.[69]

The tendency of writers like Han to measure Chinese humorists against those of the West was in part defensiveness against ongoing foreign prejudice against and contempt for China and its people. In 1930, Chinese audiences felt betrayed by the beloved comedian Harold Lloyd when they found *Welcome Danger*, Lloyd's first talkie, to be filled with offensive Chinatown stereotypes. (Lloyd's character at one point beats down a wave of attacking Chinamen with a truncheon before disrupting a human sacrifice.) Topping the list of curious factoids about "the heathen Chinee" in an advertisement for the 1932 edition of *Believe It or Not!* was that he "laughs when he is sad and cries when he is glad."[70] However tongue in cheek, Robert Ripley's cultural trivia played on stereotypes that the Chinese were perverse and backward, even inhuman. As for China's government, in 1934 Maurice Dekobra cited one American consul's opinion that the young republic was "a huge, obstreperous and tiresome baby [that is] suffering from measles and teething and is peevish and keeps crying in its cradle at Kuomintang."[71]

Lin Yutang and his fellow travelers thus spoke to two audiences. They wanted to convince self-flagellating writers like Han Shiheng to relax, stop bickering, and enjoy the pleasures of life, as a first step to changing the general cultural climate. At the same time they countered Western condescension with a humorous demeanor that was relaxed, confident, and cosmopolitan. They would turn hierarchies on their heads. In March 1936, shortly before the Shanghai release of *Modern Times*, its creator paid a short visit to Shanghai, prompting one contributor to the *China Critic* to claim the most famous entertainer in the world as China's own. As a master stylist who had perfected the archetype of a "wretched, poor soul with an eternal will to live and make good," and as an eternal vagabond who comes and goes of his own accord and who "does nothing, yet everything," Chaplin was Chinese.[72]

UNDERSTANDING SMILES AND LEADEN LAUGHTER

In introducing the word *youmo*, Lin Yutang begged the questions of why a new term was necessary, and just what was so new about it. Now it was the West's turn to be inscrutable: the one thing theorists seemed to agree on was that humor was impossible to define. Sinmay Zau, who edited the *Analects* in the late 1930s and 1940s, noted that readers often mistook *youmo* for its twin sisters, *fengci* (satire) and *huixie* (jocularity).[73] Its advocates took pains to distinguish it from *huaji*, which they considered irrelevant or injurious to contemporary life. Lao She put *huaji* at the bottom of the humor hierarchy, along with joking, claiming that both were lively but meaningless, even harmful.[74] Lin Yutang suggested in 1932 that *huaji* be translated as "trying to be funny," implying that its humor was forced and inauthentic.[75] But in his later essay "On Humor" he wrote approvingly of writings he described as "*huaji youmo.*" In 1933, Lu Xun defended *huaji*, saying that its low status was due to the public's conflating it with the "flippancy" (*youhua*) of China's many superficial comedians. The popularization of the term *youmo*, he added, had further muddied the waters. In fact, Lu Xun said, even the *Analects* included plenty of indigenous *huaji*-style humor, especially in his favorite section, "The Studio of Ancient Fragrance," which T. K. Chuan had translated as "Ye Antique Shoppe."[76] Zhou Zuoren, too, was skeptical about how broadly *youmo* could be applied. China had plenty of jokes, he wrote in 1933, but curiously little humorous narrative.[77] Though *youmo* seemed to have won the day, market demand for works advertised as *huaji* continued unabated, and for much of the 1930s many writers still preferred to translate "humor" as *huaji* or *huixie*.[78]

On 9 December 1932, Han Shiheng provided Lin with a formulation for explaining humor that remains influential even now: the "understanding smile" (*huixin de weixiao*).[79] Just five years earlier, in 1927, Sigmund Freud had opined that the pleasures of humor were less intense than those of jokes or the comic, and thus "never find vent in hearty laughter."[80] Lin was attracted by the proposition that humor involved intuitive perception, and he affirmed that its ultimate expression was the understanding smile. But, in 1932 at least, Lin's conception of humor was broader than either Han's or Freud's. The "silly laughter" (*shaxiao*) of *huaji*, he wrote, was also desirable. Humor had room too for the acidity of sarcasm.[81]

The leftist critic Xu Maoyong considered the humorous smile and the hearty laugh alike to be optimistic expressions of resistance to oppression, and thus preferable to the traditional literati tendency to greet periods of turmoil with laments.[82] For a few months in 1934, the popular pictorial monthly the *Young Companion* rebranded its regular two-page cartoon feature "The Understanding Smile."[83] The term *youmo* itself remained somewhat alien; as late as 1936, ads for Sinmay Zau's *Humor Explained*, an anthology of essays on the subject, admitted that humor was "not an authentic National Product."[84] Still, after four years of explaining, the word had caught on.

In 1934, a little over a year into the *Analects*'s life, Lin Yutang brought together some of his ideas in a three-part essay, "On Humor."[85] Invoking George Meredith's

1877 claim that laughter is an "excellent test of the civilization of a country," Lin surveys instances of humor in the philosophical, literary, and historiographical canons of Chinese civilization, drawing contrasts between major personalities in Confucian, Daoist, and Buddhist strains of thought. The essay's recurring theme is that "humor is a part of life." In its second and third parts, Lin identifies orthodox moralists as the prime foes of humor; distinguishes it from other forms of comic writing; endorses Meredith's notion that to have humor is to possess a sympathetic, cosmic view of the world and mankind; and exalts the virtues of the humorous essay. He concludes with an appeal to humor's utility: "If *The Analects Fortnightly* is able to persuade the warring politicians to cut down on their fighting, swindling and deceitful propaganda, then our accomplishments will not be insignificant."[86]

In *The Importance of Living* (1937), Lin reiterated that laughter was linked to the reality principle, its primary function being to reign in dreams. To be humorous is to catch one's own fancies in flight and ground them—a capacity lacked by all dictators. The "chemical function of humor . . . change[s] the character of our thought."[87] Its worldview, like a Midas's touch, could turn anything humorous. That's why, Xu Xu, the editor of *This Human World*, wrote, a humorist would savor a loved one's offer of a drink of dew from a leaf, whereas a scientist would see only contaminated H_2O. As a practical matter, editors like Xu Xu were compelled to quality-grade humor submissions. At the top Xu put natural products of emotional and intellectual insight; next were humorous expressions of reason; at the bottom were mere cut-and-paste jobs.[88] Even more critics were captivated by humor's moral dimensions. In a 1953 essay largely critical of Lin's views, the critic C. T. Hsia agreed with him that "humor is the most civilized form of laughter because it treats its object of ridicule with affection."[89]

Literary scholar Diran John Sohigian has argued that Lin's take on humor was about more than just the tone of debate. More fundamentally, it marked a radical departure from a cherished assumption of writers who embraced a conception of realism popularized during the May Fourth era. To those writers, truth was knowable and could be definitively represented if one only tried hard enough. Their preferred mode of laughter was satire, which "exaggerates in the service of truth," thereby revealing the gap between hypocrisy and reality.[90] Humor, in contrast, constituted an "unending discourse," an "infinite conversation" of "half-knowing" that rejected determinism and dogmatism by keeping "truth" up in the air.[91]

Many critics tried to pull humor and its promoters back down to earth. Not long after the *Analects* appeared on the scene, a backlash began. Ma Guoliang, editor of the *Young Companion*, accused Lin Yutang and Lao She of forcing people to laugh, and of offering them cigarettes when what they needed was rice. As for professional writers, it was now "an iron-clad fact that everyone should laugh," but editors' demands for humorous writings were becoming oppressive. One of

Ma's colleagues reminded advocates of "the so-called humor" that "laughter is like tobacco and alcohol: a little is a stimulant, but too much is narcotic." Sinmay Zau complained in the *Analects* that people were speaking of humor and opium in the same breath.[92]

Two years into the *youmo* craze, Lin admitted to his American readers that "one of the most difficult things for me to put over to my Chinese-reading public is to convince them that humour is a part of life and therefore should not be shut out even from serious literature." If its youths couldn't even enjoy a comic strip then "China is doomed."[93]

Humor was swept into strident rhetorical battles between the League of Left-Wing Writers, established in 1930, and the Creation Society, which promoted "art for art's sake." In 1933, the leftist playwright Yuan Muzhi dubbed Ding Xilin's plays elitist amusements that toyed with aesthetic form but failed to address social problems in a direct and meaningful way. He demanded that Ding "move from aestheticism to materialism, from the small circle of the *salon* to the large circle of society." Summing up Ding's oeuvre, Yuan declared, "We'll leave [his] six *salon* plays in the *salon*. Only when the author writes a seventh work that departs from the *salon* will we stage it for people outside the *salon* to see."[94] In July of 1932, Du Heng, a regular contributor to *Les Contemporains*, tried to avoid the crossfire by claiming to be a "third type of person" detached from partisan politics, the better to produce quality art and conscientious criticism. Lu Xun, while sympathetic to Du's predicament, judged that in China's current circumstances posing as a writer who transcends class or politics was a self-indulgent fantasy.[95]

Some of these ethical concerns echoed views voiced during the controversy over "the New Humor" in late nineteenth-century America. Scholar Henry Jenkins notes that American "proponents of 'thoughtful laughter' frequently expressed disdain for public amusements," influenced (like Lin Yutang) by the ideas of George Meredith. Their opponents tarred them all with the same brush: "the fetish of humor . . . dulls pity and stunts justice" and the public "clamor[ing] for its daily ration" would see any situation "thrown into the cauldron and cooked into some fashion of mirth."[96] But China was truly in crisis. Japan's annexation of northeast China in 1931 had put China in a state of undeclared war. The Japanese bombing of northern Shanghai in January of 1932 crippled several major publishers based in the Zhabei district. It also destroyed one of China's largest libraries, home to half a million volumes, which burned for three days and three nights.[97] The Nationalist government under Chiang Kai-shek, meanwhile, had turned with viciousness against its erstwhile allies in the Communist Party, and the 1930s saw massacres, arrests, and torture of students, unionists, and others. Chinese writers sympathetic to the left-wing cause were being assassinated with frightening regularity. There was no place for jollity either, Lu Xun wrote, among victims of bombings or floods.[98]

What's more, humor, in the eyes of another left-wing critic, was tainted by class: what would be condemned as duplicity among the common people, men of refinement passed off as "humor."⁹⁹ To be humorous was to be smug. In 1935, one critic in "Free Talk" assessed the Humor Movement as having produced only self-aggrandizing fake humorists, ineffectual petty satirists, and men of leisure who sit on their couches striking virtuous poses, slurping tea, breathing sighs of contentment, and cracking a few "light" jokes to elicit "understanding smiles." Humor would reach its potential only when it became a tool to expose the dark side of society and promote reform.¹⁰⁰

Others attacked humor on grounds of style. In a 1934 piece in Lin's "Little Critic" column, a twenty-four-year-old Qian Zhongshu deplored "this New Humor (of which Dr. Lin is himself the sponsor) as the Old Humor writ small; there is no Rabelaisian heartiness or Shakespearean broadness in it. It is full of subtle *arrièrepensées*, refined petulance, and above all . . . nostalgia" for the literary glory days of the late Ming dynasty.¹⁰¹ Xu Xu, the editor of *This Human World*, wrote after Lin's death that Lin's enthusiasm for the Ming expressivist writers had been like that of "a westerner encountering Chinese culture for the first time." To those brought up in a completely Chinese cultural environment (Lin had attended a missionary school), what Lin called humor was nothing new—it was just low-grade humor.¹⁰²

Qian Zhongshu, who would become one of modern China's literary giants, added that, "It is no sheer accident that the campaign for Humor inaugurated by the *Analects Semi-monthly* should have started among the Shanghai intellectuals." Other critics also viewed humor as a product of a "Shanghai school," though many *Analects* contributors, Lin Yutang included, were recent migrants to the city.¹⁰³ Zhou Zuoren, who lived in Beiping, rejected the association entirely: Shanghainese culture was one of vulgar extremes, while humor expressed the Doctrine of the Mean.¹⁰⁴

In Lao She's view, such attacks were a by-product of modernization. Since its transition from empire to republic, China's achievements and shortcomings alike were now invariably shoehorned into the new rubric of the nation-state. The 1911 revolution had led to the invention of concepts such as National Spoken Language, National Learning, National Writing, National Martial Arts, and National Shame. Triviality, by extension, was no longer merely a moral offence but a state offence. Lao She facetiously suggested that if little-taste essays or "middling-taste" essays (a non-existent genre) were not fulfilling the mandate for grandiosity, maybe everyone should start writing "major-taste" essays.¹⁰⁵

Criticisms of the humor movement continued long after its principals disbanded during the war. Writing in America in 1953—four years after the Communists took control of the country and the government—C. T. Hsia described the "Chinese scholar-humorist" as "invariably a Taoist hedonist": "He has none of Dickens's extroverted interest in other people, but takes pains to describe the minor pleasures and disappointments in his own life. He is often a humorist merely in the sense that he takes a philosophical, tolerant attitude toward the world's follies, superstitions, and ambitions." He is, with few exceptions, "always a minor writer. He proceeds on the assumption that man is a lovable creature and concocts a literary formula which flatters the reader's sense of superiority. His world is as mentally snug as the world of women's magazines with its cute babies, cozy living rooms, and gleaming refrigerators." The "cult of humor" was but a symptom of the banal optimism and complacency of the modern age.[106]

In 1939, Qian Zhongshu, recently returned from study overseas to teach at Southwestern United University in Kunming, wrote a brief essay entitled "On Laughter," which confirms literary scholar Richard Keller Simon's observation that the best writings on the comic "have masked their analyses in mockery, sometimes so thoroughly that there can be no simple reading of their intentions."[107] It was now the third year of the Sino-Japanese War (China having officially declared war in 1937), seven years after the *Analects* took China by storm, and the heyday of humor seemed to have already passed. "Since humor literature was first promoted, 'selling laughter' has become a profession for men of letters. Humor is, of course, vented by means of laughter, but laughter is not necessarily an indication of humor. Liu Jizhuang's *Guangyang Notes* states, 'The donkey's bray sounds like crying; the horse's whinny sounds like laughter.' Yet the horse is not celebrated as a great humorist—likely because he has a long face. In truth, most people's laughter is akin to the horse's whinny and cannot be considered humorous."[108]

Selling laughter (or smiles), as noted in chapter 1, is an activity associated with courtesans, prostitutes, and singsong girls.[109] While not naming names, Qian says that the humor movement has produced only innumerable "clowns playing with brush and ink. The clown's social status, of course, rises dramatically as he muddles his way from the theatrical stage to the literary stage under the banner of humor. Nevertheless, humor's quality deteriorates when the clown turns it into a bogus brand." Humor resides not with the clown but with his audience. Drawing on Bergson's *Le Rire*, Qian argues that promoting humor cannot help but transform the fluid into the mechanical, thereby destroying its essence. "To turn humor into a doctrine or a means of livelihood is to congeal a liquid into a solid, to transform a living thing into an artifact." German humor scholars exemplified this wrongheadedness, being "a sausage-making people who mistakenly believe that humor is like ground meat that can be wrapped up into tidy parcels of ready-made spiritual nourishment." Lin and his colleagues might seek to profit from the pleasant ring of "silvery laughter" (George Meredith's phrase), but their counterfeit humor gave forth only the dull clunk of a leaden slug.

THE PEOPLE'S HUMOR

Friends of the *Analects* anticipated criticisms like Qian's. Sinmay Zau, writing as editor in 1935, quipped that "to promote humor is supremely un-humorous, but to oppose humor is approaching humorousness."[110] Lin Yutang, too, was aware that "according to the old tradition, no one except a clown would condescend to crack a joke in public."[111] They would have been familiar with the English newspaperman W. T. Stead's famous comparison of Mark Twain to a jester, always "one of the most popular members of the community, and yet one whose popularity, strange enough, perishes with the using."[112] But by 1936 Lin had moved to America indefinitely and the *Analects* carried on without his regular contributions until war forced its closure in 1937.[113] T. K. Chuan (who had filled in for Lin before) and more than half a dozen others, including the American journalist Emily Hahn, took turns trying to keep the spirit of "The Little Critic" alive in the *China Critic*. Both journals had plenty of institutional momentum, but they missed the spark of Lin's personality. One *Critic* editorial about *The Importance of Living* observed in 1938 that the past two years "have seen more books on the enjoyment of life than any period since the Great War."[114] But by then "The Little Critic" was a thing of the past, and war news dominated the *Critic* until it too closed in 1940.

During the war, Chinese writers and artists poured scorn on phony patriots, carpetbaggers, and other opportunists. Picaresque comedy reigned in the interior, comedies of manners and *huaji* fiction in occupied Shanghai. Cartoons blanketed the land, while humor scholarship continued in reduced circumstances.[115] Qian Zhongshu, his wife, the playwright Yang Jiang (later a noted novelist, translator, and essayist), and Eileen Chang, meanwhile, hit their stride as writers of wit, humor, and pathos. In 1941, a Shanghai publisher, taking advantage of the general exodus of writers, repackaged essays from the *Analects*, along with others by Lu Xun, Liang Shiqiu, and Xuan Yongguang (author of the best-selling essay collection *Reckless Words and Crazy Talk*) under the title *How to Curse Artistically*. The *Analects* now sold not as cozy bourgeois humanism, but as guidance on how to curse like a gentleman.[116] In 1942, an unauthorized *Lao She Humor Collection* appeared in Hsinking (Changchun), the capital of the puppet-state of Manchukuo, conscripting the Manchu writer's lighter works into the Japanese imperial cause even as he was writing for the resistance down south.[117]

On 20 October 1946, one year after Japan's surrender, the *People's Daily*, the mouthpiece of the Chinese Communist Party, then published in the Communists' temporary base in Hebei province, carried a sample of what it called "The People's Humor":

> During a discussion of current events, a worker stood up and said: "Chiang Kai-shek is fighting a civil war against his daddy!" What did he mean?, the crowd asked.

He continued: "When Mr. Sun Yat-sen was alive he came up with the Three Principles of the People, implemented three great policies, and advocated the establishment of an independent, democratic, peaceful new China. After he died and came to be called Father of the Nation, his unfilial descendent Chiang Kai-shek ignored the Father of the Nation's platform and implemented a policy of selling out the nation, dictatorship, and civil war. Isn't that attacking his daddy? What's more, your parents are those who clothe and feed you. Everything Chiang Kai-shek eats and wears comes from the people, and now he's treating them as his enemy. Isn't that attacking his daddy?" Hearing this, the crowd burst into uproarious laughter.[118]

So it was that after eight years of resistance against the Japanese, in the midst of a resumed civil war, and three years before the triumph of their Revolution, the Communist Party began transforming humor from the prerogative of the urban elite to the collective property of the people.

A little over a month after that joke appeared, the *Analects* resumed publication in Shanghai. Li Qingya, a longtime contributor, became editor and began to solicit new work. Many regular contributors returned, but Lao She and Lin Yutang, both then in the United States, did not.[119] In February 1947 the *Analects* noted an overseas echo of the humor movement: the New York publication of George Kao's anthology *Chinese Wit & Humor*, which carried excerpts from the *Analects* and an introduction by Lin. The revived *Analects* flourished through civil war and hyperinflation but eventually closed with the Communist takeover in 1949.

The humor phenomenon of the 1930s was a defining moment in the modern Chinese intellectual history of the comic. It was also popular: Lin Yutang, more than any of his predecessors, made laughter a cultural issue for the general public, even if his notions about humor were not themselves particularly original.[120] Its polemics, which historians have often cast in heroic terms as a two-man battle between Lin Yutang and Lu Xun (sometimes with Lao She in a supporting role), were wide-ranging and complex—even messy—as few, if any, participants practiced as writers exactly what they preached as pundits. In the moment, humor became a proxy for other issues, such as freedom of speech. But, unlike many evanescent Shanghai cultural trends, *youmo* endured, and it changed the way Chinese people talked about humor itself.

The Year of Humor consecrated *youmo* as the new blanket term for humorous sensibilities that had been known by other names. It became a cultural standard by which China reassessed its literary traditions and its place in the world. One could dislike a particular type of *youmo*, but that was a disagreement between individuals or groups. Humor itself was inherently virtuous, an expression of broadmindedness, understanding, wisdom, reason. To possess humor was to have cosmopolitan empathy, an antidote to common contempt sprung of social divisions. Now the debate was over true humor and false, traditional and modern. *Huaji* and other indigenous terms for humor suddenly became archaic.[121]

The success of an idealized conception of humor made the promotion of humor redundant. Humor was no more in need of promotion than was kindness. Even as war and revolution relegated the 1930s humor era to a historical footnote and most of its polemics faded into obscurity, the term *youmo* became a naturalized part of the Chinese language. Yet, even though some Chinese people today are unaware of its origins, *youmo* preserves a reminder of its foreign provenance in its very sound. The proposition that Chinese culture lacked a moral outlook and sensibility to match the reasonable tolerance of humor, which proved so offensive to critics and theorists in the 1930s, is one reason why the term can inspire a sense of unease even today. *Kafei* (coffee) is a thing, but *youmo*, as a moral quality, remains in its linguistic essence one that came from without.

Epilogue
笑死

It is the hollow, reverberant laugh of old China, at the touch of whose breath, every flower of enthusiasm and hope must wither and die.
—LIN YUTANG, 1930[1]

Should we get rid of satire? [. . . No, satire is always needed.]
—MAO ZEDONG, 1943 [1953 REVISION][2]

This was modern China's first, but not last, age of irreverence. Every type of laughter surveyed in this book survived, in some form, the succession of events that ended the 1930s heyday of *youmo*. The declared war with Japan that began in 1937, the civil war that resumed in 1945, and the establishment of the Communist Party state in 1949 eclipsed some comic cultures and nurtured new ones. Just as *xin xiaoshi*, or histories of laughter, appeared again and again in the publishing market of the early twentieth century, histories of "wait till you hear this one" and "tell me another one" always look forward to the next hilarity.

Women, for example, featured frequently in the early twentieth century as the butts of misogynistic jokes. While easily explained away as mere remnants of a traditionally patriarchal mindset, they also reflect, in a backhanded way, women's growing visibility in Chinese society. The Anti-Japanese War, historian Diana Lary has shown, created opportunities for Chinese women by dispersing men and sundering the family unit.[3] It also influenced the history of modern Chinese comic writing. Xiao Hong, Yang Jiang, Su Qing, and Eileen Chang (of *Lust, Caution* fame) began producing works that were popular, funny, and "alert to the plight of Chinese women in a sexist culture" without casting women as victims.[4]

Yang Jiang wrote three comedies of manners about the urban bourgeoisie, one of which, *Sport with the World* (*Youxi renjian*), picked up a motif of frivolous play from the 1890s.[5] Su Qing's 1944 novel *Ten Years of Marriage*, a semiautobiographical satire of matrimony, was so popular that it inspired a short work called "Ten Years of Marriage Proposals," written by none other than Xu Zhuodai. Xu's parody wrote Su into a new version of his 1928 story "Women's Playthings," in which a mysterious and wildly popular female author dupes male readers into making fools of themselves in public. In this new era of inflation, Miss Peng Fuqi has twenty-five hundred suitors (compared with Qiu Suwen's 1,234) who each pay two thousand dollars for a pair of tickets for their theater date. Instead of wearing a flower, he carries a copy of Miss Peng's book, *Ten Years of Marriage Proposals*, which he bought for a fool's price of $250—*two-fifty* being Shanghai slang for "numbskull."[6] Xu Zhuodai, then sixty-six, was up to his old tricks, but hoaxing now made his heroine a millionaire.

Women responded to famous male writers, too. In the first scene of the 1947 film *Long Live the Wives*, a comedy of manners for which Eileen Chang wrote the screenplay, a young lady offers to take her mother-in-law to see the Shaoxing-style play *Xianglin's Wife*, a stage adaptation of Lu Xun's 1924 story about the woman whose son has been eaten by a wolf. "*Xianglin's Wife*?" the old lady replies. "Never heard of it." "I've heard it's a new-style play," her daughter-in-law tells her, "a real tragedy." "Oh!" the old lady exclaims, "I simply *adore* tragedies—the sadder the better!"[7] Writing for and about a public desperate for amusement, Chang portrayed Lu Xun's moral parable as having become yet another entertainment product for bourgeois consumption.

Mao Zedong is said to have requested a copy of *Which Classic?* to be sent to his wartime base of Yan'an in 1939. Though that alleged shipment of twenty books supposedly did not arrive,[8] the Communist Party later made extensive use of ghosts to reject the past and shore up its legitimacy. The government-produced 1950 film *The White-Haired Girl*, adapted from a folktale, cast the story of the Revolution as one of humans versus ghosts, an allegory of national resurrection summed up by the slogan: "The old society forced humans to become ghosts, while the new society turns ghosts into humans." The epithet *gui*, which Chinese used to revile Japanese invaders during the war, reappeared in political campaigns, most notoriously in Cultural Revolution era persecutions of "ox demons and snake spirits" (*niugui sheshen*). Just as Liu Fu's coining "Mandarin Ducks and Butterflies" eventually lost its risible aspect and came to be regarded as a neutral label for an entire class of popular literature, so these later "devils" became normative descriptors stripped of irony and humor.

In theory, the Party embraced laughter. Mao Zedong's 1942 "Talks at the Yan'an Forum on Literature and the Arts," a set of wartime speeches that shaped post-1949 cultural policy, explicitly condoned two intonations of laughter: satire (*fengci*) and eulogy (*gesong*). In a revised edition of this talk published in 1953, Mao reaffirmed that "satire is always needed," citing Lu Xun as its exemplar. Mao claimed to object only to the "indiscriminate use" of satire that did not suit its targets, be they "the enemy, friends [1953 ed.: allies], or our own ranks."[9]

Mao, notably, did not endorse *youmo*, but the Party state did become a patron of humorists, particularly practitioners of the northern-style stand-up comedy known as *xiangsheng*, which could reach even illiterate audiences. Comedy, perhaps for the first time, had major state support, and comedic performing arts soon became important mechanisms of political indoctrination at the grassroots level. But this new campaign to promote a popular form of humor—and to adapt it to serve government policy—had mixed results at best. Linguist David Moser judges that the ideological strictures and censorship of the Mao era "killed" the laughter in a once edgy and incisive form.[10] According to folklorist Marja Kaikkonen, state-backed artists compelled to clean up their acts generated few genuinely popular routines.[11] Perry Link likens the precarious existence of the handful of comic performers who enjoyed state patronage to that of the crocodile bird, which cleans the teeth of its host with the ever-present risk that its jaws might snap shut.[12]

In 1951, the Chinese Communist Party dubbed Lao She, who had returned from the United States to China to "serve the Revolution," a People's Artist, and from this pedestal he was obliged repeatedly to define humor, comedy, and satire and to explain their place in the new artistic landscape.[13] Even in the 1930s, Lao She's reputation as a genial humorist had obscured undercurrents of farce, melodrama, and nihilism in his works. For all their tears, laughter, and strivings, his characters experience the futility of human endeavor. Lao She's theater of the absurd culminated in his 1957 three-act play *Teahouse*, whose proprietor's existence becomes ever more abject despite his attempts to adapt to life in Beijing during three successive eras: the late Qing, the warlord period, and the civil war. In the final act, Wang Lifa and two aged friends, having cried themselves dry, laugh in despair and throw themselves a mock funeral. Carpetbaggers arrive to confiscate his teahouse, and Wang hangs himself offstage.[14] Nine years after *Teahouse*, the jaws snapped shut on the ever-accommodating writer himself. In the early months of the Cultural Revolution, Red Guards submitted Lao She to sustained abuse and humiliation, and on 24 August 1966 his body was found in a lake.

Writers of urban entertainment fiction were generally marginalized by the new focus on proletarians and peasants. Xu Zhuodai wrote memoirs and essays about "old" Shanghai. Already suffering from illness, he passed away in 1958, soon after his son-in-law was persecuted to death during the Anti-Rightist Movement.[15] New China also had little room for bourgeois cosmopolitans like Lin Yutang, who was written out of literary history. While the Master of Humor remained invisible on the mainland for decades, Shanghai émigrés helped to make *youmo* a staple in the press of postwar Hong Kong, which developed what was then the most freewheeling cultural climate in the Chinese-speaking world.[16] On the mainland, bureaucrats promoted a new vision of culture that drew on the folk humor of an international proletariat stretching from Estonia to Ürümqi.[17] "Uncle" Afanti, a

Uyghur and ethnic trickster figure, had his stories translated into Chinese and became wildly popular. Jokes were rebranded as a type of folk art, a "literature of the people."[18] Satirists, despite Mao's endorsement, found themselves with few safe targets, while elegiac comedy, the other state-approved option, turned humor into a tool to express reverence for government policies. Such policies and control efforts notwithstanding, comic cultures of the early Mao era were more varied than might be assumed today. Attendance at Shanghai's Great World amusement hall actually increased into the 1950s, and the ha-ha mirrors stayed up until the beginning of the Cultural Revolution, when it was deemed that they would make the proletariat "forget their class consciousness."[19]

Across the Taiwan Strait in 1957, a new Taipei monthly tried to recapture the "humor, allure, satire, and lightheartedness" of Lin Yutang's 1930s publications. Taking its Chinese title and cover calligraphy from *Renjian shi*, the *Chinese Humanist Monthly* featured essays and poems on topics such as "On Judges Dropping Drawers" and "Smelly Farts and Blushing Faces." At least twice during its quarter-century run, during the midst of a period of political repression known as the White Terror, the Kuomintang suspended it for a year for political reasons.[20] Lin's works remained in continual reprint in Taiwan, where he moved in 1966. In 1970, the Thirty-Seventh International PEN Congress convened in Seoul to discuss "Humour in Literature East and West" and Lin gave a special address that mostly revisited remarks he had made in the 1930s.[21] In the 1980s, the writer Li Ao emerged from his second period of incarceration by the Kuomintang to build a reputation as a Wu Zhihui-style renowned reviler of the famous and the powerful, giving his essay collections titles such as *Bullshit! Bullshit! Utter Bullshit!* (1984), *Yours, Mine, His Mother's* (1984), *Dog Shit, Dog Farts, Poetry* (1984), and *There Goes Li Ao, Cursing People Again!* (1999).[22]

Irreverence reemerged in China with a vengeance in the late 1970s. Following Mao's death in 1976, the Gang of Four became an officially approved target for public derision. Since the beginning of the reform era in 1978, the Chinese public sphere has seen several waves of derisive, insouciant, and playful takes on authority and convention. In the 1980s and 1990s, for example, novelist Wang Shuo made "play" (*wan'r*) a new symbol of cool urban nonchalance. In this cultural echo of late Qing *youxi*, the players now were not disaffected Shanghai literati but Beijing dropouts, hooligans, and petty entrepreneurs. Filmmakers such as Feng Xiaogang, Jiang Wen, and Xu Zheng have turned comedy into box office gold, with Jiang, in films like *Devils on the Doorstep* (2000), occasionally venturing into subversive territory.

In the twenty-first century, digital image stitching and manipulation, going beyond the techniques that created split-self photographs, have enabled online video spoofs to take off and made *e'gao* a new word for parody and derision.[23] Every day, thousands of Chinese now share their personal frustrations online in a jocular fashion through "rage comics." Created by pasting together ready-made clip art into comic strips and adding dialogue, *baozou manhua* recall the variations-on-a-theme illustration games hosted by the newspaper *Civil Rights* in the 1910s.[24] Bilingual puns like "Ma-de in China" (媽的 = "Screwed in China") have become mainstream slang among PRC citizens expressing collective exasperation, derision, humor, and solidarity.[25] The creation of new Chinese characters—portmanteaus of existing ones—is yet another online game that harkens back to the "funny words" of the 1900s and 1910s. *Naocan* 脑残 (brain-damaged), which combines the simplified characters *nao* 脑 (brain) and *can* 残 (damaged), for example, encapsulates the shoot-me-now feeling of any mind-numbing encounter, be it with deadening cliché, shameless self-promotion, or government censorship. In 2011, one artist used this term in the title of his online gallery of censorship-themed *e'gao* artworks, simultaneously invoking the government watchdog spirit of *The Travels of Lao Can*. *Lao Can youji*, as Liu E's late Qing novel is called in Chinese, follows a lonely man of conscience adrift in a chaotic age. *Naocan youji*, or "The Travels of the Brain-Damaged,"[26] offers a wander through a collection of humorous web memes that the Chinese-speaking public now uses to express the feeling of being lobotomized.

Like early twentieth-century periodicals, blogs and other online sharing platforms have promoted humor inadvertently, as in 2012, when a leading Chinese television drama was found to have plagiarized jokes from a popular internet author and blogger. Or on several occasions when tone-deaf Chinese journalists have translated bogus news items from the American satirical weekly the *Onion* and passed them off in China as real stories.[27]

Echoes of the past also resound in contemporary cultural debates. In November 2012, the Swedish Academy awarded the Nobel Prize in Literature to Mo Yan, a writer known for darkly comic novels encompassing a broad sweep of modern Chinese history. The award prompted literary critics to reappraise distinctive elements of Mo Yan's literary style: his bold corporeal imagery, his pastiche of Maoist rhetoric and folk vernacular, and what the Academy called the "hallucinatory realism" of his violent plots. For Chinese nationalists, the Nobel was a long-sought cultural consecration, the ultimate international recognition of China's literary accomplishment. Mo Yan was the first current Chinese citizen to win the prize, which in 2000 had been awarded to the playwright and novelist Gao Xingjian, who had taken up French citizenship and lived in France.

The announcement also sparked immediate controversy. Within China, a number of commentators considered Mo Yan a sellout for his endorsement of prescriptive Maoist cultural policies and for not using his position to speak out for freedom of expression. One of the most trenchant criticisms outside China came from Perry Link, who faulted Mo Yan for deflecting attention from catastrophic historical events with "daft hilarity." In one novel, the victim of a Cultural

Revolution humiliation session is accused of impregnating a donkey and is taunted by a mob that forces him to eat "fake donkey dick." Descendants of the Cultural Revolution's real victims who encounter such scenes, Link observed, "might be excused for wondering what is so funny." Mo Yan, Link contended, was doing a favor for the ruling regime, for which "to treat [potentially explosive events] as jokes might be better than banning them outright."[28] And Mo Yan was not alone, Link said. Other contemporary writers had adopted "daft hilarity" as a strategy for coping with censorship, either avoiding taboo topics or deal them only "glancing blows."[29]

Once again, laughter is being interpreted as a matter not just of literary style but of an artist's moral commitment, or lack thereof. Mo Yan is undeniably ribald, satirical, parodic, farcical, and outrageous. Is his irreverence irreverent enough? Does it express an appropriate degree of moral outrage? Will it spur social change? Not everyone, of course, endorses the notion that literature must serve a political or social agenda. But outspoken writers within China have detected similar dangers as has Link.

Liu Xiaobo, who in 2010 was awarded the Nobel Peace Prize while imprisoned on vague charges of state subversion, warned in 2006 that radical laughter in the public sphere can act as a "psychosomatic drug" to anaesthetize the populace even more readily than the vacuous official humor that saturates everyday life in China.[30] Liu also saw hope, observing that "truth-telling and joke-making have worked hand-in-hand to dismantle post-totalitarian dictatorships." A few fearless people of conscience tell the truth, while joke makers dig away "at the base of the wall by the silent majority. Without the truth-tellers, there would be no open expression of popular resistance or of moral courage; without the jokesters, the words of the truth-tellers would fall on barren ground."[31]

Prominent writers across the political spectrum continue to invoke the power of affect. In his Nobel address, Mo Yan, who occupies a leadership position in the Party-led Chinese Writers Alliance, recounted a school field trip he took in the 1960s during which he and his classmates were obliged to weep while witnessing an exhibition of how people used to suffer before Communist "Liberation." It taught him this lesson: "When everyone around you is crying, you deserve to be allowed not to cry, and when the tears are all for show, your right not to cry is greater still."[32] Yu Hua, another contemporary novelist, remembered being convulsed with mirth at the absurd spectacle of all his high school classmates weeping at the news of Chairman Mao's death in 1976. His classmates, seeing his shoulders heaving and his head buried in his arms, were moved by his sincere display of grief.[33]

If history repeats itself first as tragedy and second as farce, as the saying goes, Xianglin's wife's self-repetition in Lu Xun's 1924 story was unwitting, whereas Eileen Chang's reference to it in 1947 was intentionally farcical and mocking—the target that time round being a public eager for tears. Writers of Eileen Chang's generation used laughter to resist what literary scholar Amy Dooling calls the "drift toward banality." (During the Mao period, as may be expected, the tragedy of a poor peasant woman was played "straight.")[34] One unsettling implication of this history is that so long as writers and critics persist in endlessly rewriting its story in plaintive terms, China risks suffering a fate similar to Xianglin's wife—namely, being perceived as a culture capable of generating only what one scholar has called a literature of "tears and sniveling."[35] The irony of Mo Yan's triumph is that Chinese literature has succeeded most spectacularly in garnering international prestige when the suffering has been conveyed in a key of laughter.

Xiaosi 笑死, the Chinese phrase in the title of this epilogue, offers one rejoinder to premature epitaphs. Bringing together the characters "laugh/laughter" and "die/death," it encapsulates the ambiguity of laughter and the varying interpretations it inspires. It might mean to laugh and then die, to laugh at the dead, the laughter of the dead, to laugh at death, laughter dies, mortifying, or—as it is most often used—to laugh oneself to death. And then, for either "laugh" or "laughter" one might yet substitute in "smile" or "mock." And for "death," one might substitute in "inflexibility." Apropos of E. B. White's unfortunate frog, one might observe that is precisely through dissection—what the author of *Which Classic?* called "munching prose and chewing words"—that writers bring the thing to life and ensure the survival of the species.

It's common these days to refer to many types of intentional hilarity as *gaoxiao*, or "making people laugh." The verb *gao* (roughly, "do" or "bring about") harkens back to Mao-era revolutionary imperatives to just "get it done"—be it production or revolution—by any means necessary.[36] But even as semantics continue to shift, some refrains endure. In 2006, the prominent author Can Xue wrote in her blog that "Chinese people, by and large, have no sense of humor [*youmo*], only a sense of farce [*huaji*]."[37] Humor is alien to the Chinese temperament. Chinese people condone opportunistic behavior as an inescapable part of their national character and laugh off tragic misdeeds as a joke. Such a categorical and elitist generalization is possible, ironically, only because of the success of a humor campaign three quarters of a century old, and a Year of Humor that marked not the culmination of, but rather a new beginning for modern China's unfinished comedy.

APPENDIX ONE

Selected Chinese Humor Collections, 1900–1937

This incomplete list includes collections of jokes, essays, verse, anecdotes, and stories, as well as mixed-genre collections. It does not include any dedicated collections of humorous songs, plays, comics, or cartoons. The main selection criterion was whether or not the work is explicitly advertised in its title, subtitle, front matter, or other paratexts as being funny—not whether it actually is funny. Books are listed by earliest edition I have examined personally or found listed in reliable reference sources, such as Beijing tushuguan, ed., *Minguo shiqi zong shumu* (Comprehensive Bibliography of Books Published during the Republican Era, 1911–49). Other known editions are listed in the notes. Unknown items I have left blank.

Year	Title	Chinese	English	Editor/Author	Chinese	Place	Publisher	Notes
1903	Shixie xinji	時諧新集	Anthology of New Humor	Moyin zhuren	墨隱主人	Hong Kong	Zhonghua yinwu gongsi	Preface by Zheng Guanggong of Xiangshan 香山鄭貫公.
1906	Zhenzheng Xiaolin guangji	真正笑林廣記	The True Expanded Forest of Laughs	Youxi zhuren	遊戲主人	Shanghai	Shanghai shuju	4 juan. Ed. of an 18th-century joke collection. Digital version available via HathiTrust Digital Library.
1909	Qiaopi hua	俏皮話	Wisecracks	Wu Jianren	吳趼人	Shanghai	Qunxueshe	More than 100 jokes on 183 pages. Jokes first appeared in *Yueyue xiaoshuo*.
1909	You yu lu	優語錄	Sayings of Jesters	Wang Guowei	王國維			Photolithographic reprint of 1909 manuscript held at Cambridge University Library. Title also appears as 優語錄一卷. Preface by Wang Guowei dated 宣統改元 [1909]. Appears in 1932 ed. by Shanghai's Six Arts Press 六藝書同 as 16 pages of anecdotes from classical sources, one of five works in collection entitled *Drama of the Tang and Song* 唐宋大曲考, 1940 ed. by Shanghai's Commercial Press.
1910	Huaji wenji	滑稽文集	Humor Collection	Yanyun jushi	硯雲居士	Shanghai		3 prefaces; 1 dated 1910. 1980 Taipei reprint.

Year	Title	Chinese	English	Editor/Author	Chinese	Place	Publisher	Notes
1910	Huitu xuetang xiaohua, yiming xuetang xianxingji	繪圖學堂笑話，一名學堂現形記	Illustrated Amusing Stories from New-Style Schools; or, An Exposé of New-Style Schools	Lao Lin	老林	Shanghai	Gailiang xiaoshuo she	Reprint. 134 pages in 2 vols. 6 illustrations in front matter. Page 1 identifies author as "Old Lin" 老林 and gives the book's "original title" 原名 as "The Mercurial Pedant" 學究變相. Subtitle: "Comic Novel" 滑稽小說. 25 chapters. National Library of Australia.
1911	Xiaohua qitan	笑話奇談	Jokes and Remarkable Stories			Shanghai	Yixin shuju	Listed in Terumoto (2002) x 0623. Illustrated.
1911	Xinxian xiaohua qitan	新鮮笑話奇談	Fresh Jokes and Remarkable Stories			Shanghai	Zhensheng xiaoshuo she	2 vols. 52 pages, 55 pages. Illustrated. Lithographic printing. Possibly based on above ed. National Library of China.
1911	Xing Han mie Man huaji lu	興漢滅滿滑稽錄	Funny Stories from the Restoration of the Han and Extermination of the Manchus					12 pages. Wenyan. Lithographic printing.

(continued)

Year	Title	Chinese	English	Editor/Author	Chinese	Place	Publisher	Notes
1912	Xiaohua xintan	笑話新談	Jokes and New Stories	Li Jiezhai	李節齋	Shanghai	Guangyi shuju	1st ed. 2 vols. of 52 pages each. Lithographic printing. Illustrated. Running title: "Newest jokes and stories" 最新笑話新談. 1913 ed. by Shanghai's 沈鶴記書局.
1913	Daizi de xiaohua	呆子的笑話	Jokes on Simpletons					130 pages. Dating and English title from 1974 facsimile ed. by Taipei Orient Cultural Service 東方文化書局; series editor: Lou Tsu-k'uang 婁子匡 (1907–2005).
1913	Huaji congshu	滑稽叢書	Humor Anthology	Hu Jichen	胡寄塵	Shanghai	Guangyi shuju	A 2-volume book published by Guangyi shuju in 1914 under the same title credits author Haike 海客.
1913	(Gongheguo) Xin haha xiao	(共和國)新哈哈笑	New Laughs (of the Republic)	[Li] Jiezhai	[李]節齋	Shanghai	Shenheji shuju	42 pages. Lithographic printing. Illustrated.
1913	Lengxiao congtan	冷笑叢談	A Collection of Cold Laughs	Qunxueshe tushu faxingsuo	羣學社圖書發行所	Shanghai	Qunxueshe tushu faxingsuo	196 pages. Contains 13 translated stories. 2nd ed.: 1914.
1913	Minguo xin haha xiao	民國新哈哈笑	New Laughs of the Republic	[Li] Jiezhai	[李]節齋	Shanghai	Shiyin ju	1 vol. Illustrated. Bibliographic information from National Library of China online catalog. Compare with (共和國)新哈哈笑.

Year	Title	Chinese	English	Editor/Author	Chinese	Place	Publisher	Notes
1913	Pengfu tan	捧腹談	Side-Splitting Chats	Hu Jichen	胡寄塵	Shanghai	Guangyi shuju	Subtitle: "New Stories to Raises a Smile" 新解頤語. 100 pages. 117 jokes. Wenyan. Preface written in *National Herald* 神州報 editorial office. 1st ed.: June 1913; 2nd ed.: December 1913; new ed: 1923 (price: 0.15 yuan). 10th ed.: 1927.
1913	Yuan Xiangcheng zhengzhi xiaohua	袁項城政治笑話	Political Jokes about Yuan Shikai	Changqiu Shi	常秋史	Beijing	Xianfa huabaoguan	70 pages. Illustrated.
1914	Poti lu	破涕錄	Laughing Through Tears	Li Jingzhong; Shen Ganruo	李警眾 沈肝若	Shanghai	Minquan chubanshe	6 juan, plus one-section *Laughing Through More Tears* 破涕續錄. Prefaces by Xu Zhenya, Hu Jichen, Li Dingyi; 1923 ed. published by Shenbao. Eds. held at Columbia University's C.V. Starr East Asian Library and National Library of Australia have different cover illustrations. *(continued)*

Year	Title	Chinese	English	Editor/Author	Chinese	Place	Publisher	Notes
1914	Wenyuan huaji tan	文苑滑稽談	Funny Chats from the Garden of Literature	Yunjian diangong [Lei Jin]	雲間顛公 [雷瑨]	Shanghai	Saoye shanfang	6 vols. 2nd ed.: 1924. Includes ad for Yunjian diangong's *Zuixin huaji zazhi*. Price given in Saoye shanfang shumu (1915): 1.2 yuan.
1914	Xiao shijie chubian	笑世界初編	World of Laughs, vol. 1	Shaoxing Xiao shijie bianjibu	紹興《笑世界》編輯部	Shaoxing	Xiaobao	172 pages. Wenyan. Compiled by the editors of Shaoxing's *World of Laughs* magazine.
1914	Xiaolin shize	笑林十則	Forest of Laughs: Ten Jokes	Handan Chun	邯鄲淳	Shanghai	Shangwu yinshuguan	Ed. of earliest known Chinese joke collection, ca. 3rd century CE.
1914	Zuixin huaji zazhi	最新滑稽雜誌	Newest Humor Assortment	Yunjian diangong [Lei Jin]	雲間顛公 [雷瑨]	Shanghai	Saoye shanfang	6 vols. Price given in Saoye shanfang shumu: 0.8 yuan.
1915	Duiyi Taiwan xiaohua ji	對譯臺灣笑話集	Collection of Taiwanese Jokes, with Parallel Translation	Kawai Sanenaga	川合真永	Taipei	Taiwan nichinichi shinbōsha 臺灣日日新報社	50 jokes. Preface dated 1914. A copy of a 1919 ed. by same publisher is held at the National Taiwan Library. 1920 ed. by Taipei's 河野道忠 is 125 pages and contains text in Chinese and katakana. Distributor is given in some online sources as Saitsujisei tarou 柴辻誠太郎.

Year	Title	Chinese	English	Editor/Author	Chinese	Place	Publisher	Notes
1915	Huaji wenxuan	滑稽文選	Literary Humor Selections	[Lei Jin]	[雷瑨]	Shanghai	Saoye shanfang	6 vols. Preface by Yunjian diangong, aka Lei Jin. Price given in Saoye shanfang shumu: 1.2 yuan.
1915	Wofoshanren Huaji tan	我佛山人滑稽談	Wofoshanren's Funny Chats	Wu Jianren	吳趼人	Shanghai	Saoye shanfang	More than 100 jokes in 2 vols. Preface by Yunjian diangong. Contains ads for other titles. Price given in Saoye shanfang shumu: 0.3 yuan. 1926 ed. has 74 pages.
1916	Guwen huaji leichao	古文滑稽類鈔	Assorted Collection of Humorous Writings in Classical Chinese	Gu Yu	顧餘	Shanghai	Zhonghua shuju	Preface dated September 1913. 7th ed.: 1930; 9th ed.: 1936. Contains 90 items from Han to Qing dynasties. Authors credited.
1917	Guang xiaolin	廣笑林	Expanded Forest of Laughs	Li Dingyi	李定夷	Shanghai	Guohua shuju	206 pages. More than 200 jokes. 4 juan. 1st ed.: April 1917; 2nd ed.: July 1917. Title from *Minguo shiqi zong shumu*. National Library of Australia holds an undated book by Li Dingyi entitled *Guang xiaofu* 廣笑府 (Expanded Treasury of Laughs), which might be the same. *(continued)*

Year	Title	Chinese	English	Editor/Author	Chinese	Place	Publisher	Notes
1917	Qing bai lei chao	清稗類鈔	Assorted Collection of Unofficial Sources on the Qing	Xu Ke	徐珂	Shanghai	Shangwu yinshuguan	This 48-volume anthology includes sections containing over 550 satirical 譏諷 and over 350 humorous 詼諧 short narratives. See vol. 4 of Taiwan Shangwu yinshuguan 1983 reprint.
1917	Pengfu ji	捧腹集	Side-Splitters	Guo Yaochen	郭堯臣	Shanghai	Saoye shanfang	1st ed. Wenyan.
1917	Xiaohua shijie	笑話世界	World of Jokes	Guohua shuju bianjisuo	國華書局編輯所	Shanghai	Guohua shuju	2 juan. 156 pages. 1st juan: jokes; 2nd juan: songs. Wenyan.
1917	Xiewen daguan	諧文大觀	Panorama of Humorous Prose	Aofeng laoren; Zhen Xiage	鰲峰老人; 枕霞閣	Shanghai	Zhenxiage	158 pages. 2nd ed.: 1926. Zhen Xiage is also credited as punctuator.
1917	Xiewenci leizuan	諧文辭類纂	Collection of Humorous Writings, by Genre	Li Dingyi	李定夷	Shanghai	Guohua shuju	2 vols. 300 pages. Divided into 8 genres. Appendix: Zhu Zuolin's 朱作霖 Parody of Dream of the Red Chamber 紅樓夢游戲文
1918	Kefa yixiao	可發一笑	Worth a Laugh	Qinshi shanren	琴石山人	Shanghai	Huiwentang shuju	Other eds.: 1921, 1922, 1928. 1922 ed. of 252 pages contains 582 items and editor's preface.

Year	Title	Chinese	English	Editor/Author	Chinese	Place	Publisher	Notes
1919	Guai hua	怪話	Bizarre Tales	Hu Jichen	胡寄塵	Shanghai	Guangyi shuju	Author credit: Mr. Bizarre 怪人. 188 pages. Preface by Li Dingyi 李定夷. 3rd ed.: 1921. 140-page eds. published by Shanghai's Xinmin shuju in 1924 and Dada tushu gongyingshe in 1935 both credit Hu Jichen as author.
1919	Huaji shijie	滑稽世界	Funny World	Jiang Hangong	江漢公	Shanghai	Guangyi shuju	2 vols. 84 pages. Subtitle: "Playful Jottings" 游戲札記. 2nd ed.: 1933. 1935 ed. by Shanghai's Xinmin shuju has 4 illustrations and subtitle: "Humorous Writings" 幽默文章. Parodies organized by genre.
1919	Huaji conghua	滑稽叢話	Funny Stories	Chen Yan	陳琰	Shanghai	Dadong shuju	1st ed. Reprinted 1923. 1935 ed. published by Shanghai's Datong tushushe and held at Yale University Library has different cover illustration.
1919	Huaji hun	滑稽魂	The Comic Spirit	Li Dingyi	李定夷	Shanghai	Gujin shushi	
1920	Huaji xinyu	滑稽新語	New Funny Stories			Shanghai (?)	Xinhua shudian	124 pages. Subtitle: "New King of Comedy" 新編滑稽大王.

(*continued*)

Year	Title	Chinese	English	Editor/Author	Chinese	Place	Publisher	Notes
1920	Qianjin yixiao lu	千金一笑錄	Priceless Laughs			Shanghai	Guohua shuju	Cover reprinted in front matter of Hou Xin (2008).
1920	Xiaolin guangji	笑林廣記	Expanded Forest of Laughs	Cheng Shijue [uncredited]	程世爵	Shanghai	Jinbu shuju	90 pages. Inscription: "Illustrated Funny Stories" 繡像繪圖滑稽小說. Ed. of late Qing joke collection.
1921	Gujin huaji shihua	古今滑稽詩話	Comic Verse and Prose, Ancient and Modern	Fan Fan	范范	Shanghai	Huiwentang shuju	1st ed. 98 pages. Wenyan. 3rd ed.: 1922; 15th ed. published in 1928 by Shanghai's 會文堂新記書局 (95 pages); 52-page Huiwentang ed.: 1938.
1921	Gujin xiaohua daguan	古今笑話大觀	Compendium of Jokes, Ancient and Modern	Li Xiaowu	李笑吾	Shanghai	Dalu tushu gongsi	
1921	Miben Huaji wenfu daguan	秘本滑稽文府大觀	Secret Vast Treasury of Comic Writing	Zou Diguang	鄒迪光	Shanghai	Guangyi shuju	Author dates: 1550–1626. 10 juan.
1922	Nannü xin xiaohua	男女新笑話	New Jokes about Men and Women	[Lin] Buqing (narrator); Qian Xiangsi (transcriber)	[林]步青、錢相似	Shanghai	Shijie shuju	7th ed. 1st ed. date given as 1920. Poor paper quality and binding errors. 7th ed. price: 0.5 yuan.

Year	Title	Chinese	English	Editor/Author	Chinese	Place	Publisher	Notes
1922	Xiasan huasi	瞎三話四	Shooting the Breeze	Dong Jianzhi	董堅志	Shanghai	Xinhua shuju	50 pages. 1st ed.: January; 2nd ed.: August. 50 pages. Subtitle: "Funny New Book" 滑稽新書. Wenyan stories, baihua verse. Likely unrelated to the Shanghai tabloid *Shooting the Breeze* 瞎三話四 (1927) listed in Li Nan (2005), 348. Copy held in National Taiwan Library.
1922	Qingdai mingren xiaoshi daguan	清代名人笑史大觀	Compendium of Funny Stories about Celebrities of the Qing Dynasty	Xi Xutao	席嘯濤	Shanghai	Zhonghua yinshuguan	2nd ed.
1923	Haha lu	哈哈錄	Ha! Ha!	Yan Fusun	嚴芙孫	Shanghai	Yunxuan chubanbu	Publication date tentative. Advertised in the 3rd ed. (1924) of Yan's *Dictionary of Shanghai Slang* 上海俗語大辭典.
1923	Huaji shijie	滑稽世界	Funny World	Zhao Tiaokuang	趙苕狂	Shanghai	Shijie shuju	4 vols. Subtitle: "Diversion for the Traveler" 客中消遣. Stories in baihua.

(*continued*)

Year	Title	Chinese	English	Editor/Author	Chinese	Place	Publisher	Notes
1923	Qian xiao ji	千笑集	One Thousand Jokes	Yugong (Mr. Foolish)	愚公	Shanghai	Guangyi shuju	5th ed. More than 500 wenyan jokes on 170 pages. New ed.: 1932. 1940 ed. by same publisher carries alternative title: *Changxin Forest of Laughs: 1,000 Jokes* 長新笑林一千種. Editor's preface dated spring 1917.
1923	Zengguang gujin xiaolin xinya yiqianzhong	增廣古今笑林新雅一千種	Enlarged and Expanded Forest of Laughs, Featuring One Thousand New Elegant Jokes from Collections Ancient and Modern	Chenhai Chixiaosheng	塵海痴笑生	Shanghai	Xinxin shuju	Preface by the Smiling Elder 繁然叟. "4 thick volumes for 0.4 yuan" 大洋四角 四厚冊定價. Title of every joke in Contents uses the formula "Funny . . ." "…有趣."
1924	Renren xiao	人人笑	Everyone Laughs	Zhao Tiaokuang	趙苕狂	Shanghai	Shijie shuju	This is the listing for vol. 2 下冊 only from *Minguo shiqi zong shumu*. 75 entries on 116 pages. Inscription: "The #1 Miracle Book to Cheer You Up" 解悶消憂第一奇書.

Year	Title	Chinese	English	Editor/Author	Chinese	Place	Publisher	Notes
1924	Tiaoxiao lu	調笑錄	Laugh-Getters	Xu Zhuodai	徐卓呆	Shanghai	Dadong shuju	1st ed. 159 jokes on 81 pages. Wenyan. Price: 0.3 yuan.
1924	Xin Xiaolin	新笑林	New Forest of Laughs	Xu Zhuodai	徐卓呆	Shanghai	Dadong shuju	Dating tentative. Advertised in *Banyue* 3, no. 16 (4 May 1924).
1924	Xin xiaoshi	新笑史	A New History of Laughter	Xu Zhuodai	徐卓呆	Shanghai	Dadong shuju	Dating tentative. Advertised in *Banyue* 3, no. 16 (4 May 1924).
1925	Huaji shiwen ji	滑稽詩文集	Comic Poems and Prose	Fan Zengxiang	樊增祥	Shanghai	Guangyi shuju	68 pages. Alternate title: *Comic Poems and Prose of Fan Shan, Vol. 1* 樊山滑稽詩文集初編. Contains studio photo of author. Title page says it was "written in jest" 戲著 by Mr. Fan (1846–1931), a poet and former high-ranking Qing official. 1935 and 1936 eds. by Shanghai's Dada tushu gongyingshe carry title *Comic Poems and Prose of Fanfan Shan* 樊樊山滑稽詩文集.

(continued)

Year	Title	Chinese	English	Editor/Author	Chinese	Place	Publisher	Notes
1925	Xiaohua	笑話	Jokes	Li Jinhui; Lu Yiyan	黎錦暉, 陸衣言	Shanghai	Zhonghua shuju	7th ed. 24 pages. Subtitle: Vol. 1 第一集. Series: Children's Literature Series 兒童文學叢書.
1926	Xiao Chan lu	笑禪錄	Mocking Zen Buddhism	Pan Youlong	潘游龍	Shanghai	Saoye shanfang	Ed. of a Ming dynasty work, appearing in book entitled *Story Compendium 2: Stories from Five Temples* 小說叢書之二：五廟小說大觀. Vol. 40 in a series.
1926	Xinshi biaodian Huaji tan	新式標點滑稽談	Funny Chats, with New-Style Punctuation	Wu Jianren	吳趼人	Shanghai	Saoye shanfang	Preface by Wuliaozi 無聊子 (Mr. Bored/Boring).
1927	Guifang xiaoshi	閨房笑史	Funny Stories from the Ladies' Chambers	Zhao Tiaokuang	趙苕狂	Shanghai	Dadong shuju	7th ed. Preface dated 1921 mentions a book of *Courtship Jokes* 情場笑話 that Zhao wrote in spring 1927 that was reprinted thrice within a week.
1927	Huaji qushi	滑稽趣史	A Funny and Amusing Tale	Zhao Zhongxiong	趙仲熊	Shanghai	Shijie shuju	7th ed. 14 chapters. 8th ed. by 普益書局 carries additional title: "Instant Laughs from the King of Comedy" 一見入笑滑稽大王.
1927	Jiao she lu	嚼舌錄	Eat Your Tongue	Li Jingzhong	李警眾	Shanghai	Zhenya tushuguan	

Year	Title	Chinese	English	Editor/Author	Chinese	Place	Publisher	Notes
1927	Xiaohua daguan	笑話大觀	Panorama of Jokes	Wu Gechang	吳個廠	Shanghai	Guangyi shuju	Information from Chen and Guo (1996: 4:759).
1927	Xiaolin guangji	笑林廣記	Expanded Forest of Laughs			Luzhou (?)		17 pages. Woodblock ed. Supertitle: "Complete Revised Edition" 改良全本. Location Luzhou 爐洲 appears on cover. Fu Sinian Library, Academia Sinica. Different from *Xiaolin guangji* by Youxi zhuren and Cheng Shijue.
1928	Xiaohua sizhong	笑話四種	Four Joke Books	Zhang Xiaochao	張笑潮			1974 facsimile reprint by Taipei's Dongfang wenhua chubanshe also carries English title "Four Jest-books."
1928	Zhenzheng Xiaolin guangji	真正笑林廣記	The True Expanded Forest of Laughs			Shanghai	Shenheji shuju	Contains preface. 1974 facsimile reprint by the Orient Cultural Service, Taipei. Series editor: Lou Tsu-k'uang.
ca. 1900s–1920s	Jingxuan yijian haha xiao	精選一兒哈哈笑	A Selection of Instant Laughs			Shanghai		Verse. Woodblock ed. Fu Sinian Library, Academia Sinica.

(continued)

Year	Title	Chinese	English	Editor/Author	Chinese	Place	Publisher	Notes
ca. 1910s–1920s	Pai zhang ji	拍掌集	Applause!	Zhuoyin caotang	拙吟草堂	Guangzhou	Wuguitang	14 pages. Verse. Supertitle: "Hilarious and Remarkable" 好笑奇談. Fu Sinian Library, Academia Sinica.
ca. 1910s–1920s	Xiao ci du	笑刺肚	Bust a Gut in Laughter	Sanmen zhuren	散悶主人	Guangzhou	Yiwentang	6 pages. Publisher name 以文堂 appears on contents page. Fu Sinian Library, Academia Sinica.
ca. 1910s–1920s	Xiao luan chang	笑攣腸	Double Over in Laughter	Sanmen zhuren	散悶主人	Guangzhou (?)	Yiwentang (?)	7 pages. Appears to be from same series as *Xiao ci du*. Fu Sinian Library, Academia Sinica.
ca. 1910s–1920s	Huaji ximi zhuan	滑稽戲迷傳	The Comical Biography of an Opera Fan			Shanghai	Putong shuju	Folk songs. Lithographic printing. Fu Sinian Library, Academia Sinica.
ca. 1920s	Xiaohua qiguan	笑話奇觀	Jokes and Bizarre Sights	Li Dingyi	李定夷	Shanghai	Guohua shuju	52 pages. Over 150 jokes. UC Berkeley Library.
ca. 1928–37	Xiaohua daguan	笑話大觀	Panorama of Jokes			Beiping	Baowentang	Subtitle: "Contemporary Satirical Ballads; Civilized Amusements" 時調一覽, 文明消遣. Fu Sinian Library, Academia Sinica.

Year	Title	Chinese	English	Editor/Author	Chinese	Place	Publisher	Notes
1930	Xiaolin yiqianzhong	笑林一千種	Forest of Laughs: One Thousand Jokes	Taicang Tang Zhenru	太倉唐真如	Shanghai	Jiaotong tushuguan	Wenyan. Title page note: "Edition Based on Manuscript of Shanghai Zhenru Editing and Translation Bureau" 上海真如編譯社藏版. Contains author's preface.
1930	Dasha xiaoshi	大傻笑史	Hilarious Tales of Idiocy	Huang Yanqing	黃言情	Hong Kong	Yanqing chubanbu	194 pages. Stories. Author's preface says he drew material over 3 years from periodicals 香江晚報 and 南中晚刊. Advertisements interspersed throughout. Detailed antipiracy notice on copyright page. Published on Double-Tenth National Day (October 10). Price: 0.6 Hong Kong dollars.
1931	Yikan jiuxiao	一看就笑	Instant Laughs	Cui Bingleng	崔冰冷	Shanghai	Da Zhonghua shuju	Subtitle: "Rare and Bizarre" 稀奇古怪.
1931	Youxi wenxue congkan	游戲文學叢刊	Compendium of Playful Literature	Cao Xiujun	曹誘君	Shanghai	Wenming shuju	2 vols. 280 pages, 290 pages. Contents divided into 8 categories, each with editor's preface.

(*continued*)

Year	Title	Chinese	English	Editor/Author	Chinese	Place	Publisher	Notes
1932	Minzhong xiaolin	民衆笑林	Laughs for the Masses	Zhao Shuicheng	趙水澄	Beiping	Zhonghua pingmin jiaoyu cujinhui	2nd ed. Series: Everyman's Library 平民讀物, no. 29.
1932	Xiao zan	笑贊	In Praise of Jokes	Qingdu sanke (compiler); [Lu] Huiyin (ed.)	清都散客; [陸]會因	Beiping	Xingyuntang shudian	1st ed. 72 jokes on 76 pages, plus 4 pages of back matter. Contains Ming dynasty compiler's preface 題詞; preface by editor Lu Huiyin's husband, Zhang Shoulin 張壽林; and list of corrections 正誤表. Original compiler identified as Zhao Nanxing 趙南星 (1550–1627). Price: 0.2 yuan. Print run: 1,000 copies.
1933	Huaji gushi leibian	滑稽故事類編	Compendium of Funny Stories	Yang Ruquan	楊汝泉	Tianjin	Dagongbao she	254 pages. Editor's preface. Same publisher as newspaper *L'Impartial*.
1933	Jie yan	解顏	Smile-Raisers	Zhonghua yingwen zhoubao she	中華英文週報社	Shanghai	Zhonghua shuju	Jokes and sketches excerpted from *Chung Hwa English Weekly* 中華英文週報.
1933	Kucha'an xiaohua xuan	苦茶菴笑話選	Selected Jokes from the Bitter Tea Studio	Zhou Zuoren	周作人	Shanghai	Beixin shuju	208 pages, plus 20 pages of front matter. Selections from four Ming and Qing joke and story collections, with editor's preface and commentary.

Year	Title	Chinese	English	Editor/Author	Chinese	Place	Publisher	Notes
1933	Minzhong xiaolin erji	民眾笑林二集	Laughs for the Masses, vol. 2	Liu Shiru et al.	劉世如等著	Beiping	Zhonghua pingmin jiaoyu cujinhui	Series: Everyman's Library 平民讀物, no. 166.
1934	Huaji wenxuan	滑稽文選	Literary Humor Selections	Huang Fuquan	黃馥泉	Shanghai	Minzhi shudian	50 pages. 50+ poems and essays. Microform of 5th ed. (1936) held at Yale University Library.
1934	Jie ren yi	解人頤	Smile-Raisers	Qian Decang	錢德蒼	Shanghai	Dada tushu gongyingshe	175 pages. 7 juan. Preface dated Qianlong 26 (1761). Subtitle: "Humorous Stories" 幽默文學說部. Punctuator: Pan Gongzhao 潘公昭. Punctuated, eds. also published by Shanghai's Guangya shuju (1934) and Dawen shudian (1935).
1934	Jie ren yi guangji	解人頤廣集	More Smile-Raisers	Bao Gengsheng	鮑賡生	Shanghai	Xin wenhua shushe	164 pages. Only punctuator is credited. 1935 ed. by Shanghai's Dada tushu gongyingshe.
1934	Lao She youmo shiwen ji	老舍幽默詩文集	Humorous Poems and Prose by Lao She	Lao She	老舍	Shanghai	Shidai shuju	Published by publisher of the *Analects Fortnightly* 論語半月刊.

(*continued*)

Year	Title	Chinese	English	Editor/Author	Chinese	Place	Publisher	Notes
1934	Xiaolin guangji	笑林廣記	Expanded Forest of Laughs	Cheng Shijue	程世爵	Shanghai	Qizhi shuju	2nd ed. 131 pages. Ed. of late Qing joke book.
1934	Xiaolin guangji	笑林廣記	Expanded Forest of Laughs	Cheng Shijue	程世爵	Shanghai	Dada tushu gongyingshe	Contains Cheng Shijue preface dated Guangxu 25 (1899). Possible reprint of 1911 Guangyi shuju ed., since Guangyi distributed books for Dada. 2nd ed.: 1935.
1934	Xiaoxiao lu	笑笑錄	Laugh upon Laugh	Duyiwo tuishi (Happily Retired Cave-Dwelling Hermit)	獨逸窩退士	Shanghai	Dada tushu gongyingshe	2nd ed. Subtitle: "Notes and Stories" 札記小說. Punctuator: Zhou Mengdie 周夢蝶. Author preface dated 1879 (Guangxu 5) says 6-juan book was compiled over 30 years. 224-page 3rd ed. published by Shanghai's Xin wenhua shushe in April 1935 in "Biji Fiction Series" 筆記小說叢畫. Reprinted with introduction by Changsha's Yuelu shushe in 1985.

Year	Title	Chinese	English	Editor/Author	Chinese	Place	Publisher	Notes
1934	Youxi wenzhang	游戲文章	Playful Writings	Li Dingyi	李定夷	Shanghai	Guohua xinji shuju	4th ed. Reprinted in 2010 by Beijing's Guotu shudian.
1935	Guang Xiaofu	廣笑府	Expanded Treasury of Laughs	Feng Menglong	馮夢龍	Shanghai	Zhongyang shudian	More than 400 jokes on 139 pages. Editor: Shen Yagong 沈亞公. 2nd ed.: 1936. Author's preface. Series: "Treasury of Rare Chinese Classics" 國學珍本文庫. Bowdlerized version of Ming dynasty joke collection. See Pi-Ching Hsu (1998: 1048n13).
1935	Modeng xiaohua	摩登笑話	Modern Jokes	Cui Bingleng	崔冰冷	Shanghai	Jiaotong shuju	Editor's preface dated 1933. Subtitle: "Absolutely Bizarre and Hilarious" 絕妙絕趣. 1937 ed. by Shanghai's Wenye shuju.
1935	Youmo biji	幽默筆記	Humorous Jottings	Hu Shanyuan	胡山源	Shanghai	Shijie shuju	408 pages. Author's preface dated January 1935. Published in November 1935. New ed.: 1939.
1935	Youmo xiaohua	幽默笑話	Humorous Jokes	Dong Zhenhua	董振華	Shanghai	Da Zhonghua shuju	190 items. 1936 ed. by Shanghai's Wenye shuju has 122 pages. Editor's preface dated 13 August 1935, Suzhou. Price: 1.20 yuan.

(continued)

Year	Title	Chinese	English	Editor/Author	Chinese	Place	Publisher	Notes
1935	Xin xiaohua	新笑話	New Jokes	Hu Jichen	胡寄塵	Shanghai	Shangwu yinshuguan	2 vols. 22 pages each. 1st ed.: September 1935; 3rd ed.: November 1935. Contains *zhuyin* romanization next to characters.
1935	Jiang Bao xiaoji	江鮑笑集	Laughs from Jiang and Bao	Jiang Xiaoxiao; Bao Lele	江笑笑 鮑樂樂	Shanghai	Zilin shuju	Comic routines from performing comedians. 1941 ed.
1935	Jiemen xiaochou lu	解悶消愁錄	Relieving Boredom and Dispelling Worry	Huaji shanren	滑稽山人	Shanghai	Weiyi shuju	8 juan. 119 jokes on 98 pages. Price: 1.60 yuan.
1935	Kuaihuo lin	快活林	Happy Times	Wu Gehan	吳個厈	Shanghai	Xinmin shuju	4 juan, 32 pages. Subtitle: "Funny Short Stories" 滑稽短篇小說. Running title: "Comic Panorama" 滑稽大觀. Republished in 1936 by Shanghai's Dada tushu gongyingshe.
1935	Lidai huaji gushi xuanji	歷代滑稽故事選集	Selected Comical Stories from the Imperial Period	Fang Cheng	方成	Nanjing	Zhongzheng shuju	227 pages. More than 200 items, with annotations. 1947: first Shanghai ed.
1935	Xiao quan	笑泉	Fount of Laughter	Li Xinyan	李心炎	Shanghai		Subtitle: "Precious Treasury of Humor, vol. 1" 幽默寶庫第一輯. Cover reprinted in Hou Xin (2008).

Year	Title	Chinese	English	Editor/Author	Chinese	Place	Publisher	Notes
1935	Xiaohua - disan ce	笑話第三冊	Jokes, vol. 3	Ji Zhizhong; Xu Banmei (a.k.a. Xu Zhuodai)	計志中 徐半梅	Shanghai	Shangwu yinshuguan	32 pages. Ed.: "2nd ed. after the National Difficulties [i.e., Japan's 1932 invasion]" 國難後一版. Series: "Children's Literature Compendium" 兒童文學叢書.
1935	Xiaohua	笑話	Jokes	Mark Twain	馬克吐溫	Shanghai	Zhonghua shuju	In November 1934, Zhonghua also published *Humorous Stories* 幽默小說集 by Twain and others (Zhang Menglin 張夢麟 et al., trans.).
1935	Xiaohua sanqian	笑話三千	Three Thousand Jokes	Xu Zhuodai	徐卓呆	Shanghai	Zhongyang shudian	1st ed. 3 vols. Art deco cover illustration. Contains author's preface 自序 consisting entirely of grammatical particles and dated "Written in the Broken Chamber Pot Studio on the day the news of the butterflies' marriage was announced, October 1935." Price: 5 yuan.
1935	Qianqi baiguai modeng da xiaohua	千奇百怪摩登大笑話	Absolutely Bizarre and Hilarious Modern Jokes			Shanghai	Yuxin shuju	86 pages.

(*continued*)

Year	Title	Chinese	English	Editor/Author	Chinese	Place	Publisher	Notes
1936	Jia lao'er wenda	家老二問答	Q&A with the Folks	Jia Lao'er	家老二	Shanghai	Xin shidai shuju	208 pages. First serialized in the supplement of *Wanjiang Daily* 皖江日報.
1936	Xiaohua ku	笑話庫	Warehouse of jokes	Jieyisheng	解頤生	Shanghai		Dating and author from preface (23 December 1936). 192 pages; est. 600 jokes. National Library of Australia.
1936	Xiaohua qitan	笑話奇譚	Jokes and Remarkable Stories	Yiqingshizhu	怡情室主	Shanghai	Wenye shuju	1st ed. Subtitle: "Fresh and Original" 別開生面.
1936	Xinxian xiaohua yi da xiang	新鮮笑話一大箱	A Crate of Fresh Jokes	Jin Zuxin	金祖馨	Shanghai	Yuxin shuju	2nd ed. 93 pages. Subtitle: "Funny Jokes" 滑稽笑話. Wenyan. Contents page credits "King of Jokes" 笑話大王. National Library of Australia. WorldCat lists a book by Zhao Zhuding 趙鑄鼎 with same title and subtitle (Shanghai: Zhongya shuju, ca. 1911–49).
1936	Youmo xiaohua ji	幽默笑話集	Humorous Jokes	Guo Boliang	郭伯良	Shanghai	Jingwei shuju	4 vols. 360 pages. More than 200 jokes. Preface dated 1936.
1937	Huaji lianhua	滑稽聯話	Comic Couplets	Dong Jianzhi	董堅志	Shanghai	Zhongyang shudian	102 pages. 4th ed. Subtitle: "New and Brilliant" 新編絕妙. Collator: Chu Juren 儲菊人.

Year	Title	Chinese	English	Editor/Author	Chinese	Place	Publisher	Notes
1937	Xiaohua xiaohua	笑話笑畫	Illustrated Jokes	Xu Zhuodai	徐卓呆	Shanghai	Zhongyang shudian	Illustrator: Zhou Hanming 周汗明. 82 pages. Illustrated. C.V. Starr Library, Columbia University.
1937	Xiao hai	笑海	Ocean of Laughs	Zhang Jizu	張繼祖	Shanghai	Zhongguo jiyu cujinshe	Subtitle: "Vol. 1" 第一集. Hou Xin (2) gives author as Zhang Jieyao 張杰耀.
1937	Xiaolin guangji	笑林廣記	Expanded Forest of Laughs	Cheng Shijue	程世爵	Shanghai	Dawen shudian	6th ed. Subtitle: "Comic Short Stories" 滑稽短篇小說. Ed. of late Qing joke book. Cheng is credited only in preface, not on cover or title page. Punctuator: Secret Fisherman of the Lake 湖上漁隱; Collator: Fan Shuhan 范叔寒.
1937	Xinxian xiaohua dawang	新鮮笑話大王	King of Fresh Jokes	Zou Mengxia	鄒夢霞	Shanghai	Xingmin chubanshe	67 pages. Dating from Hou Xin (2008), page 2. Subtitle: "Humorous and funny" 詼諧滑稽. 4th ed: 1948.

(continued)

Year	Title	Chinese	English	Editor/Author	Chinese	Place	Publisher	Notes
1937	Youmo de jiaomai-sheng	幽默的叫賣聲	Humorous Vendor Calls	Xia Gaizun, et al.	夏丏尊等著	Shanghai	Shenghuo shudian	60 entries on 304 pages by various authors, including Chen Zizhan, Hong Shen, Lao She, Li Jianwu, Li Liewen, and Wu Zuxiang.
1937	Youxi wenzhang	游戲文章	Playful Writings	Li Dingyi	李定夷	Shanghai	Guohua xinji shuju	2 vols. New ed. of 1917's *Xiewenci leizuan*, with new title. According to *Minguo shiqi zong shumu*, only vol. 2 is extant.
ca. 1920s–1930s	Dazhong xiaohua	大衆笑話	Jokes for All			Shanghai (?)		Supertitle: "Head Rush!" 血頭血腦. Series: "Humorous Jokes Collection, no. 1" 幽默笑話叢書之一. Cover reprinted in Hou Xin (2008).
ca. 1920s–1930s	Xinxian xiaohua louzi	新鮮笑話簍子	Basket of Fresh Jokes			Shanghai (?)		Cover reprinted in Hou Xin (2008).

APPENDIX TWO

Which Classic? Editions and Paratexts

I. EDITIONS

This list of editions, which follows the citation format used in Altenburger (2001–2), augments those previously compiled by Roland Altenburger and Chen Yingshi (Chen 2005). One important but overlooked early edition is *HD* 1928a, printed in Guangzhou, which contains three exuberantly mocking prefaces. Also notable is a 2003 Braille edition. Several Taipei editions published between 1954 and 1980 disprove the claim (in *HD* 2000: 289) that *He Dian* "ceased circulation" between 1949 and 1981. Chinese characters and English translations appear only in the first instance.

- *HD* 1878—(Anonymous). *He Dian* 何典 (Which Classic?). Edited by Guoluren 過路人; comm. Chanjia er xiansheng 纏夾二先生. Shanghai: Shenbaoguan. Reprint: Shanghai: Shanghai guji chubanshe, 1990. (Guben xiaoshuo jicheng, vol. 92.)

- *HD* 1894a—(Anonymous). *He Dian*. Shanghai: Tushu jicheng yinshuju.

- *HD* 1894b—Edited by Zhang Nanzhuang 張南莊. *Di shiyi caizi shu guihua lianpian lu* 第十一才子書鬼話連篇錄 (The Eleventh Book of Genius: A Pack of Lies). Comm. Chen Deren 陳得仁. Lithographic printing. Shanghai: Jinji shuzhuang.

- *HD* [ca. 1911–25]—*Shuo guihua zushi* 說鬼話祖師 (The Devil-Talk Master). *Xiuxiang zhenzheng guihua lianpian* 繡像真正鬼話連篇 (The Illustrated Authentic Chains of Devil Talk). 2 vols. Lithographic printing. Shanghai: Wenyi shuju.

- *HD* 1926a—Zhang Nanzhuang. *He Dian*. Edited by Liu Fu 劉復. Shanghai: Beixin shuju. Some words censored. Printed May 1926.

HD 1926b—Zhang Nanzhuang. *He Dian*. Edited by Liu Fu. Shanghai: Beixin shuju. Printed July 1926.

HD 1926c—Zhang Nanzhuang. *He Dian*. Edited by Lu Youbai 陸友白. Shanghai: Qingyun tushu gongsi. First printing: July 1926. Third printing: May 1928. Sheep leather cover. Text based on Beixin edition.

HD 1928a—Zhang Nanzhuang. *He Dian?* 何典? Edited by Chang Chao 昶超. Guangzhou: Shoukuang chubanbu. Print run: 2,000 copies. Hong Kong distribution.

HD 1928b—Guoluren. *He Dian*. Shanghai: Qingyun tushu gongsi.

HD 1929—Zhang Nanzhuang. *He Dian*. Edited by Liu Fu. Shanghai: Beixin shuju. 3rd printing.

HD 1932—Zhang Nanzhuang. *He Dian*. Collected in *Shijie youmo quanji* 世界幽默全集 (An Anthology of World Humor). Edited by Masuda Wataru 増田渉. (Publisher unknown).

HD 1933—Zhang Nanzhuang. *He Dian*. Edited by Liu Fu. Revised edition: censored words restored. Shanghai: Beixin shuju.

HD 1934—Zhang Nanzhuang. *He Dian*. Punct. Zhou Yuhao 周郁浩; collat. Ma Juren 馬舉仁. Shanghai: Dada tushu gongyingshe. Cover advertises "new-style punctuation" (新式標點). Second ed.: 1935.

HD 1946—Zhang Nanzhuang. *He Dian*. Collected in *Wan ren shouce di yi ji* 萬人手冊第一輯 (A Handbook for All: Volume One). Shanghai: Youlian. Cover inscription: "The Immortal Masterpiece Recommended by Mr. Wu Zhihui" (吳稚暉先生推薦不朽傑作). Bowdlerized edition.

HD 1949—Zhang Nanzhuang. *He Dian*. Shanghai: Beixin shuju. 6th edition. Cover inscription: "Recommended by Wu Zhihui" (吳稚暉推薦).

HD [ca. 1911–49]—(unknown). *He Dian*. (Publisher unknown). Cover inscription: "Mr. Wu Zhihui's Writing Teacher" (吳稚暉先生的文學老師). Color cover illustration of two skulls.

HD 1954—Zhang Nanzhuang. *He Dian*. Punct. Liu Bannong; supplemental punct. Lou Tsu-k'uang 婁子匡; comm. Chen Deren; comm. Chanjia er xiansheng; essay by Zhu Jiefan 朱介凡. Cover inscription by Jingheng 敬恆 [Wu Zhihui]. Genre: "A Curious Novel of Chinese Proverbs" (中國諺語長篇奇情小説). Taipei: Dongfang wenhua gongying she. (Dongfang wencong, no. 19.) Based on 1933 Beixin edition.

HD 1955—Zhang Nanzhuang. *Ren gui zhi jian* 人鬼之間 (Between Men and Devils). Taipei: Qiming shuju.

HD 1970—Zhang Nanzhuang. *He Dian*. Edited by Lou Tsu-k'uang. Annot. Liu Fu. Taipei: Dongfang wenhua gongying she. (Minsu congshu, no. 8.)

HD 1973—Zhang Nanzhuang. *He Dian ji qita* 何典及其他 (*Which Classic?*, Etc.). Comm. Chen Mingcheng 陳明誠. Taipei: Tianren chubanshe.

HD 1976—Zhang Nanzhuang. *He Dian*. Taipei: Changge chubanshe. (Changge Zhongguo gudian ming zhu congkan.)

APPENDIX 2   195

HD 1977—Zhang Nanzhuang. *He Dian*. Edited by Guoluren; comm. Chanjia er xiansheng. Taipei: Xinxing shuju. (Biji xiaoshuo daguan, vol. 20, no. 6, pp. 3707–3810.) Facsimile reprint of 1878 edition. Reprinted in 1990.

HD 1980—Zhang Nanzhuang. *He Dian*. Taipei: Heluo tushu chubanshe.

HD 1981a—Zhang Nanzhuang. *He Dian*. Beijing: Renmin wenxue chubanshe. (Zhongguo xiaoshuo shiliao congshu.)

HD 1981b—Zhang Nanzhuang. *He Dian*. Comm. Chen Deren. Beijing: Gong-shang chubanshe.

HD 1985—Zhang Nanzhuang. *He Dian*. Shanghai: Shanghai shudian. Series: "Selected Books with a Preface or Afterword by Lu Xun" (魯迅作序跋的著作選輯).

HD 1990—(Anonymous). *Gui hua lian pian* 鬼話連篇 (Chains of Devil Talk). Edited by Chen Guohui 陳國輝. Hong Kong: Jinhui chubanshe. Series: "Huangdan qi shu" 荒誕奇書 (Fantastic and Remarkable Books).

HD 1995—(Anonymous). *He Dian*. Edited by Zhang Nanzhuang. Beijing: Huaxia chubanshe. (Zhongguo gudian xiaoshuo mingzhu bai bu.)

HD 1996—Zhang Nanzhuan. *He Dian*. Shijiazhuang: Hebei jiaoyu chubanshe. (Lidai biji xiaoshuo jicheng, vol. 87.)

HD 1998—Zhang Nanzhuang. *He Dian*. Annotated by Huang Lin 黃霖; reviewed Miao Tianhua 繆天華. Taipei: Sanmin shuju. Combined volume with *Zhan gui zhuan* 斬鬼傳 (Smashing the Demons) and *Tang Zhong Kui ping gui zhuan* 唐鍾馗平鬼傳 (Zhong Kui of the Tang Quells the Demons). Series: "Famous Classical Chinese Novels" (中國古典名著).

HD 2000—Zhang Nanzhuang. *He Dian: Xin zhu ben* 何典新注本 (Which Classic?: Newly Annotated Edition). Edited by Cheng Jiang 成江. Shanghai: Xuelin chubanshe. (Zhongguo youmo wenxue jingdian zhuzuo.)

HD 2003—Zhang Nanzhuang. *He Dian*. Edited by Ye Mang 野莽. Beijing: Zhongguo mangwen chubanshe. Copyright page: "Braille edition published simultaneously."

HD 2009—Zhang Nanzhuang. *He Dian*. Beijing: Airusheng shuzihua jishu yanjiu zhongxin. Digital edition based on *HD* 1878.

II. PARATEXTS

Paratexts listed here include advertisements, introductions, postscripts, commentaries, publishers' notices, and illustrations that appear in editions of *Which Classic?* They are listed chronologically by date of composition or first publication. Dates in parentheses at end of each line indicate the earliest known edition of *Which Classic?* in which the paratext appears. Chinese characters are given only in the first instance.

(Anonymous). "*He Dian* guanggao" 何典廣告 (Advertisement for *Which Classic?*). (1878).

Taiping keren 太平客人. "Xu" 序 (Preface). (1878).

Guoluren 過路人. "Xu" (Preface). (1878).

Haishang can xia ke 海上餐霞客 (The Shanghai Traveler Who Dines on Rosy Clouds). "Ba" 跋 (Afterword). (1878).

Wu Zhihui 吳稚暉. "Gui pi" 鬼屁 (Ghost Farts). Written 1907. (1980).

Wu Zhihui. "Fengshui xiansheng" 風水先生 (Mr. Fengshui). Written 1909. (1980).

Liu Fu 劉復. "*He Dian* zhong guilian yi ban" 何典中鬼臉一斑 (Devil Faces from *Which Classic?*). (1926a).

Beixin zhanggui 北新掌櫃 (Head of Beixin Books). "Xiang duzhemen daoqian" 向讀者們道歉 (An Apology to the Reader). (1926a).

Lu Xun 魯迅. "Ti ji" 題記 (Preface). (1926a).

Liu Fu. "Chong yin *He Dian* xu" 重印何典序 (Preface to the Reprint of *Which Classic?*). (1926b).

Beixin zhanggui 北新掌櫃 (Head of Beixin Books). "Zai xiang duzhemen daoqian" 再向讀者們道歉 (Another Apology to the Reader). (1926b).

(Liu) Dabai (劉)大白. "Du *He Dian*" 讀何典 (Reading *Which Classic?*). First published 26 June 1926. (2000).

Liu Bannong 劉半農. "Guanyu *He Dian* li fangfangfang ji qita" 關於何典裡方方方及其它 (On the Empty Squares and Other Things in *Which Classic?*). First published 27 June 1926. (2000).

(Pu) Zhishui (浦)止水. "Cong *He Dian* xiangdao *Ping Gui Zhuan*" 從何典想到平鬼傳 (Thinking from *Which Classic?* to *Quelling the Demons*). Dated 31 June 1926. (1980).

Liu Fu 劉復. "You shi guanyu jiaokan *He Dian* de hua" 又是關於校勘何典的話 (More Comments on the Collation of *Which Classic?*). (1926b).

(Liu) Dabai. "Liangge quanr he yibaiyishige kuangr" 兩個圈兒和一百一十個框兒 (Two Circles and 110 Squares). First published 8 August 1926. (2000).

(Liu) Dabai. "Zaihe 'wu jia' Liu Fu boshi kai hui wanxiao (xuqian)" 再和「吾家」劉復博士開回頑笑 (續前) (More Joking with "My Relative" Dr. Liu Fu [Continued]). First published 8 August 1926. (2000).

(Lin) Shouzhuang 林守庄. "Guanyu Liu jiao *He Dian* de jige kaodezhu de zhengwu" 關於劉校何典的幾個靠得住的正誤 (Regarding a Few Reliable Corrections to Liu's Collation of *Which Classic?*). First published 9 August 1926. (2000).

Liu Fu. "Bu yu Liu Dabai xiansheng banzui" 不與劉大白先生拌嘴 (No More Bickering with Mr. Liu Dabai). First published 23 August 1926. (2000).

(Liu) Dabai. "Jieshao 'wu jia' Liu Fu boshi di ji zhong qiaomiao famen" 介紹「吾家」劉復博士底幾種巧妙法門 (Introducing a Few of the Clever Methods of "My Relative" Dr. Liu Fu). First published 29 August 1926. (2000).

Lin Shouzhuang. "Xu" (Preface). Dated 27 October 1926. (1933).

Huang Tianshi 黃天石. "Xu" (Preface). (1928a).

Zheng Tianjian 鄭天健. "Xu" (Preface). (1928a).

Chang Chao 昶超. "Xie zai *He Dian* jiaoding xinben zhiqian" 寫在何典校訂新本之前 (Foreword to the Newly Collated and Revised Edition of *Which Classic?*). (1928a).

Yuan Zhenying 袁振英. "*He Dian?* xu" 何典?序 (Preface to *Which Classic?*). (1928a).

Liu Fu. "Guanyu *He Dian* de zai ban" 關於何典的再版 (About the Second Edition of *Which Classic?*). (1933).

Lu Xun. "Wei Bannong ti ji *He Dian* hou, zuo" 為半農題記何典後作 (A Follow-Up to My Preface to Bannong's *Which Classic?*). (1933).

Zhitang 知堂 (Zhou Zuoren 周作人). "Zhongguo de huaji wenxue" 中國的滑稽文學 (China's Comic Literature). First published in *Yuzhou feng* 宇宙風 (Cosmic Wind) serial *Fengyu hou tan* 風雨後談 (Chats after the Storm), issue 24 (1937), pp. 544–46. (2000).

Zhu Jiefan 朱介凡. "Lun *He Dian* de yuyan yunyong" 論何典的語言運用 (On the Use of Language in *Which Classic?*). (1954).

(Lou) Tsu-k'uang. "Juantou yu" 卷頭語 (Preface). (1954).

Lou Tsu-k'uang. "Dai xu: Liang wei su wenxue de zhu shuai: Zhang Nanzhuang he Feng Menglong" 代序: 兩位俗文學的主帥: 張南莊和馮夢龍 (In Lieu of a Preface: Two Masters of Low Literature: Zhang Nanzhuang and Feng Menglong). (1970).

(Anonymous). "Jianjie *He Dian*" 簡介何典 (A Brief Introduction to *Which Classic?*). (1976).

Zhao Jingshen 趙景深. "Ba" (Afterword). Written 1979. (1981a).

Ning Yuan 寧遠. "*He Dian* tiyao" 何典提要 (A Synopsis of *Which Classic?*). (1980).

Pan Shen 潘慎. "Jiao zhu houji" 校注後記 (Editor's Afterword). (1981a).

(Anonymous). "Chuban shuoming" 出版說明 (Publication Notes). (1981b).

Lin Chen 林辰. "Huangdan qishu xu" 荒誕奇書序 (Preface to the "Fantastic and Remarkable Books" Series). (1990).

Gu Xinyi 顧歆藝. "Qianyan" 前言 (Foreword). (1990).

Huang Lin 黃霖. "*He Dian* kaozheng" 何典考証 (Textual Research on *Which Classic?*). (1998).

Huang Lin. "Yinyan" 引言 (Foreword). (1998).

Cheng Jiang 成江. "Dianzhu houji" 點注後記 (Editor's Afterword). (2000).

Ye Mang 野莽. "Ci chu he dian, he chu ci dian" 此出何典, 何出此典 (Which Classic Did This Come From, How Did This Classic Emerge). (2003).

ABBREVIATIONS

CC	*The China Critic*
HD	*He Dian*
HM	*Hong meigui*
HZ	*Hong zazhi*
LBQJ	*Li Boyuan quanji*
LXSW	*Lu Xun: Selected Works*
LY	*Lunyu banyuekan*
QDBK	*Qingdai baokan tuhua jicheng*
SB	*Shenbao*
THRB	*Tuhua ribao*
WJQJ	*Wu Jianren quanji*

NOTES

PREFACE

1. Harris, *Humbug*, 3.
2. White, *Essays of E. B. White*, 303 (originally, "Preface" to White and White, *A Subtreasury of American Humor* [1941]).

ACKNOWLEDGMENTS

1. "Satire 2" (Satyre II), lines 25–30, in Donne, *The Major Works*, 22.

CHAPTER 1. BREAKING INTO LAUGHTER

1. *Tong shi* was serialized from 1903 to 1905. Wu's joke series *Xin xiao shi* appeared in *Xin xiaoshuo* under the pen name Wofoshanren in 1903 and 1905 (vol. 1, issues 8, 17, and vol. 2, issue 11). On Wu Jianren's (Wu Woyao, 1866–1910) narrative innovations, see Hanan, *Chinese Fiction of the Nineteenth and Early Twentieth Centuries*, chaps. 8 and 9.

2. Liu E (1857–1909) wrote *Lao Can youji* between 1903–4; it was first published in 1907. On Liu as passionate weeper, see Hsia, C. T. *Hsia on Chinese Literature*, 247–68, esp. 263. Translation of book title and preface is modified from Liu, *The Travels of Lao Ts'an*, 1–2. Cf. Lee, *Revolution of the Heart*, 1–4.

3. Several versions of this legend from the late imperial and Republican periods are translated in Idema, *Meng Jiangnü Brings down the Great Wall*; for a contemporary novelistic retelling, see Su, *Binu and the Great Wall*.

4. See Xidi (Zheng Zhenduo [1898–1958]), "Xue he lei de wenxue" ("A Literature of Blood and Tears"), *Wenxue xunkan* 6 (30 June 1921), n.p.

5. Emphasis added. Cheng Zhanlu, "Kexi de xuelei wenzhang," *HM* 21 (20 December 1924), n.p. In issue 26 (24 January 1925), Cheng published a companion piece, "A Painful Story of Happy Laughter" ("Ketong de xixiao wenzhang"), which mocks the false cheer of purportedly comic stories.

6. Sabina Knight explains the debt concisely: "Born with a piece of jade in his mouth and a consuming need to love and be loved, Baoyu (Precious Jade) shares a predestined association with his cousin Daiyu. She owes him a cosmic debt because when he was a stone and she a flower in their prior existence, he awoke her to sentience by watering her with dew. Determined to return his kindness, the flower-turned-fairygirl had resolved to repay his sweet dew with a lifetime of human tears." Knight, *Chinese Literature*, 93. Qian Zhongshu uses the terms *maiku* (selling crying), *maixiao* (selling smiles), *chang leizhai* (repay a debt of tears), and *xing leihui* (bribe with tears). See Qian, *Guanzhui bian*, 4:1435–38; addendum, and 5:251–52. English translation modified from Qian, *Limited Views*, 416. See also Cao, *The Story of the Stone*, vol. 1, chaps. 1 and 5.

7. Lengxue (Cold-Blooded) was a pen name of Chen Jinghan (1878–1965). Bao's pen name was inspired by a passage in the *Shenyi jing*. See Zheng, *Zheng Yimei xuanji*, 1:115–16. The ginger joke appears in Li, *Poti lu*, juan 1, 5. Liu E's translator cites his "pervading sense of humor" and C. T. Hsia his "genial sense of humor." See Shadick, "Translator's Introduction," in Liu, *The Travels of Lao Ts'an*, xxxiii; and Hsia, *C. T. Hsia on Chinese Literature*, 251. Lu Xun, as noted in chapter six, nominated *Lao Can* to a Japanese friend as an exemplar of Chinese literary humor.

8. *LXSW*, 1:182. The story is also reprinted on the website www.marxists.org.

9. See Berry, *A History of Pain*, especially the discussion of "centripetal" and "centrifugal" traumas on pages 21–28; Wang, *The Monster That Is History*.

10. Inspired by Benjamin's reading of Paul Klee's painting *Angelus Novus*, Wang likens modern Chinese writers' attitude toward history to the angel's paralyzed, terror-stricken gaze at historical catastrophe. See Wang, *Illuminations from the Past*, 97–98. Trauma also drives the interpretive rubric of studies focused on other aspects of modern Asian literary culture. Karen Thornber, for example, makes the sweeping comment that "it is as difficult to imagine a literature that does not discuss suffering as it is to imagine a life without suffering"—though she later acknowledges that in the early twentieth-century Chinese context the experience of suffering was sometimes "lampooned." See Thornber, *Empire of Texts in Motion*, 251–90 ("Spotlight on Suffering"), esp. 252 and 266–70.

11. White, *Essays of E. B. White*, 304.

12. See Li Shizhen (1518–93), *Bencao gangmu*, "Grass" (cao) section, *juan* 17, entry: *mantuoluo* flower. Online at www.theqi.com/cmed/oldbook/book132/b132_20.html. Li's self-experiment with adding this poisonous flower to an alcoholic drink is mentioned in Nappi, *The Monkey and the Inkpot*, 48, 178n64.

13. On the etymological links between words for *smile* and *laugh* in various European languages, see Trumble, *A Brief History of the Smile*, 79; chapter 4 of Trumble's book discusses changes in smile/laugh/smirk terminology over time. For a detailed survey of varied uses of the word *xiao* in Ming and Qing sources, see Santangelo, *Laughing in Chinese*, 29–203.

14. The couplet is *tao zhi yaoyao, zhuozhuo qi hua*. The homophone *yao* 㜳 referred specifically to a girl's smile, and the Ming dynasty 芺, which removed the female radical, leaves

us with the precursor to the graph used today, which substitutes a bamboo radical for the grass radical. See Qian, *Guanzhui bian*, 1:70–72. In the section on *The Correct Meaning of the Classic of Poetry* (*Maoshi zhengyi*), "Peach Blossoms Open, Flowers Smile" ("Tao yao: hua xiao"), Qian Zhongshu also cites Joseph Addison's 1711 observation that "the Metaphor of Laughing, applied to Fields and Meadows when they are in Flower, or to Trees when they are in Blossom, runs through all Languages." Addison's essay "Laughter" may be found online at http://essays.quotidiana.org/addison/laughter_1/. Another variant, *xiao* 咲, substitutes a mouth radical for the bamboo radical, an oral metaphor.

15. Wang Anshi (1021–86) included this anecdote about Su Shi's (1037–1101) criticism of his *Zishuo* in a collection of Su's witticisms, *Humorous Jests* (*Tiaoxue pian*). In 1937, a contributor to the humor magazine the *Analects Fortnightly* (see chapter 6) provided a facetiously literal explanation to meet Su's challenge: seeing someone drive an ox or sheep through the marketplace with a bamboo stick won't raise an eyebrow, but driving a dog will make people laugh. See Guanjin, "Xin *Zishuo*" ("A New *Chinese Characters Explained*"), *LY* 116 (16 July 1937), 929. Explaining characters solely based on their visual components is a popular practice but, as these examples suggest, potentially misleading.

16. Emperor Xuanzong's (posthumous name: Xuande, r. 1426–35) "Yi xiao tu" is held in the Nelson-Atkins Museum of Art under the title *Dog and Bamboo*. My thanks to Jocelyn Chey for bringing this painting to my attention and to Stacey Sherman for assistance in obtaining the image. Images of a Japanese toy based on the 竹+犬=笑 rebus, a dog wearing a bamboo basket on its head, can readily be found by searching those three Kanji on the Internet.

17. For an amusing reading of this plot, including the detective's reconstruction of a book he hasn't read, see Bayard, *How to Talk about Books You Haven't Read*, 32–46.

18. Zhu Ziqing, "Xiao de lishi" ("A History of Laughter"), *Xiaoshuo yuebao* 14, no. 6 (10 June 1923), n.p. Zhu's (1898–1948) story is dated 28 April 1923.

19. Four pseudonymous reviews of the story appeared in the pages of *Fiction Monthly*, each under the title "Zhu Ziqing jun de 'Xiao de lishi'" ("Mr. Zhu Ziqing's 'A History of Laughter'"): one in vol. 14, no. 8 (August 1924); two in vol. 14, no. 10 (October 1924); and one in vol. 14, no. 12 (December 1924). The first reviewer states that his lessons about women's liberation and family reformation are drawn from the story's "naked instructions." The second recounts the story's invigorating effect—it was literally a wake-up call that shook him out of his summer lethargy. Reviewers praise the story for its psychological and emotional realism and its implicit castigation of "old-style" families. Reviewer Four remarks that "laughter and tears are both expressions of extreme emotion."

20. The anthology appeared in several volumes in 1935–36. See Mao Dun (Shen Yanbing, 1896–1981), *Zhongguo xin wenxue daxi—xiaoshuo juan*, 3:326–34. Zhu Ziqing served as the editor of the poetry volume (vol. 8). Zhu's story also lent its name to the title of a 1925 collection of short stories by Zhu, Lu Xun, Ye Shaojun, and two other authors edited by Xiaoshuo yuebao she. The English title of the collection is given on the copyright page incorrectly, but suggestively, as *"The History of a Woman" and Other Stories*.

21. See "Zhenglizhe de hua" ("A Few Words from the Editor"), in the front matter of Bao and Wang, *Huoshao doufudian*. *Zhengli* means to put in order, tidy up, clean up, or revise. The play's Chinese title is "Shaoxing Aguan cheng huoche."

22. See, for example, Cohen, *History in Three Keys*.

23. These and other cases of "laughing disorders" diagnosed as early as the third century CE are discussed in Lee, "'Xiaoji' kao." The description of the laughing woman in *Bencao gangmu* (*shibu, juan* 11) can be found online at www.theqi.com/cmed/oldbook/book132/b132_14.html. One of the *Strange Tales from the Liao Studio*, a Qing dynasty collection, features a bewitching girl who laughs too much. After marrying, she reveals that she is part fox and was raised by a ghost mother. See Pu, *Strange Tales from a Chinese Studio*, 152-67.

24. White, *Essays of E. B. White*, 305.

25. Zhang, *Guitu riji*, 2.

26. Feng Menglong's *Gujin xiaoshi* was originally titled *Survey of Talk Old and New* (*Gujin tangai*) and also known as *Jokes Old and New* (*Gujin xiao*). The collection was dubbed a "history of laughter" by the comic writer and bon vivant Li Yu (1610-80), who wrote a preface included in a 1667 edition. Another partially extant Qing dynasty collection is entitled *Three-Mountain's History of Laughter* (*Sanshan xiao shi*). Excerpts from these collections appear in Yang, *Zhongguo xiaohua shu*, 14-15, 89, 137-38, 211-34, 410. Chen Geng's *Xiao shi* (A History of Laughter) contains six *juan* (four extent), seven prefaces, the earliest dated Daoguang 22 (1841), and an afterword dated 1844. Preface 2 contrasts "orthodox" (*zheng*) imperially commissioned histories with "miscellaneous" (*za*) histories, including histories of laughter. A copy is held at the University of Alberta. The book is reprinted in Chen and Guo, *Zhongguo lidai xiaohua jicheng*, 4:252-341. A notice appearing on the front page first column of *Shun Pao* beginning in 3 May 1879 (issue 2155) mentions that a book entitled *Xiao shi* will be available for sale on 15 May; this is likely Chen Geng's.

27. One 1914 parody, "Biography of Mr. Good-for-Nothing," includes a commentary by the Historian of Laughter (*Xiaoshi shi*). See Cunxin, "Fantong liezhuan," *SB* 14861 (25 June 1914), 14. Many *xiaoshi* can be found in the 1920s magazine the *Recreation World*, discussed in chapter 3.

28. See "'Wenming jiehun' zhi xin xiaoshi" ("The Latest 'Civilized Marriage' Absurdity"), *SB* 15076 (27 January 1915), 10.

29. See Diegengsi (Dickens), *Lüxing xiaoshi*; *Kancainu xiaoshi*. *Luoke xiaoshi* appeared in *Famous Funnies* (*Huaji huabao banyuekan*, 1936-37), a short-lived fortnightly magazine of translated Western cartoons, which is reprinted in Jiang et al., *Minguo manhua qikan jicui*, vol. 4. China's "history of pain" was also the subject of cartoons. The inaugural issue of the *True Record* (discussed in chapter 3), for instance, featured a nine-panel cartoon depicting "the painful history of the Republic's indebtedness" to foreign countries during the regime of Yuan Shikai. See [Ma] Xingchi, "Minguo jiezhai zhi tongshi," in *Zhenxiang huabao* 1, no. 1 (5 June 1912), after page 20.

30. Zeitlin, *Historian of the Strange*, 2.

31. See the first preface to Chen, *Guang xieshi*, n.p. This preface is dated 1615. A second preface is dated 1579 (Wanli 7). The collection is made up almost entirely of parodic pseudobiographies (Biography of Mr. Kettle, Biography of Madame Bamboo, Biography of a Coin, Biography of Dragon Sperm, etc.).

32. On the global flows that contributed to openness during the Republican period, see Dikötter, *The Age of Openness*.

33. Contemporary reports estimated *Shun Pao*'s daily circulation at between fifty-six hundred and seven thousand copies. See Wagner, "The Shenbao in Crisis," 108. On its institutional history, see Mittler, *A Newspaper for China?*

34. Tabloid count is from Wang, "Officialdom Unmasked," 86.

35. Reed, *Gutenberg in Shanghai*, 17. As Reed notes, publishers, printers, retail outlets, and other parts of the publishing supply chain were often vertically integrated.

36. Rea and Volland, *The Business of Culture*, 186.

37. For full bibliographic details of these tabloids, see Li, *Wan Qing, Minguo shiqi Shanghai xiaobao yanjiu*, 335–68. Their titles are: *Xiao wutai* 笑舞臺, *Huangtang shijie* 荒唐世界, *Huangtang xiaobao* 荒唐笑報, *Xiasan huasi* 瞎三話四, *Huli hutu* 糊里糊塗, *Xin Xiaolin* 新笑林, *Xin xiaobao* 新笑報, *Feihua* 廢話, *Zhuo Bieling* 卓別靈 (two), *Zhen kuaihuo* 真快活, *Zhen kaixin* 真開心, *Kuaihuo shijie* 快活世界 (two), *Kaixin shijie* 開心世界.

38. See Jones, *Yellow Music*, 53.

39. These and other productions of the Shanghai-based Asia Film Company dating from 1913 onward, some of which had multiple titles, are listed in Huang Xuelei, "Zhongguo diyi? *Nanfu nanqi* yu tade 'jingdianhua'" ("China's First Film? The Canonization of *The Difficult Couple*"), in Wong, *Zhongguo dianying suyuan*, 17.

40. Quoted in the epigraph to Hanan, *The Invention of Li Yu*.

41. The physician Ding Fubao (1874–1952) cites a New York report about the health benefits of laughter in a 1902 publication. See Lee, "'Xiaoji' kao," 136.

42. This description of the popular response to Johnson's addictive chorus is from page 31 of Tim Brooks's *Lost Sounds*, part 1 of which discusses in detail Johnson's career and the history of his laughter song, which dates to the early 1890s.

43. Zhang, *Zhongguo xiju guannian de xiandai shengcheng*, 6; Bergson, *Xiao zhi yanjiu*. (A Japanese translation of Bergson's work appeared in 1914.)

44. *Yi yixiao zhizhi*. For both the original and a translation of this essay, dated 13 November 1929, see "Yaba lizan" ("In Praise of Mutes") in Zhou, *Zhou Zuoren: Selected Essays*, 248–49.

45. Laughter might be interpreted in terms of interpellation, a term from social theory that refers to how a speaker addresses a listener and, by eliciting a response, fits the listener into the speaker's own value system. In Louis Althusseur's formulation, *interpellation* refers to the moment in which an individual acknowledges that he or she is being addressed by an authority and implicitly accepts his or her own subjugation. See Althusseur, *Lenin and Philosophy and Other Essays*, 127–86, especially 170–77. I do not share Althusseur's presumption that an insidious ideology is at work in all acts of interpellation. To take just one Chinese example: literary scholar Charles Laughlin writes of an essay by Liang Yuchun that "the beauty of its comic rhetoric . . . is that it would be foolish to try to 'refute' his arguments, because in doing so you would be playing the 'straight man' to his comic, thereby only helping his cause." Laughlin, *The Literature of Leisure and Chinese Modernity*, 121.

46. Postman, *Amusing Ourselves to Death*.

47. Paolo Santangelo counts 2,234 instances of *xiaodao* and its equivalents in *Dream of the Red Chamber*. See the detailed linguistic typology beginning on page 31 of Santangelo, *Laughing in Chinese*. David Tod Roy interprets the pen name Lanling Xiaoxiaosheng as an allusion to the Confucian philosopher Hsün-tzu (Xunzi, 3rd c. BCE), who

scoffed at false doctrines and amoral status-seekers. See Roy, *The Plum in the Golden Vase*, vol. 1, xxiii–xiv.

48. Gatrell, *City of Laughter*, 5.

CHAPTER 2. JOKES

1. This couplet from Li Yu's *Xianqing ouji* (Casual Expressions of Idle Feeling) was reprinted on the cover of the sixtieth issue of the *Analects Fortnightly*. See Li, *Li Yu quanji*, 3:58; *LY* 60 (1 March 1935). Title translation and dating of Li's work are from Hanan, *The Invention of Li Yu*, 1.

2. Wu's three other occasional joke columns were the following: *Xin Xiaolin guangji* (New Expanded Forest of Laughter) was first published under the pen name Wofoshanren in *Xin xiaoshuo* 1903 and 1905 (vol. 1, issue 10; vol. 2, issue 10); on *Qiaopi hua* (Wisecracks), see next note; *Huaji tan* (Funny Chats) first appeared in the periodical *Yulun shishi bao* (Editorials on Current Events) in 1910, and was published as the single volume *Wofoshanren Huaji tan* (Wofoshanren's Funny Chats) in 1915. Punctuation and emphasis in all Chinese excerpts follows the original. Full citations for all joke collections published between 1900 and 1937 appear in appendix 1.

3. [Wu] Jianren, "Zalu yi: Qiaopi hua" ("Miscellany 1: Wisecracks"), *Yueyue xiaoshuo* 1 (September 1906). See vol. 1, p. 251 of the Dongfeng shudian reprint. Wu's preface mentions by name a Hong Kong *Anthology of New Humor* (*Shixie xinji*), which contains songs, ditties, poems, and letters, as well as a variety of parodic prose that recently appeared, the editor says, in various papers. Few entries in that book are credited, despite the editor's promise. A copy is held at the Stanford Library. A short-lived periodical with a similar title, *New Humor Pictorial* (*Shixie huabao*), circulated in Guangdong and Hong Kong in 1907. See Jiang, *Baojie jiuwen*, 208–11. According to an editorial note in Wu's collected works, *Qiaopi hua* appeared in various periodicals during the Guangxu reign period (1875–1908) before Wu revised, edited, added to, and published the joke series in the *All-Fiction Monthly* between 1906 and 1908. See *WJQJ*, 7:5. *Wisecracks* appeared as a book in 1909.

4. "Zhaozu si," in Wu, *Wofoshanren Huaji tan*, 41.

5. "Xiaoniu xiaoma," in Wofoshanren, "Zalu: Xin Xiaolin guangji," *Xin xiaoshuo* 2:10 (1905), 149.

6. "Shang chuan huang magua," from *Yueyue xiaoshuo* 5 (15 January 1907), 234; reprinted in *WJQJ*, 7:365.

7. The above jokes are republished with minor modifications in *WJQJ*, 7:478, 341, 365, 358–59, respectively.

8. "You ma ziji le" ("Cursing Myself Again") is one of the last jokes in Wu's *Funny Chats*. See Wu, *Wofoshanren Huaji tan*, 45.

9. Reed, *Gutenberg in Shanghai*, 5.

10. Zhang Dai's (1597–1689) account of uproarious times in his second uncle's *xueshe* appears in Santangelo, *Laughing in Chinese*, 18.

11. Wang, "The Weight of Frivolous Matters," 87.

12. Christie Davies writes: "Jokes differ from comedies, cartoons, caricatures, and humorous essays in that, especially when taken in aggregate, they are authorless and it is

pointless to look behind them for the kinds of motives, purposes, and feelings that characterize a single author." See Davies, *Ethnic Humor around the World*, 3. In a later study, Davies endorses the observation of another scholar that "it is impossible to trace the originators of jokes and futile to try to do so." See Davies, *Jokes and Targets*, 10. Ruth Wisse fills her pail with Jewish jokes. See Wisse, *No Joke*, 245.

13. Li Dingyi (1890–1963), a prolific joke anthologizer of the Republican period, for example, credited the author of every joke in his collections *Expanded Treasury of Laughs* (*Guang xiaofu*) (ca. 1910s) and *The Comic Spirit* (1919) (though not "funny news items"). Many journals of the era also credit jokes to specific authors.

14. *Joe Miller's Jests* (1739), a book of jokes posthumously attributed to a beloved English comedian, Joe Miller (d. 1738), is a prime example of editors using the name of a famous personality to boost joke book sales. See Wardroper, *Jest upon Jest*, 12–14. Scholarly debate about the editorship of some late Ming joke collections suggests a similar practice at work in China almost a century earlier. Patrick Hanan, for example, believes that the *Expanded Treasury of Laughs*, usually attributed to the famous writer-editor Feng Menglong, who had compiled a *Treasury of Laughs* in the late Ming, is not Feng's work. See Hanan, *The Chinese Vernacular Story*, 225n67. Stories about Dongfang Shuo's (ca. 154–ca. 93 BCE) facility with jokes and riddles appear in chapter 65 of the *History of the Former Han*, whose author comments that people "have invented all sorts of odd sayings and outlandish tales and attached Shuo's name to them." See Watson, *Courtier and Commoner in Ancient China*, 79–106, esp. 106.

15. Wu, who arrived in Shanghai in 1883 and worked briefly as a journalist in Hankou in 1902, had worked as an editor for multiple tabloid periodicals and began writing fiction in earnest in 1903, maintaining a feverish productivity until his death in 1910. For a brief biography, see Huters, *Bringing the World Home*, 124–27.

16. Lu Xun's letter to Tao Kangde is dated 1 April 1934 (i.e., April Fool's Day). See Lu Xun, *Lu Xun shuxinji*, 1:514–15.

17. Untitled preface to "Zalu yi: Xin *Xiaolin guangji*" ("Miscellany 1: *New Expanded Forest of Laughs*"), *Xin xiaoshuo* 10 (25 July 1905), 153.

18. "Shengguan," from Youxi zhuren's *Xiaolin guangji*, is reprinted in Chen and Guo, *Zhongguo lidai xiaohua jicheng*, 4:3. On sex jokes in this and other works from imperial China, see: Levy, *Chinese Sex Jokes in Traditional Times*; Huang and Lee, "Ming-Qing xiaohua zhong de shenti yu qingyu"; Hinsch, *Passions of the Cut Sleeve*, chap. 5 (on homosexuality in humor).

19. In 1897, Li Boyuan founded a newspaper called *Play* and adopted the pen name Master of Play (see chapter 3). Around 1900, a certain Cheng Shijue (fl. 1890s) compiled a humor collection under the same title but with different jokes. A 1928 edition of the Master of Play's compilation distinguished it from Cheng's and other competitors' by calling it *The True Expanded Forest of Laughs* (*Zhenzheng Xiaolin guangji*).

20. Wu writes of *gailiang*, *yishi*, and *quwei*. Lydia Liu identifies *yishi* as a "return graphic loan"—a category of "classical Chinese-character compounds that were used by the Japanese to translate modern European words and were reintroduced into modern Chinese." See Liu, *Translingual Practice*, 302, 310.

21. A translation of Liang's influential essay, "On the Relationship between Fiction and the Government of the People," appears in Denton, *Modern Chinese Literary Thought*,

74–81. The wine/bottle point is made in Lu and Yang, *Zhongguo youmo wenxue shihua*, 311.

22. If you enjoyed "Promoted," see the joke-telling party in chapter 15 of *Shenlou zhi* (1804), translated by Patrick Hanan as Anonymous, *Mirage*, 226–28. Jokes appear in chapters 73–78, 81, 83–87, 90–93 of Li, *Jinghua yuan* (Flowers in the Mirror, 1828). On that novel's varied forms of humor, see Elvin, *Changing Stories in the Chinese World*, 40–48. An abridged English translation cuts most of the jokes. See Li, *Flowers in the Mirror*. For a sampling of another type of humorous riddle that circulates widely in popular culture, see Rohsenow, *A Chinese-English Dictionary of Enigmatic Folk Similes*.

23. This inspired translation by David Hawkes appears in chapter 38 of Cao, *The Story of the Stone*, 2:256.

24. Translation from Wu, *The Scholars*, 73–76.

25. On this fragmentary collection, and its reconstruction by many hands over the centuries, see Baccini, "The Forest of Laughs (*Xiaolin*)," especially the textual history and translation on 151–92.

26. Translations of section titles in this list are from Hsu, "Feng Meng-lung's *Treasury of Laughs*," 1048. As Pi-Ching Hsu notes, later editors and anthologizers who drew on Feng Menglong's (1574–1646) material altered the classifications.

27. "Haojing," from *Xiaofu*, in Feng, *Feng Menglong quanji*, 11:96.

28. Cohen, *Jokes*, 10.

29. Wang, *Lidai xiaohua ji*, xv. Other scholars have subsequently conducted systematic comparisons of dynastic joke books to identify repetition and adaptation. Yang, *Zhongguo xiaohua shu*, 478–526, also includes Zhou Zuoren's 1936 *Kucha'an xiaohua xuan*.

30. Ming dynasty joke books and encores include *Treasury of Laughs* (*Xiaofu*), followed by an *Expanded Treasury of Laughs* (*Guang Xiaofu*), and *Forest of Laughs* (*Xiaolin*), followed by *Sequel to the Forest of Laughs* (*Xu Xiaolin*). Li Yu, who in the early Qing dynasty edited and retitled one of Feng Menglong's joke collections, mentions in his preface that of Feng's "playful laughter and furious mockery" he had "just cut out the mockery." See Chen and Guo, *Zhongguo lidai xiaohua jicheng*, 2:713. On the question of laughter versus mockery in Chinese joke books, see chapter 4 in this book. *Chats from a Night in the Mountains* (*Shanzong yixihua*, ca. 1621–44), also known as *Open the Book and Laugh* (*Kaijuan yixiao*), is another product of several hands. Compiled by the late Ming philosopher Li Zhi (1527–1602), it was later edited and expanded by Mr. Laughter (Xiaoxiao xiansheng) and collated by the Ha-Ha Daoist (Haha daoshi), a pen name of playwright Tu Long (1542–1605).

31. Eight *Xiaolin*s dating from before 1900 are listed in the modern anthologies Chen and Guo, *Zhongguo lidai xiaohua jicheng* and Wang, *Lidai xiaohua ji*. The *Expanded Forest of Laughs* drew on *Xiaofu*, Li Zhuowu's *Xiao dao*, and Shi Tianji's *Xiao de hao*, respectively. See Yang, *Zhongguo xiaohua shu*, 601. The title of one Qing edition, *The Newly Engraved (xinjuan) Expanded Forest of Laughs*, distinguished it from earlier woodblock editions.

32. The Ming collection *Shixing xiaohua* (Fashionable Jokes), compiled by Chen Meigong, is a rare exception. See Chen and Guo, *Zhongguo lidai xiaohua jicheng*, 761–74. *Paidiao* and *paiyu* are other terms for humorous utterances that appear in dynastic joke

collections. See Huang, "Jokes on the Four Books," 31. The term *xiaohua ji*, or collection of jokes, was commonly added by editors of twentieth-century editions.

33. Respectively, *lin, hai, lang, shi, fu, lu, ji, cong.*

34. The 1616 preface to *Three Collections of Jokes to Snap the Strings on Your Hat* (*Jueying sanxiao*) mentions Feng Menglong's *Treasury of Laughs*, which itself contained material from more than twenty earlier joke collections. See Hsu, "Feng Meng-lung's *Treasury of Laughs*," 1045–46.

35. The Korean word *sohwa*, which again uses the same Chinese characters, also has the same meaning of "laughter-inducing stories." The term *showa* appears in the title of many premodern Japanese humor collections.

36. See, for example, Sun, *Amulin xiaoshi* (The Hilarious Story of a Moron, 1923); Huang, *Dasha xiaoshi* (Hilarious Tales of Idiocy, 1930); [author unknown], *Kancainu xiaoshi* (The Hilarious Story of a Miser, 1920).

37. These include prose, rhapsodies, disquisitions, poems, jokes, stories, lantern riddles, and drinking songs. See Jiang Hangong, *Huaji shijie*. *Panorama of Play* (*Youxi daguan*), a six-volume book of amusements published in 1919, includes "joke games" (*xiaohua youxi*), along with word games, lantern riddles, drinking songs, science experiments, and athletic games.

38. Davies, *Jokes and Targets*, 11. A notable exception to this consensus is the capacious amusement-based definition offered by the psychologist Christopher P. Wilson: "any stimulation that evokes amusement and that is experienced as being funny." Wilson treats "joke" as synonymous with "humor." See Wilson, *Jokes*, 2.

39. Cohen, *Jokes*, 1–2.

40. Ibid., 4.

41. Wang Liqi has gone so far as to claim that the vast majority of *xiaohua* created by literati during the dynastic period were about "real people and real events." See Wang, *Lidai xiaohua ji*, i.

42. "*Xiaobao* fu" ("Rhapsody to *Laughter*"), cited in *Zhongguo wenxue da cidian*, 6:4373. "Xiaohua ze xinwen" in the first line could also be interpreted as "news items-cum-jokes."

43. Zheng, *Zheng Yimei xuanji*, 1:802.

44. See Jian [Wu Jianren], "Pingbu qingyun (xiaobing)," *Yueyue xiaoshuo* 5 (27 February 1907), 189–92. A modern edition changes *bing* 枋 in the title to the common variant *bing* 柄. See *WJQJ*, 7:42–44.

45. Part 1 of *Huitu xuetang xiaohua, yiming xuetang xianxingji* contains an additional title on the first page of its main text, "The Mercurial Pedant" ("Xuejiu bianxiang"); identifies the author as a certain Old Lin (Lao Lin); and identifies the genre of the book as *huaji xiaoshuo*. See chapters 3 and 5 on *xiaohua*, *youxi*, and *huaji* being used interchangeably as markers for the comic genre.

46. See Xu, *Huaju chuangshiqi huiyilu*, 9. The 10 April 1914 issue of the *Chinese Students' Monthly* (9, no. 6, 494) contains in the column "Wit and Humor" an example of what might be called an English-language *xiaohua* in the form of an amusing anecdote about "Why John Wang Ordered His First Pair of Glasses":

> Mr. John Wong is a mighty jolly fellow as everybody knows. Why he ordered his first pair of glasses is rather amusing. While in Peking he was once

asked to a banquet, and for one thing or another he was rather late in coming. When he came in the guests had all been seated, and looked upon him rather reproachfully. John, being somewhat embarrassed, turned round to find a place to hang up his coat. All the hooks were taken. On the side of the wall John discovered a black spot, and thinking this must be a nail, he began to lift his coat to it. It was nothing but a fly. This caused an uproar. Turning around he saw yet another black spot just like the first one. To avenge himself he gave this spot a hard blow. It turned out to be a real nail in the wall this time. He bought a pair of glasses after the banquet that very day.

47. Chen Pingyuan identifies three types of jokes: those adapted from previously published jokes, those already in oral circulation that had not yet been written down, and newly authored jokes. See Chen, *Zhongguo xiaoshuo xushi moshi de zhuanbian*, 163–65.

48. Wu, *Ershi nian mudu zhi guai xianzhuang*, 49–52.

49. "Ni shuo zhe bushi qiren bai jiazi de pingju me?" (ibid., 52). A conversation in chapter 7 further illustrates how Wu Jianren uses *xiaohua* in two senses, as true funny story and as made-up joke. The narrator runs into the servant who witnessed the incident. Gao Sheng confirms that the story "is true, not just a joke" (*shi shishi, bing bushi xiaohua*) and then proceeds to tell him about "another funny incident" (*haiyou ge xiaohua ne*) that happened the night before (59–60).

50. This includes both Chinese and non-Chinese readers. See Huang, "Qintai keju"; Bishop, "Some Limitations of Chinese Fiction," 240–41.

51. See Elliott, *The Manchu Way*, chap. 4, especially p. 176 on Lao She's humorous accounts of his Manchu bannerman relatives' indolence.

52. On *guanchang xiaohua* in *Yuyan bao* (1901–5), see Wang, "The Weight of Frivolous Matters," 93. English translation of the journal title is from the Heidelberg Chinese Entertainment Newspapers (*xiaobao*) database: www.sino.uni-heidelberg.de/xiaobao/index.php?p=start.

53. These two episodes appear in Wu, *Ershi nian mudu zhi guai xianzhuang*, 95, 202–3.

54. Chen, *Zhongguo xushi moshi de zhuanbian*, 163.

55. *Jianguai buguai*. See Wang, *Fin-de-siècle Splendor*, 189, 200. On the literariness of late Qing journalism, and the blurring of fictional and factual, see Mittler, *A Newspaper for China?*, chap. 1, esp. 86–104, 113–17. Other studies of Chinese novelistic satire and exposé up to the late Qing, discussed under various generic rubrics, include: Hsia, *C. T. Hsia on Chinese Literature*, 30–49; Huters et al., *Culture & State in Chinese History*, chap. 2. Abridged English translations of the two most famous exposé novels of this period are available as Wu, *Vignettes from the Late Ch'ing*, and Yang, *Officialdom Unmasked*.

56. See Wu, *Ershi nian mudu zhi guai xianzhuang*, 602–6. The narrator's joke features several of the types of social "devils" (drunk devil, and so on) mentioned in chapter 4.

57. Chen, *Zhongguo xushi moshi de zhuanbian*, 165.

58. The writer emotes: "Alas for self-governance! For it I shed tears." The term *guaizhuang* is virtually equivalent to Wu's *guai xianzhuang*. See "Zizhiju yiyuan zhi jinq-

ianzhuyi" ("Self-Governance Bureau Representative's Money-ism"), reprinted in *THRB*, 4:142.

59. Periodicals that regularly carried jokes include, to name a few, *New Fiction*, the *True Record*, the *Recreation World*, the *Scarlet Magazine*, *Red Rose*, the *Sunday*, the *China Critic*, the *Analects Fortnightly*, and *Shun Pao*.

60. *Forest of Laughs* (*Xiaolin bao*, 1901–10) "had a national distribution network of twenty-two cities and locales" within two years of its inauguration. See Wang, "Officialdom Unmasked," 89. *Variety News* (*Caifeng bao*, 1898–1911), which Wu Jianren edited for a time, promised to feature "jokes and amusing stories" along with strikingly original opinion pieces. Its promise of *xiaohua xietan* appears in the preface (*xu*) to issue 1 (July 1898). A daily newspaper, it later carried the English title of *Cha Fung Poa*. Another tabloid called itself simply *Laughter* (*Xiao bao*, est. 1897).

61. This claim covers only works from the imperial period that have been anthologized (or mentioned) in modern collections under the rubric of *xiaohua*. The number of actual joke collections produced during the imperial period is of course impossible to calculate, since many have been lost. Around one hundred joke books dating between the second century BCE and 1910 are mentioned in the following modern collections: Chen and Guo, *Zhongguo lidai xiaohua jicheng* (5 vols.) (1996); Wang, *Lidai xiaohua ji* (1957); Yang, *Zhongguo xiaohua shu* (2002). This count includes thirty-six presumed joke books listed in *Lidai xiaohua ji* (576–80) whose titles are extant but whose contents are not. Some "joke collections" in this count include caches of jokes appearing in encyclopedia (*leishu*). One Ming encyclopedia (not extant) is said to have contained 18,890 jokes. (See Mair, *The Columbia History of Chinese Literature*, 135.) Of these secondary sources, the most complete collection of premodern Chinese jokes is Chen and Guo's. However, Guo explains in a preface (5) that the editors included "more high-level and elegant" jokes from the Ming-Qing period, suggesting that they excluded jokes they considered to be unfunny or dirty.

62. Zhou, *Kucha'an xiaohua xuan*, 4. Joke anthologists, to name a few, came from the following hometowns: Cheng Zhanlu, Cui Bingleng, Hu Shanyuan (see chapter 6), Li Boyuan, Li Dingyi, Xu Zhuodai, and Zheng Yimei were from Jiangsu. Lei Jin (aka Li Junyao) was from Songjiang County, and Wang Dungen from Qingpu, both just outside Shanghai. Wu Jianren's family was from Guangdong, though he was born in Beijing. T. K. Chuan, Fan Fan, Yan Fusun, Zhao Tiaokuang, and Zhou Zuoren were from Zhejiang. Hu Jichen, editor of *The Story World*, and Li Jingzhong were from Anhui.

63. *Po ti lu* takes its title from the expression *po ti wei xiao*, or "to go from crying to laughing." The cover described here is from the third edition. The National Library of Australia holds a copy with a different cover featuring a Western child yelling "Hooyeema!" An advertisement pasted to the inside of the cover says that *Laughing Through Tears* is meant to make up for the inadequacies (*buzu*) of books like *The Expanded Forest of Laughter*. In the first joke in the collection, a foreigner moves into the house of the new republic only to discover that its "paper walls and clay government" disintegrate at the touch. More allegorical metaphors of this sort are discussed in chapter 3. Lu Xun, as discussed below, later more famously likened China to a suffocating "iron house." On *Civil Rights* and the Civil Rights Press, see Zheng, *Shubao huajiu*, 253–55.

64. See the copyright pages in Qinshi shanren's *Kefa yi xiao* (1921 ed. [1st ed. 1918]) and Hu Jichen's (1886–1938) *Pengfu tan* (1927 ed. [1st ed. 1913]).

65. Zhao, *Guifang xiaoshi*. Zhao's preface, dated 1921, says that in the spring he had written a book of jokes about love and courtship for fun and that within a week of publication it had been reprinted three times. Urged by friends, he put together the current book in the matter of a few days, drawing material from conversations with his friend Mr. Zhou (likely Zhou Shoujuan, a fellow writer and colleague). Zhao edited, among other popular magazines, *The Recreation World* and *Red Rose*, both published by World Books, and was a friend of Xu Zhuodai, discussed in chapter 5.

66. Chenhai Chixiaosheng, *Zengguang gujin xiaolin xinya yiqianzhong*.

67. One nineteenth-century scholar estimated that less than 1 percent of unsolicited jokes submitted to London's *Punch* by readers made it to press and contrasted *Punch*'s selectivity with the purportedly more liberal editorial culture of the United States. He further speculated that "Though undoubtedly many of *Punch*'s jokes are deliberately manufactured, or else improved from actual incidents, a vast number ... are used with but slight textual editing, just as they occurred." One *Punch* editor is said to have placed a wholesale order of five jokes only to discover that three were "former *Punch* friends, and the remaining two were old ones of his own invention!" See Spielmann. *The History of "Punch,"* 139, 143. From chapter 6: "*Punch*'s Jokes—Their Origin, Pedigree, and Appropriation."

68. A colleague responded by publishing a handful of "Jokes in Western Dress." See Bucaizi, "Yangzhuang de xiaohua" ("Jokes in Western Dress"), *HM* 2:10 (24 October 1925).

69. The author of the story about Xiong (1870–1937) also cites an anecdote about the female education reformer and journalist Zhang Mojun (1883–1965) (founder of the *National Herald*), who, while serving as a school principal, told a stale joke about Su Dongpo at a banquet but was lauded for her originality by a group of sycophants. Cuixiu, "Zhang Mojun yu Xiong Xiling de xiaohua" ("Zhang Mojun and Xiong Xiling: Two Jokes"), *Sanri huabao* 11 (1 September 1925), 2.

70. "Sha zhu yingxiong," from *Xiaoquan*, reprinted in Hou, *Hou Baolin jiucang zhenben minguo xiaohua xuan*, 253.

71. Yugong, *Qian xiao ji*.

72. Literary historian Patrick Hanan notes that "if a broad distinction is drawn between the comic anecdote, told of famous figures, and the joke, which is about social types, the anecdote can be seen to predominate in virtually all joke books up until the last part of the Ming." Hanan adds that Feng Menglong "actually made the distinction in his own practice; [one collection] consists of anecdotes, mostly comic, while the *Treasury [of Laughs]* is entirely jokes." See Hanan, *The Chinese Vernacular Story*, 90.

73. Jenkins, *What Made Pistachio Nuts?*, 38–39.

74. Zheng Yimei (1895–1992), Shanghai's *bubai dawang*, remembered his colleague Xu Zhuodai closing letters by wishing him "happy space-filling!" (*bu'an*). See Zheng, *Qingmo Minchu wentan yishi*, 193.

75. For more on the influence of *Punch* from Turkey and Egypt to India, China, and Japan, see Harder and Mittler, *Asian Punches*. On *China Punch* and *Puck, or the Shanghai Charivari*, see my chapter in that volume (389–422): "'He'll Roast All Subjects That May Need the Roasting': Puck and Mr Punch in Nineteenth-Century China."

76. Parton, *Caricature and Other Comic Art in All Times and Many Lands*, 196–97. *Anatheum* appeared from 1828–1921.

77. This account of a conversation about jokes (*xiaobing*) with Zhang Ziwei (fl. 1900s) appears in the preface to *Zhongguo zhentan an* (Chinese Detective Cases), in *WJQJ*, 7:71.

78. [Lin] Buqing, "Xieyin quyu" (Puns), *Yuxing* (Amusements) 1 (1914), 96.

79. Make Tuwen [Mark Twain], *Xiaohua* (1935).

80. "Wit and Humor," *Chinese Students' Monthly* 9, no. 4 (10 February 1914), 312. The locations of the *Monthly*'s editorial and business office changed over the years, its longest run being at Columbia University. Most of the jokes in the column rely on puns. See issues 9, no. 4 (10 February 1914), 311–12; 9, no. 5 (10 March 1914); 9, no. 6 (10 April 1914), 494–95.

81. "80 Marriages," *CC* 10, no. 7 (15 August 1935), 147. Some contributors to the *China Critic*, such as T. K. Chuan, had previously written for the *Chinese Students' Monthly*.

82. "Annexation," *CC* 10, no. 8 (22 August 1935), 175.

83. Longxiyishi, "Fakanci" ("Publishing Manifesto"), *Yican* 1 (5 November 1927).

84. The joke is entitled "Funei kong luosuo." See *Duiyi Taiwan xiaohua ji*, listed in appendix 1.

85. Zhou Zuoren, "Ren de wenxue," in Zhou, *Zhou Zuoren jingdian zuopin xuan*, 7–8.

86. See Zhou, *Kucha'an xiaohua xuan*. Zhou had published some of these serially in Beijing's *Morning Post* in the 1920s, until its general editor discontinued the series. Sun Fuyuan, the editor of the *Post*'s literary supplement, protested this action and, in Zhou's account, was forced to leave the paper. Sun went on to be the inaugural editor of the magazine *Threads of Discourse*, discussed in chapter 4. See Denton and Hockx, *Literary Societies of Republican China*, 175.

87. Zhou's annotation to one of the Xu Wenchang stories describes their value as being in their "Rabelaisian" energy of the people and their inclusion of many "elements unsuitable for moral instruction" (*buke weixun de fenzi*). See Zhou, *Kucha'an xiaohua xuan*, 206.

88. Ibid., 5.

89. See the introduction to the 1932 edition of Qingdu sanke, *Xiao zan*. *Xiao zan* drew on at least ten earlier joke books. See Yang, *Zhongguo xiaohua shu*, 516–18.

90. T. K. Chuan, "The Little Critic: 'Chinese Humor,'" *CC* 6, no. 3 (19 January 1933), 69–70. Commentary appears in Qingdu sanke, *Xiao zan*, 14–15.

91. The preface to Duyiwo tuishi's *Xiaoxiao lu* is also reprinted in a 1985 edition by Changsha's Yuelu shushe, which carries different punctuation.

92. This anecdote is related by Hou Baolin's (1917–93) child, Hou Xin, in the preface to Hou, *Hou Baolin jiucang zhenben Minguo xiaohua xuan*, 3.

93. Lin Buqing (1860–1917) is credited as narrator (*koushuzhe*) and the pseudonymous Qian Xiangsi (Moneylike) as transcriber (*bishuzhe*) in Lin and Qian, *Nannü xin xiaohua*.

94. "Epianzi zhi xiaohua: pianshu qiaomiao" ("Jokes about Swindlers: A Brilliant Trick"), in ibid., 21. A version of this joke from the Ming collection *Elegant Banter* (*Yanuë*) is translated in Kowallis, *Wit and Humor from Old Cathay*, 64–65. Other jokes from imperial collections are translated in Giles, *Quips from a Chinese Jest Book*.

95. Ye Qianyu's (1907–95) cartoon might also have been inspired by "Catching Fools" ("Zhuo hutuchong"), a version of the same joke appearing in Xiaoshi daoren's *More Truly*

Delightful Chats (*Zhengxu Xitan lu*, ca. 1882–84), in which it is a local official, rather than a fellow peasant, who tells the man to cut the pole in half.

96. Xu Xu, "Lunzhan de wenzhang yu maren de wenzhang" ("Literary Debating and Literary Mud-Slinging"). In Xu, *Xu Xu wenji*, 9:490.

97. Taozhui [Zhou Shuren], "Bangxianfa fayin" ("The Secret to Promoting Leisure"), *SB* 21695 (5 September 1933), 19. Title translation of this essay from *LXSW*, 3:346–47. Even some of Lin Yutang's fellow travelers in the humor movement used similar language. Decades later, Xu Xu (1908–80), who served as editor of Lin Yutang's 1930s magazine *This Human World*, distinguished between "telling the truth" (*zhenhua*) and "telling jokes" (*xiaohua*). See Xu Xu, "Zhenhua yu xiaohua" ("Telling the Truth and Telling Jokes") (1968), in Xu, *Xu Xu wenji*, 10:328–29.

98. Frankfurt, *On Bullshit*, 38, 60–61. Frankfurt adds that although bullshit is "produced without concern with the truth, it need not be false. The bullshitter is faking things. But this does not mean that he necessarily gets them wrong" (47–48).

CHAPTER 3. PLAY

1. Lin, *The Importance of Living*, 65.

2. A tangram is a paper-folding game also known as "seven-piece puzzle." *Daguan*, literally "grand view," was, similar to "world," a common trope that periodicals used to signal their comprehensiveness.

3. Chiung-yun Liu notes that the author's "play" includes alteration of an earlier narrative of a Dharma-seeking pilgrimage; inclusion of "humorous episodes with dubious religious meanings"; and mixing of categories and discourses. She adds that the author "delights in playing with the established meanings of various religious signifiers to highlight the incompleteness of the journey." See Liu, "Scriptures and Bodies," 17, 21.

4. On Crazy Ji, see Shahar, *Crazy Ji*.

5. *Woyou*, as used in pictorials such as the *Shun Pao*'s *Dianshizhai huabao*, is discussed in several studies in Wagner, *Joining the Global Public*, esp. 154–55, 194, 200, 204.

6. Riddle-poems and line-matching games (often involving spontaneous composition) were popular with the literati and appear in novels such as *Dream of the Red Chamber* and *Flowers in the Mirror*. Acrostic poems with hidden political messages date as early as the first century CE. On these and other varieties, see Wolfgang Behr's chapter in Voogt and Finkel, *The Idea of Writing*, 281–314. Anne Birrell has shown that the ludic mode "dominates" one influential medieval literary anthology, in which she finds "verbal games, poetry competitions, riddles, parody, illusory play, artifice, performance play, and . . . the representation of desire as a power game." All of these varieties of play appear in the early twentieth century as well. See Birrell, *Games Poets Play*, 13, and chap. 1, esp. 41–42 on postmodern theories about the relation between play and laughter.

7. On the reception of Han Yu's (768–824) "E'yu jiwen," see Owen, *The End of the Chinese "Middle Ages*,*"* 60.

8. Translation of *Zhongguo zuida youxi zhi chang* modified from Wagner, *Joining the Global Public*, 204. On late Qing literati's use of playground symbolism, see also Yeh, *Shanghai Love*; Zhang, *Zhongguo jindai chengshi qiye, shehui, kongjian*, 308–35.

9. *Jishi xingle bao* was established in 1901. See Wang, "The Weight of Frivolous Matters," 8, 68.

10. The title *Youxi bao* has been translated as *Entertainment* (by Catherine Yeh), *Fun* (by Juan Wang), and *Recreation News* (by Theodore Huters). While the periodical's ethos and self-marketing encompasses all of these elements, I translate it as *Play* to emphasize the semantic continuity with the various practices of "playing" that use the same Chinese word. As these scholars note, *Play* was the most influential of several periodicals Li founded between the 1890s and 1900s.

11. Li went by Youxi zhuren. The guidebook was coauthored. See Haishang youxizhu, *Haishang youxi tushuo* (Illustrated Guide to Shanghai Game Playing) Shanghai, (lithograph), 1895. Cited in the bibliography of Yeh, "Reinventing Ritual."

12. Wagner, *Joining the Global Public*, 209-10.

13. See Yeh, "Reinventing Ritual."

14. Li's words, from an 1899 announcement accompanying the printing of *Play* contents in book form, were *yi huixie zhibi, xie youxi zhi wen*. Quoted in *LBQJ*, 5:37. One essay prescribed that works be profound (*hou* 厚), insightful (*tou* 透), fluid (*liu* 溜), grounded (*kou* 扣), witty (*dou* 逗), and concise (*gou* 夠) while proscribing vulgarity (*lou* 陋), cliché (*cou* 湊), inchoateness (*lou* 漏), and ugliness (*chou* 丑). See Baiyun ciren, "Youxi wenzi zhi liufa siji" ("Six Techniques and Four Prohibitions for Playful Writings"), in *LBQJ*, 5:154-55. The editors note that Li Boyuan's authorship of this piece is probable but not definitive.

15. *Xiaobao, Xiaoxianbao, Xiaolin bao* were three of more than three dozen that appeared within fifteen years. See Wang, "Officialdom Unmasked," 85-86. The journal's popularity is also mentioned in *LBQJ*, 5:37. Years later, Zheng Yimei, a participant, gadfly, and historian of Republican Shanghai's literary sphere, remembered that the paper's "humorous writings, jokes, and biographies of courtesans bowled over society." See Wei, *Li Boyuan yanjiu ziliao*, 22.

16. Sixteen issues of *Youxi shijie*, edited by Yin Bansheng (fl. 1900s), are reprinted in *Minguo tiyu qikan wenxian huibian* (Collection of Republican Sports Periodicals), vols. 55-60, a series published by China's Quanguo tushuguan wenxian suowei fuzhi zhongxin (Nationwide Library Materials Microfilm and Facsimile Reproduction Center).

17. World affairs, in Li's words, *zhen yi youzi zhi ju ye*. See "Lun *Youxi bao* zhi benyi" ("On the Fundamental Significance of *Play*"), *Youxi bao* 63 (25 August 1897). Reprinted in *LBQJ*, 5:27-28; "Lun benbao zhi bu he shiyi" ("Why This Paper Is Ahead of Its Time"), *Youxi bao* 149 (19 November 1897). Reprinted in *LBQJ*, 5:28-29.

18. *Fang zi taixi*. See *LBQJ* 5:27.

19. "Editorial," *The Rattle* 2, no. 1 (November 1900), 1. For an in-depth discussion of F. & C. Walsh's *Puck*, see Harder and Mittler, *Asian Punches*, 389-422.

20. Pope, *An Essay on Man*, 57.

21. This is the final stanza of "Pom Pom," *The Rattle* 2, no. 4 (May 1901), 51.

22. Judge, *Print and Politics*, 1. *The Future of New China* (*Xin Zhongguo weilai ji*) began serialization in issue 1, which also carried Liang's influential treatise "On the Relationship Between Fiction and the Government of the People" and three "New Examination Jokes" (*kaoshi xin xiaohua*). Its third chapter appeared in issue 2 and its fourth and final chapter in issue 3, which carried two of Wu Jianren's joke series. The following discussion

of Liang's novel is based on the original version serialized in *Xin xiaoshuo*, which was credited "by Yinbingshi zhuren [Liang Qichao]; commentary by Pingdengge zhuren [Di Baoxian]."

23. Liang was on record as saying that all Manchus and most women were idlers who did not contribute to national production. See Wang, *Chinese Intellectuals and the West*, 217. *New Fiction* was published in Yokohama until 1903 (after *The Future of New China* ceased publication), when it shifted to Shanghai. Another of Liang's magazines was *Sein Min Choong Bou* (*Xinmin congbao*, 1902–7), whose title Rudolf Wagner translates as *Reform the People Collecteana*. See Wagner, "China 'Asleep' and 'Awakening,'" 124.

24. Wang, *Chinese Intellectuals and the West*, 226.

25. Discussing education reform later in his speech (chap. 2), Old Mr. Kong makes the audience laugh by observing that when universities were first being founded across China in the early twentieth century, professors' qualifications were inferior to those of elementary school students today. See Yinbingshi zhuren, "Xin Zhongguo weilai ji," *Xin xiaoshuo* 1 (15 October 1902), 71. In 2004, about a century after Liang Qichao, China's central government began promoting overseas Confucius Institutes, reviving the image of the Sage as the international face of Chinese culture and learning.

26. On political thought in the novel, see Tang, *Global Space and the Nationalist Discourse of Modernity*, 165–223. Liang's setting proved attractive enough to inspire imitations. These include Chen Tianhua's novel *The Roar of the Lion* (*Shizi hou*, 1906), which was first serialized in Tokyo's *Minbao* (est. 1905). See Wagner, "China 'Asleep' and 'Awakening,'" 120–22.

27. With the notable exception of Beijing chubanshe's *Complete Works of Liang Qichao* (*Liang Qichao quanji*, 1999), most later editions of the novel omit these commentaries, thus giving the misimpression that the original work had only one voice.

28. Hill, "New Script (Sin Wenz) and a New 'Madman's Diary,'" 1. Futuristic fantasy was a major trend in late Qing fiction writing, inspired by foreign science fiction as well as domestic antecedents, such as Li Ruzhen's picaresque 1827 novel *Jinghua yuan*, which combines geographic travel with progressive social and political fantasy. A partial translation is available as Li, *Flowers in the Mirror*. On late Qing fantasy novels, see Wang, *Fin-de-siècle Splendor*, chap. 5. A translated selection of late Qing science fiction appears in the journal *Renditions* 77–78 (Spring–Fall 2012).

29. Wang, *Fin-de-siècle Splendor*, 23. See Wang's analysis of Liang's novel in chapter 5, esp. 302–6; also, 351n37, 354n89.

30. *New Fiction* often missed its monthly publication deadline, suggesting that Liang was simply overworked, not out of ideas for a new China. See Shi, *Liang Qichao yu Riben*, 218. Other examples of commentarial play may be found in *New Fiction* and its Shanghai successor, the *All-Story Monthly*, edited by Wu Jianren.

31. Di Chuqing (1873–1941), as he was also known, styled himself Pingdengge zhuren. While at *Eastern Times* (*Shibao*, 1904–39), he created a two-page daily supplement of funny stories, jokes, and advertisements called *Funny Eastern Times* (*Huaji Shibao*), which was anthologized in several volumes in 1915. Di split with Liang and Kang over ideological differences and control of *Eastern Times*, and he founded a rival version in northern China. For a detailed study of *Eastern Times*, Di Baoxian's involvement with the periodical, and

its turn from politics to general interest and entertainment after 1912, see Judge, *Print and Politics*, esp. 46–50, 195–97, 208.

32. On changes in Liang's political thinking from the 1890s through the 1900s, see Zarrow, *After Empire*, chap. 2, esp. 76. Liang himself contributed to the future of a new China, if briefly, as a member of the Beiyang government. After fourteen years abroad, he returned to China in October of 1912 and was appointed minister of justice in Yuan Shikai's cabinet. In 1915, he publicly opposed Yuan's bid to reestablish the monarchy, resigning his post and taking refuge in the Japanese concession in Tianjin. After Yuan's death he focused on scholarship and writing reformist essays. See Young, *The Presidency of Yuan Shih-k'ai*, 122; Ch'en, *Yuan Shih-k'ai*, 171–72.

33. As other scholars have pointed out, the late Qing genre of futuristic fiction was closely tied to the fantastical graphic images popularized by *Dianshizhai Pictorial* in the 1880s of spacecraft and other technological novelties. Futurism extended to drama too. In late 1906 or early 1907, young drama students in Shanghai mounted a play called *China Ten Years Hence*. See Huang, *Chinese Shakespeares*, 61. Wu Jianren's *Xin Shitouji* began serialization in issue 28 of *Nanfang bao* on 19 September 1905, less than a month after the daily's launch, and continued in *New Fiction* in March of the following year. It was published as an illustrated forty-chapter book in 1908.

34. On the anachronistic and paradoxical figure of Lao Shaonian, see Song, "Long Live Youth," chap. 1.

35. Jones, *Developmental Fairy Tales*, 31. *Haidi lüxing* was retranslated from an 1884 Japanese translation of the French original, known in English as *Twenty Thousand Leagues under the Sea*. It began serialization in *New Fiction* in 1902 in the same issue as *The Future of New China*.

36. Wang, *Fin-de-siècle Splendor*, 282. Andrew Jones echoes this view in characterizing Baoyu as a figure tortured by his own impotence: "Haunted by the past, a belated bystander to a history that has yet to unfold, Bao-yu is ultimately denied even the consolation of agency and consigned to the scrap heap of evolutionary history." See Jones, *Developmental Fairy Tales*, 62.

37. Wang, *Fin-de-siècle Splendor*, 273.

38. Harris, *Humbug*, 61–89. Harris's study extends beyond Barnum the man to analyze nineteenth-century American culture, beginning in the pre–Civil War Jacksonian era (ca. 1828–50s).

39. Chapters 12–17 of *New Story of the Stone*, for instance, include a protracted revenge subplot set against the Boxer Rebellion.

40. The *zazhi* (literally, miscellaneous records), which would usually be translated as "magazine," was in fact a six-volume book, published in March 1914 by Shanghai's Saoye shanfang. The phrase on everyone's lips is *wuzu gonghe le*.

41. "Renshi nanfeng kaikou xiao" is from Du Mu's "Climbing Mount Qi on the Double-Ninth Holiday" ("Jiuri Qishan denggao") (the author modifies "in the mortal realm" *chenshi* to "in a lifetime" *renshi*). "Shenmei yixiao qi yide" is from Su Dongpo's "Dengzhou: A City on the Sea" ("Dengzhou haishi"). Du Mu's line alludes to a comment in one of the "miscellaneous chapters" of the Warring States era Daoist text *Zhuangzi* that given the illnesses and worries one faces in life, "one might laugh no more than four or five days a month."

42. The British pressed their territorial interests in Tibet after its de facto independence from China in 1912. Though Mr. Tottering would not have anticipated it, the Simla Accord would cede South Tibet to British India in 1914. A cartoon of foreigners carving up Tibet appears in *Illustration Daily*, circa 1910. See *THRB* 215, 9, in Shanghai guji reprint, 5:177.

43. "The Bird and the Shell-Fish," for example, draws on an old parable to show the North and South quarreling and thereby making themselves "the easy prey of some covetous fishermen," Japan and Russia, while the boyish nation-state of New China and his Western adviser look on. This bilingual cartoon originally appeared in the *National Review*, a Shanghai-based paper supportive of Yuan Shikai, on 3 February 1912, a month after the founding of the Republic of China. The image is reprinted in VALDAR and others, *The History of China for 1912 in Cartoons, with Explanatory Notes in Chinese and English*, n.p. Cartoons of the Qing empire being carved up also circulated on postcards. Several French and German examples are reprinted in Zeng, *Bengkui de diguo*, 55–57, 179.

44. *Guafen*, or "to carve like a melon," became a generic term for partition in the nineteenth century. Early Republican examples can be found in the series "The Melon Game" ("Gua xi"), which appeared in the newspaper *Civil Rights*. On this transnational motif, see Wagner, "China 'Asleep' and 'Awakening.'" The term *pogua*, or "break the melon," appears in literature as early as the Ming dynasty; see Feng, *Feng Menglong quanji*, 23:1298. On its use in Shanghai brothels, see Hershatter, *Dangerous Pleasures*, 107; cf. Wang and Xu, *Shanghai suyu tushuo*, 11. Chinese cartoons occasionally applied the split melon motif to foreign countries. In one cartoon dating from 1918, America uses the sword of democracy to carve the melon of Kaiserism, draped with a German flag, at a post–World War I "peace banquet" attended by various foreign leaders. See *Shanghai Puck* 1, no. 3 (November 1918), 22.

45. Saoye shanfang's offerings for 1914 included Wu Jianren's *Funny Chats* and a thicker book of *Funny Chats from the Garden of Literature* edited by Lei himself (2nd ed., 1924). In 1917 it issued Guo Yaochen's joke book *Bowled Over*. See appendix 1. On the history of the press, which saw its business decline in the 1920s, see Reed, *Gutenberg in Shanghai*, 101–2, 287, 321n51.

46. An advertisement for Yunjian diangong's *Man-Qing guanchang baiguai lu* (Myriad Oddities of Manchu-Qing Officialdom) appears at the back of Saoye shanfang's 1914 edition of Wu Jianren's *Wofoshanren's Funny Chats*. It was reprinted in 1925. Lei later worked for many years as an editor at *Shun Pao*.

47. "Free Talk" was first edited by Wang Dungen (1888–1950). Editorship later passed to the popular writer Zhou Shoujuan (1919–32), followed by the author and translator Li Liewen (1932–34). "On Playful Writings," a parodic essay that appeared in "Free Talk" in 1917, echoes Wu Jianren's argument that a comical style is the most effective way to get a point across, claiming that playful writings have the capacity "first, to save the nation and second, to change the culture" (*da ze jiuguo, ci zu yifeng*), and citing the antecedent of Sima Qian's "Biographies of Court Wits." See Jihang, "Youxi wenzhang lun—fang Ouyang Xiu huanzhe zhuanlun" ("On Playful Writings: In Imitation of Ouyang Xiu's 'Discourse on Eunuchs'"), *SB* 16037 (6 October 1917), 14. On the contributions of "Free Talk" to the development of China's public sphere, see Lee, *Xiandaixing de zhuiqiu*, chap. 1. Li Boyuan's

personal literary fame also continued posthumously. In the early 1920s, for example, the *Recreation World* featured a "Famous Work" (*mingzhu*) column dedicated to Li's "humorous writings" (*xiewen*).

48. Tong Ailou, "*Ziyou zazhi* zhushi" ("Congratulatory Poem for *Free Magazine*"), *Ziyou zazhi* 1 (October 1913), 2.

49. On mockery in the late Qing tabloids, see Juan Wang's book *Merry Laughter and Angry Curses*.

50. The original English title of *Youxi zazhi* was *The Pastime*. Haiyan Lee translates *Ziyou zazhi* as *Liberty Magazine*; I translate it as *Free Magazine* (though it did cost money) to illustrate the link with *Shun Pao*'s "Free Talk." Lee notes that Wang Dungen's coeditor at *Free Magazine* (*Ziyou zazhi*), Tong Ailou, promoted the conceit that *Free Magazine* offered a "dime store of words" for readers to browse at their leisure. See Lee, "A Dime Store of Words," 54. The metaphor of miscellany (*za*) found in the words *magazine* (*zazhi*) and *dime store* (*zahuodian*) is, to me, also emblematic of *youxi* culture's emphasis on experimentation and exploration. The choose-your-own-amusement ethos is akin is to the variety structure of American vaudeville shows that, for a flat fee, allowed customers to enter and exit the venue at any point to watch a repeating series of acts. *Illustration Daily* had in 1909–10 employed the same metaphor in the series "A Dime Store of New Knowledge" ("Xin zhishi zhi zahuodian"), which contained comical, satirical, and allegorical cartoons.

51. Wu Jianren's *Xin Fengshen zhuan* appeared in *Yueyue xiaoshuo* in 1907. Bao Tianxiao's *Xin Xiyouji*, serialized in *Youxi shijie* beginning in issue 9 (February 1922), is advertised as having been "narrated in jest" (*xishu*) (see issue 10). Part of Bao's *Xin Jinghua yuan* appears in *Huaji* 1 (1923). Yet another *New Journey to the West*, by Huang Yanqing, was published in Hong Kong by Yanqing chubanbu in 1934. Novelistic mash-ups continued to be popular in 1950s Hong Kong, in which the experience of postwar exile contributed to the popularity of a genre John Christopher Hamm calls "comedies of displacement." See Hamm, *Paper Swordsmen*, chap. 3.

52. Numerous pieces with these prefaces appear in Yanyun jushi's *Huaji wenji* (preface 1910), for example, 49–50, 62, 93–96, 125–28, 130–32, 134–35, 145–46, 149–50, 177, 202. The following definition of parody, an evaluative mode, is probably accurate, though as Simon Dentith notes elsewhere, the devil is in the cultural work it does: "Parody includes any cultural practice which provides a relatively polemical allusive imitation of another cultural production or practice." Dentith, *Parody*, 9.

53. The parody substitutes well-known Shanghai place-names and retains rhyming words of the original. The parodist even places *paiban* (pimp) to alliterate with *jiangnan* (the south) in the third line. See Du Fu, *Du Shaoling xiangzhu*, 2, 1199; Ma Er xiansheng, "Fang Tangshi: Yeji" ("Parody of a Tang Poem: Street-Walker"), *Shanghai Puck* 1, no. 1 (1 September 1918), 25. The parody might have been improved further by substituting *xunjing*, which has a similar meaning to *xunbu* (policeman on the beat), so as to alliterate with Du Fu's *fengjing* (scenery). The first issue of *Free Magazine* five years earlier contained a piece entitled "Whoring (a New *Classic of Poetry*)" ("Piao [xin *Shijing*]").

54. *Mi zhuchong*, *Fantong* (literally, rice bucket), and *Renmian xie* appear in the "playful writings" section of *Ziyou zazhi* 1 (September 1913). Haohao xiansheng, Gui xiansheng,

Mapi xiaojie, and *Koutou chong* appear in the first section in Li, *Huaji hun* (1919). On the mid-Tang dating, see Franke, "Literary Parody in Traditional Chinese Literature," 24.

55. "Zujie malu fu" (in the style of "Afang gong fu"), appeared on the front page of *Xiaolin bao* (1901–10) on 2 April 1901. Tao Baopi's [Newspaper Addict] "He qiong wen" ("In Praise of Poverty") is collected in Yanyun jushi, *Huaji wenji* (1910), 11–13.

56. Jiaoxin, "Shi tan" ("Louse Chat"), *Yuxing* 1 (1914), 54.

57. *Huaji hun*'s credited authors include Li Boyuan, Li Dingyi, Gong Shaoqin, and Lu Wanliang. Other pseudonyms include Hilarious, Poetry Addict, Weeping Ape, and Sick Man. News items are uncredited. A second edition appeared in 1923, and another in 1935.

58. Zhe Lu, "Yangui wei kexue quancai shuo," in Li, *Huaji hun*, section 1, 4–5. The table of contents gives the title as "The Opium Addict Master of the Female Sciences" ("Yangui nü kexue quancai"), likely an editing error, as gender is not its focus. This parody bears some resemblance to the facetious praise of Chinese scientific ingenuity with opium in Peng Yang'ou's 1909 novel *Souls from the Land of Darkness* (*Heiji yuanhun*), summarized in McMahon, *The Fall of the God of Money*, 146–47. Wu Jianren's modest proposal to solve the opium problem was to open an opium den and sell a cut-price product with a time-delay poison that kills the addict. See "Jue yapian miaofa" ("An Ingenious Solution to the Opium Problem"), in Wofoshanren, "Zalu: Xin Xiaolin guangji," *Xin xiaoshuo* 17 (May 1905), 159.

59. Xiangsan, "Zhi yatong," in Li, *Huaji hun*, section 3, 5. A different funny practical advice column appeared in the *Scarlet Magazine* in the 1920s.

60. Motifs of illness and cure have permeated literary and pictorial representations of China since the nineteenth century. See, for example, Schonebaum, "Fictional Medicine"; Heinrich, *The Afterlife of Images*.

61. One notable defection was Wu Youru (1840?–93?), a chief illustrator of *Dianshizhai Pictorial*, who left in 1890 to found his own pictorial, *Feiyingge huabao*. On the history of the former institution, see Ye, *The Dianshizhai Pictorial*.

62. Founded in Shanghai by Tongmeng hui member Yu Youren (1879–1964), the *National Herald* (*Shenzhou ribao*, 1907–47) began as an anti-Qing daily and reached a circulation of more than ten thousand copies. After the founding of the republic, Yuan Shikai (1859–1916) purchased the *Herald* and installed a sympathetic legislator as editor. For more on its history, see Wagner, "China 'Asleep' and 'Awakening,'" 101; Jing and Ke, *Diguo bengkui qian de yingxiang*, 3.

63. [Ma] Xingchi, "Fang chuan," *Shenzhou huabao* (10 August 1909). Reprinted in *QDBK*, 5:269.

64. Liu E's novel contains several autobiographical episodes, like this one, based on the personal experiences of the author. Political cartoonists renewed the free speech theme in the 1910s when factions of the Beiyang government began to repress journalists and publishers. See, for example, the cartoons in the October 1918 issue of Shen Bochen's (1889–1920) *Shanghai Puck* protesting the mass arrest of journalists and closure of newspapers following their disclosure of the premier's acceptance of secret loans from Japan.

65. Information on Ma Xingchi (1873–1934) is from a Shandong Provincial Government website about historical figures and personalities from the Jining locality: http://sd.infobase.gov.cn/bin/mse.exe?seachword=&K=a&A=84&rec=1350&run=13. *The True Record*'s publishing manifesto: Yingbo, "Fakanci," *Zhenxiang huabao* 1 (5 June 1912), 4–6. Ed-

ited and printed in Shanghai, it had a Guangdong bureau and was distributed nationwide and in colonial Hong Kong.

66. Ma Xingchi, "Eguo yuyan/The Unwholesome Fruit (A Metaphor)," *Zhenxiang huabao* 17 (1 March 1913), n.p.

67. A regular Chinese-drawn comic strip did not appear until Ye Qianyu's *Mr. Wang* debuted in *Shanghai Sketch* in 1928. The character was so popular that Ye was contracted to create multiple versions of the strip for newspapers in Shanghai, Nanjing, and Tianjin. In the 1930s and 1940s, films were made based on the character. A comic strip entitled *Taishi xiansheng*, whose hero is clearly based on Mr. Wang, followed shortly on *Mr. Wang*'s heels, debuting in Guangzhou's *The Sketch* (*Banjiao manhua*) in 1929. Chinese versions of *The Katzenjammer Kids* and *Mutt and Jeff* (ca. 1910s), are reprinted in *QDBK*, 10:76–77, 80–81.

68. *Civil Rights*, which was shut down after the failed Second Republican Revolution of 1913, also serialized Xu Zhenya's blockbuster novel *Jade Pear Spirit* (*Yuli hun*, 1912). *Minhu ribao*, a contemporary, was similarly aggressive in its political cartooning.

69. Several illustrations depicting the ape sleeping reinterpret the long-standing "China asleep and awakening" paradigm of international discourse about China. Some show Yuan Shikai's awakening as too early and him as *insufficiently* passive—he should be waiting for natural processes to run their course. See *QDBK*, 11:43. A cartoon published on 2 October 1912, "Dreaming of Being at the Center" ("Zhongyang meng"), shows the ape reaching for a placard reading "Long live the emperor," indicating that Yuan's imperial ambitions were evident soon into his presidency.

70. See, for example: "Qingting wudao, yousha weixin" 凊廷無道又殺維新 ("The Qing Court Again Wantonly Slaughters Reformists") in *Meilibao bu Aiguo bao* (5 August 1903), 2–3. I am grateful to Luo Haizhi of the University of New South Wales for alerting me to this common practice in Australia-based Chinese-language newspapers of the era, and for sharing this source with me.

71. In September of 1908, the court belatedly announced principles for a proposed constitution that reserved ultimate power for itself. See Ch'en, *Yuan Shih-k'ai*, 71, 79–82.

72. The image appears as Zhenye, "Yuanzi zhi jieguo" ("Yuan's End"), *Minquan bao* 50 (16 May 1912). Funny words appeared in a variety of publications, including *Illustration Daily*, *Eastern Times*, *Civil Rights*, *The True Record*, *Tee Ooh Pao* (*Tianduo bao* 天鐸報, 1910s; literally *Heavenly Bell*), *People's Cry Daily* (*Minhu ribao*, 1909), *People's Sigh Daily* (*Minxu ribao*, 1909), and the *National Herald*. One example from *Eastern Times* is reprinted in Judge, *Print and Politics*, 164. For examples from *Illustration Daily*, see issues 238, 239, 243, reprinted in *THRB*, 5:450, 462, 510. I am grateful to I-Wei Wu for alerting me to funny words in *Tee Ooh Pao* and the *People's Cry/Sigh* papers, as well as others not listed here.

73. A literary parody of the practice of *chaizi* appears in the "Xielin" ("Grove of Humor") section of *Youxi shijie* 7 (December 1921).

74. Japanese examples from the Meiji era and later appear in a catalog published by the Museum of Modern Art, Saitama, *Subtle Criticism*.

75. My thanks to I-Wei Wu for drawing my attention to this image.

76. In November and December 1933 (issues 75 and 76), a Guangzhou cartoon weekly carried ten faces drawn using Chinese characters, such as thief (*dao* 盜), wealthy (*fu* 富),

poor (*pin* 貧), and malicious (*e* 惡). The full list includes: friendly, elderly, wealthy, thief, poor, laughing, rapist, brain-dead, evil, suffering. They appear as miscellany on a crowded page rather than as a feature, and evince only a tinge of social satire, lacking the polemical edge of their predecessors. See Fanneng, "Xiang zhi zhongzhong" ("Various Visages"), *Banjiao manhua* 7, no. 3 (issue 75, 26 November 1933) and 7, no. 4 (issue 76, 2 December 1933).

77. Reprinted in *QDBK*, 12:1076–77. One series featured a puppet motif; another a circular latticed window bordered by a spray of flowers framing a lump-shaped figure; and a third series the bust of a Western woman with a long braid of hair resting on her shoulders. Facsimile copies appear in *QDBK*, 12. *Shanghai Puck* held a cartoon caption contest in 1918 but did not last long enough to publish winning entries. See *Shanghai Puck* 1, no. 1 (1 September 1918), 27.

78. Small-font teaser descriptions above story titles hint at their themes, which include: "Reborn after a Fake Death," "Unstoppable and Peerless," "A World Apart," "Spousal Liberation," and "Romance on a Moonlit Night." See *Kuaihuo* 1 (1922). This publication of the World Book Co., edited by Li Hanqiu (1873–1923), was reportedly popular but closed abruptly because of an editorial dispute. Its thirty-sixth issue announces that a reorganized version of the magazine, which I have not seen, would carry several new novels, including three encores of popular works: Li Hanqiu's *Strange Events Eyewitnessed in the Past Ten Years* (*Jin shinian muxian zhi guai xianzhuang*), Hanqiu's *New Guangling Tides* (*Xin guangling chao*), and Yang Chengyin's *New Travels of Lao Can* (*Lao Can xin youji*). See "Benkan gaizu tebie qishi" ("Special Announcement of This Magazine's Restructuring"), *Kuaihuo* 36 (1922), n.p. The copies held at the ANU's Menzies Library do not give month of publication.

79. See "Feilongdao youji" ("My Visit to Flying Dragon Island"), *SB* 6194 (19 July 1890), 1.

80. "Feilong qiji" ("Miraculous Encounters at Flying Dragon Island"), *SB* 6200 (25 July 1890), 2.

81. Chinese periodicals that used the motif of "the world" in their title include the Shanghai entertainment tabloid *World Vanity Fair* (*Shijie fanhua bao*, 1902–10) and the newspapers issued by the New World (*Xin shijie*) and the Great World (*Da shijie*). Amusement halls also probably played a role in influencing Shanghai slang, which referred to the city itself as a "world of play" (*baixiang shijie*). The two characters that make up the Shanghainese term for *play* (*baixiang* in Mandarin), imply that this type of play is cheap, mutual or relativistic, and oriented toward the visual. See Li, *Wan Qing, Minguo shiqi Shanghai xiaobao yanjiu*, 199.

82. The comic performer Yang Huasheng (1918–2002) cites a Republican era survey estimating that the clientele of the large entertainment halls was 80 percent male. See Yang and Zhang, *Shanghai lao huaji*, 41.

83. Qingyun, "Youxi chang: Xin nian zhi Xin shijie" ("Amusement Halls: New World at New Year's"), *Minguo ribao* 1092 (6 February 1919), 8.

84. *Xiuyuntian youxichang* and *Quanyechang* are both mentioned in 1917 issues of *Shun Pao*. On Flower World, see "Youxi chang: Hua shijie kaimu zhi suojian" ("Amusement Halls: Sights at the Opening of Flower World"), *Minguo ribao* 1090 (4 February 1919), 8. A comical piece on *Quanyechang* appears in the first section of Li, *Huaji hun*. Ads describ-

ing the offerings at *Xianshi leyuan*, including its *moxing gaota* and five-cent elevator, appear in 1919 issues of the *Republican Daily News* (*Minguo ribao*). On newspapers published by Shanghai amusement halls, see Catherine Yeh's chapter in Brosius and Wenzlhuemer, *Transcultural Turbulences*, chap. 5.

85. Rabinovitz, *Electric Dreamland*, 4.

86. Amusement parks in Singapore and Malaya featured Malay *bangsawan*, indoor and outdoor spaces for Western ballroom dance, mechanized rides, and movies. As in Shanghai, these were backed by major capital, such as the Shaw Brothers, who established amusement parks in cities across Southeast Asia in order to expand the distribution network for their films. On Singapore's New World, Great World, and Happy World amusement parks, see Wong and Tan, "Emergence of a Cosmopolitan Space for Culture and Consumption," 279–304; Krishnan, *Looking at Culture*, 21–33. The Tiger Balm Gardens were also known as the Haw-Par Villas (*Hu-Bao bieshu*), after the Aw brothers, Boon Haw (Hu Wenhu, 1882–1954) and Boon Par (Hu Wenbao, 1884–1944), for whom they doubled as residences. On the Aw brothers' entrepreneurial activities in philanthropy, newspapers, and public culture, see Rea and Volland, *The Business of Culture*, chap. 5. Theme parks in Japan, like amusement parks in the United States, were often built by tram and train companies hoping to boost ridership. See Ogawa, "History of Amusement Park Construction by Private Railway Companies in Japan"; Rabinovitz, *Electric Dreamland*, chap. 1. Ogawa (on p. 31) lists thirty-seven amusement facilities built by private railway companies between 1899 and 1924.

87. See the front page of the amusement hall's daily newspaper, *Xin shijie* 2911 (14 September 1917).

88. Scott, *Actors Are Madmen*, 75.

89. The elevator was copied from the New World, which charged twenty cents for admission to the premises and an additional ten cents to ride the elevator. See Xiao, *Hubin lüeying*, 230–31. Teahouses and story houses in the metropolis suffered a decline during this period, with the cinema rather than the amusement hall as the primary competition. On one form of Suzhou opera, see Bender, *Plum and Bamboo*, 15 and 50, on the formal categories of humor (*xuetou*) in the Suzhou chantefable.

90. Scott, *Actors Are Madmen*, 78; Liang, *Liang Yuchun sanwenji*, 15.

91. Huang Chujiu's (1872–1931) 1921 foray into banking proved to be his undoing when, in 1930, a group of investors with underworld ties engineered a run on the bank, bankrupting him. Huang died soon thereafter. Martin, *The Shanghai Green Gang*, 193.

92. The description appears in Eileen Chang's (1920–95) semi-autobiographical novel Chang, *The Fall of the Pagoda*, 232. On Huang and the mob, see Wakeman, *Policing Shanghai*, 106.

93. Dating from Pang, *The Distorting Mirror*, 5; source of mirrors from Wakeman, *Policing Shanghai*, 105.

94. Yang and Zhang, *Shanghai lao huaji*, 41. As a foreign product that enabled Chinese to view distorted reflections of themselves, the ha-ha mirror might be taken as the symbol of distorted self-perception caused by technological modernity, one with overtones of Western hegemony. Yet the testimony of Yang Huasheng and other contemporaries suggest that the encounter with the ha-ha mirror was generally positive.

95. Pang, *The Distorting Mirror*, 5. Pang also discusses the "distorting mirror" as a metaphor for "the complex cultural mechanisms that mediate the amalgamation of the self, the mirror, and the world" (7).

96. "Xin haha jing," *SB* 17440 (10 September 1921), 18. The cartoon appeared in the "Free Talk" section.

97. Scottish physician and missionary John Dudgeon compiled *Tuoying qiguan* (On the Principles and Practice of Photography, 1873) while working in Beijing. Shanghai-based translators John Fryer and Xu Shou published a book on photography in 1887. See Roberts, *Photography and China*, 41–42; see also Jiao and Su, *Wan Qing shenghuo lüeying*, 18–21.

98. On courtesan photographs since the 1890s, see Yeh, *Shanghai Love*; Hershatter's *Dangerous Pleasures* contains a sampling of photographs from 1917 after page 177. Costume photos may be found in the bound (and undated) republished editions of *Youxi shijie* (1921–23).

99. Some of these costumes and settings are listed in the advertisement for Shanghai minying zhaoxiangguan on the inside cover of *Huaji shibao* 2 (May 1915).

100. For a detailed textual analysis of Xunling's (1874–1943) photographs of Cixi (1835–1908), see Rojas, *The Naked Gaze*, 1–28. On their context, see Roberts, *Photography and China*, 34–39, 56.

101. These *youxi zhao* appear in *Xiaoxian yuebao* 4 (1921), 1. My thanks to H. Tiffany Lee for sharing this image and the accompanying citation. Yu Tianfen's pen name, "Heavenly Indignation," is likely in imitation of Bao Tianxiao's pen name, "Heavenly Laughter."

102. Zhou Yaoguang's 1907 photography guide *Shiyong yingxiangxue* (Practical Photography) calls the multiple exposure photograph (*huashen xiang*) "the cleverest thing in the world" (*tianxiashi moyou qiqiao yu cizhe yi*). Zhou is credited as the "editor and author" (*bianzhu*), and the book carries a cover inscription by "The Father of the Apparatus" (Qifu). My thanks to H. Tiffany Lee for bringing this book to my attention. For a global history of photographic manipulation, see Fineman, *Faking It*.

103. A Japanese photomontage from 1893 appears in Tucker et al., *The History of Japanese Photography*, 42. A revised and expanded 1922 ninth edition of Walter E. Woodbury's *Photographic Amusements* is available online at Project Gutenberg.

104. On Hangzhou's Erwo xuan and split-self photography in Lukang, circa 1916, see Roberts, *China and Photography*, 59–60, 69.

105. Lu Xun, "Lun zhaoxiang zhi lei" ("On Types of Photography"), *Yusi* 9 (12 January 1925), 1–3. (Date of composition is given as 11 November 1924.) For a translation, see Denton, *Modern Chinese Literary Thought*, 196–203. H. Tiffany Lee quotes an unpublished study by photography historian Oliver Moore, who points out that turn-of-the-century studios in Hangzhou, Kunming, Taiwan, and Shanghai named themselves *Erwo* in order to market photographic portraiture's ability to create a "second self." Self-splitting capacity, in other words, was central to the reception of the medium itself. See Lee, "One, and the Same," 2.

106. Lu Xun, "Lun zhaoxiang zhi lei," 2. The notion that novelty photographs were a bourgeois plaything is echoed in Su et al., *Zhongguo sheying shilüe*, 16.

107. Another photo taken in Shanghai in 1912 by the American Luther Knight (1879–1913) and captioned "Two Sisters of Shanghai," is a rare example of the photographic sub-

ject actually smiling. H. Tiffany Lee judges that its focus and shading reveals the photograph to be of one woman in two poses rather than a photograph of identical twins, as advertised. See Lee, "One, and the Same," 5. The different eye line of the two figures also suggests separate sittings by one individual.

108. *Lunyu*, Weilinggong chapter: "Gentlemen ask of themselves, while inferior men ask of others"; Wenzi shangde chapter: "It is better to blame oneself than to blame others, just as it is better to ask of oneself than to ask of others."

109. Jin Nong (1687–1773), who hailed from what is now Hangzhou, earned much of his living from painting and often sold self-portraits. As several scholars have noted, however, Jin's works were often forged. See the studies cited in Cahill, *The Painter's Practice*, 167nn90,95,98.

110. See *THRB* 205 (1910), 7, in Shanghai guji reprint, 5:7. Beginning in 1906, Xu Yongchang (1887–1959) kept a journal entitled *Journal of the Ask of Oneself Studio (Qiujizhai riji)*, a copy of which is held in the Institute of Modern History Library, Academia Sinica.

111. Claire Roberts cites one 1844 photograph as evidence of "the important role that decorum plays in Chinese portraiture and the seriousness with which portraiture in general was regarded." Her book also includes a reprint of the Puyi photograph. See Roberts, *Photography and China*, 12, 68.

112. Actors used the doppelgänger effect to allude to their multiple roles on- and offstage and screen by sitting for split-self photos and with mirrors as props. Film historian Zhang Zhen writes that Lu Xun's comments on the genre "called attention to an at once fragmented and recomposed subject caught between separate yet superimposed worlds, or, in Homi Bhabha's phraseology, on the 'split screen of the self and its doubling' in a colonial setting." See Zhang, *An Amorous History of the Silver Screen*, 164, and 163–69 passim.

113. One critic wrote in 1934: "This type of photograph is precisely an expression of split personality—a satirical portrait of such ironic subtlety that even the world's greatest caricaturists couldn't render it." See Mengruo, "Liangzhong renge" ("Split Personality"), *SB* 21947 (26 May 1934), 20.

114. The author of a 1934 *Shun Pao* article (which plagiarizes verbatim some of Lu Xun's comments on photography), for example, refers to split-self photography as a practice of the past. See ibid. Recent Chinese critics have judged the split-self photo by the standards of realism and found it artistically wanting. The authors of *A History of Photography in China, 1840–1937* comment, "The various dress-up and self-splitting portraits that appear in China's early photographic history express different philosophies and allegories of human life and also criticize some social phenomena. However, the thematic ideas expressed in these works are idealized products of their creators, which consequently diminish their significance as realistic photographic art" (Ma, *Zhongguo sheying shi*, 112).

115. In *Illustration Daily*, the X-ray is the central motif in several satirical cartoons revealing what is inside the heart of the official, including opium and, as in the example in chapter 2, money. See *THRB* 190, no. 9, Shanghai guji reprint, 4:142, 477.

116. On early Chinese trick photography, see Zhang Zhen's *An Amorous History of the Silver Screen*, chaps. 3 and 5; and Dong, "The Laborer at Play," both of which discuss the

film *Laogong zhi aiqing*, which was codirected by Zheng Zhengqiu (1888–1935) and Zhang Shichuan (1890–1954). Xu Banmei's (aka Xu Zhuodai) book *The Science of Shadowplay* (*Yingxi xue*, 1924), as Zhang (161–169) points out, includes detailed discussion of trick cinematography. Film historian Jubin Hu writes that "as applied to film, the conceptual emphasis was on 'play' (*xi*) rather than on 'shadow' (*ying*)." See Hu, *Projecting a Nation*, 32, and 30–33 passim. On playfulness in early Chinese cinema, and its connections to world cinema, see Dong, "China at Play."

117. Zhang, *An Amorous History of the Silver Screen*, 116. Zhang's observation that the film places "emphasis on *mechanical* movement and optical experiment" (109) anticipates Xinyu Dong's (2008) argument that the film exhibits an operational aesthetic shared by early mischief comedies of world cinema.

118. Huizinga's (1872–1945) 1938 book, adapted from lectures first given in 1933, appears in English as Huizinga, *Homo Ludens*.

119. Wang Guowei (1877–1927) limited his claims to lyrical literature, saying that narrative fiction was underdeveloped in China. See Denton, *Modern Chinese Literary Thought*, 90–95.

120. On this account (one of several) of the magazine's founding, see Denton and Hockx, *Literary Societies of Republican China*, 174.

121. Zhang's novel about this Don Quixote-like figure, which makes extensive use of dialect burlesque, was serialized in *Xiandai* in 1933–34. The 1936 book version includes a preface addressed to China's "Big Children." For the thermos episode in *Yangjingbang qixia*, see Zhang, *Zhang Tianyi wenji*, 6, 61–63. Title translation is David Hull's.

122. See Lu, *Old Tales Retold*. Cf. Widmer and Wang, *From May Fourth to June Fourth*, 249–68.

123. Other publications featuring *youxi kexue* and *kexue youxi* include the compendium *Panorama of Play* and the *Recreation World*.

124. Zhou Shoujuan, "*Youxi shijie* fakanci" ("Introducing the *Recreation World*"), *Youxi shijie* 1 (July 1921), 1. Confucian allusions: "You yu yi," *Lunyu* 7, no. 6 ("Shu Er"); "Shanxi xue xi, buwei nue xi", *Shijing*—"Weifeng," "Qi Yu." Translations from Slingerland (Confucius, *Analects*, 65) and Legge (modified). The *Recreation World* featured fiction, essays, poetry, jokes, anecdotes, and news about the literary scene, as well as illustrations and photographs. Zhou's coeditor was fellow popular writer Zhao Tiaokuang (1892–1953). Contributors were some of the biggest names in Shanghai's popular literature scene, including detective fiction specialist Cheng Xiaoqing; novelist and translator Bao Tianxiao; the humor specialists Cheng Zhanlu, Xu Zhuodai, and Gong Shaoqin; and writer-editors Li Dingyi, Yan Duhe, Hu Jichen, and Yan Fusun.

125. "Games of China," an essay by Rubbish New and Old, which appeared in the inaugural issue, for example, itemizes the "games" played in China recently. Yuan Shikai, who pronounced the Empire of China in 1915 and General Zhang Xun, who attempted to put Puyi back on the throne in 1917, treated the emperor as a game. Xu Shichang (1855–1939) and Sun Yat-sen, elected president of Beijing and Guangzhou-based governments in 1917 and 1918, respectively, treated the presidency as a game. Governors, legislators, the military, unification, self-governance, rule of law, opium suppression, national debt—all

were being treated as games—hence the need for this new magazine. See Xinjiu feiwu, "Youxi zhi Zhongguo" ("Games of China"), *Youxi shijie* 1 (July 1921), n.p.

126. Other translated archetypes of the "new woman" influential in early twentieth-century China are discussed in Hu, *Tales of Translation*. Lu Xun's 1923 lecture ("What Happens after Nora Leaves Home?") famously doused the enthusiasm of would-be Chinese Noras by pointing out that without money her options were prostitution and returning home. See *LXSW*, 2:85–92.

127. Image source: *Shanghai poke* 1, no. 4 (December 1918), 28. In April 1927, the year of the Northern Expedition, a cartoon reprinted in *La Satire de Pékin* captured the rising and falling fortunes of warlords by depicting them as children on a seesaw, with the caption: "Chez les militaristes l'un monte, l'autre descend" ("As one militarist rises, the other falls"). *La Satire de Pékin*, a supplement to *La Politique de Pékin*, a French-language journal based in Beijing, reprinted cartoons from the Chinese press on matters related to warlord fighting, social issues, and freedom of the press with French captions. The cartoon mentioned here (image quality is, unfortunately, too poor to reproduce) may be found in *La satire chinoise, politique et sociale, anné 1927*, 10. My thanks to Rudolf G. Wagner for bringing this source to my attention, and to Paize Keulemans for assistance in obtaining it.

128. A photomontage depicting the vices of "drinking, lusting after women, smoking, and gambling" appears in *Liangyou huabao* 70 (October 1932), 15. My thanks to Gary Wang of the University of Toronto for bringing this image to my attention.

129. On *Xiao wanyi*, see Fernsebner, "A People's Playthings"; Jones, *Developmental Fairy Tales*, chap. 4.

130. Barmé, *An Artistic Exile*, 23. As a *manhua* sketch artist, Feng himself largely avoided the mode of satire, which fixes people in an unchanging mold.

131. Palindromic poems go by various names, including *huiwen shi* (reversible poem) and *yuanquan shi* (circular poem). Meow Hui Goh notes in a study of late fifth-century poetry that the palindrome in some poems is "facilitated not only by its syntactical structures but also its tone patterns." See Goh, *Sound and Sight*, 102. On palindromic poems in the early nineteenth-century novel *Flowers in the Mirror*, see Elvin, *Changing Stories in the Chinese World*, 38–40. Thomas Mullaney argues that "In the 1920s, non-verbal commentary [such as punctuation] was used to unlock meanings and/or resolve ambiguities ... [that were treated as being] the inherent fault and deficiency of the Chinese language itself." See Mullaney, "The Semi-Colonial Semi-Colon." Phonologists gravitated to aural word games. The linguist Y. R. Chao (Zhao Yuanren, 1892–1982), who promoted a standard Chinese dialect, for example, in 1930 wrote "The Story of Mr. Shi Eating a Lion" ("Shishi shishi shi"), which consisted of ninety-two characters pronounced *shi* in Mandarin (albeit with different tones). For a translation and discussion, see Voogt and Finkel, *The Idea of Writing*, 283–86. The professional punctuator Zhu Taimang (1895–1939) published a collection of palindromic poems in 1933. See Zhu, *Xiandai wubai jia yuanquan shi ji*, cited in Mullaney, "The Semi-Colonial Semi-Colon." A pair of "New Reversible Poems: Flight of the Wild Goose and the Swallow" appears at the back of the second issue of *Free Magazine*. See Hong, "Xin huiwenshi: hong yan fen fei," *Ziyou zazhi* 2 (December 1913), n.p.

CHAPTER 4. MOCKERY

1. Huang Tianshi (1898–1983), "He Dian *xu*" ("Preface to *Which Classic?*"). In *HD* 1928a, 2.

2. Ran [Inflamed], "Zhusheng gouyang zhi Zhongguoren" ("Chinese Swine and Sons of Bitches"), *Xin shiji* 91 (3 April 1909), n.p.

3. Writing about continuities between the 1920s and nowadays, for example, Gloria Davies observes that despite hand-wringing by intellectuals "the vituperative nature of Chinese intellectual debates ... remains a feature of present-day critical discourse." See Davies, *Worrying about China*, 10.

4. Pollard, *The True Story of Lu Xun*, 109. Michel Hockx's *Questions of Style*, discussed below, is one prominent exception: a study that takes mockery seriously as style.

5. See the extensive reception history in Foster, *Ah Q Archaeology*.

6. Lu Xun, "'Ah Q zhengzhuan' de chengyin" ("How 'The True Story of Ah Q' Was Written"), *Beixin* 18 (18 December 1926), 545–55. For an English translation, see *LXSW*, 2:313–20. "Ah Q" moved from the column "Kaixin hua" to "Xin wenyi" (New Literature). For more on Lu Xun's "innovative play on traditional biographical forms," see Cheng, *Literary Remains*, 73–78.

7. John Morreall identifies three dominant Western theories of laughter. Superiority is the first. The second is Francis Hutcheson's (1694–1746) "incongruity" theory, a critique of Hobbes (1588–1679) developed in *Thoughts on Laughter* (1725), which roots laughter in man's sense of the ridiculous and proposes that laughter arises from recognition of a disjunction between one's concept of a thing and the thing itself. The third, known as the "relief" theory (or the "hydraulic" or "economic" theory), grew out of Freud's notion that joking was primarily a function of releasing pent-up psychic tension. For representative primary texts, see Morreall, *The Philosophy of Laughter and Humor*, 9–126. The classification first appeared in Morreall, *Taking Laughter Seriously*.

8. Wen-hsin Yeh notes that Liu Dabai (1880–1932), for one, "was ready to hail the victory of the Northern Expedition of the Guomindang in 1927 as a victory of the New Culture Movement, which he thought the Nationalists had more or less championed after May Fourth." See Yeh, *Provincial Passages*, 318n24. On Lu Xun's views, see Pollard, *The True Story of Lu Xun*, 112.

9. Liang Shiqiu (1903–87) wrote this 1926 essay in New York: Liang Shiqiu, "Xiandai Zhongguo wenxue zhi langman de qushi" ("The Romantic Trend in Modern Chinese Literature"). In Li, *Lu Xun Liang Shiqiu lunzhan shilu*, 1–28.

10. Hockx, *Questions of Style*, 186, 220. For an analysis of abusive criticism in the poetry community of this period, see chapter 6 of Hockx's study.

11. The Chinese phrase is *ren ru qi wen, wen ru qi wen*. See ibid., 191.

12. "Ma chusheng" ("Beast Curses"), *Xin Xiaolin guangji*, *Xin xiaoshuo* 2, no. 5 (May 1906), 157.

13. See Lu Xun, "Lun 'tamade!'" *Yusi* 37 (27 July 1925), 4–6. English translation in *LXSW*, 2:192–97. The first copy of *Yusi* reportedly sold fifteen thousand copies. See Denton and Hockx, *Literary Societies of Republican China*, 203.

14. *Lengchao refeng* and *xixiao numa*, respectively. On the popularity of the latter phrase in Shanghai tabloids of the late Qing, see Wang, *Merry Laughter and Angry Curses*.

15. Lin Yutang, "Chalun *Yusi* de wenti—yinjian, maren, ji fei'e polai" ("An Intervention Regarding *Threads of Discourse* Style: Moderation, Cursing, and Fair Play"), *Yusi* 57 (24 December 1925), 3–6. A partial translation of Lin's essay, which I draw on here, appears in Sohigian, "The Life and Times of Lin Yutang," 329–30. In the essay, Lin cites Wu Zhihui, discussed below, as an exemplary curser. Lu Xun's rebuttal: Lu Xun, "Lun fei'e polai yinggai huanxing" ("On Deferring Fair Play"), *Mangyuan* (Wilderness) 1 (January 1926), 5–16. Sohigian remarks: "The dog-in-the-water or 'fair play' debate seemed to be about the nature of discourse. Was the text to be a savage battleground or a convivial forum for the exchange of ideas? Should discourse be an ongoing playful sparring game where none seemed to win (Lin Yutang) or a fight to the death in which a winner had the final word (Lu Xun)? Could both kinds of discourse coexist?" See Sohigian, "Contagion of Laughter," 161n44.

16. Lee-hsia Hsu Ting judges that in addition to submitting to haphazard warlord censorship, "a subservient press not only connived at, but even abetted, corruption." See Ting, *Government Control of the Press in Modern China*, 57–60; see also 55 on an attempt to arrest Wu Zhihui in 1924 for having "insulted the government."

17. Liang, *Ma ren de yishu*. The essay, first published in Shanghai in 1927, was translated into English and published in 1936 with the author listed as "unknown." See Liang, *The Fine Art of Reviling*.

18. It recounts, for example, a fourth-century emperor's courtiers being described as "a gelded bull weighing a thousand catties" and another, a ladies' man, as "a curly-horned cow pirouetting round and round." In another episode, an old man asks an eight-year-old boy about a gap in his teeth: "What's that dog hole in your mouth for?" and he replies "For letting in and out dogs like you!" Translations adapted from Liu, *Shih-shuo hsin-yu*, 409, 413.

19. See Feng Zhiyu [Lu Xun], "Erchou yishu," *SB* 21616 (18 June 1933), 18. Translated as "The Art of the Number-Two Clown" in *LXSW*, 3:312–13.

20. Lu Xun's essay distinguishes between indiscriminate and apropos abuse; to wit: to mock someone's surname is meaningless, since he inherited it, but mocking his style name (such as "Sick Cuckoo" [*bingjuan*]—likely a jab at the popular writer Zhou Shoujuan ["skinny cuckoo"] or "Sick Crane" [the cartoonist Qian Binghe (1879–1944)])—is fair game, since it targets his self-image. Mocking reproaches (*xiaoma*) are also acceptable. See Lu Xun, "Ruma he konghe jue bushi zhandou—zhi *Wenxue yuebao* bianji de yi feng xin" ("Insults and Threats Are Certainly Not Fighting the Good Fight: A Letter to the Editors of *Literature Monthly*"), *Wenxue yuebao* 1, nos. 5–6 (25 December 1932), 247–49.

21. Tang Tao, "Piping yu ma" ("Criticism and Mockery"), *Taibai banyuekan* 2, no. 9 (20 July 1935), 378–79.

22. Lu, *A Brief History of Chinese Fiction*, chap. 28. On Lu Xun's reception compared to his predecessors, see, for example, the essay "Satirical Fiction and *The Scholars*," which calls Li Boyuan and Wu Jianren's novels "heated invective" (*rema*) and "True Story of Ah Q" "the pinnacle of cold satirical fiction." Bihui, "Fengci xiaoshuo yu *Rulin waishi*" ("Satirical Fiction and *The Scholars*"), *LY* 58 (1 February 1935), 495.

23. Wang, *Fin-de-Siècle Splendor*, 205–6. For consistency, devil names have been changed to match my translations.

24. *HD* 1878, chap. 1, 4. Pagination restarts at 1 in every chapter of this edition. Full bibliographical citations for *Which Classic?*'s editions (identified as "*HD* [year]") and paratexts are listed in appendix 2.

25. On the slang terms *mapi jing* and *peng luanzi guoqiao*, see Xue, *Shanghai xianhua*, 154, 242.

26. Idema and Haft, *A Guide to Chinese Literature*, 228.

27. The devil names are, respectively, *Se gui, Esha gui, Maoshi gui, Ci gui, Liu Dagui, Huo siren, Heiqi datougui, kongxin gui, xiao gui, lao gui, ye gui, Cuiming gui, Gui jian, Kangsang gui,* and *Liushi gui*.

28. See *HD* 1878, chap. 6, 4–5. On "four-eyed dog," see Xue, *Shanghai xianhua*, 81. Thanks to Veronica Ye Zhengdao for assistance with determining the meaning of some of these terms.

29. Idema and Haft, *A Guide to Chinese Literature*, 228.

30. Earlier phrases are *goubi zi, zhishang kongyan*, and *fangpi wenzhang*, respectively. Several appear in chapter 6, where the wandering Daoist Crab Shell mocks Living Devil's book learning before giving him a pill to make him smarter. See *HD* 2000, 112.

31. Upon the scholar's second death he swaggers into an audience with the King and is reintroduced as "the scholar who composes farts." "Pi song" ("In Praise of Farts") appears in Qingdu sanke, *Xiao zan*, 7. See appendix 1.

32. The treatise, structured as a formal parody of the thirty-six-part Daoist canon, did not go over well: the emperor who had commissioned it had it burned. For a translation and discussion, see Kohn, *Laughing at the Dao*.

33. Zhu Jiefan, "Lun *He Dian* de yuyan yunyong" ("On the Use of Language in *Which Classic?*"), in *HD* 1980, 131.

34. Altenburger, "Chains of Ghost Talk," 35.

35. Judith Zeitlin discusses the connection between the phrase "ghost of a ghost," nonsense, comedy, and "play with infinity" in seventeenth-century literature in Zeitlin, *The Phantom Heroine*, 178.

36. *Which Classic?* is recognized as a key text in the history of Shanghai/Wu dialect. See Qian, *Shanghai yuyan fazhan shi*, 24, 78–80, 104.

37. Altenburger points out that its "artificial vernacular" relies heavily "on punning and on the use in a literal sense of figurative expressions, producing a multiplicity of lexical meaning, oscillating between mere nonsense and sophisticated irony." Altenburger, "Chains of Ghost Talk," 39–40.

38. Examples include the Ming dynasty *Smashing the Demons* (*Zhan gui zhuan*, first extant ed., 1688) and the Qing dynasty Qianlong era *Zhong Kui of the Tang Quells the Demons* (*Tang Zhong Kui ping gui zhuan*, 1st extant ed., 1785). On the ghost-novel genre, see Chen, *Qingdai guilei fengci xiaoshuo sanbuqu*. Altenburger (34) gives several examples of plot elements derived from "the minor narrative tradition of ghost novels," to which one more may be added: in chapter 1 of *Which Classic?*, a middle-aged ghost who is lamenting his lack of a son is urged by his wife to make an offering to the spirits. Soon after he does, his wife is visited in a dream by a spirit and becomes pregnant. The same chain of events appears in the opening chapter of the Ming novel *The Complete Biography of Zhong Kui of the Tang*. See *Dingqie quanxiang anjian Tang Zhong Kui quanzhuan*, 2013–19.

39. Wang, *Fin-de-Siècle Splendor*, 207.

40. The earliest surviving Chinese dictionary/encyclopedia, the *Erya* (ca. third century BCE), for example, glosses *ghost* as "that which returns" (*gui zhe, gui ye*). David Wang cites this homophonic conceit in his discussion of memories of violence in modern Chinese literature, noting intersections between "haunting" and the Freudian notion of "the return of the repressed." See Wang, *The Monster That Is History*, chap. 8.

41. For a partial translation of Pu Songling's (1640–1715) *Liaozhai zhiyi*, see John Minford's *Strange Tales from a Chinese Studio*. Yuan Mei's (1716–97) *What Confucius Didn't Talk About* proved successful enough that the editor-compiler put together an encore volume with more tales in 1796. A punctuated edition appeared in 1935; see Yuan, *Zi bu yu*. For a bilingual edition, see Santangelo and Yan, *Zibuyu*.

42. *Jing guishen er yuanzhi*. See *Lunyu*, "Yongye" chap., 6. For background on Chinese ghosts and the role of *gui* in popular religion and literature, see Huntington, *Alien Kind*; Chan, *The Discourse of Foxes and Ghosts*.

43. Zeitlin, *The Phantom Heroine*, 4–5.

44. McKeown, *Chinese Migrant Networks and Cultural Change*, 126, and 125–30 passim. McKeown notes that as a part of late imperial and early twentieth-century Chinese kinship networks, *gui* occupied that intermediary space within a different cosmological framework made up of not just ghosts and men, but also gods and ancestors.

45. Ibid., 126.

46. A pioneer in commercial book publishing, Shenbaoguan played a crucial role in the retrieval and publication of lost books and obscure manuscripts following the destruction of private and public libraries during the Taiping Rebellion (1850–64). It also had a transformative influence on how literature was published and marketed in China in the late nineteenth century. By soliciting manuscripts through advertisements in its affiliate newspaper *Shun Pao*, the press was reportedly able to attract five hundred usable manuscripts per month in the mid-1870s. According to Rudolf Wagner, from the beginning, its British proprietor, Ernest Major (1841–1908), demonstrated admirable marketing savvy: print runs were sometimes limited to one or two thousand copies to ensure a sellout, and high-quality materials were used to appeal to book collectors. Readers of *Shun Pao* were informed about the impending release of a book through printed advertisements in the pages of the newspaper. See Chen et al., *Wan Ming yu wan Qing*, 169–78, esp. 174–75. *Which Classic?* was one of six books Shenbaoguan published in 1878. Other titles included *Heroic Sons and Daughters (Ernü yingxiong zhuan)* and *Dream of the Green Chamber (Qinglou meng)*. See Han and Wang, *Xiaoshuo shufang lu*, 80–81. Three years earlier, in 1875, Shenbaoguan published *Xi you bu*, another novel that Liu Fu, discussed below, was to edit, punctuate, and republish.

47. *Guihuo*, also known as *linhuo*, is a phosphorescent light thought to emanate from graves.

48. Originally published in the *Shun Pao Publishing House Continued Book Catalog*, 1878; reprinted in *HD* 2000, 195. "Three-family village," akin to "one-horse town," refers to a tiny rural settlement.

49. Gérard Genette defines paratexts as "those liminal devices and conventions, both within and outside the book, that form part of the complex mediation between book, author, publisher, and reader." He notes that titles, prefaces, forewords, commentaries,

and other such packaging collectively represent "a discourse that is fundamentally heteronymous, auxiliary, and dedicated to the service of something other than itself ... [that is,] the text." See Genette, *Paratexts*, 1, 12. Paratexts, as the discussion below shows, may reveal as much about authors, editors, publishers, and readers as about the main text.

50. Pen names and pseudonyms had long been common in Chinese vernacular narrative—the famous Ming dynasty literatus Feng Menglong, for example, had more than a dozen aliases—and by the nineteenth century, the pseudonym was de rigueur for novels' authors, commentators, and preface writers alike. *Dream of the Green Chamber* and *Dream of Romance* (translated by Patrick Hanan as *Courtesans and Opium*), are two prominent examples of novels published under pseudonyms. For a discussion of the pseudonym as riddle in late imperial pornographic fiction, see Wang and Shang, *Dynastic Crisis and Cultural Innovation*, 235–63.

51. The pseudonyms are *Guoluren*, *Taiping keren*, *Haishang canxiake*, and *Chan Jia er xiansheng*. The Confucian classics were usually read with commentaries, glosses, and other interpretive aids. Vernacular novels also appeared in editions with prefaces, afterwords, and illustrations. On the importance of paratexts in premodern literature, see David Rolston's *Traditional Chinese Fiction and Fiction Commentary*, as well as his edited volume, *How to Read the Chinese Novel*. Other studies, such as Robert Hegel's *Reading Illustrated Fiction in Late Imperial China*, explain how visual paratexts—particularly woodblock prints and illustrations—in Ming-Qing vernacular novels influenced how those texts were read and experienced. On commentaries on the Confucian classics, see Makeham, *Transmitters and Creators*. Since 1878, *Which Classic?* has accumulated over three dozen commentaries, about half of which date to the 1920s and 1930s. Especially valuable is *HD 2000*, which includes 141 pages of main text, 38 pages of endnotes and glosses, and 111 pages of other paratextual materials, comprising 22 documents and 11 illustrations.

52. Taiping Traveler's preface, like Passerby's, repeatedly refers to "making stories out of nothing" and "making classical allusions without alluding to anything," treating the question of whether or not ghosts exist as a proxy for whether or not *Which Classic?* has antecedents. A similar teasing tone appears in a preface to the novel *Fengyue meng*: "Dream is in fact reality, reality is in fact a dream; if you call it real it is real, if you call it a dream it is a dream. Heh heh, ha ha!" Translation from Des Forges, "From Source Texts to 'Reality Observed,'" 82.

53. *HD* 1894b attributes the chapter-end commentaries to an individual named Chen Deren. Altenburger renders the pseudonym as "Mr. Argumentative Interferer" ("Chains of Ghost Talk," 27), though it mentions "two gentlemen" (*er xiansheng*).

54. *Guoluren* appears to have been a popular literary appellation. The courtesan novel *Dream of Romance* (preface 1848), published by Shenbaoguan in 1883, is attributed to Guolairen 過來仁 (bringer of benevolence), a pun on *guolairen* 過來人 (passerby) and Han Bangqing's (1856–94) *Flowers of Shanghai* (*Haishang hua lie zhuan*, 1894) also carries a preface by a Guolairen 過來人. See Des Forges, "From Source Texts to 'Reality Observed,'" 69; Hanan, *The Invention of Li Yu*, 347. On the likelihood of Guoluren being the author, see *HD* 2000, 290.

55. "Munching prose and chewing words" refers to philological quibbling; "*zhi, hu, zhe, ye*" refers to the "empty" grammatical particles of the classical language. This usage means to show off one's literary virtuosity via the empty manipulation of language.

56. *Di shiyi caizi shu guihua lianpian lu* (*HD* 1894b). The phrase "pack of lies" (*guihua lianpian*) may be translated literally as "chains of ghost talk" (Altenburger, "Chains of Ghost Talk," 42). *Love among the Courtesans* (*Hualiu shenqing zhuan*, preface 1897), is another late-nineteenth-century novel that was retitled to improve its marketability.

57. Liu is generally credited with having in 1920 suggested splitting China's third-person pronoun *ta* 他 into female (她), neuter (它), animal (牠), and divine (祂) variants, which served to "gender" 他 retroactively as male. Cf. Liu, *Translingual Practice*, 37–39. On Liu's poetry, see Hockx, "Liu Bannong and the Forms of New Poetry." Cai's dates are 1868–1940. Liu wrote a book on photography: Liu, *Bannong tan ying*.

58. Liu was for several years a staff writer and editor for the commercial publishing house China Books (Zhonghua shuju) and wrote for a number of its magazines, including *Zhonghua xiaoshuojie*. On Liu's early career, see Xu, *Huaju chuangshiqi huiyi lu*, 146–48. In one of his comic pieces from 1914, inspired by Hans Christian Andersen's "The Emperor's New Clothes," a character wears "trick glasses" (*tuolike yanjing*), a type of comedic ocular gadget like those discussed in chapter 3. See Bannong, "Yangmi xiaoying" ("Portrait of an Afficionado of Things Western"). In Yu, *Qingmo Minchu xiaoshuo shuxi—huaji juan*, 123–26. One typo silently corrected. A story by Liu Bannong appears in the first issue (January 1917) of the *Illustrated Novel Magazine*, edited by Bao Tianxiao and published by Shanghai's Wen Ming Press. A 1918 translation by Liu appeared in *The Eden* (1918–27), published by Shanghai's Sincere Amusement Park. On the latter, see Catherine Yeh's chapter in Brosius and Wenzlhuemer, *Transcultural Turbulences*, 117.

59. On *yuanyang hudie pai*, see Hsia, *C. T. Hsia on Chinese Literature*, 480n6; Denton and Hockx, *Literary Societies of Republican China*, chap. 2. One of its main representatives was the "Butterfly Immortal," Chen Diexian (1879–1940), author of *The Money Demon*. Qian Xuantong's (1887–1939) comments are reprinted in Qian, *Qian Xuantong wenji*, 1:292–93.

60. *Bu yong dian*. Hu Shi remarked that of the eight prohibitions, the sixth—proscribing allusions—was the one "most singled out for attack" and "most misunderstood." As such, he took pains to outline five types of allusions "in the broad sense" that were permissible and five types that fit a "narrow definition," which he further subdivided into permissible and impermissible based on originality and skill of usage. See Hu Shi, "Wenxue gailiang chuyi" ("Some Modest Proposals for the Reform of Literature"), *Xin qingnian* 2, no. 5 (January 1917), n.p. For an English translation, see Denton, *Modern Chinese Literary Thought*, 123–39. In a revised version of this list published in *La Jeunesse* in April 1918, Hu moved "Don't use allusions" from number six up to number three.

61. *Si gudian*. See Lu Xun, "Tiji" ("Preface"). Dated 25 May 1926. In *HD* 1926a.

62. *HD* 1928a, 2.

63. 儂多拆拆尿, 早點評上教授. *Chainiao* (piss) and *chushu* (put out books) rhyme in Shanghainese. See Qian, *Shanghai yuyan fazhan shi*, 76.

64. As Perry Link has described, popular literature of the 1910s and 1920s was subject to aggressive promotion tactics: "Advertisements filled with extravagant praise for particular works appeared in magazines, newspapers and the backs of books. Publishers devised catchy names for magazines … and used attractive pictures for their covers. They also made the most of well-known names. The manuscript of a third-rate or unknown writer would, for example, be published behind a cover carrying the conspicuous an-

nouncement 'Revised by so-and-so' (a leading name)." See Link, *Mandarin Ducks and Butterflies*, 149.

65. On irregular salary payments to academic staff and other employees of the Beiyang government during the 1920s, see studies by Chen Mingyuan. Peking University professor Gu Jiegang recorded in his diary that his salary for 1925 was up to eight months late, and even then he had to make multiple trips to collect it. In August 1926, Gu left for a new job at Amoy University. See Chen, *Wenhuaren de jingji shenghuo*, 170–71.

66. *Yusi* 69 (8 March 1926), 2–3. Variations of this advertisement, which highlight the celebrity of Wu Zhihui (discussed below) or Liu Fu and riff on lines from the novel, appear in issues 70–72.

67. Beixin zhanggui (Head of Beixin Books), "Xiang duzhemen daoqian" ("An Apology to the Reader"). *HD* 1926a.

68. One reviewer laments the missing Qian Xuantong preface twice in his review. See Lan Hua, "He Dian," *SB* 19239 (23 September 1926), 22. Cheng Jiang follows this credible interpretation. See *HD* 2000, 286. The second apology, Beixin zhanggui, "Zai xiang duzhemen daoqian" ("Another Apology to the Reader"), originally appeared in *HD* 1926b and also appears in *HD* 2000, 284. To my knowledge, no preface by Qian appears in *Threads of Discourse*, extant editions of *Which Classic?*, or his collected works, Qian, *Qian Xuantong wenji*.

69. Wang Jingxuan [Qian Xuantong], "Wenxue geming zhi fanxiang" (A Voice Opposed to the Literary Revolution), *Xin qingnian* 4, no. 3 (15 March 1918), 265–68. For an in-depth analysis of Lin Shu's (1852–1924) role in this hoax, see Hill, *Lin Shu, Inc.*, 178–229. The hoax is also mentioned in Liu, *Translingual Practice*, 233–34.

70. Liu's response to Wang appears in *Xin qingnian* 4, no. 3 (15 March 1918), 268–85.

71. Zhang Kebiao, a contributor to the *Analects* magazine in the 1930s, said that Wang Jingxuan ended up *xuechu guluo*. Zhang, *Zhang Kebiao wenji*, 2:450. The exchange was canonized in volume 1 ("Literary Debates," edited by Zheng Zhenduo) of the 1935 *Compendium of China's New Literature* under the heading "From Wang Jingxuan to Lin Qinnan [Lin Shu]").

72. "Diary of a Madman" was Zhou Shuren's first story to appear under the pen name Lu Xun. Lu Xun's obituary also mentions that the frank words he made in his preface to Liu's edition led to their later estrangement: "When he later punctuated *Which Classic?*, still thinking of him as a friend, I made a few frank comments in my preface. I heard afterwards that he took offence, but 'what's said cannot be undone'—it was too late." See Lu Xun, "Yi Liu Bannong jun" ("In Memory of Liu Bannong"), *Qingnian jie* (Youth World) 6, no. 3 (October 1934), 2–4. Translation from *LXSW*, 4:78–79. The back cover of the preceding issue of *Youth World* 6, no. 2 (September 1934) carries a death-notice-cum-advertisement by Beixin Bookstore featuring a photograph of Liu and a price list for thirteen of his books, including *Which Classic?*

73. On Lu Xun's activities during this period, see Pollard, *The True Story of Lu Xun*, 97–112. On Lu Xun's opinion of the university chancellor, Lim Boon Keng (Lin Wenqing, 1869–1957), who is further discussed in chapter 6, see Kowallis, *The Lyrical Lu Xun*, 31.

74. *Which Classic?* has become part of the Lu Xun canon. Based on a bibliographic survey, most editions since 1926 have included Lu Xun's preface, and the book is included in a series of "Selected Works with Prefaces or Postscripts by Lu Xun" (*HD* 1985). Lu Xun

was conscious of how his prestige was used to market others' products. Likening himself to a beast of burden, he wrote in 1926, "if the Zhaos want me to stand in front of their shop with an advertisement on my back, saying, 'This dairy has excellent cows and sells first-rate, pasteurized, nourishing milk,' though I am lean and a bull and have no milk, so long as they do not sell poison I shall not protest for I sympathize with their wish to enlarge their business." Translation source: *LXSW*, 2:314.

75. Lu Xun wrote:

> So in my understanding, [Bannong's] main enterprise is still teaching these curvatures [of Chinese phonology] to his students. But now—oh joy—Peking University is about to close its doors, and he doesn't have any outside employment. Thus, while I don't claim to be a superior individual, I have no problem with him publishing and selling books. And if you're going to publish books, naturally you'll want them to sell well; and if you want them to sell well, naturally you'll want to advertise; and if you advertise, naturally you'll want to say the book's good. Do you think anyone would publish a book and take out an ad that said "This book is boring, please don't read it"?

This essay was reprinted in the July 1926 Beixin edition, as well as most subsequent editions. See Lu Xun, "Wei Bannong ti ji *He Dian* hou, zuo" ("Postscript to My Preface to Bannong's *Which Classic?*"), *Yusi* 82 (7 June 1926), 19–21. Preface dated "Night of 25 May 1926." As for Liu's alleged profiteering, one of his obituaries reads: "Like the true scholar that he was, he had a great contempt for money. To his family, therefore, he left practically nothing except his books." See Wen Yuan-ning, ed., "Intimate Portraits: Dr. Liu Fu (劉復)," *CC* 7:32 (9 August 1934), 778.

76. Both Liu Fu and Hu Shi wrote prefaces to *Flowers of Shanghai*, the great Wu dialect novel of the 1890s, and both saw in the "living language" (*huode yuyan*) of dialect literature great potential to spur innovation in Mandarin writing. They nevertheless worried that the potential readership for Wu dialect works was too limited—hence the need for punctuation and annotation. Their *Flowers of Shanghai* appeared in four volumes in December 1926, but *Which Classic?*, out for half a year, goes unmentioned. See Han, *Haishang hua liezhuan*, 30, 32, 36. Hu's preface is dated 30 June 1926, so he might not even have seen Liu Fu's edition of *Which Classic?*, which had just been published that month; Liu's preface is dated "1925 Tianjin." Volume 1 also contains a "Collator's Postscript" by Wang Yuanfang and advertises the same type of value-added editorial work that Liu Fu did for *Which Classic?*: "With new-style punctuation and paragraph breaks." Tempering his earlier criticism of Liu Fu's punctuation of *Which Classic*, Lu Xun jokes in an essay included in the July 1926 Beixin edition of *Which Classic?*: "I feel that for many things you really have to be a specialist to do them well. For instance, punctuating must be left to Wang Yuanfang, no one but Hu Shi should write the preface, and only Yadong tushuguan should publish it; neither Liu Bannong, Li Xiaofeng, nor myself are worthy." See Lu Xun, "Wei Bannong tiji *He Dian* hou zuo," 19.

77. See *HD* 2000, 10. Blood-drenched pig's head is likely a variation of the saying *gou xue lin tou*, which refers to severe verbal abuse, meaning literally to curse someone till "dog's blood drenches his head." On the meanings of these terms, see Pan Shen's gloss in *HD* 1981a.

78. For other examples of Rabelaisian lists besides the Passerby preface, Devil Incarnate's birthday, and the dog curses, see *HD* 2000, 17, 22, 57–58, 59–60, 122, 127.

79. Zhou's comments are reprinted in *HD* 2000, 274; Zhao's (1902–85) appear in *HD* 1981, 128.

80. [Liu] Dabai, "Du *He Dian*" ("Reading *Which Classic?*"), *Liming* 33 (26 June 1926), 97–100.

81. [Lin] Shouzhuang, "Guanyu Liu jiao *He Dian* de ji ge kaodezhu de zheng wu" ("Regarding a Few Reliable Corrections to Liu's Collation of *Which Classic?*"), *Yusi* 91 (9 August 1926), 177–78. Liu Bannong later invited Lin to write a preface to the 1933 edition of *Which Classic?*, in which Lin notes the difficulty of collating a work written in dialect.

82. See Liu Fu, "Bu yu Liu Dabai xiansheng banzui," *Yusi* 93 (23 August 1926), 207–9; [Liu] Dabai, "Jieshao 'wu jia' Liu Fu boshi di ji zhong qiaomiao famen" ("Introducing a Few of the Clever Methods of 'My Relative' Dr. Liu Fu"), *Liming* 44 (5 September 1926), 11–13; reprinted *HD* 2000, 261–66.

83. Cf. the entry on "Abdomen" in Ambrose Bierce's *The Devil's Dictionary* (serialized intermittently, 1881–1906): "The temple of the god Stomach, in whose worship, with sacrificial rights, all true men engage."

84. The terms in this passage are *dingbi chong*, *luanmao li tiaoshi*, and *pabi heshang*. Lascivious monks appear, for example, in chapters 24–25 of *The Water Margin* and chapters 95–96 of Wu Jianren's *Strange Events Eyewitnessed over Twenty Years*.

85. See Lu Xun, "Tiji" ("Preface"), *HD* 1926a, 1; [Liu] Dabai. "Du *He Dian*," *HD* 2000, 218. Liu's response: Liu Bannong, "Guanyu *He Dian* li fangfangfang ji qita" ("About the Empty Squares in *Which Classic?*"), *Yusi* 85 (27 June 1926), 69–75. Page 71 of this issue includes a notice from Liu requesting help from Shanghai natives surnamed Zhang in tracking down information about Zhang Nanzhuang.

86. See the 1926 Beixin edition of Zhang, *Xing shi*. The book appeared in multiple editions (some pirated) and reprintings in its first year, including one by Beijing's You zhong she, a copy of which is held at the ANU's Menzies Library. Beixin, which published *Which Classic?*, also published one of Zhang's earlier books, *An Aesthetic Philosophy of Life* (*Mei de renshengguan*, 1924). For a history of modern Chinese attitudes and public discourse about on sex that covers influential figures including Zhang Jingsheng (1888–1970), eugenicist Quentin Pan (Pan Guangdan, 1899–1967), and birth control advocate Margaret Sanger, who had visited China in 1921, see Dikötter, *Sex, Culture, and Modernity in China*. On Zhang Jingsheng, *Sex Histories*, and their reception, see Rocha, "Sex, Eugenics, Aesthetics, Utopia in the Life and Work of Zhang Jingsheng 張競生 (1888–1970)"; Larson, *From Ah Q to Lei Feng*, 54–59; Chen and Dilley, *Feminism/Femininity in Chinese Literature*, 159–78; and Leary, "Sexual Modernism in China."

87. The 1926 Beixin edition of Zhang Jingsheng's *Sex Histories* is advertised in issue 73 (5 April 1926), the same issue that carried Liu Bannong's preface to his new edition of *Which Classic?* In June, Beixin Books began taking advance orders in *Threads of Discourse* for a translated book on sex education. An advertisement for *Xing jiaoyu* (Sex Education), by Stowell, translated by a certain "YD," appears in the last page of *Yusi* 83 (14 June 1926). Later that year, Beixin released three more books on sex: Chen Laoxin's *Xingyu yu xing'ai*

(Sexual Desire and Sexual Love), and two translated works on *A Healthy Sex Life* (*Jiankang de xing shenghuo*) and *The Female Sexual Urge* (*Nüzi di xing chongdong*), advertisements for which appear in *Yusi* issue 95 (4 September 1926).

88. See Larson, *From Ah Q to Lei Feng*, 54–59; Leary, "Sexual Modernism in China," chap. 7.

89. Poyu, "Jinren zhi: Liu Fu (Bannong)" ("Contemporary Personages: Liu Fu [Bannong]"), *Renjian shi* 9 (5 August 1934), 43. Poyu was a pen name of Xu Xu, the editor of *Renjian shi*. Lin Yutang, a colleague at *Threads of Discourse*, considered Liu to have a fragile ego. See Sohigian, "The Life and Times of Lin Yutang," 325.

90. Anderson, *The Limits of Realism*, 37.

91. Zarrow, *Anarchism and Chinese Political Culture*, 198.

92. Qian Xuantong's praise appears in *Xin qingnian* 4, no. 2 (15 February 1918), 150. Qian Xuantong and Wu Zhihui were well acquainted as participants in language reform efforts, including the Esperanto movement, and published open letters to each other on matters of language policy. See also Hu Shi's approving comments on Wu's deploring of the effects of Buddhism on Chinese culture in Hu's essay "China's Sterile Inheritance," in T'ang, *China's Own Critics*, 64–73. The Confucian shop comment appeared in a preface Hu wrote for one of Wu's books. See Liu and Zhang, *Xiu yuan zhi lu*, 205.

93. Dorp, "Wu Chih-hui and the Late Nineteenth Century Gentry," 119. Among his later academic honors, Wu was in 1948 elected to the inaugural class of Academicians of the Academia Sinica (est. 1928), the Republic of China's premier research institution.

94. Wu-isms such as *gouride, ganku laopozi, maiyin, huhou shudi,* and *wenqi yuxing shi wo hou zhong e buzhi* appear in various issues of *Xin shiji*; see especially issues 74–76.

95. The comment about Cao Kun (1862–1938) being the *jingchong zongtong*, as well as other anecdotes, continue to circulate on websites, such as Taiwan's *Apple Daily* (www .appledaily.com.tw/appledaily/article/headline/20110802/33569399/) and China Central Television's discussion forum: http://bigs.cctv.com/gate/bigs/bbs.cntv.cn/thread-14468662 -1-1.html.

96. Wu's essay about Zhang Shizhao (1881–1973), "Yousang: zhi *Guoyu zhoukan* jizhe" ("Bereft of a Friend: A Letter to the Journalists of *National Spoken Language Weekly*"), is reprinted in Wu, *Wu Zhihui yanlun ji*, 1:127.

97. The incident resulted in the newspaper *Subao* (1896–1903) being shut down by the Qing government on 7 July 1903. On the incident, see Wang, *Subao an yanjiu*.

98. Yi [Wu Zhihui], "Maiyin shizhuang" ("The Whore Revealed"), in *Xin shiji* (*La Novaj Tempoj*) 76 (5 December 1908), 6–8.

99. Ran [Wu Zhihui], "Zhusheng gouyang zhi Zhongguoren," n.p. This essay is part of a series, which included titles such as "Zhusheng gouyang zhi renzhong" ("Human Swine and Sons of Bitches"), *Xin shiji* 33 (8 February 1908), n.p.

100. Wu's specific phrases include: *goubao, piqi jingjin, lan goufen chou, shuangla, suan er xuannao*. See Ran, "Zhusheng gouyang zhi Zhongguoren."

101. Ch'en, *Yuan Shih-k'ai*, 78.

102. Ran, "Gui pi," *Xin shiji* 74 (21 November 1907), 5–9. Another essay in a similar style is "Fengshui xiansheng," *Xin shiji* 88 (1909), 11–15. The essays are reprinted in *HD* 1980, 117–22 and 118–27, respectively.

103. Representative of dozens of similar pieces is Zhongren, "Wu Zhilao: miaoren, miaoyu!" ("Old Wu: Brilliant Words from a Brilliant Man!"), *Kuaihuo lin* 34 (14 December 1946), 9. Reprinted in Meng, *Fangxing zhoubao*, 5:71. In the 1930s, the magazine the *Saturday* also carried anecdotes about Wu's wit, unintentional humor, and slovenly dress.

104. Lin, *A History of the Press and Public Opinion in China*, 159.

105. Zhou's phrase is *luru shigu*. In Zhou's September 1927 essay, "The Cruelty of Dishonoring the Dead" ("Wuru sizhe de canren"), he recounts a friend's objections to Wu's mockery of purged communists who had begged for their lives. See Zhou, *Zhou Zuoren: Selected Essays*, 82–87.

106. Translation from Kowallis, *The Lyrical Lu Xun*, 19–20.

107. Dating from Chen and Chen, *Wu Zhihui xiansheng nianpu*, 71. For versions of the story of Wu's discovery of *Which Classic?*, see Zhang, *Zhilao xianhua*, 68; Wu, *Wu Zhihui xiansheng yishi*, 28; [Liu] Dabai, "Du *He Dian*," 97. Some versions of this story, including in the chronology, mistakenly claim that the line "Bullshit! Bullshit! How truly absurd!" is the first line in *Which Classic?* when it in fact appears at the end of the opening lyric.

108. *Youhua zhishuo, youpi zhifang*. See Zhang, "Zhengzhiquan wai de Wu Zhihui."

109. "Liyan" ("General Remarks"), "Wu Zhihui xiansheng shudu" (Letters by Wu Zhihui"). In Shi, *Wu Zhihui yanxing lu*, 1.

110. Lu Xun's pseudonymous doggerel "Ode to 'a Verbal Spat,'" written in 1932, alludes to Wu's heated invective at a recent KMT assembly, and KMT faction leader Wang Jingwei's diabetes: "Cures and solidarity might be easy, / If you toss the 'verbal spat' into the privy. / Fart, fart, fart like a farting doggie; / It's all as absurd as absurd can be!" See A Er (Number Two) [Lu Xun], "'Yanci zhengzhi' ge," *Shizi jietou* (Crossroads) 3 (5 January 1932). Cited in Lu and Yang, *Zhongguo youmo wenxue shihua*, 238.

111. On Wu's work on *Guoyin zidian* and opinions of its competitors, see Chen, "The Sounds of 'Mandarin' in Gramophone Records and Film, 1922–1934," 10.

112. The preface was first printed on the front page of *Threads of Discourse*. See Liu Bannong, "Chongyin *Hedian* xu" ("Preface to the Reprint of *Which Classic?*"), *Yusi* 73 (5 April 1926), 103–4. The phrase *qiyou cili* appears in the title of two works of humorous literature published during the reign of the Jiaqing emperor (1796–1820): *How Absurd!* (*Qiyou cili*, 1799) and the encore volume *Even More Absurd!* (*Geng qiyou cili*, 1800).

113. Yuan Zhenying (1894–1979), "He Dian? xu" ("Preface to *Which Classic?*"). *HD* 1928a, 20. For a recent biography of Yuan written by a Communist Party historian. See Li et al., *Yuan Zhenying zhuan*.

114. Zheng Tianjian (Zheng Shuixin, 1900–75), "Xu" ("Preface"). *HD* 1928a, 5. Zheng later worked as propagandist for the KMT.

115. Zheng Tianjian, "Xu" ("Preface"). *HD* 1928a, 4. While no preface writer in the 1928 edition directly acknowledges the existence of Liu Fu's edition, Chang Chao (fl. 1920s), alludes to Wu Zhihui by means of a proverb that Liu had used in his original preface to convey that the student (Wu) had surpassed the teacher (*Which Classic?*): "Reading *Which Classic?* can't help but make one think of Old Wu. It's been said that *Which Classic?* was Wu's composition teacher. His essays read just like *Which Classic?*, but his diction is even more natural, not to mention more delightful and skillful! To express this with an allusion: 'Green comes from blue but is lovelier; ice is made of water but is colder.' But

making allusions is such a pain—an 'absurdity' indeed! Which allusion? 'Bullshit! Bullshit!'" See Chang Chao, "Xie zai *He Dian* jiaoding xin ben zhi qian" ("Foreword to the Newly Collated and Revised Edition of *Which Classic?*"), *HD* 1928a, 14. At the end of his preface (15), Chang also alludes to Wu Zhihui's "Ghost Farts."

116. See *HD* 1928a, 16–23; cf. *The Tragedy of King Lear* 1.2.334–55; apropos of bountiful billingsgate, see Kent's tirade against Oswald in 2.2.1087–95. A 1931 issue of the literary magazine *Big Dipper* (*Beidou*, 1931–32), edited by Ding Ling (1904–86), contains a short story, "A Comedy" ("Xiju"), written by a certain "Which Classic?" (Hedian). See *Beidou* 1, no. 2 (20 October 1931), 1–8. "Space-fillers" (*bubai*) by a writer using the pen name "Which Classic?" also appear regularly in 1926 in the leftist literary magazine *Zhongliu*, whose regular contributors included Lu Xun, Mao Dun, Ba Jin, Xiao Hong, Chen Baichen, Hu Feng, and Ye Shengtao.

117. The poet Pu Zhishui coined the term *devil-talk novel* (*guihua xiaoshuo*) to liken *Which Classic?* to *Quelling the Demons*, another novel he fondly recalled encountering in his youth. See [Pu] Zhishui, "Cong *He Dian* xiang dao *Ping gui zhuan*" ("Thinking from *Which Classic?* to *Pacifying the Devils*"), *Yusi* 87 (12 July 1926), 105–8. Signed "Tianjin 31 June 1926." Zhou Zuoren nominated it as an example of "comical literature" (*huaji wenxue*) analogous to Japanese *kōkkei*. See Zhitang [Zhou Zuoren], "Zhongguo de huaji wenxue" ("China's Comical Literature"), *Yuzhou feng* 22 (1 August 1936), 544–46.

118. Altenburger, "Chains of Ghost Talk," 24.

119. *HD* 1946 reportedly had a print run of ten thousand copies; Cheng Jiang. "Editor's Afterword," *HD* 2000, 288. The cover of *HD* 1954, printed in Taipei, is inscribed in the hand of "Jingheng," aka Wu Zhihui.

120. Notably, not until the 1980s do editions of *Which Classic?* mention Lu Xun on the cover. See *HD* 1985 and *HD* 2000. More than half a century later, the writer Zhang Kebiao, who was associated with the *Analects* school in the 1930s, mentions Wu Zhihui but not Lu Xun in his positive recollection of the novel: "Following the New Culture Movement of the May Fourth period, Liu Bannong even republished a comical novel, *Which Classic?* He went all-out on publicity and it seems even old Mr. Wu Zhihui praised it highly—I'm sure that people more advanced in years will remember. That work was also written by someone from the Qianlong-Jiaqing era. I very much enjoyed the book myself and re-read it many times." Zhang Kebiao, "Fulu: *Wentan denglongshu* de jingyan ("Appendix: How I Wrote *How to Become a Famous Writer*"), in Zhang, *Zhang Kebiao wenji*, 1:586. (Essay dated "First draft: 17 October 1988; Revised: 1998.")

121. In 1929, for example, sociologist Li Jinghan (Franklin C. H. Lee, 1895–1986) used the term *living devils* (*huogui*) to refer to the tens of thousands of indigent poor of Beiping, the phrase encapsulating Li's sympathy for individuals and families along with his horror at the broader sociological phenomenon they represented. While mockery was undoubtedly the furthest thing from Li's mind, his choice of phrase nevertheless is objectifying and connotes a similar categorical logic. See Chen, *Guilty of Indigence*, 94.

122. Playwright Bai Wei's (1894–1987) *Dachu Youlingta* (Breaking Out of Ghost Pagoda) originally appeared in *Torrent* (*Benliu*, 1928–29) between June and September of 1928. For a translation see Chen, *The Columbia Anthology of Modern Chinese Drama*, 165–226. The implied author of Zhang Tianyi's novel *Ghostland Diary* (*Guitu riji*), first published in 1931,

in an undated, prefatory "Letter about *Ghostland Diary*" ("Guanyu 'Guitu riji' de yifeng xin"), advises the reader baldly: "At first glance, their society might appear different from that of our mortal world. But, Sir, I must ask you to look closer. When you do, you'll discover that the seeming differences between the societies of ghosts and men are merely superficial matters of form. In fact, everything in these two societies—be they people or events—works on the same principles." See Zhang, *Guitu riji*, front matter.

123. On the "fundamental opposition" between ritual insults, which have little bearing on reality and are swapped with in a play frame, and personal insults, which cut too close to home and thus break that frame, see Labov, *Language in the Inner City*, 297–353.

124. Zheng, *Zheng Yimei xuanji*, 1:891–92. *Shehui yuebao* (1934) reportedly lasted only six issues, but *Shehui ribao* (the *Social News Daily*, 1929–37) spanned almost the entire Nanjing Decade.

125. "Tongren jietiao" (Prohibitions for Members), *LY* 1, no. 1 (16 September 1932). T. K. Chuan's translation of this list appears in chapter 6.

126. The play was first published in the magazine *Torrent*, which Lu Xun edited. See [Lin] Yutang, "Zi jian Nanzi" ("Confucius Saw Nancy"), *Benliu* 1, no. 6 (November 1928), 921–53. For Lu Xun's defense of the play and Lin, see Lu Xun, "Guanyu *Zijian Nanzi*" ("Regarding *Confucius Saw Nancy*"), *Yusi* 5, no. 24 (19 August 1929), 24–48. A short account of the play's reception in Qufu, Shandong is given in the prefatory remarks to Lin's English translation: Lin, "Confucius Saw Nancy," v–vi.

127. Lin Yutang, "On Freedom of Speech," reprinted in Lin, *With Love and Irony*, 133. A modified version of the Chinese phrase *xiaoma you ta xiaoma, haoguan wo zi wei zhi* appears in a poem Liang Qichao inserted in chapter 2 of *The Future of New China*, which satirizes cigar-chomping, diamond-ring-wearing opportunists who "fawn on devils but gnash their teeth at humans." See Yinbingshi zhuren [Liang Qichao], *Xin Zhongguo weilai ji, Xin xiaoshuo* 1 (15 October 1902), 74.

128. Cheng Shijue, "Xu" ("Preface"). In Cheng, *Xiaolin guangji* (1934, Dada tushu ed.), 1. As mentioned in chapter 2, this collection is different from the early Qing work of the same title compiled by the Master of Play.

CHAPTER 5. FARCE

1. Lin Yutang, "Chinese Realism and Humour," *CC* 3, no. 39 (25 September 1930), 924–25. The essay is reprinted in Lin, *The Little Critic: Essays, Satires and Sketches on China (First Series: 1930–1932)*, 86–95, though it did not actually appear in the Little Critic column.

2. [Xu] Zhuodai, "Shangxia liangdui" ("Two Couples"), *Xiaoshuo shijie* 1, no. 6 (9 February 1923), n.p.

3. Xu Zhuodai, "Nüxing de wanwu," *HM* 5, no. 3 (2 March 1928), n.p. The first page of the story includes a small illustration of a young woman sitting on a chair playing with a doll, as a dog looks on expectantly. The same issue carries chapter 2 of Cheng Zhanlu's novel *A New History of Comedy* (*Huaji xin shi*).

4. Lu Xun describes his addition of comedic material as *huluan* or haphazard. See Lu Xun, "'Ah Q zhengzhuan' de chengyin," 548.

5. Shirley Chan notes in her study of the classical Daoist text *Liezi* that, in its premodern usage, "*huaji* does not differ in essence from what is now generally understood as humour in contemporary China." See Chey and Davis, *Humour in Chinese Life and Letters*, 73. *Huixie* is now sometimes cited as the closest indigenous Chinese approximation of the English word *humor* before the introduction of the transliteration *youmo*. Some humor columns of the 1900s and 1910s were entitled "Humorous Writings" (*xiezhu*, *xiewen*), and the *All-Story Monthly* serialized "humorous novels" (*huixie xiaoshuo*). Few periodicals or literary works of that period, however, contain the term *huixie* in their title. In the 1920s Anglophile essayist Liang Yuchun (1906–32) used *huaji* and *huixie* interchangeably as translations for *humor*. In 1927 he translated *humorist* as *huajijia* and in 1929 translated *humor* as *huaji* and *humorist* as *huixiejia*. See Liang, *Liang Yuchun sanwenji*, 18, 70–72.

6. Several parodies from *Huaji hun*, written by many hands and edited by Li Dingyi, are discussed in chapter 3. A 1921 retranslation from English of Henri Bergson's essay *Le Rire* rendered "the comic" as *huaji*. See Bergson, *Xiao zhi yanjiu*.

7. Perry Link estimates that the Shanghai book-publishing industry as a whole grew more than sixfold from 1910 to 1930, from revenue of 4–5 million *yuan* to 30 million *yuan*. See Link, *Mandarin Ducks and Butterflies*, 92–93. Alexander Des Forges notes that the so-called petty urbanites (*xiao shimin*) were defined by their consumption practices, "depend[ing] not primarily on their occupations, but rather on the kinds of housing they occupied, and, significantly, on the kinds of books and magazines they read." See Des Forges, *Mediasphere Shanghai*, 127.

8. Lin Yutang, "Unconscious Chinese Humor," *CC* 7, no. 45 (8 November 1934), 1098.

9. The "Guji liezhuan" chapter of Sima Qian's *Shiji* (chap. 126) is translated in Baccini, "The Forest of Laughs (*Xiaolin*)," 193–203. Stories of Baldy Chunyu (Beatrice Otto's translation) and other jesters also appear in Otto, *Fools Are Everywhere*, 88, 105–6, 122–23, 177, 232.

10. This meaning is found in literature as recently as the nineteenth century. *Guji* is used to refer to a wine vessel in the novel *Heroic Sons and Daughters* (*Ernü yingxiong zhuan*, nineteenth century). Individually, *gu* 滑 meant "to bubble like a spring" and *ji* 稽 "continuous and unceasing." See the entries on *huaji* and *guji* in Luo, *Hanyu da cidian*, 1481; compare Tang, *Zhongguo xiandai huaji wenxue shilüe*, 1. The use of *huaji* as a noun to mean comic performer continues today, as seen in the title of actor Yang Huasheng's (1918–2012) autobiography *An Old Comic Performer of Shanghai* (2005). See Yang and Zhang, *Shanghai lao huaji*.

11. In an eighth-century commentary, Sima Zhen remarked: "Those adept at speech and argumentation make the false appear true and the true appear false, throwing the similar and the dissimilar into confusion" (*yanbian jie de ren yan fei ruo shi, shuo shi ruo fei, yan luan yitong ye*). Literary theorist Liu Xie (ca. 465–522 CE) shared this moralistic view of humor, giving pride of place to corrective satire. See Liu, *The Literary Mind and the Carving of Dragons*, 154–65.

12. Mr. Bored's (or Mr. Boring's, Wuliaozi) "New Preface" to the 1926 Saoye shanfang edition of *Funny Chats*, for example, compares Wu Jianren to Baldy Chunyu and Dongfang Shuo. Wu, *Xinshi biaodian Huaji tan*. (See appendix 1.)

13. Wang Guowei (1877–1927), retranslating the philosopher and psychoanalyst Harald Höffding (1843–1931) from English, used the term *huaji zhi qing*. Haifuding, *Xinlixue gailun*, 395.

14. Zhitang [Zhou Zuoren], "Zhongguo de huaji wenxue" (see appendix 2). *Kōkkei shinbun*, founded by author and journalist Miyatake Gaikotsu (1867–1955), was an immediate nationwide success and lasted 173 issues before it was banned in 1908 for printing a "suicide issue." A new edition took its place shortly thereafter.

15. *Huaji dawang*. Chaplin's films screened in China in the late 1910s, but it was likely not until movie house infrastructure became more established in the 1920s that they reached a broader audience. Reviews of and stills from Chaplin's films, as well as news and gossip about his personal life appeared regularly in magazines such as *Stage and Screen* (*Xiju dianying*, est. 1926).

16. The manifold meanings, connotations, and interpretations of *quwei* are discussed at length in Daruvala, *Zhou Zuoren and an Alternative Chinese Response to Modernity*, 138–52, and Zhao, *Zhongguo xiandai quwei zhuyi wenxue sichao*. Daruvala notes that *quwei* "draws on a host of related words carrying the associations of taste (*qu*) and flavor (*wei*). These are words with a large and overlapping semantic range that includes the senses of interest, piquancy, delight, and delectation" (145). I use the imperfect translation "taste" to indicate *quwei*'s strong association in Shanghai popular fiction magazines with the idea of individual sensibility. This usage differs significantly from idealized conceptions of elite Beijing-based aesthetic theorists. For Zhou Zuoren, "taste" was an innate and inalienable quality that could not be cultivated. Daruvala endorses Jonathan Chaves's formulation that "*qu* is the ineffable essence at the heart of things and even partakes of a spiritual quality" (145). For cultural entrepreneurs, however, taste was a function of a market shaped by the relentless pursuit of novelty. In his work on the artist and essayist Feng Zikai, Geremie Barmé translates it as "allure," among other renderings. See Barmé, *An Artistic Exile*, 95. A Shanghai tabloid calling itself *Qubao* (Amusement) appeared in 1898. See Wang, "The Weight of Frivolous Matters," 65.

17. Wu Jianren's *Xin Fengshen zhuan* appeared in *Yueyue xiaoshuo* (*All-Story Monthly*). See Tang, *Zhongguo xiandai huaji wenxue shilüe*, 69–70. Wei Yi (1880–1932) translated Dickens's prose orally, and Lin Shu, who knew no foreign languages, converted Wei's vernacular rendering into classical Chinese. On their improvised humor, see Qian Zhongshu's study of Lin Shu's translations, "Lin Shu de fanyi" in Qian, *Qizhui ji*, 77–114; translated in Qian, *Patchwork*, 139–88.

18. *Huaji* works include Yanyun jushi's *Huaji wenji* (1910), *Xing Han mie Man huaji lu* (1911), Hu Jichen's *Huaji congshu* (1913, repub. 1914), Chen Yan's *Huaji conghua* (1919), and *(Miben) Huaji wenfu daguan* (1921). See appendix 1.

19. In 1915, the daily newspaper *Eastern Times* (*Shibao*, 1910–39) released four issues of *Funny Eastern Times* (*Huaji shibao*), each well over one hundred pages. The pictorial magazine *Shanghai Puck* (1918) carried the alternate title *Bochen's Funny Pictorial* (*Bochen huaji huabao*). During its two-year run, the fiction weekly the *Sunday* (*Xingqi*, 1922–23) issued an annual subscriber freebie entitled *Funny* (*Huaji*), which featured color cartoons,

stories, and comic play scripts. A 1922 advertisement in the *Sunday* advertises the supplement as being in the style of "the European *Puck*, the American *Puck*, and *Life*," and claims that the *Sunday* has more than three thousand subscribers.

20. The supertitle *huaji xiaohua* appears on the cover of Zhao, *Xinxian xiaohua yi da xiang*.

21. Fan and Kong, *Tongsu wenxue shiwu jiang*, 251. Wei Shaochang's list of popular authors who wrote *huaji* works—which he says tended to be short pieces—includes, in addition to Cheng (1879/82–1943), Gong (1879–1939) and Wu (1884–1934), Li Dingyi, Li Hanqiu, Bao Tianxiao, Hu Jichen, Fan Yanqiao (1874–1967), Zhang Chunfan, Bi Yihong (1892–1926) (founder of *Shanghai Pictorial* [est. 1925]), Liu Tieleng (1881–1961) (editor of an encore to *Civil Rights*), Xu Jinfu (1891–1953) (editor of *Fiction Daily*), Yan Duhe (1889–1968), Ping Jinya (1892–1980), Ye Xiaofeng (1887–1946), Wang Zhongxian, You Bankuang, and Huang Zhuantao. At the top of his list is Xu Zhuodai. See Wei, *Wo kan yuanyang hudie pai*, 176. Geng Xiaodi's dates are 1907–94.

22. See Tang, *Zhongguo xiandai huaji wenxue shilüe*, 34; Lee, "A Dime Store of Words," 59.

23. Pronounced Xu Zuo'ai in Wu dialect. The following biographical material is drawn primarily from four sources: Xu, *Huaju chuangshiqi huiyi lu*; Zheng, *Qingmo minchu wentan yishi*, 187–94; Tang, *Zhongguo xiandai huaji wenxue shilüe*, 147–71; Tian, "Xu Zhuodai yu Zhongguo xiandai dazhong wenhua."

24. Jonathan Kolatch writes that "The [Xus] were truly the first family of Chinese physical education." The sports academy that Xu founded in 1904 graduated more than fifteen hundred students before it closed in 1928. The girls' sports academy founded by Tang Jianwo (d. 1932) in 1905 remained in continuous operation until 1937. See Kolatch, *Sports, Politics, and Ideology in China*, 6–7. According to a Suzhou local gazeteer, Tang, who also studied in Japan, was the first principal of a girls' sports academy in China. See Deng, "'Dongfang Zhuobielin' Xu Zhuodai" ("'Oriental Charlie Chaplin' Xu Zhuodai"), online at: http://122.11.55.148/gate/big5/www.dfzb.suzhou.gov.cn/zsbl/1677127.htm. The date that Xu founded his first school is given in most sources as 1905, the year he returned from Japan. In 1907, Xu Zhuodai cofounded another school with Xu Yibing (1881–1922) and others and briefly served as its principal. Xu's book *Gymnastics Physiology* appeared in 1909. Andrew D. Morris's *Marrow of the Nation* does not mention the Xus' pioneering work in the field of physical education but discusses the importance of sport in the discourse of nation building. One of Xu's daughters, Xu Zhongqi, was also an athletic champion; photographs of her with track and field trophies (next to samples of her calligraphy in oracle bone style) and in swimwear appear in the *Liengyi's Tri-Monthly* (*Lianyi zhi you*, 1925–31).

25. Xu wrote *Wireless Broadcasting* (*Wuxiandian boyin*) for the Commercial Press's "social education short book series" (*shehui jiaoyu xiao congshu*). The copy held in the Shanghai Library lacks a date, but the thread binding and traditional character font mark it as a Republican era publication. The eighth edition (1935) of Xu's book on judo is held at the Shanghai Library: Xu, *Riben roudao*.

26. Chinese titles: *Shishi xinbao*, *Shanghai chenbao*, *Xiao hua*, and *Xin Shanghai*.

27. These include *Banyue, Chahua, Dazhong, Haifeng, Haiguang, Hong meigui, Hong zazhi, Kuaihuo shijie, Lianyi zhi you, Libailiu, Qiri tan, Shenbao, Shibao, Wanxiang, Xiao hua, Xiaoshuo daguan, Xiaoshuo shijie, Xin Shanghai,* and *Zazhi.*

28. Chinese titles: *Qiyoucili zhi riji, Buzhi suoyun ji, Zuihou xiu pingguo, Xiaohua sanqian.*

29. See Hu Jichen, "Hu xu" ("Hu Jichen Preface"), in Xu, *Qiyou cili zhi riji*, n.p. Zhao's words are *mihan zheli.* See Zhao Tiaokuang, "Benji zhuzhe Xu Zhuodai jun zhuan" ("A Biography of the Author of this Collection, Mr. Xu Zhuodai"), in Xu, *Zhuodai xiaoshuo ji*, 1–2 (January 1926 reprint). Zhu Shoutong makes the Molière comment in his preface to a collection he edited: Xu, *Qiyou cili zhi riji*, n.p.

30. Link, *Mandarin Ducks and Butterflies*, 163. This anecdote appears as early as 1923. See Yan Fusun, "Xu Zhuodai," in *Quanguo xiaoshuo mingjia zhuanji* (Biographies of Famous Chinese Fiction Writers), reprinted in Yuan, *Huo zai weixiao zhong*, 36–37. A 1924 advertisement for two of his joke books echoes the common view that Xu's "every move was funny." The ad for Xu's *Laugh-Getters* (*Tiaoxiao lu*) and *New Forest of Laughs* (*Xin xiaolin*), both published by Shanghai's Dadong shuju, appeared in *Banyue* 3, no. 16 (4 May 1924), on the fifth anniversary of the May Fourth Movement. An identical claim appears a month later in a literary gossip column written by Xu's editor at *Red Rose*. See Shi Jiqun, "Wentan quhua: Xu Zhuodai zhi huaji" ("Literary Anecdotes: Funny Man Xu Zhuodai"), *HM* 94 (6 June 1924), n.p.

31. Xu Fulin (aka Zhuodai) is to be confused with Xu Fulin (1879–1958), an early chairman of the Democratic Socialist Party. Clumsiness, in the sense of simple and uncultivated naiveté, is also a long-prized quality in literati art. See Barmé, *An Artistic Exile*, 116.

32. Xu's pen names include *po yehushi zhu, banlao Xuye, maiyou lang,* and *jiangweng.* In regional opera and vernacular fiction, *maiyou lang* is an oil seller (*you* can refer to oil or sauce). See Xu Zhuodai, "Miao buke jiangyou" ("Marvelous Soy Sauce!"), *Chahua* 18 (10 November 1947), 40–48. The title of Xu's essay is a pun on "Too marvelous for words!" since words (*yan*) sounds like salt (*yan*), and soy sauce is salty. Another variant on the salty theme, "Marvelous beef soup!" (*miao buke niuroutang*)—which deliberately sabotages the pun—appeared in the first installment of Xu's 1946 advice column, "Li Ah Mao's Mailbox: Special Edition" ("Li Amao Xinxiang haowai"), in the tabloid *Haiguang* 10 (6 February 1946), 10; reprinted in Meng, *Fangxing zhoubao*, 2:492.

33. On Xu's work with Huo Yuanjia (1868–1910), see Deng, "'Dongfang Zhuobielin' Xu Zhuodai."

34. On Huang's employment of Xu, see Cochran, *Chinese Medicine Men*, 52, 182n51.

35. A photograph of Xu in costume also appears in the first issue of the short-lived magazine *The Happy World* (*Kuaihuo shijie*, 1914). In 1917 he and the female impersonator Ouyang Yuqian (1889–1962) traveled together to Japan to study how Japanese actors were trained. Four years later, he joined a short-lived theater research group founded by Wang Zhongxian (1888–1937) called the Masses Drama Society (*Minzhong xijushe*), whose members included the Anglophile playwright Xiong Foxi (1900–1965) and New Literature advocates such as the realist writer Zheng Zhenduo and the leftist novelist Mao Dun, who later became the People's Republic of China's minister of culture.

36. The origins of *huaji xi* are as contested as those of vaudeville in America. A summary and analysis of leading theories of origin appears in Fan and Wei, "Huaji xi qiyuan yu xingcheng chutan." See also Shanghai wenhua chubanshe, *Huaji luncong*. Zhang Jian credits the coining of the term *huaji xi* to Wang Guowei, from Wang's famous study of Song and Yuan drama. See Zhang, *Zhongguo xiju guannian de xiandai shengcheng*, 54. Historians have applied the term retroactively to comedic drama dating as early as the Tang dynasty (617–907). See Luo, *Hanyu da cidian*, 1482.

37. Laughing Jiang (Jiang Xiaoxiao, 1900–1947) and Boisterous Bao (Bao Lele, 1902–63) produced a series of books featuring their routines, *Laughs from Jiang and Bao* (*Jiang Bao xiaoji*), the first volume of which was published by Shanghai's Zilin shuju in 1935. A two-volume 1941 edition, which I have seen only the cover of, appears to have been issued by a paper-cutting company, Zhongguo qiezhi gongsi. Another edition features prominent ads for cigarettes, wireless radios, and other commodities. Liu Chunshan (1902–42), like Xu Zhuodai, founded his own Happy Film Company (Kuaile yingpian gongsi) specializing in comic shorts. Wimpy Wang's (Wang Wuneng, d. ca. 1939) stage routines are discussed in Shanghai wenhua chubanshe, *Huaji luncong*. According to one cultural history of Shanghai, *huaji* stage performance reached its peak of popularity in amusement halls in the late 1920s and waned after the Mukden Incident of 1931. See Shanghaishi wenshi yanjiuguan, *Hubin lüeying*, 228.

38. For an example of this usage, see chapter 43 of Zhuang Binghai's (pen name of Tao Juyin, b. 1898) unfinished novel *Yuan Shikai yanyi* (Shanghai: Jiaotong tushuguan, 1917); cited in Luo, *Hanyu da cidian*, 1482.

39. Xu reportedly began playwriting in 1909. His plays can be found in more than half a dozen magazines and journals, including the *Story World*, the *Grand Magazine*, *Funny* (a supplement of the *Sunday*), the *Half Moon Journal*, *Wan hsiang*, and the *Masses*. Play count is from Zheng, *Qingmo Minchu wentan yishi*, 189; estimate that this was more than any other contemporary playwright is from Tang, *Zhongguo xiandai huaji wenxue shilüe*, 41.

40. Xu remembered the phrase as "tian yao luoyu, niang yao jiaren." The Laughter Stage (*Xiao wutai*) troupe later expanded from seven to nine members, including Ouyang Yuqian. Xu mentions that its newspaper advertisements "read like playful writings" (*youxi wenzhang*) and succeeded in drawing full houses. See Xu, *Huaju chuangshiqi huiyilu*, 88.

41. See ibid., 87–93. Laughter Stage's production of Hong Shen's *Yama Zhao*, premiered on 6 February 1923 and starred the playwright himself. See "Guchui caibing zhi xinzi kaiyan zaiji" ("Premiere of Another New Drama Play Advocating Disarmament"), *SB* 17944 (4 February 1923), 18.

42. Zheng and Xu, *Shanghai jiuhua*, 104.

43. [Xu] Zhuodai, "Juhun shizhe," *Xiaoshuo shijie* 1, no. 1 (5 January 1923), n.p.

44. Davis, *Farce*, 7. In another reversal farce pitting father against son, "A Father's Duty," Chen Weimei and his father, Chen Jinping (a pun on "neurotic," *shenjing bing*), encounter each other at the entrance to a brothel. Each dispatches the other with the excuse that he just happened to be passing by, only to return separately and sneak into the brothel one after another. The prostitute Big Pretty Flower receives son and father in turn. Weimei informs Big Pretty Flower of his plan to trick his greedy father into allowing them to marry by telling him that his unnamed fiancée will bring a large dowry. When his father,

Jinping, arrives, Weimei hides in the wardrobe and overhears his father tell Big Pretty Flower that his son is engaged, and that as soon as Weimei is out the door he will bring her in as his concubine. She feigns delight and convinces Jinping to give her three thousand dollars to prepare for their wedding and settle her debts. In the final scene, Weimei's bride is revealed to be none other than Big Pretty Flower herself, and since the father cannot admit that he knows this prostitute in the presence of the wedding party, the couple succeeds in relieving the father of both money and concubine. See [Xu] Zhuodai, "Fuqin de yiwu," *Xiaoshuo shijie* 2, no. 4 (1923), n.p.

45. Performance notices and reviews in *Shun Pao* record that the play was performed a Shanghai girls' school in 1923 and staged at least four times by the Morning Star Acting Troupe in 1926 and 1927. Morning Star's second staging was at Shanghai's Guangdong Baptist Society; in the fourth, in February 1927, featured Xu Tianneng as Ah Ba and Ouyang Yuqian in the ensemble. Notices for these performances appear in *Shun Pao*: "Wujing nüxue kai shizhou jinian youyihui" ("Wujing Girl's School Holds Tenth Anniversary Gala"), *SB* 18049 (27 May 1923), 19; "Chenxing yanjutuan zhi 'Juhun shizhe'" ("Morning Star Theatrical Troupe's *The Devil Messenger*"), *SB* 19021 (17 February 1926), 19; "'Juhun shizhe' jinri fuyan" ("*The Devil Messenger* Returns to the Stage Tonight"), *SB* 19108 (15 May 1926), 22; "Juchang xiaoxi" ("Theater News"), *SB* 19712 (3 February 1927), 21–22. The script dubs the work a "laughter play" (*xiaoju*), or farce, while the newspaper notices refer to it as a "delightful play" (*quju*).

46. [Xu] Zhuodai, "Shangxia liangdui." The play is advertised as a comedy (*xiju*) in one act and three scenes.

47. Shameless's italicized words, here and below, appear as English in the original.

48. Second sentence rendered phonetically to preserve the rhyme and the imitation of foreign sounds.

49. Inflated food prices and their effects on the common people was one of Xu's recurring concerns. Commodity inflation appears in many of his other works, including the novel *Omnipotence* (*Wanneng shu*, 1926), serialized in the *Story World*, and the series *The Unofficial Story of Li Ah Mao* (1940–41), which is discussed below. In the story "The International Currency Reform Conference," a beat reporter daydreams that the hyperinflation that followed World War I will be solved by inverting the value of currency, making a dime worth one hundred dollars, and vice versa. See Xu Zhuodai, "Wanguo huobi gaizao dahui," *HM* 19 (1922), 1–10. The title character of the *Ah Mao* stories, which were written in occupied Shanghai, dreams up ways to trick people so he can fill his poor friends' bellies. In the eleventh episode, for example, Ah Mao opens a Japanese-language school, charges his students a bag of rice as tuition, and then (since he does not speak Japanese himself) spends a month teaching them how to pronounce the Japanese word for "rice," which he learned from a Japanese soldier.

50. See Tang, *Zhongguo xiandai huaji wenxue shilüe*, 51, 150.

51. On the links between vaudeville and cinema, see Trav S. D., *No Applause*; Jenkins, *What Made Pistachio Nuts?*

52. Happy Film Company (*Kaixin yingpian gongsi*) issued its own special handbook-size periodical to accompany each new release, which contained still photographs and articles about the production. The handbook for *He-Wife* (*Xiong xifu*, 1926) contains a piece

by a member of the acting company who mentions that Zheng Zhengqiu introduced him to join Laughter Stage before he joined Happy Film Company. See Wu Jichen, "Wode dianying mi" ("My Cinephilia"), *Kaixin tekan* 2 (1 May 1926), 21–22. Xu's own piece, "She xiangyan pigu zhuyi," appears on pages 4–8. A copy is held at the Shanghai Library. The Chinese names of the films mentioned below are *Aishen zhi feiliao* and *Guai yisheng*.

53. A still from *Gangda zhuozei* appears in the front matter of *Banyue* 2, no. 21 (14 July 1923).

54. Zhang, *An Amorous History of the Silver Screen*, 163. Zhang includes an illustration from *The Science of Shadowplay* (*Yingxi xue*) and a photograph of Xu in costume for a female role on pages 165–66. Not all *tuolike* lenses were funny. A 1914 advertisement in the *Happy World* by "China's first producer of trick lenses," for example, referred to multiple-focal eyeglasses. See *Kuaihuo shijie* 2 (18 October 1914), n.p.

55. See Karnick and Jenkins, *Classical Hollywood Comedy*, 87–105; compare also Dong, "The Laborer at Play."

56. Zheng Yimei relates an anecdote indicative of the culture of joking that surrounded Xu. At a party to celebrate the launch of the Candle Film Company (*Lazhu yingpian gongsi*), his friend presented him with two big candles, an allusion to the phrase "light the big candles" (*dian da lazhu*), Shanghai slang for a virgin prostitute's first night with a john, which Xu happily accepted. See Zheng, *Qingmo Minchu wentan yishi*, 191; for a 1935 gloss of the candle expression, see Wang and Xu, *Shanghai suyu tushuo*, 10–12.

57. Two of Xu's later "delightful plays" (*quju*) appear in the August 1941 and February 1942 issues of *Wanxiang* during the period that magazine was serializing Xu's twelve-part story series *The Unofficial Story of Li Ah Mao*. Xu's comments on fiction appear in [Xu] Zhuodai, "Xiaoshuo wuti lu" ("Untitled Notes on Fiction"), *Xiaoshuo shijie* 1, no. 7 (1923), n.p.

58. Xu Zhuodai, "Kaimu guanggao," *HM* 1, no. 1 (2 August 1924), n.p. In-text quotations are from this version. The story is reprinted in Wei and Wu, *Yuanyang hudie pai yanjiu ziliao*, 2:1149–58.

59. A cartoon of a rickshaw puller with "Your Ad Here" on his back appears, for example, in *Yuxing* 1 (1914), 52. Zhou Shoujuan's 1917 novella *The Intimate Beauty* (*Hongyan zhiji*) also uses the newspaper advertisement as a device to reunite the lovers. See Mostow, *The Columbia Companion to Modern East Asian Literature*, 355–63.

60. On the rise of the Chinese cultural entrepreneur, see Rea and Volland, *The Business of Culture*.

61. Guides to letter writing were a new commodity in the Republican period, occasioned by a broad shift from the classical language to a vernacular style of writing. Advertisements appeared regularly in magazines like *Red Rose*. The *Half Moon Journal*, for example, in 1923 carried a standing advertisement for a guide to writing *Letters for All Social Occasions* (*Jiaoji chidu daquan*) by a certain Letter-Writing King (*chidu dawang*).

62. Zhang Yingjin notes that male writers often used the trope of an absent woman who must be constructed purely through text to configure Republican Shanghai in gendered terms. Zhang quotes Teresa de Lauretis: "The city is a text which tells the story of male desire by performing the absence of woman and by producing woman as text, as pure representation." Zhang adds that "woman is repeatedly inscribed as absent, as ultimately

unattainable in narrative or in the city—'repeatedly,' because the more unattainable the goal appears, the stronger the (male) desire burns, and the more urgent the task of constructing the narrative/city becomes." See Zhang, *The City in Modern Chinese Literature and Film*, 186. Xu's narrative encapsulates the patterns of absence and repetition but differs in that Qiu controls the interaction.

63. Recent studies of the figure of the "modern woman" (*modeng nüxing*), "new woman" (*xin nüxing*), and "modern girl" (*moga*), as she is variously called, include Weinbaum, et al., *Modern Girl around the World*; Hu, *Tales of Translation*; Des Forges, *Mediasphere Shanghai*, 131–59.

64. Xu's story nevertheless differs from mainstream cautionary tales about duplicitous females, like the gold-digging confidence women that appear in Zhu Shouju's story "The Confidence in the Game" ("Cizhong mimi," 1922), translated in Wong, *Stories for Saturday*, 5–27; or Zhang Henshui's novel *Ping-Hu tongche* (1935), translated as Zhang, *Shanghai Express*.

65. Davis, *Farce*, 7.

66. According to notices in *Shun Pao*, *Morning Post* (*Chenbao*) carried an Ah Mao column in 1933 and one of its sister publications carried "Li Ah Mao's Experiments" ("Li Amao ceyan") in 1935. "Li Ah Mao's Notebook" ("Li Amao suibi") appeared in *Social News Daily* (*Shehui ribao*) in 1937. The *Hai Kwang Weekly*, a postwar tabloid, contains a series of more than twenty "Li Ah Mao's Mailbox: Special Edition" ("Li Amao xinxiang haowai"), credited to Big Brother Ah Mao (Amao ge). A second series, "Biographies of New Theater Aficionados" ("Xin ximi zhuan"), is credited to Li Amao with illustrations by Dong Tianye. Other contributions appear under Xu's pen name Old Man Soy Sauce (Jiangweng).

67. Chinese film titles: *Li Ah Mao yu Tang Xiaojie*, *Li Ah Mao yu jiangshi*, and *Li Ah Mao yu Dongfang Shuo*. The latter ranked as the sixth-highest-grossing film in the first half of 1940. On the Ah Mao films, see Tian, "Xu Zhuodai yu Zhongguo dazhong wenhua," 195; Rao, *Zhongguo xiju dianying shi*, 95. Li Ah Mao's leap from page to silver screen followed close on the heels of "Mr. Wang," the titular protagonist of 1930s Shanghai's most popular comic strip who became the central character in at least a dozen live-action (as opposed to animated) films. Zheng Xiaoqiu's dates are 1910–89.

68. Xu Zhuodai, *Li Amao waizhuan* (The Unofficial Story of Li Ah Mao). Serialized in the first twelve issues of *Wanxiang*, July 1941 to June 1942.

69. See Xu Zhuodai, *Li Amao waizhuan* (yi): "Yuren jie" ("The Unofficial Story of Li Ah Mao [1]: April Fool's Day"), *Wanxiang* 1, no. 1 (1 July 1941), 195–97. Xu also wrote other "stories in playscript form" (*jubenti xiaoshuo*), including "Splash" ("Shuisheng") and "One Part of the Heart" ("Yi fangmian de xin"). None of the Li Ah Mao films or scripts appear to be extant, so we do not know whether any of the scenarios of *The Unofficial Story* appeared on-screen.

70. Xu Zhuodai, *Li Amao waizhuan* (ba): "Qing zou houmen chuqu" ("The Unofficial Story of Li Ah Mao [8]: Please Exit through the Back Door"), *Wanxiang* 1, no. 8 (February 1942), 208–10. The story is illustrated.

71. Ibid., 209–10.

72. One example of deceptive medicinal advertising from this period is the Western-sounding product Ailuo Brain Tonic (*Ailuo bunaozhi*) developed by the "King of Adver-

tising" (*guanggao dawang*) Huang Chujiu, founder of the Great World amusement hall. The importance of textual packaging is evident from Huang's marketing techniques: "He distributed the drug in bottles under a Chinese name ... which sounded like a Chinese transliteration of a Western name, and he had China's biggest publishing house, the Commercial Press, print instructions on the label in English. On the label and the outer paper wrapper he added, also in English, that the product was invented by Dr. T. C. Yale. Thus, on the outside, this medicine gave every indication of being Western." See Yeh, *Becoming Chinese*, 63.

73. See Fan Boqun, "Dongfang Zhuobielin, huaji xiaoshuo mingjia—Xu Zhuodai" ("The Oriental Charlie Chaplin and Famous Comic Fiction Writer: Xu Zhuodai"), in Xu, *Huaji dashi Xu Zhuodai daibiao zuo*, 4–5; Tang, *Zhongguo xiandai huaji wenxue shilüe*, 147–72. Later in the war period, Xu wrote essays offering readers practical advice on nutrition and how to fill their bellies while saving money. See, for example, "Shengmi chifan fa" ("How to Make Your Rice Last"), *Dazhong* (December 1944), 115–16; and "Baojian shiliao" ("Healthful Foods"), *Dazhong* (January 1945), 113.

74. On ruses, strategies, and tactics, see Certeau, *The Practice of Everyday Life*, xix, 29–42, 52–56. Translation from Schor and Holt, *The Consumer Society Reader*, 309.

75. Hyde adds, "Trickster starts out hungry, but before long he is master of the kind of creative deception that [has long been] a prerequisite of art." See Hyde, *Trickster Makes This World*, 17.

76. *Jiejue shi*. Tian, "Xu Zhuodai yu Zhongguo xiandai dazhong wenhua," 125.

77. Xu Banmei, "Xiaoshuo cailiao pifasuo," *Banyue* 1, no. 3 (15 October 1921), 13–28. In-text quotations are from this version. The story is one of two that Zhou Shoujuan singled out for praise upon the journal's first anniversary. See Zhou Shoujuan, "*Banyue* zhi yinian huigu" ("Looking Back at the *Half-Moon Journal*'s First Year"), *Banyue* 2, no. 1 (20 November 1923), n.p. Wengong (Lit-Man) carries the dual meanings of "literary worker" (*wenxue gongren*) and "good at literature" (*gong yu wen*). The name Yang Lanwu, below, puns on *yang lanwu*, or "Western moral depravity." My thanks to Eva Hung for suggesting renderings of some character names in this story, my translation of which appears in *Renditions* 67.

78. For a history of foreign consumer good boycotts and Buy "Made in China" movements in early twentieth-century China, see Gerth, *China Made*, especially chaps. 3 and 4.

79. Xu Zhuodai, "Yangzhuang de chaoxijia," *HZ* 33 (1923), n.p. In-text quotations are from this edition.

80. Xu Zhuodai, "Gaofa chaoxi," *HZ* 34 (1923), n.p. The dictionary is "Gaofa yong xiao zidian."

81. The episode appears in chapter 19. For a translation, see Cao, *The Story of the Stone*, 1:375–99, especially 383–92.

82. Davis, *Reading the Text That Isn't There*, chap. 4.

83. Twain's passage ends: "far in the empty sky a solitary oesophagus slept upon motionless wing; everywhere brooded stillness, serenity, and the peace of God." Davis includes the full text of Twain's letter to readers in ibid., 179–80.

84. The notice, addressed to *maozei* who *guaipian*, first appears in its tenth issue of 8 August 1914. See "Jinggao chaoxijia" in *Libailiu* 10 (8 August 1914), six pages before copyright

page. *The Liengyi's Tri-Monthly*, a Shanghai entertainment publication that featured both writings by and news items about Xu Zhuodai, carried a regular notice warning against plagiarism or unauthorized reproduction of its contents, as did many of its peers.

85. The alleged plagiarism of the Zhous's *Yuwai xiaoshuo ji* occurred in 1914 but is not supported by a comparison of the two translations. The collection is reprinted in Zhou, *Zhou Zuoren yiwen quanji*, 11, 441–559. As literary scholar Yu Ling points out, the story of Li's alleged misdeed was even embellished later by other writers. In 1942, Ping Jinya, one of Xu Zhuodai's associates, and the distributor of *Wan Hsiang*, wrote a gripping but highly dubious account of Li Dingyi being confronted by the (unnamed) translator. Yu points out that not only is Ping's account improbable, but that even Lu Xun's 1920 preface misleads the reader into thinking that he himself did the translation (of a Polish story, retranslated from English), when the translator was in fact Zhou Zuoren. For details, see Yu Ling, "Dengqing Li Dingyi dui *Leren yangke* de chaoxi gong'an" ("Sorting Out the Case of Li Dingyi's Alleged Plagiarism of *Sielanka*"), in Chen and Wang, *Jiangou Zhongguo xiandai wenxue duoyuan gongsheng tixi de xin sikao*, 264–70.

86. Yunjian diangong, *Shanghai zhi pianshu shijie*.

87. Xu's "Zuixin jinyanshu" and Chunmeng's "Zuixin jinyanshu buyi" appear in *HZ*, issues 39–41, 45, and 47. Hu Jichen's "Xujun xiaoshuo de fanmian" rewrote Xu's "It's a Small World" ("Xizhai de shijie," issue 3) as "It's Not a Small World" ("Bu xiazhai de shijie") and his "A Frantic New Year's Day" ("Jixing de yuandan," issue 28) as "A Slow-Paced New Year's Eve" ("Manxing de chuxi"). Works on the plagiarism theme from this period include Gengkui's "Ni chaoxijia bianyuan chengwen" ("A Mock Petition in Defense of Plagiarists"), *HZ* 28 (1923); and Chi Hen's "Ci chaoxi wen" ("A Jibe at Plagiarism"), *HZ* 34 (1923).

88. See the anonymous piece: "Huaji boshi qushi: Li Amao qingchang baibeiji" ("A Funny Anecdote about Dr. Funny: Li Ah Mao Unlucky in Love"), *SB* 22501 (15 December 1935), 21.

89. Xu's emphasis on the craft and technique of trickery, for example, bears close resemblance to early comic films such as *Laborer's Love* (1922), discussed in chapter 3, in which a carpenter turned fruit seller uses the tools of his carpentry trade to bring down his tormentors and attain his desired object. In one fast-forwarded sequence, the carpenter rebuilds a staircase so that it can be converted into a slide with a push, and back to a staircase with a pull. His victims, patrons of a nightclub above his room who have kept him awake all night, slip their way down his contraption to become clients of his would-be father-in-law, a doctor. His enterprise brings the match about.

90. On this culture, and on Gu Mingdao's (1879–1944) stunt, see Link, *Mandarin Ducks and Butterflies*, 171.

91. Zau's (Shao Xunmei, 1906–68) prank on Zeng Pu (1871–1935) is described in Jonathan Hutt's article, "*Monstre Sacré*." Hutt notes that Zau's "penchant for [literary] pranks was soon at odds with the heated stylistic debates and political confrontations that characterized the increasingly acrimonious literary arena." The case of Xu Zhuodai shows that such pranks were by no means an expression of an exclusively "bourgeois" humor, as Zau's critics in the League of Left-Wing Writers might have imagined. It is also worth mentioning that readers tricked staff writers and editors too. Perry Link notes that when Chen Diexian was a columnist for *Shun Pao*, he was embarrassed to discover that a reader-

submitted poem that he had given a poor grade turned out to have been written by the famous Tang writer Liu Zongyuan (773–819). See Link, *Mandarin Ducks and Butterflies*, 171.

92. In 1908 or 1909, Xu was backstage at a Shanghai performance of the Enlightenment Troupe when a teenage Liu Bannong (see chapter 4), was thrust into his hands to have his face painted for a comic role. A month later, Xu, then an editor at the *China Times* (*Shishi xinbao*, 1907–49), helped Liu to get several translations published in that major newspaper. When Xu was hired by the publishing house China Books (*Zhonghua shuju*), he brought Liu along, and the two worked together for several years before Liu moved to Beijing. See Xu, *Huaju chuangshiqi huiyilu*, 46–48. For a study of "Shanghai modern" focused on cosmopolitan literary modernists of the 1930s and 1940s, see Lee, *Shanghai Modern*.

93. Bakhtin, *Rabelais and His World*, 92. Perry Link notes that Xu's fiction "drew heavily upon the device of abrupt surprise, every page turning the reader's expectations upside down." See Link, *Mandarin Ducks and Butterflies*, 158. But Xu's plots tend to be driven by problem solving rather than by coincidence, and the surprises result from the clever machinations of an enterprising character who exploits commercial print media for his or her own ends.

94. Kern, *The Absolute Comic*, 208. Edith Kern follows Charles Baudelaire in making a distinction between farcical and realistic modes of comedy: "the absolute comic, or farce, [is] highly creative from an artistic point of view, [while] the significant comic [is] mainly imitative and mimetic" (3). The distinction, in my opinion, is not hard and fast.

95. This is a bonus endnote.

96. Tang, *Zhongguo xiandai huaji wenxue shilüe*, 38.

97. As mentioned earlier, Xu Zhuodai used the Li Ah Mao pen name from the mid-1930s to the late 1940s. He used it, for example, in his contribution to *The Foreign Concessions Illustrated and Explained* (*Yangjingbang tushuo*), an illustrated and annotated dictionary of Shanghai slang. The series was an encore and tribute to Wang Zhongxian's *A New Illustrated and Annotated Dictionary of Shanghainese Expressions* (*Huyu xin cidian tushuo*), which was originally serialized in the *Social News Daily* from 28 November 1932 to 18 June 1935 and published as the book *Shanghai Slang Illustrated and Explained* (*Shanghai suyu tushuo*) in 1935. The author's preface to the Li Ah Mao slang series says that Wang's work was written "fifteen years earlier," so Li Ah Mao's likely dates to between 1947 and 1950. For a modern edition, see Meng, *Lao Shanghai suyu tushuo daquan*. Big Brother Ah Mao (*Ah Mao ge*)—the name Li Ah Mao's friends use to address him in Xu's stories—also appears as author of short pieces in *Tea Talk* and several other postwar magazines and newspapers. Some of these are reprinted in Meng, *Fangxing zhoubao*.

98. Cheng, *Literary Remains*, 188. See chapter 7 of Eileen Cheng's study for an extended analysis of mockery, satire, wordplay, and irreverence in *Old Tales Retold*, whose Butt of Laughter spoke for promoters of "art for art's sake."

CHAPTER 6. THE INVENTION OF HUMOR

1. Ch'ien Chung-shu, "The Little Critic: Apropos of 'The Shanghai Man,'" *CC* 7, no. 44 (1 November 1934), 1076–77. On the *China Critic* (*Zhongguo pinglun zhoubao*, 1928–40, 1945), see the combined issue of *China Heritage Quarterly* 30–31 (June–September 2012).

2. [Chen] Zizhan, "Qulu xuyu ershiliu" ("Scattered Sayings from My Humble Dwelling #26"), *SB* 21581 (13 May 1933), 17. Chen (1898–1990) phrased his question in archaic literary Chinese: "Jinnian henian hu?" One critic looking back on 1933 judged that the success of the Year of Humor had far outstripped that of Buy "Made in China" Year. See Xu Maoyong, "Zatan youmo" ("Random Thoughts on Humor"), *SB* 21866 (5 March 1934), 19. Xu (1911–77), who borrows part of Chen Zizhan's quip, notes that the most popular literary works of 1933 were works of humor.

3. Humor arrived "with a resounding bang" (Lu Xun), "like a live cinder that flitted its way toward the gasoline fumes" (Sun Junzheng). See Sohigian, "Contagion of Laughter," 137–38, 159.

4. Dekobra (1885–1973) was known for, among other works, *Le Rire dans le brouillard: anthologie des meilleurs humorists anglais et américains* (Foggy Notions of Laughter: An Anthology of the Best English and American Humorists, 1926), and *Le Rire dans la steppe: L'humour russe* (1927; English translation: *The Crimson Smile*, 1929). Dekobra's 1934 book about his trip to China, *Confucius en pull-over, ou le beau voyage en Chine*, was translated in 1935 as *Confucius in a Tail-Coat: Ancient China in Modern Costume*.

5. See Lin Yutang's exchange of letters with Dekobra in the *China Critic*, which are reprinted online in *China Heritage Quarterly* 30–31. Lin Yutang, "The Little Critic: An Open Letter to M. Dekobra," *CC* 6, no. 51 (21 December 1933), 1237–38; Maurice Dekobra, "Chinese Girls on Toast," *CC* 7, no. 8 (18 January 1934), 69.

6. See Sohigian, "The Life and Times of Lin Yutang," 466; Crespi, "China's *Modern Sketch*." This period coincided with the stricter implementation of the 1930 Publication Law, a censorship mechanism which required all periodicals to register with the government. See Ting, *Government Control of the Press in Modern China*, 86.

7. Zau's Xiandai yinshua gongsi (Modern Press) began printing the *Analects* with issue 11 (16 February 1933) and his Shidai tushu gongsi (Modern Publications) began distributing it with issue 28 (1 November 1933). Other participants in Zau's salon included Lin Yutang, T. K. Chuan (Quan Zenggu, 1903–84), Quentin Pan (Pan Guangdan, 1899–1967), Zhang Kebiao (1900–2007), and Li Qingya (1886–1969). On Zau's salons, see Hutt, "*Monstre Sacré*."

8. The literary magazine *Les Contemporains* (*Xiandai*, 1932–35), founded in Shanghai a few months earlier, to name one contemporary, professed a similar hostility to factions, cliques, and ideological schools.

9. *Zhongyong banyuekan* lasted less than a year. *Tanfeng youmo banyuekan*, which was also based in Shanghai, closed upon the outbreak of war with Japan. Sohigian mentions a third imitator entitled *Liaozhai*, which I have not seen. See Sohigian, "Contagion of Laughter," 138. The ad for *Shidai manhua* (1934–37), of the Modern Publications family, appears in *LY* 94 (16 August 1936). The full text of *Modern Sketch* is available on the MIT Visualizing Cultures and Colgate University websites, with an introductory article by John Crespi.

10. A brief notice about the launch of the *Analects* in Singapore's *Sin Kok Min Jit Pao* (*Xin guomin ribao*) on 11 October 1932 (issue 3, no. 821) does not mention *youmo* but predicts that *The Analects* will contribute to the "field of literary satire" (*fengci wentan*). The term *youmo* appeared in the Hong Kong press in the 1930s as well. See, for example, Wang Wan, "Youmo" ("Humor"), *Xingdao ribao* 55 (24 September 1938), "Xingzuo" ("Constellation") column.

11. Lin Yutang, "Zhengyi sanwen bing tichang 'youmo'" ("Soliciting Translated Essays and Promoting 'Humor'"), *Chenbao fukan* 115 (23 May 1924), 3–4. In a follow-up essay that June Lin admitted that readers had not been satisfied with his claim that someone not in the know would fail to recognize humor "even if you slap his palm a hundred times." But instead of defining it himself, he referred interested parties to the theories of Henri Bergson, George Meredith, Theodore Lipps, and Sigmund Freud (who would write in 1927 that "not everyone is capable of a humorous attitude. It is a rare and precious gift. . . ." See Freud, *The Standard Edition of the Complete Psychological Works of Sigmund Freud*, 21, 166.) Lin Yutang, "Youmo zahua" ("Random Comments on Humor"), *Chenbao fukan* 131 (9 June 1924), 1. In 1935, the *Analects* reprinted extracts of these pieces in its third anniversary issue under the title "The Two Earliest Essays to Promote Humor." See Lin Yutang, "Zuizao tichang youmo de liangpian wenzhang," *LY* 73 (1 October 1935), 3–5.

12. In 1926, reviewers for the *Shun Pao* described Lewis Carroll's *Alice in Wonderland* and foreign film comedies as examples of "*youmo* Humor." A 1927 notice announced that the new cartoon magazine *Shanghai Sketch* "specialized in *youmo* writings and illustrations." See Dao, "Ou-Mei zuijin shezhi zhi wenyi yingpian" ("Recently Produced Art Films from Europe and America"), *SB* 19490 (5 August 1926), 22–23; Zhang Yi'an, "Huaji yingpian de youmo ji zimu" ("Humor and Subtitles of Film Comedies"), *SB* 19213 (28 August 1926), 22; "Shanghai manhua dingqi chuban" ("*Shanghai Sketch* Begins Regular Publication"), *SB* 19686 (30 December 1927), 16. In September 1931, Lu Xun introduced Mark Twain as a famous "*youmojia* Humorist" and teller of jokes in his introduction to Li Lan's translation of *Eve's Diary*, published by Shanghai's Hufeng shuju as *Xiawa riji* (October 1931). Humor was also becoming a topic of discussion in neighboring countries. The Korean transliteration *yumoŏ* 유-모어 (humor) is mentioned in a 5 February 1930 article appearing in the reader Q&A section of Seoul's *Tonga Ilbo* under the title "Additional Answers in the Reception Room" ("Ŭngjŏpsil pyŏltam"). A reader mentions that "I hear this word often these days," and the journalist replies that "Humor is like salt to literature; without it, a piece of writing lacks taste," and then suggests that the newspaper have more of it. Thanks to Selina Lai-Henderson for the Twain reference and to Si Nae Park for the *Tonga Ilbo* reference.

13. See chapter 2; cf. Harder and Mittler, *Asian Punches*.

14. Ding Xilin (1893–1974), "Yizhi mafeng" ("A Wasp"), in Ding, *Ding Xilin xiju ji*, 1–34. My translations of dialogue are based on this edition. A full translation of the play appears in Chen, *The Columbia Anthology of Modern Chinese Drama*, chap. 5. On Ding Xilin and his "comedy of ethics," see Weinstein, "Directing Laughter," 32–100.

15. Ding Xilin, "Yapo" ("Oppression"), in Ding, *Ding Xilin xiju ji*, 133–46. My translations of dialogue are from this edition. Full translations of the play include the following: Gunn, *Twentieth-Century Chinese Drama*, 41–52; Ting, "Oppression," 117–24; Chen, *The Columbia Anthology of Modern Chinese Drama*, chap. 6. In dedicating the play to a deceased friend in 1925, Ding praised his sense of humor, not *youmo*, suggesting that he was unaware of Lin Yutang's 1924 transliteration. See Ting, "Oppression," 117.

16. Lao She, *Lao Zhang de zhexue*.

17. Lao She's (1899–1966) *Er Ma* is translated as Lao She, *The Two Mas*; on the novel and the *Fu Manchu* context, see Witchard, *Lao She in London*, chaps. 4 and 5, esp. 90, 118–22. See also Mather, "Laughter and the Cosmopolitan Aesthetic."

18. Lao She, *Laoniu poche*, 43–49. On Japan's 1932 attack on Shanghai, see Jordan, *China's Trial by Fire*.

19. Lao She's first piece for the *Analects* was published in November 1932. A December 1932 photo caption in *Les Contemporains* identifies Lao She as a *youmojia*. See the photo insert after page 94 in *Xiandai* 2, no. 1 (1 November 1932). In August 1934, the *Young Companion* dubbed Lao She a "humorous writer of satire," before soon changing that to "humor writer" (*youmo zuojia*). See *Liangyou* 90 (15 July 1934), 11; *Liangyou* 92 (15 September 1934), 6. Zhang Tianyi, who gained prominence in the 1930s as a writer of satirical fiction, was also sometimes was lumped in with the humorists. See the editor's preface to his 1936 selected works: Zhang, *Zhang Tianyi xuanji*. Even one of Xu Zhuodai's short stories of the 1940s was billed a "*youmo* short story." (Most were still called *huaji*.) See Zhuodai, "Meirongshu" ("Plastic Surgery"), *Xin Shanghai* 32 (1946), 6.

20. Preface to *Lao She youmo shiwenji*.

21. Lin Yutang, "The Little Critic: Confessions of a Nudist," *CC* 9, no. 12 (20 June 1935), 281.

22. Lin, *The Importance of Living*, 78–79. The final section of the book is entitled "Be Reasonable."

23. T. K. Chuan, ed., "The Little Critic: Laugh and You Laugh Alone," *CC* 5, no. 1 (7 January 1931), 14. "In humor," Chuan wrote, "there can be no internationalism . . . it is not laughter that brings men together."

24. Early discussions of humor terminology appear in the letters to the editor sections of *LY* 1 (16 September 1932); *LY* 4 (1 November 1932), 142–43. In "The *yumiao* [humor] of Stalin" a woman's request to have a baby is passed up the Communist bureaucratic hierarchy to Stalin, who decides: "This isn't in the Five-Year Plan—request denied!" See [Li] Qingya, "Shidalin de yumiao" ("The Humor of Stalin"), *LY* 7 (16 December 1932), 222. Li Qingya was the *Analects*'s main advocate of *yumiao* over *youmo*. *Youma* is said to have been a nomination of I Pei-chi (Yi Peiji, 1880–1937), then head of the National Palace Museum in the Forbidden City. In the Lao She story, father laughs when he comes home to discover that the boys have painted their faces like opera roles, leading them to reply, "Dad, yours is pretend *youmo*, but we're really *youmo*!" See Lao She, "Dang youmo biancheng youmo" ("When Humor Turns into Applying Paint"), *LY* 11 (16 February 1933), 368–71. Zhang Jian of Beijing Normal University, as I've noted previously, appears to be the first scholar to have noted Wang's coining. See Zhang, *Zhongguo xiju guannian de xiandai shengcheng*, 56; Rea, "Comedy and Cultural Entrepreneurship in Xu Zhuodai's *Huaji* Shanghai," 47n9. Wang used the term again in his 1907 retranslation of Harald Höffding's *Outlines of Psychology*, mentioned in chapter 5. See Haifuding, *Xinlixue gailun*, 401, and Wang's essay "Wenxue xiaoyan" ("Incidental Remarks on Literature"), translated in Denton, *Modern Chinese Literary Thought*, 90–95. Höffding's ideas about the comic spirit greatly influenced Wang, whose argument that literature is rooted in the ludic impulse (see chapter 3) drew on Kant.

25. On Georgii Avksent'ievich Sapojnikoff (d. 1949), who began doing cartoons for the *News* in 1925, see Rigby, "Sapajou's Shanghai."

26. Wang Tiran's translation of Ramón Gómez de la Serna's (1888–1963) essay appeared as "Lun youmo" in *LY* 32 (1 January 1934), 386–89; and *LY* 33 (16 January 1934), 452–55. The first part of Lin's essay appeared in *LY* 33. Serna's essay contains ideas similar to Lin's, such

as that humor is a product of natural, individual observation and that it has a chemical function.

27. T. K. C. "The Little Critic: Introducing 'The Analects,'" *CC* 5, no. 49 (8 December 1932), 1303. I have not corrected Chuan's grammar. The editors of the *Critic* had in fact introduced the new magazine a few days after its launch. See "A Chinese Humorous Fortnightly," *CC* 5, no. 38 (22 September 1932), 981.

28. *LY* 2 (1 October 1932), 12. The original news report about *fenni juan* appeared in Hong Kong's *Chaoran bao*, and the couplet is attributed to Chen Xiazi (n.d.), founder of the tabloid the *Crystal* (*Jing bao*, 1919–40).

29. T. K. Chuan prefaced one translation for the *China Critic* with a note that some *Analects* readers had failed to detect as parody a supposed elegy to Xu Zhimo, which had quoted the deceased poet as being uncharacteristically humble, saying that only the author's poems "can truly be called poetry; compared to them, mine are not worth a cent," and asking the *Analects* editors to "please have the title changed to 'Myself and Hsu Tsumo'?" See Han Moh-sun, "The Little Critic: Hsu Tsumo and Myself," translated by T. K. Chuan, *CC* 6:15 (13 Apr. 1933), 381–82.

30. See "Liang Zuoyou changyou Daguanyuan" ("Liang Zuoyou's Happy Sightseeing Trip to the Grand View Garden"), *LY* 3 (16 October 1932), 84.

31. "Guiqu tu" ("Curious Ghosts"), *LY* 91 (1 July 1936), 892.

32. Huang Yao, "Guitian guidi" ("Land of Devils"), *LY* 91 (1 July 1936), 902–3.

33. The close link between these two publications has been noted by Charles Laughlin (2008), Qian Suoqiao (2011), and other scholars. Lin Yutang, T. K. Chuan, Quentin Pan, Lin Yu (Lin Yutang's younger brother), and several other writers wrote for both the *China Critic* and one or more of Lin Yutang's Chinese-language magazines, the *Analects*, *This Human World*, and *Cosmic Wind*.

34. This ironic definition of *zuo wenzhang* appears in the condensed translation of the speech published as Lin Yutang, "The Function of Criticism at the Present Time," *CC* 3, no. 4 (23 January 1930), 78–81. In-text quotes in this and the next paragraph are from this edition.

35. Lin Yutang, "Chinese Realism and Humour," *CC* 3, no. 39 (25 September 1930), 924. The lecture occurred on 22 September 1930.

36. Ibid., 926.

37. On Lin's income, see Xu Xu, "Zhuisi Lin Yutang xiansheng" ("Remembering Mr. Lin Yutang"), in Xu, *Xu Xu wenji*, 11:157; Qian, *Liberal Cosmopolitan*, 105–6; Chey and Davis, *Humour in Chinese Life and Letters*, 195–96. The 23 January 1930 issue of the *China Critic* contains on page 91 a half-page advertisement for the first three volumes of Lin's Kaiming textbooks.

38. Lin Yutang, "The Little Critic: On Shaking Hands," *CC* 10, no. 8 (22 August 1935), 180.

39. Lin Yutang, "The Little Critic: How I Bought A Tooth-Brush," *CC* 5, no. 35 (18 August 1934), 850–51.

40. Lin Yutang, "I Moved Into a Flat," *CC* 5:38 (22 September 1932), 991–92.

41. The five essays listed here were first published in English (e) and Chinese (c) in the following years, respectively: 1932e/1933c; 1933e/1934c; 1935e/c; 1935e/1936c; 1935e/c. Chinese versions of Lin's essays were published variously in the *Analects Fortnightly*, *Shun Pao Monthly*, and *Cosmic Wind*. Datings from Qian, *Selected Bilingual Essays of Lin Yutang*, 232–34.

42. See both volumes of Lin, *The Little Critic*, for which Buck wrote a preface. Buck's second husband, Richard Walsh, an editor at John Day publishers, would later publish many of Lin's English-language books. Buck won the Nobel Prize for Literature in 1938.

43. Liang Shiqiu, "Wenxue li de 'youmo'" ("'Humor' in Literature"). In Liang, *Liang Shiqiu wenji*, 7:51. Originally appeared in *Yishi bao—wenxue zhoukan* (Tianjin) on 31 December 932.

44. Dog collar: L. Y. [Lin Yutang], "Introducing 'The Little Critic,'" *CC* 3, no. 27 (3 July 1930), 636–37. Un-buttoned moods: Lin Yutang, preface to Lin, *The Little Critic: Satires and Sketches on China (First Series: 1930–1932)*.

45. Wen Yüan-ning (1899–1984) is listed as a "contributing editor" of the China Critic from 4 January 1934 until its final issue of 27 December 1945, but his last contribution appears to have been a book review in the 6 July 1936 issue. On *T'ien Hsia* (1935–41), most of whose editorial board members had worked at the *Critic*, see Shen, *Cosmopolitan Publics*, chap. 2.

46. Qian Zhongshu discusses Wen's fondness for Lamb in his review of Wen's book: Zhongshu jun [Qian Zhongshu], "Bugou zhiji" (Imperfect Understanding), *Renjianshi* 29 (5 June 1935), 41.

47. Wen Yüan-ning, ed., "Intimate Portraits: Dr. Lim Boon Keng 林文慶," *CC* 7, no. 22 (31 May 1934), 519. In *The Merchant of Venice* (1.1.99–100), Gratiano mimics phony wise men with the line: "I am Sir Oracle / And when I ope my lips, let no dogs bark!" Subsequent quotations are from this edition.

48. On Lim Boon Keng's (Lin Wenqing, 1869–1957) alleged conflict with Lu Xun, and the general contempt with which he has been treated by Chinese critics and historians, see Wang, *China and the Chinese Overseas*, 147–65.

49. Wen Yüan-ning, ed., "Intimate Portraits: Dr. Lim Boon Keng, Once More" *CC* 7, no. 23 (7 June 1934), 542–43. Letter from F. T. Wang is dated 1 June, Shanghai.

50. [Wen Yüan-ning], "Unedited Biographies: Dr. Hu Shih, A Philosophe," *CC* 7, no. 9 (1 March 1934), 208; [Wen Yüan-ning], "Unedited Biographies: Mr. Wu Mi 吳宓, a Scholar and a Gentleman," *CC* 7, no. 4 (25 January 1934), 86; [Wen Yüan-ning], "Unedited Biographies: Mr. Chou Tso-jen 周作人, Iron and Grace," *CC* 7, no. 13 (29 March 1934), 304; Wen Yüan-ning, ed., "Intimate Portraits: Mr. Wu Chih-hui (吳稚暉)," *CC* 7, no. 37 (13 September 1934), 906; [Wen Yüan-ning], "Unedited Biographies: Emperor Malgre Lui," *CC* 7, no. 6 (8 February 1934), 135–36.

51. [Wen Yüan-ning], "Unedited Biographies: Liang Yu-ch'un (梁遇春), A Chinese Elia," *CC* 7, no. 15 (12 April 1934), 353. Liang Yuchun (1906–32) himself anticipated the humor trend. In 1927 he noted that "Since China's 'Literary Renaissance' (an overblown phrase if ever there was one), plenty of people have promoted literature of blood and tears, realist literature, aestheticism, and so on . . . never has anyone promoted harmless laughter." (Liang mentioned in passing that "recently someone has advocated *youmo*" but he himself did not adopt the term.) Liang was keenly interested in laughter and its relation to grief, consulting Lamb, Carlyle, Brontë, Emerson, Barrie, Hazlitt, Gorki, and others. Thomas Hobbes he took to task for being too much a fool to enjoy life—Hobbes's notion that laughter was a product of arrogance was "the type of stupid thing only a philosopher could say." See Liang, *Liang Yuchun sanwenji*, 15–17, also 109–12. Liang uses the term *youmo* once but, as mentioned in chapter 5, uses *huaji* as a direct translation of *humor*.

52. Wen's column inspired a similar series in *This Human World*, "Contemporary Personages" (*jinren zhi*), which included Chinese translations of Wen's profiles of Wu Mi, Hu Shi, and Xu Zhimo. Twenty were later collected in Renjian shi she, *Ershi jinren zhi* (*Twenty Contemporary Personages*, 1935). A translation of Wen's profile of Zhou Zuoren appeared in Yijing 17 (1936), 70–71. A bilingual edition of the full *Critic* series has been published as Wen, *Imperfect Understanding/Bugou zhiji*. In the 1930s Wen became a member of the *Legistlative* Yuan, and during the war he headed the Hong Kong office of the Ministry of Information; in 1947, he was appointed Ambassador to Greece, a post he held for over twenty years.

53. Zizhan, "Qulu xuyu ershiliu," 17.

54. Qian Suoqiao interprets *youmo* as being part of a "creative re-interpretation of Chinese culture," citing in particular Lin's radical take on the character of Confucius as being motivated by a "spirit of reasonable tolerance." See Qian, "Translating 'Humor' into Chinese Culture," esp. 288, 292–93.

55. The English title of the play is from Lin's own modified translation, which appeared in the 1937 collection Lin, *Confucius Saw Nancy, and Essays about Nothing*. On the play and the controversy sparked by its performance in Qufu, see Sohigian, "Confucius and the Lady in Question." Lin discussed the sage's run-in with the Queen of Wei again in a speech delivered at the Shanghai YMCA on 25 November 1930, in which he suggests that Confucius and his followers incurred the contempt of others for using "unscrupulous methods" to ingratiate themselves and coming across as "a class of capped and gowned wandering hobos." See Lin Yutang, "The Little Critic: Confucius as I Know Him," *CC* 6, no. 1 (1 January 1931), 5–9. Lin later extensively translated and discussed examples of Confucius's sense of humor. Cf. Christoph Harbsmeier's studies "*Confucius Ridens*" and "Humor in Ancient Chinese Philosophy."

56. Lin, *The Gay Genius*. On Zhuangzi, see Watson, *Chuang Tzu*.

57. Essays discussed Confucius, Lao Tzu (Lin: "the first ancestor of Chinese humor"), satirical fiction and *The Scholars*, humorous couplets, the humor of the late Ming, and humorous poems of the Qing dynasty. The two special issues are: "Xiyang youmo zhuanhao," *LY* 56 (1 January 1935); "Zhongguo youmo zhuanhao," *LY* 58 (1 February 1935).

58. [Lin] Yutang, "Wode hua: Youbuwei zhai jie" ("My Words: On the Name Some Things Left Undone Studio"), *LY* 31 (16 December 1933), 304.

59. Zhitang [Zhou Zuoren], "Tan Mengzi de maren" ("On Mencius's Curses"), *LY* 116 (16 July 1937), 912–14. Zhou's discussion focuses on Mencius's critique of the philosophers Yang Zhu and Mozi: "Now, Yang's principle is 'Each one for himself,' which does not acknowledge the claims of the sovereign. Mo's principle is 'to love all equally,' which does not acknowledge the particular affection due to a father. But to acknowledge neither king nor father is to be in the state of a beast." *Mencius—Teng Wen Gong* 2, 14; Chinese Text Project (Legge, trans.): http://ctext.org/mengzi/teng-wen-gong-ii. In the same essay, Zhou quips that cursing unfilial people as being like beasts who cannibalize their parents was ineffective because "in beast society, going out of your way to find your father in order to eat him is no mean task."

60. Chen surmised that Chinese scholarship had made no progress in the last two thousand years because scholars struggled against each other, rather than against nature. See

Chen Zizhan, "Wenren xiangma lun" ("On Writers Cursing Each Other"), *Taibai* 2, no. 4 (5 May 1935), 145–46.

61. Zizhan, "Qulu xuyu ershiliu."

62. Hu Shanyuan (1877–1988) speaks of a *youmo wangguo*. See the preface to Hu, *Youmo biji*. In the front matter, Hu says that he excluded "low-class" (*diji quwei*) works like *Expanded Forest of Laughs* and *Instant Laughs* (*Yijian haha xiao*). Hu also edited a separate volume of *Humorous Poems* (*Youmo shihua*, 1936), and in 1938 briefly edited "Free Talk."

63. For Lu Xun's side of the exchange about *Shijie youmo quanji* with Masuda (1903–77), see the letters dated 13 May, 22 May, 31 May, 28 June, 18 July, 2 October, and 19 December 1932 in Lu Xun, *Lu Xun shuxin ji*, 2:1098–1112, 1120–22, 1108–9.

64. Yu Dafu's "Er shiren" first appeared in 1928 and Zhang's "Xiao bide" in 1931.

65. Lu Xun, *Lu Xun shuxin ji*, 2:1111–12, 1126–27.

66. Ibid., 1108–9.

67. Ibid., 1123–24. Lu Xun signs off *mo'an* in his letter to Lin dated 6 January 1934. See ibid., 1:475.

68. T. K. Chuan, "The Little Critic: 'Chinese Humor,'" *CC* 6, no. 3 (19 January 1933), 69.

69. [Han] Shiheng, "Tan 'youmo'" ("On 'Humor'"), *SB* 21436 (9 December 1932), 17. In his essay, which appeared in "Free Talk," Han (1908–87) cites Lu Xun's essay on China's "national curse" to bolster a point about sex curses.

70. The advertisement is reprinted in Rojas, *The Great Wall*, 25.

71. Dekobra, *Confucius in a Tail-Coat*, 16.

72. Yao Hsin-nung (Yao Ke, 1905–91), "The Chinese in Chaplin," *CC* 12, no. 13 (26 March 1936), 296–98. Yao was an editor at *T'ien Hsia Monthly*, a friend and translator of Lu Xun's, and later a famous playwright and screenwriter.

73. Shao Xunmei, "Youmo zhendi" ("The True Meaning of Humor"), *LY* 90 (16 June 1936), 821.

74. Lao She, for instance, dubbed farce, which he translates as both *huaji ju* and *nao xi*, "the lowest-grade humor" in both drama and fiction. See Lao She, *Laoniu poche*, 81.

75. Lin, "Fanyi zhi nan" ("Translation Troubles"), *SB* 21445 (18 December 1932), 18. In the same essay, Lin facetiously suggests translating *huoche* (train) as "wheelbarrow," since Chinese trains are slow, and "Please arrive at precisely 7:00 p.m." into Chinese as "Please arrive at 5:30," since Chinese are always late.

76. In this essay Lu Xun notes that the Japanese defined *youmo* as "sympathetic *huaji* [*kokkei*]" (*youqing huaji*). Wei Suo [Lu Xun], "'Huaji' lijie" ("Examples of '*huaji*'"), *SB* 21745 (26 October 1933), 19.

77. Zhou, *Kucha'an xiaohua xuan*, 3. The introduction is dated 27 July 1933, Beiping.

78. Comic Mountain Man's (Huaji shanren) *Relieving Boredom and Dispelling Worries* (*Jiemen xiaochou lu*, 1935), for example, is targeted at readers with a traditional comic literary sensibility, written in classical Chinese, and divided into thematic sections (romance, crimes, ghosts, bizarre events, animals, anomalies, etc.) like a traditional joke collection. According to the copyright page, the book was distributed in Canton, Hong Kong, and Shanghai. Shi Zhecun in 1932 noted the "revival of the *Saturday* school," suggesting that the playful style of literary entertainment examined in chapter three was alive

and well. See Shi Zhecun, "Bianji zuotan" ("Editor's Forum"), *Xiandai* 1, no. 1 (1 May 1932), 197. Zhu Guangqian's (1897–1986) 1936 textbook on Western literary aesthetics, *The Psychology of Art and Literature* (*Wenyi xinlixue*), which covers foreign notions of play, laughter, and comedy from Plato, Socrates, and Aristotle to Hobbes, Kant, Bergson, and Freud, for example, translates both *humor* and *wit* as *huixie*. See chapter 12, "Play and the Origins of Art" ("Yishu de qiyuan yu youxi"), and chapter 17, "Laughter and Comedy" ("Xiao yu xiju"). See Zhu, *Zhu Guangqian quanji*, 1:368–85, 455–77, esp. 469, 471.

79. [Han] Shiheng, "Tan 'youmo'," 17. The phrase, which might be rendered more literally as a "smile of the meeting of the hearts/minds," is said to have originated with Ming dynasty essayist Yuan Hongdao (1568–1610). See Sohigian, "Life and Times of Lin Yutang," 35n45. It was Han, and not Lin, as is often thought, who first connected the phrase with *youmo*.

80. Freud, *The Standard Edition of the Complete Psychological Works of Sigmund Freud*, 21, 166.

81. Lin Yutang, "Huixin de weixiao" ("The Understanding Smile"), *LY* 7 (16 December 1932), 214.

82. Xu Maorong, "Xiao" ("Laughter"), *SB* 21823 (15 January 1934), 17. Xu's article appeared in "Free Talk."

83. This title appears intermittently from January through September, beginning with *Liangyou huabao* 84 (30 January 1934), 32–33.

84. See the advertisement for *Youmo jie* in *LY* 100 (16 November 1936), 191. In 1946, Zau repackaged many of these essays under a new title, *On Humor* (*Lun youmo*), which was reprinted in February 1949. It included essays by Lin Yutang, Zhou Gucheng, Xu Xu, Sinmay Zau, Yu Dafu, Lu Xun, and others.

85. See Lin Yutang, "Wode hua—Lun youmo" ("My Words—On Humor"), *LY* 33 (16 January 1934), 434–38; Lin Yutang, "Wode hua—Lun youmo (xia)" ("My Words—On Humor, Part III"), *LY* 35 (16 February 1934), 522–25. For a critical modern edition of Meredith's essay, see Ives, *George Meredith's Essay on Comedy and Other New Quarterly Magazine Publications*.

86. The last line is modified from Joseph C. Sample's translation; see Chey and Davis, *Humour in Chinese Life and Letters*, 189.

87. Lin, *The Importance of Living*, 80.

88. Xu Xu, "Tan youmo" ("On Humor") (1934), in Xu, *Xu Xu wenji*, 9:245–46.

89. Hsia, "The Chinese Sense of Humor."

90. The phrase is film scholar Joan Mellen's. See Mellen, *Modern Times*, 42.

91. Sohigian, "Contagion of Laughter," 140–44.

92. See, respectively, Ma Guoliang, "Mei quwei de wenzi" ("Insipid Writing"), *SB* 21836 (28 January 1934), 17; Xu Yuehong, "Ganlan" ("Olives"), *Liangyou huabao* 105 (May 1935), 44; Shao, "Youmo zhendi," 821. Xu Yuehong urged the humor literati to try harder, and to emulate Shaw's satirical piquancy instead of laughing at random (*luanxiao*).

93. See Lin, *With Love and Irony*, 67, 71.

94. Yuan Muzhi, "Zhongguo juzuojia jiqi zuopin" ("Chinese Dramatists and Their Works"), in Sun, *Ding Xilin yanjiu ziliao*, 142–43. Words in italics appear in English in Yuan's (1909–78) original 1933 essay.

95. See Su Wen, "Guanyu 'wenxin' yu Hu Qiuyuan de wenyi lunbian" ("On 'Wenxin' and Hu Qiuyuan's Polemic on Literature and Art"), *Xiandai* 1, no. 3 (July 1932), 378–85; and Lu Xun, "Lun 'disanzhong ren'" ("On the 'Third Type of Person'"), *Xiandai* 2, no. 1 (1 December 1932), 162–65. See also Su Wen, "'Disanzhong ren' de chulu" ("A Way Out for the 'Third Type of Person'"), *Xiandai* 1, no. 6 (1 October 1932), 767–79 (this issue contains related essays by Su Wen and Shuyue). Su Wen (aka Du Heng, 1907–64) took over editorship of *Les Contemporains* from the modernist writer Shi Zhecun. In 1935, the magazine was taken over by the Nationalist Party, which installed a new editor. The KMT-run version lasted only three issues. Thanks to Richard King for sharing his copy of the magazine with me.

96. See Jenkins, *What Made Pistachio Nuts?*, 31 and 26–58 passim.

97. Zheng, *Zheng Yimei xuanji*, 1:762–3.

98. Lu Xun, "*Lunyu* yinian—jieci youtan Xiao Bona" ("One Year of the *Analects*—and a Few More Words on Bernard Shaw"), *LY* 25 (16 September 1933), 16–18. In contrast to the state-sponsored violence, one independent female assassin who took revenge on a warlord in 1935 garnered public support thanks in part to sympathetic media coverage. See Lean, *Public Passions*, especially chap. 2.

99. Yizhi, "Lun 'yasu gongshang'" ("On 'Appealing to Both Refined and Vulgar Tastes'"), *Taibai* 2, no. 3 (20 April 1935), 100–101.

100. Mengjia, "Zalun youmo" ("Miscellaneous Thoughts on Humor"), *SB* 22264 (19 April 1935), 17. One reader comment from Korea reinforces the impression that by early 1935 the *Analects* might have started to lose its way: "Lin Yutang's *Analects* is the best representative of humorous (*yumoŏ*) literature.... At the beginning, the magazine had a good political and satirical edge, but its quality has recently deteriorated into the realm of lowbrow taste and mockery." See Kim Kwangju, "Chungguk mundan ŭi hyŏnse ilbyŏl (4)" (A Glimpse of the Trends in the Chinese Literary Sphere [4]), *Tonga Ilbo* (8 February 1935), 3.

101. Ch'ien, "The Little Critic: Apropos of 'The Shanghai Man,'" 1076–77.

102. Xu, *Xu Xu wenji*, 11:150.

103. Xu Maoyong, "Zatan youmo."

104. Zhou Zuoren, "Shanghai qi" ("Shanghai Style"), in Zhou, *Zhou Zuoren jingdian zuopin xuan*, 132–33. (Essay dated "Beiping, 27 February 1936.")

105. "Lao She laixin shuo" ("A Letter from Lao She"), *SB* 21459 (1 January 1933), 23. In the essay, Lao She likens the made-up genre of *dapinwen*, Major Taste Essays, to "unicorn feathers and phoenix horns" (*linmao fengjiao*) and "major trifles" (*da wanyi*), intentionally mixing up common metaphors for rarity and triviality.

106. See Hsia, "The Chinese Sense of Humor." Hsia echoes a theme in Van Wyck Brooks's 1933 verdict on Mark Twain that "the making of the humorist was the undoing of the artist." Brooks, *The Ordeal of Mark Twain*, 265.

107. Simon, *The Labyrinth of the Comic*, 243.

108. The earliest version of this essay appeared in May of 1939 in "Cold Room Jottings" ("Lengwu suibi"), a series published in the Kunming literary journal *Criticism Today* (*Jinri pinglun*). The title, "Shuo xiao," was added when a revised version appeared in 1941 in Qian's essay collection, *Written on the Margins of Life* (*Xie zai rensheng bianshang*). The title contains two additional meanings besides "On Laughter": telling jokes or funny stories and,

most literally, talking and laughing. Jizhuang is the style name (*zi*) of the early Qing scholar Liu Xianting (1648–95). *Guangyang Notes* (*Guangyang zaji*) is a collection of "notes" (*biji*) on various historical, legal, administrative, geographical, agricultural, medical, and artistic topics. Southwestern United University was a wartime amalgamation of several universities with Qian's alma mater, Tsinghua. Translations in this and the following paragraph are from Qian, *Humans, Beasts, and Ghosts*, 47–49. On Qian Zhongshu's hostility to Lin Yutang, which is also evident in Qian's later works *Ren shou gui* and *Weicheng* (which places Lin's *My Country and My People* alongside other such "immortal classics" as *Interior Decorating* and *Teach Yourself Photography*), see my essay "The Critic Eye 批眼."

109. A singsong girl might clarify to clients that "I sell smiles but not my body" (*maixiao bu maishen*).

110. Shao, "Youmo zhendi," 821.

111. Lin, *With Love and Irony*, 81.

112. W. T. Stead, "Mark Twain," *Review of Reviews* 16 (August 1897), 123.

113. Lin edited the *Analects* only until 1933. Later editors in the 1930s include Tao Kangde (1908–83), Sinmay Zau, and Lin Dazu, who replaced Lin Yutang's column "My Words" ("Wode hua") with one of his own called "His Words" ("Tade hua").

114. "Humor and Humanity," *CC* 20, no. 1 (6 January 1938), 3.

115. In 1944, for instance, the Commercial Press published Feng Yuanjun's comparative study of jesters from pre-Qin to Western Han China and European *fou* (fools) from the Middle Ages. See Feng, *Guyou jie*. Feng's essay is dated summer 1941, Guangdong (page 91).

116. Shu Yiqiao's *Zenyang shi maren yishuhua* is divided into five parts, the first of which is Liang Shiqiu's *The Fine Art of Reviling*, retitled as "Maren de jishu" ("Techniques of Reviling"); part 2 is called "Humorous Reviling Techniques" ("Youmo de marenshu"). Xuan Yongguang (1886–1960) was the author of *Wangtan fenghua*. As mentioned earlier, contributors to the *Analects* were less opposed to cursing than its Ten Commandments suggest. Near the end of its revived run, one contributor suggested keeping Chinese cursing in perspective. The frequency with which Harry S. Truman uttered "son of a bitch" proved that "the moon doesn't necessarily shine brighter abroad than in our China!" See Peng Xuehai, "Cong 'S.O.B.' dao 'guoma'" ("From 'S.O.B.' to 'National Oaths'"), *LY* 174 (1 April 1949), 2434–35.

117. Lao She, *Lao She youmo ji*. A certain Yin Xi is credited as the "editor-author" (bianzhu) of this work, a copy of which is held at the Library of the Institute of Chinese Literature and Philosophy, Academia Sinica. The work appears in my bibliography under Lao She's name, even though he is not credited on the book's copyright page.

118. Jinbo, "Renmin de youmo" ("The People's Humor"), *Renmin ribao* 154 (20 October 1946), 3. The 20 December 1946 and 5 January 1947 issues of *People's Daily* (which then carried the masthead *Rhenmin Rhbao*) also carried comic pieces "in imitation of humorous *xiaopin*" (*ni youmo xiaopin*), the style popularized by the *Analects Fortnightly*.

119. Li Qingya (1886–1969), a translator of French literature, had in 1932 advocated *yumiao* (witty speech) over Lin Yutang's *youmo*. As editor in 1946, he revived his preferred transliteration. See Qingya and Yutang, "*Youmo* yu *yumiao* zhi taolun" ("A Discussion of *youmo* and *yumiao*"), *LY* 1 (16 September 1932), 44–45. The first piece in the relaunched *Analects* to broach the topic of humor was Li Qingya's review essay "Dazhan zhong de yumiao

xiaopin zhi yiban" ("A Few Humorous Sketches from the Great War"), *LY* 118 (1 December 1946), 38–39. A note from distributor Sinmay Zau appearing in issue 119 exemplifies the publication's terminological inconsistency, promising subscribers a complementary calendar with "*youmo*" illustrations, but soliciting essays and cartoons in a "*yumiao* humor" style. Though Li stepped down as editor after only a few issues, the magazine used both terms until the end of its run. Returnees included Chen Zizhan, Ding Cong, Feng Zikai, Wu Zuguang, Yu Pingbo, Zhang Leping, Zhao Jingshen, and Shen Congwen.

120. Qian Suoqiao, for example, argues that Lin's significance lies in his success in making humor relevant to Chinese people and not "his original contribution to the notion of humor as such." Qian, "Translating 'Humor' into Chinese Culture," 279.

121. George Kao, a friend of the *Analects*, wrote in 1946 that the 1930s humorists discovered *huaji* to be "obsolete and corrupted." See the "Editor's Preface" in Kao, *Chinese Wit & Humor*, xxii.

EPILOGUE

1. Lin Yutang, "Chinese Realism and Humour," *CC* 3, no. 39 (25 September 1930), 926.

2. For a translation of the 1943 transcript of Mao's 1942 speeches, as well as the revisions published in 1953, see McDougall, *Mao Zedong's "Talks at the Yan'an Conference on Literature and Art,"* 80–81 and 102n235.

3. See Lary, *The Chinese People at War*, 6, 97–98.

4. On anti-patriarchal laughter in the works of Su Qing, Yang Jiang, and Eileen Chang, see chapter 4 of Amy Dooling's *Women's Literary Feminism in Twentieth Century China* (quotation is from page 140) and her article "In Search of Laughter."

5. Yang's *Youxi renjian*, unfortunately, is no longer extant. On Yang's (b. 1911) stage comedies of the 1940s, see Amy Dooling, "Yang Jiang's Wartime Comedies; Or, the Serious Business of Marriage," in Rea, *China's Literary Cosmopolitans*, chap. 1, as well as the book and article cited in the preceding note. Yang's plays brought her fame as a comic talent before her husband, Qian Zhongshu.

6. Su, *Jiehun shinian*. Zhuodai, "Qiuhun shinian" ("Ten Years of Marriage Proposals"), *Qiri tan* 8 (6 February 1946), 8. Reprinted in Meng, *Fangxing zhoubao*, 3:360. Miss Peng Fuqi's name sounds like both "untouchable" and "uninflatable."

7. The old lady affirms her love of "kuxi." *Taitai wansui* (Sang Hu, dir. 1947).

8. See Liu, "Mao Zedong weihe ai du qishu *Hedian*?"

9. See McDougall, *Mao Zedong's "Talks at the Yan'an Conference on Literature and Art,"* 80–81 and 102n235.

10. Moser, "Stifled Laughter."

11. In early years theaters would sometimes advertise the new politically-correct routines, but artists would perform the old ones, and just start singing *The East is Red* if a cadre happened to walk in the door. Kaikkonen, *Laughable Propaganda*, 76.

12. Brown and Pickowicz, *Dilemmas of Victory*, 207–31.

13. In his preface to *Humorous Poems and Prose by Lao She*, he notes, "People are always asking me: What is humor? I don't have an American PhD in humor, so I can never answer." Lao She's other representative pieces on the topic from the 1930s include "Laoniu

poche (shi): tan youmo" ("Old Ox Pulling a Rickety Cart [10]: Chatting about Humor"), *Yuzhou feng* 22 (1 August 1936), 547–50; and "Youmo de weixian" ("The Dangers of Humor"), *Yuzhou feng* 41 (16 May 1937), 208–9. His letters and essays from the 1950s and 1960s about humor, satire, comedy, and *xiangsheng* appear in Lao She, *Lao She quanji*, 14, 433–34; 17, 419–21, 422–24, and 649–51; 18, 15–17, 25–26, and 27–28.

14. See Lao She, *Teahouse*; on Lao She's farce, see Wang, *Fictional Realism in Twentieth-Century China*, 111–56. The Mao era may be taken as *Teahouse*'s implied fourth act.

15. A biographical profile published by the Suzhou Local Gazetteer Office says that Xu died of esophageal cancer. An account by Xu's friend Zheng Yimei implies that his final decline was related to depression after his son-in-law's suicide. See Deng, "'Dongfang Zhuobielin' Xu Zhuodai"; Zheng, *Qingmo minchu wentan yishi*, 194. *Tales of Old Shanghai*, which Zheng and Xu co-wrote during the 1950s, was not published until 1986.

16. Hong Kong's *Xinsheng wanbao* (1945–76), and *Qingnian wenyou* (est. 1952), for example, regularly carried humor features in the early 1950s. Shanghainese émigrés like Zhang Xianli, publisher of *Xinsheng wanbao*, dominated Hong Kong literary supplements in the 1950s and 1960s. See Ma, *Xianggang baotan huiyilu*, 151–53. Xu Xu, a veteran of the *Analects Fortnightly* and former editor of *This Human World*, launched a short-lived revival of the *Analects* in Hong Kong in the 1950s, with different contributors.

17. On transnational culture of the new PRC, see Nicolai Volland's forthcoming book, *Cold War Cosmopolitanism*.

18. Joke books entitled *Minjian xiaohua* (roughly, Jokes from among the People, or Folklore Jokes) were published in Shanghai and Hong Kong in 1951 and in Taipei in 1952. The Taipei joke collection is reprinted in Zhang, *Xiaohua sizhong* (see appendix 1). Virtually all PRC scholarship on jokes from the 1950s refers to them as *minjian*, with some scholars identifying literati jokes as a separate category.

19. The Great World reportedly sold a daily average of 7,000 tickets in 1946 and 13,000 tickets between 1 May 1955 and 1 May 1956, or 4,380,000 for that one-year period. Other sources give daily attendance figures for 1955 ranging from 10,000 to 15,000. Shanghai's Culture Bureau took over the Great World in July 1954 and changed some of its content (ridding it of prostitutes and slot machines, for example), but retained the ha-ha mirrors until the beginning of the Cultural Revolution, when one Party organ declared that "Laughing at the ugly image of themselves in the ha-ha mirror at the entrance of the Great World, proletarians not only deface themselves but become vulnerable to bourgeois attack, since they are likely to forget their class consciousness" (translation modified). See Liang, "The Great World: Performance Supermarket," 103, 108, 110–11, 114. My thanks to Jake Werner for sharing this source.

20. See Li Shifu, "Lun faguan tuoku," *Renjian shi* (Taiwan) 9, no. 1 (January 1969), 4–6 (a sequel by a different writer appears in *Renjian shi* 9, no. 2 (February 1969), 8–10); Long Buwang, "Pichou yu lianhong," *Renjian shi* 9, no. 5 (May 1969), 23. The periodical, whose cover motto was *youmo, fengqu, fengci, qingsong*, lasted until 1983. Xu Xu, editor of the 1930s *Renjian shi*, from which *Chinese Humanist Monthly* drew its Chinese title, wrote from Hong Kong in 1968 that in the second case an offending article had objected to a high official's son being admitted to Taiwan's top university without having to sit for the entrance examination. (That official, Kung Te-ch'eng, later became head of the Examination Yuan.)

The reason given for the suspension was that the publication had violated its mandate, which was "light humor." See Xu Xu, "Qingsong youmo" ("Light Humor"), in Xu, *Xu Xu wenji*, 10:337.

21. Lin Yu-tang, "Humor in East and West," in *Humour in Literature East and West*, 167–82. Lin cofounded the Chinese branch of PEN with Hu Shi and Xu Zhimo in Shanghai in 1924. In 1970 he was elected president of the Chinese PEN Center based in Taiwan.

22. Li Ao (b. 1935), who was imprisoned for political reasons from 1972–76 and 1981–82, has authored or coauthored over one hundred books. Since the 1980s Li has been a frequent candidate for political office in Taiwan, serving briefly in the Legislative Yuan, as well as a ubiquitous media personality.

23. Dress-up-and-touch-up bridal photos, now a middle-class rite of passage, have also become a major industry in Chinese communities worldwide, their fantasy settings recalling the various fun studio photos of the Republican era. For the best study to date of the *hunsha* industry, see Adrian, *Framing the Bride*. On *e'gao*, a term that encompasses various types of spoofs, puns, parodies, and mash-ups, see my chapter, "Spoofing (*e'gao*) Culture on the Chinese Internet," in Davis and Chey, *Humour in Chinese Life and Culture*, chap. 7.

24. Chen, "*Baozou manhua* (Rage Comics)."

25. On these and many more slang neologisms, see the "Grass-Mud Horse Lexicon," compiled by *China Digital Times* (www.chinadigitaltimes.net).

26. The Hong Kong-born artist Kenneth Tin-Kin Hung's self-translation of *Naocan youji* is "The Travelogue of Dr. Brain Damages." See his online gallery at www.tinkin.com/arts/the-travelogue-of-dr-brain-damages/.

27. On the joke plagiarism case, see Wang, "Much Ado about TV Plagiarism." For a study tracking the popularity of jokes as internet memes ("small units of culture") across languages, including Chinese, see Shifman and Thewall, "Assessing Global Diffusion with Web Memetics." The tone-deaf journalism is discussed in Wong, "Kim Jong-un Seems to Get a New Title: Heartthrob." For a nineteenth-century case of translating the content but missing the humorous intent, see the discussion of *Puck, or the Shanghai Charivari* in chapter 3.

28. Link writes in this piece for the *New York Review of Books* that, given that the Chinese Communist Party proscribes writing about Party-caused disasters, "Mo Yan's solution (and he is not alone here) has been to invoke a kind of daft hilarity when treating 'sensitive' events." Mo Yan's treatment of the famine caused by the Great Leap Forward, for example, "has great fun with the craziness but leaves out the disaster." See Link, "Does This Writer Deserve the Prize?"

29. Link, "Politics and the Chinese Language." In this online essay from December 2012, Link clarifies and expands on his *NYRB* piece, several times citing the phrase "daft hilarity."

30. Liu Xiaobo's essay, "From Wang Shuo's Wicked Satire to Hu Ge's E'gao: Political Humor in a Post-Totalitarian Dictatorship," is dated 18 September 2006. Translation from Liu, *No Enemies, No Hatred*, 184.

31. Ibid., 186. Notably, Liu ultimately concludes that "the benefits of *e'gao* [online spoofs] outweigh the costs" and that their sarcasm constitutes a constructive form of antitotali-

tarian resistance. On *e'gao*, see also Davis and Chey, *Humour in Chinese Life and Culture*, chap. 7.

32. Mo Yan, "Nobel Lecture: Storytellers," 10. Mo Yan is one of fourteen vice chairpersons of the Chinese Writers Alliance, which is described on its website as a "professional, voluntary-participation people's group comprised of writers from China's various ethnicities and led by the Chinese Communist Party." See www.chinawriter.com.cn/zxjg/.

33. Yu Hua, *China in Ten Words*, 34–35. Yu's book was first published in Taiwan and is currently banned in China.

34. Quote from Dooling, *Women's Literary Feminism*, 143. A teachable moment involving Lu Xun's story appears in Xie Jin's 1964 film *Stage Sisters* (*Wutai jiemei*), which is set between 1935 and 1950. In 1946, on the tenth anniversary of Lu Xun's death, a radical woman journalist takes a young actress from the countryside to a Shanghai exhibition of artworks inspired by Lu Xun's works. Looking at an etching of Xianglin's wife, the actress sees herself (and eventually appears onstage) as the "doomed peasant widow." Despite its avocation of the revolutionary cause, Xie's film was banned. See Marchetti, "*Two Stage Sisters*." The line about repetition is often attributed to Karl Marx: "Hegel remarks somewhere that all great world-historic facts and personages appear, so to speak, twice. He forgot to add: the first time as tragedy, the second time as farce." See "The Eighteenth Brumaire of Louis Bonaparte" (1852), online at www.marxists.org/archive/marx/works/1852/18th-brumaire/ch01.htm. On the misquotation of this line, see www.marxists.org/glossary/terms/h/i.htm#history-repeats.

35. The phrase is Joseph Lau's. See Liu, *Tilei jiaoling de xiandai Zhongguo wenxue*. David Wang, who quotes Lau, also cites this conundrum, noting that "a muffled tradition of laughter" has coexisted with "tears and cries of indignation." See Wang, *The Monster That Is History*, 7, also 2, 4, 294n6. As we've seen, laughter was muffled only intermittently.

36. On this "dummy verb" and its connection to official culture, see Link, *An Anatomy of Chinese*, especially 17–19, 271–72.

37. See Can Xue, "Youmo" ("Humor"), posted on *Can Xue de BLOG* (Can Xue's BLOG) on 22 June 2006 (http://blog.sina.com.cn/s/blog_46eacfc90100048p.html).

GLOSSARY

Names and titles that appear in the bibliography and appendixes, as well as names of well-known places and people, do not appear in the glossary.

A Er 阿二
"Afang gong fu" 阿房宮賦
Alaoda 阿老大
Ah Mao ge 阿毛哥
"Ah Q zhengzhuan" 阿Q正傳
"*Ah Q zhengzhuan* de chengyin" 《阿Q正傳》的成因
Ailuo bunaozhi 艾羅補腦汁
aiqing xiaoshuo 哀情小說
Aishen zhi feiliao 愛神之肥料
Bai Wei 白薇
baixiang shijie 白相世界
Baiyun ciren 白雲詞人
"Bangxianfa fayin" 幫閑法發隱
banlao Xuniang 半老徐娘
banlao Xuye 半老徐爺
"*Banyue* zhi yinian huigu" 半月之一年回顧
Bao Tianxiao 包天笑
"Baojian shiliao" 保健食料

Bencao gangmu 本草綱目

"Benkan gaizu tebie qishi" 本刊改組特別啟事

Bi Yihong 畢倚虹

"Bianji zuotan" 編輯座談

bianzhu 編著

Bihui 碧暉

Bing Xin 冰心

bingjuan 病鵑

bishuzhe 筆述者

bizhan 筆戰

Bochen huaji huabao 伯塵滑稽畫報

"Bu xiazhai de shijie" 不狹窄的世界

"Bu yu Liu Dabai xiansheng banzui" 不與劉大白先生拌嘴

bu yong dian 不用典

bu'an 補安

bubai 補白

bubai dawang 補白大王

Bucaizi 不才子

"Bugou zhiji" 不夠知己

buke weixun de fenzi 不可為訓的分子

Can Xue de BLOG 殘雪的 BLOG

ceyan xingzhi jing 測驗性質鏡

chaizi 拆字

"Chalun *Yusi* de wenti—yinjian, maren, ji fei'e polai" 插論《語絲》的文體——隱健、罵人、及費厄潑賴

chang leizhai 償淚債

chao de tai guohuo le 炒[吵]得太過火了

Chaoran bao 超然報

chaoxi 抄襲

Chen Jinghan 陳景韓

Chen Laoxin 陳勞薪

Chen Meigong 陳眉公

Chen Tianhua 陳天華

Chen Xiazi 陳霞子

Chen Zizhan 陳子展

Cheng Zhanlu 程瞻廬

chenshi 塵世

"Chenxing yanjutuan zhi 'Juhun shizhe'" 晨星演劇團之"拘魂使者"

Chi Hen 恥痕

chidu dawang 尺牘大王

chitiaotiao de zhishi 赤條條的指示

Chuanjiabao 傳家寶

"Chungguk mundan ŭi hyŏnse ilbyŏl (4)" 中國文壇의現勢一瞥 (四)

Chunmeng 春夢

"Ci chaoxi wen" 斥抄襲文

ciwu 此物

"Cong 'S.O.B.' dao 'guoma'" 從「S.O.B.」到「國罵」

Cuixiu 翠袖

Cunxin 寸心

da nao 大鬧

Da shijie 大世界

da wanyi 大玩意

da ze jiuguo, ci zu yifeng 大則救國，次足移風

Dachu youling ta 打出幽靈塔

"Dang youmo biancheng youmo" 當幽默變成油抹

Dao 燾

dapinwen 大品文

"Dazhan zhong de yumiao xiaopin zhi yiban" 大戰中的語妙小品之一斑

Deng Wengong 鄧文工

"Dengqing Li Dingyi dui *Leren yangke* de chaoxi gong'an" 澄清李定夷對《樂人揚珂》的抄襲公案

"Dengzhou haishi" 登州海市

Di Baoxian 狄葆賢

Di Chuqing 狄楚青

dianwei 顛危

Ding Fubao 丁福保

Ding Ling 丁玲

"'Disanzhong ren' de chulu" "第三種人"的出路

dongfang huaji zhi feng 東方滑稽之風

"Dongfang Zhuobielin, huaji xiaoshuo mingjia—Xu Zhuodai" 東方卓別林, 滑稽小說名家—徐卓呆

Du Heng 杜衡

dujiao xi 獨角戲
e 鵝
e'gao 惡搞
"Epianzi zhi xiaohua: pianshu qiaomiao" 惡騙子之笑話：騙術巧妙
"Er shiren" 二詩人
erwo tu 二我圖
Erwo xuan 二我軒
Erya 爾雅
e'zuoju 惡作劇
fa qing 發情
"Fakanci" 發刊詞
Fan Yanqiao 范煙橋
fang 仿
"Fang chuan" 防川
"Fang Tangshi: Yeji" 仿唐詩：野雞
Fang zi taixi 仿自泰西
Fantong 飯桶
"Fantong liezhuan" 飯桶列傳
"Fanyi zhi nan" 繙譯之難
Fei Chunren 費純人
fei'e polai 費厄潑賴
"Feilong you qiji" 飛龍游奇蹟
Feilongdao 飛龍島
"Feilongdao youji" 飛龍島游記
Feng Xiaogang 馮小剛
Feng Zhiyu 豐之餘
fengci 諷刺
fengci hua 諷刺畫
fengci wentan 諷刺文壇
"Fengci xiaoshuo yu *Rulin waishi*" 諷刺小說與儒林外史
fengshi 諷世
"Fengyu hou tan" 風雨後談
fenni juan 冀溺捐
fenshen xiang 分身像 / 分身相
fu 賦

"Fulu: *Wentan denglongshu* de jingyan" 附錄：《文壇登龍術》的經驗
"Funei kong luosuo" 腹內空哆嗦
"Fuqin de yiwu" 父親的義務
fuzhang 拊掌
"Gaige xuanyan" 改革宣言
gailiang 改良
Gangda zhuozei 戇大捉賊
"Ganlan" 橄欖
Geng qiyou cili 更豈有此理
Geng Xiaodi 耿小的
Gengkui 賡夔
Gong Shaoqin 貢少芹
gong yu wen 功於文
Gong Zizhen 龔自珍
gou xue lin tou 狗血淋頭
goubao 狗報
Gu Mingdao 顧明道
"Gua xi" 瓜戲
Guai yisheng 怪醫生
guai zhuang 怪狀
guaipian 拐騙
Guanchang xianxing ji 官場現形記
Guang Xiaofu 廣笑府
guanggao dawang 廣告大王
Guanjin 觀今
"Guanyu 'Guitu riji' de yifeng xin" 關於"鬼土日記"的一封信
"Guanyu 'wenxin' yu Hu Qiuyuan de wenyi lunbian" 關於文新與胡秋原的文藝論辯
"Guanyu *Zijian Nanzi*" 關於《子見南子》
"Guchui caibing zhi xinzi kaiyan zaiji" 鼓吹裁兵之新戲開演再既
Gui xiansheng 龜先生
gui zhe, gui ye 鬼者，歸也
guihua lianpian 鬼話連篇
guihuo 鬼火
guizi 鬼子
guji 滑稽

"Guji liezhuan" 滑稽列傳
Guohua yingpian gongsi 國華影片公司
"Guolian kaobuzhu le" 國聯靠不住了
Haha daoshi 哈哈道士
Haidi lüxing 海底旅行
"*Haishang hua liezhuan* liyan" 海上花列傳例言
haiyou ge xiaohua ne 還有個笑話呢
[Han] Shiheng [韓]侍桁
Han Yu 韓愈
Han Ziyun 韓子雲
Hanfeizi 韓非子
Haohao xiansheng 好好先生
"Haojing" 好靜
"He qiong wen" 賀窮文
Heiji yuanhun 黑籍冤魂
heping xi 和平席
Hong 紅
Honglou meng 紅樓夢
Hongyan zhiji 紅艷知己
hua 畫
Hua Duancen 華端岑
huaji 滑稽
"Huaji boshi qushi: Li Amao qingchang baibeiji" 滑稽博士趣事：李阿毛情場敗北記
huaji dawang 滑稽大王
Huaji dawang youhu ji 滑稽大王游滬記
huaji ju 滑稽劇
"'Huaji' lijie" 滑稽例解
huaji xi 滑稽戲
huaji xiaohua 滑稽笑話
huaji xiaoshuo 滑稽小說
"Huaji yingpian de youmo ji zimu" 滑稽影片的幽默及字幕
huaji zhe 滑稽者
huaji zi 滑稽字
huajijia 滑稽家
Hualiu shenqing zhuan 花柳深情傳
Huang Chujiu 黃楚九

Huang Xuelei 黃雪蕾

Huang Zhuantao 黃轉陶

Huangjin sui 黃金祟

huashen xiang 化身相

Hu-Bao bieshu 虎豹別墅

huhou shudi 狐后鼠帝

Hui 回

huimo 詼摹

huiwen shi 迴文詩

huixie 詼諧

huixie wenzi 詼諧文字

huixie xiaoshuo 詼諧小說

huixiejia 詼諧家

huluan 胡亂

Huo Yuanjia 霍元甲

huode yuyan 活的語言

Hu Wenbao 胡文豹

Hu Wenhu 胡文虎

"Hu xu" 胡序

Huyu xin cidian tushuo 滬語新詞典圖說

Ji Dian 濟癲

"Ji e'yu wen" 鱷魚祭文

Ji Gong 濟公

jia xinshi biaodian fuhao fenduan de 加新式標點符號分段的

Jiang Jinbao 江金寶

"Jiangnan feng Li Guinian" 江南逢李龜年

Jiankang de xing shenghuo 健康的性生活

"Jiaodu houji" 校讀後記

Jiaoji chidu daquan 交際尺牘大全

Jiaoxin 焦心

jiawen 夾文

jie'e 解額

jiejue shi 解決士

"Jieshao 'wu jia' Liu Fu boshi di ji zhong qiaomiao famen" 介紹 "吾家" 劉復博士底幾種巧妙法門

jieyan 解顏

jieyi 解頤

Jihang 濟航

Jin Nong 金農

Jin shinian muxian zhi guai xianzhuang 近十年目睹之怪現狀

Jinbo 金波

Jing bao 晶報

jingchong zongtong 精蟲總統

Jingu qiguan 今古奇觀

Jingwo 鏡我

Jinnian henian hu 今年何年乎

jinren zhi 今人志

"Jinren zhi: Liu Fu (Bannong)" 今人志: 劉復 (半農)

Jishi xingle bao 及時行樂報

"Jiu hou" 酒後

"Jiuri Qishan denggao" 九日齊山登高

"Jixing de yuandan" 急性的元旦

jubenti xiaoshuo 劇本體小說

"Juchang xiaoxi" 劇場消息

"Jue yapian miaofa" 絕鴉片妙法

jueying 絕纓

Jueying sanxiao 絕纓三笑

"Juhun shizhe" 拘魂使者

"'Juhun shizhe' jinri fuyan" "拘魂使者"今日復演

junzi dong kou budong shou 君子動口不動手

Kaiming shetuan 開明社團

"Kaimu guanggao" 開幕廣告

Kaixin yingpian gongsi 開心影片公司

"Kaixinhua" 開心話

kaoshi xin xiaohua 考試新笑話

"Ketong de xixiao wenzhang" 可痛的嬉笑文章

"Kexi de xuelei wenzhang" 可喜的血淚文章

Kim Kwangju 金光洲

Kong Juemin 孔覺民

koushuzhe 口述者

Koutou chong 叩頭蟲

Kung Te-ch'eng 孔德成

lan goufen chou 爛狗糞臭

Lan Hua 蘭華

Lanling Xiaoxiaosheng 蘭陵笑笑生

Lao Shaonian 老少年

"Lao She laixin shuo" 老舍來信說

"Laoniu poche (liu): wo zenyang xie *Maocheng ji (chuangzuo jingyan)*" 老牛破車（六）— 我怎樣寫《貓城記》（創造經驗）

"Laoniu poche (shi): tan youmo" 老牛破車 (十)—談幽默

Lazhu yingpian gongsi 蠟燭影片公司

Lei Jin 雷瑨

leishu 類書

lengchao refeng 冷嘲熱諷

Li Ah Mao 李阿毛

Li Ah Mao waizhuan 李阿毛外傳

Li Ah Mao yu Dongfang Shuo 李阿毛與東方朔

Li Ah Mao yu jiangshi 李阿毛與僵屍

Li Ah Mao yu Tang Xiaojie 李阿毛與唐小姐

Li Amao boshi 李阿毛博士

"Li Amao ceyan" 李阿毛測驗

"Li Amao suibi" 李阿毛隨筆

"Li Amao xinxiang haowai" 李阿毛信箱號外

Li Duo 李鐸

Li Fanfu 李凡夫

Li Hanqiu 李涵秋

Li Lianying 李蓮英

Li Liewen 黎烈文

Li Qingya 李青厓

Li Shifu 李石福

Li Shizhen 李時珍

Li Zhi 李贄

Li Zhuowu 李卓吾

"Liang Zuoyou changyou Daguanyuan" 梁作友暢遊大觀園

lianhuanxi 連環劇

liansuoxi 連鎖劇

"Lieyan" 列言
Lin Dazu 林達祖
"Lin Shu de fanyi" 林紓的翻譯
Lin Wenqing 林文慶
Lin Yutang 林玉堂
linhuo 磷火
linmao fengjiao 麟毛鳳角
Liu Tieleng 劉鐵冷
Liu Xichun 劉繫春
Liu Yin 留隱
Liu Yuan 劉元
Liu Zongyuan 柳宗元
"Liyan" 例言
Long Buwang 龍不王
Longxiyishi 隴西一士
luanxiao 亂笑
"Lun benbao zhi bu he shiyi" 論本報之不合時宜
"Lun 'disanzhong ren'" 論"第三種人"
"Lun fei'e polai yinggai huanxing" 論費厄潑賴應該緩行
"Lun xiaoshuo yu qunzhi zhi guanxi" 論小說與羣治之關係
"Lun 'yasu gongshang'" 論"雅俗共賞"
"Lun *Youxi bao* zhi benyi" 論《遊戲報》之本意
"Lun zhaoxiang zhi lei" 論照相之類
"*Lunyu* yinian—jieci youtan Xiao Bona" 論語一年—借此又談蕭伯納
"Lunzhan de wenzhang yu maren de wenzhang" 論戰的文章與罵人的文章
Luoke 羅克
Luoke xiaoshi 羅克笑史
Lu Wanliang 陸萬良
"Ma chusheng" 罵畜牲
Ma Er xiansheng 馬二先生
Ma Guoliang 馬國亮
Ma Xingchi 馬星馳
"Ma zongtong de ziyou" 罵總統的自由
maiku 賣哭
maixiao 賣笑

maixiao bu maishen 賣笑不賣身
"Maiyin shizhuang" 賣淫實狀
maiyou lang 賣油郎
manli 鰻鱺
mantuoluo 曼陀羅
"Manxing de chuxi" 慢性的除夕
Maoshi gui 冒失鬼
Maoshi zhengyi 毛詩正義
maozei 蟊賊
Mapi xiaojie 麻皮小姐
"Maren de jishu" 罵人的技術
Masuda Wataru 增田涉
Mei de renshengguan 美的人生觀
"Mei quwei de wenzi" 沒趣味的文字
meipi 眉批
"Meirongshu" 美容術
Meishushi quge 梅墅石渠閣
Mengjia 孟加
Mi zhuchong 米蛀蟲
miao buke jiangyou 妙不可醬油
miao buke niuroutang 妙不可牛肉湯
"Mimi shi" 秘密室
Minbao 民報
"Minguo jiezhai zhi tongshi" 民國借債之痛史
mingzhu 名著
Minhu ribao 民呼日報
minjian 民間
Minxu ribao 民吁日報
Minzhong xijushe 民眾戲劇社
miyao 秘鑰
Miyatake Gaikotsu 宮武外骨
mo'an 默安
modeng nüxing 摩登女性
moxing gaota 摩星高塔
mudu 目睹

Nanfang bao 南方報
Nanshe 南社
nao xi 鬧戲
Naocan youji 腦殘遊記
naoju 鬧劇
neng dong ren ganqing ye 能動人感情也
ni 擬
"Ni chaoxijia bianyuan chengwen" 擬抄襲家辯冤呈文
"Ni shuo zhe bushi qiren bai jiazi de pingju me" 你說這不是旗人擺架子的憑據麼？
ni youmo xiaopin 擬幽默小品
ningmengguo 檸檬果
"Nüxing de wanwu" 女性的玩物
Nüzi di xing chongdong 女子底性衝動
"Ou-Mei zuijin shezhi zhi wenyi yingpian" 歐美最近攝製之文藝影片
oumuya 歐穆亞
Ouyang Yuqian 歐陽予倩
paidiao 排調
paiyu 俳語
Pan Guangdan 潘光旦
Pan Shen 潘慎
penfan 噴飯
peng 捧
Peng Xuehai 彭學海
Peng Yang'ou 彭養鷗
pengfu 捧腹
"Piao [xin *Shijing*]" 嫖（新詩經）
Ping Jinya 平襟亞
"Pingbu qingyun" 平步青雲
Pingdengge zhuren 平等閣主人
Ping-Hu tongche 平滬通車
"Piping yu ma" 批評與罵
piqi jingjin 屁氣淨盡
po yehushi zhu 破夜壺室主
pogua 破瓜
poti 破題
po ti wei xiao 破涕爲笑

Poyu 迫迂
"Qi Yu" 淇奧
qiang 強
qiaopi 俏皮
qi'e 啟額
Qifu 器父
"Qing zou houmen chuqu" 請走後門出去
"Qingsong youmo" 輕鬆幽默
Qingya 青崖
Qingyun 慶雲
Qiu Suwen 邱素文
"Qiuhun shinian" 求婚十年
qiuji tu 求己圖
qiuren buru qiuji 求人不如求己
qiyan 啓顏
qiyi 奇異
Qiyou cili 豈有此理
Quan Zenggu 全增嘏 [T. K. Chuan]
Quanguo xiaoshuo mingjia zhuanji 全國小說名家傳集
Quanyechang 勸業場
quju 趣劇
"Qulu xuyu ershiliu" 蘧廬絮語二十六
quwei 趣味
Ran 燃
rema 熱罵
"Ren de wenxue" 人的文學
ren ru qi wen, wen ru qi wen 人如其文, 文如其文
renjian 人間
Renmian xie 人面蟹
"Renmin de youmo" 人民的幽默
rensa-geki 連環戲
renshi 人世
renshi nanfeng kaikou xiao 人世難逢開口笑
"Ruma he konghe jue bushi zhandou—zhi *Wenxue yuebao* bianji de yi feng xin" 辱罵和恐嚇決不是戰鬥一致《文學月報》編輯的一封信
"Sha zhu yingxiong" 殺豬英雄

"Shang chuan huang magua" 賞穿黃馬褂

shangai 刪改

"*Shanghai manhua* dingqi chuban" 上海漫畫定期出版

"Shanghai qi" 上海氣

"Shanghai: 'Shijie youxi chang'—Wan Qing jinü shengyijing" 上海："世界游戲場"—晚清妓女生意經

"Shangxia liangdui" 上下兩對

"Shanxi xue xi, buwei nue xi" 善戲謔兮，不為虐兮

Shao Xunmei 邵洵美 [Sinmay Zau]

"Shaoxing Aguan cheng huoche" 紹興阿官乘火車

"She xiangyan pigu zhuyi" 捨香煙屁股主義

shehui jiaoyu xiao congshu 社會教育小叢書

"Shenbaoguan zaoqi de shuji chuban (1872–75)" 申報館早期的書籍出版 (1872–75)

"Shengguan" 升官

"Shengmi chifan fa" 省米吃飯法

shenjing bing 神經病

Shenlou zhi 蜃樓志

shenmei yixiao qi yide 伸眉一笑豈易得

Shenyi jing 神異經

sheta'er 射他耳

Shi Jiqun 施濟群

shi shishi, bing bushi xiaohua 是實事，並不是笑話

"Shi tan" 蝨談

Shi Tianji 石天基

"Shidalin de yumiao" 史達林的語妙

shihua 詩話

Shijie fanhua bao 世界繁華報

Shijing 詩經

shimpa-geki 新派劇

"Shishi shishi shi" 施氏食獅史

Shizi hou 獅子吼

Shu Qingchun 舒慶春

shuangla 爽辣

"Shuisheng" 水聲

"Shuo xiao" 說笑

Shuyue 舒月
Sima Zhen 司馬貞
siren 私人
sishu 四書
sishu 死書
Song Jiaoren 宋教仁
suku 訴苦
Su Wen 蘇汶
suan er xuannao 酸而眩腦
Sun Wukong 孫悟空
Taiping guanji 太平廣記
Taishi xiansheng 太史先生
"Tan Mengzi de maren" 談孟子的罵人
"Tan 'youmo'" 談"幽默"
Tang Jianwo 湯劍我
Tang Tao 唐弢
Tao Baopi 陶報癖
Tao Juyin 陶菊隱
Tao Kangde 陶亢德
"Tao yao: hua xiao" 桃夭 花笑
tao zhi yaoyao, zhuozhuo qi hua 桃之夭夭, 灼灼其華
Taozhui 桃椎
tianxiashi moyou qiqiao yu cizhe yi 天下事莫有奇巧於此者矣
Tiaoxue pian 調謔篇
tiezheng 鐵證
Tong Ailou 童愛樓
Tong shi 痛史
Tongjian xuexiao 通鑒學校
"Tongren jietiao" 同仁戒條
Tu Long 屠隆
tuolike 托里克
tuolike yanjing 托力克眼鏡
Tuoying qiguan 脫影奇觀
"Ŭngjŏpsil pyŏltam" 應接室別答
Wang Dungen 王鈍根

Wang Jingxuan 王敬軒
Wang Shuo 王朔
Wang Tiran 汪侗然
Wang Wan 王宛
Wang Yuanfang 汪原放
wanjinyou dawang 萬金油大王
wanshi 玩世
wanyi 玩藝
Wei Suo 葦索
"Weifeng" 衛風
wen 文
"Wenming jiehun zhi xin xiaoshi" 文明結婚之新笑史
wenming xi 文明戲
wenren 文人
"Wenren xiangma lun" 文人相罵論
"Wentan quhua: Xu Zhuodai zhi huaji" 文壇趣話：徐卓呆之滑稽
wentan xiaojiang 文壇笑匠
Wenxin diaolong 文心雕龍
"Wenxue gailiang chuyi" 文學改良芻議
"Wenxue geming zhi fanxiang" 文學革命之反響
wenxue gongren 文學工人
"Wenxue li de 'youmo'" 文學裡的"幽默"
"Wenxue xiaoyan" 文學小言
Wenyi xinlixue 文藝心理學
"Wenzhang wuwei" 文章五味
"Wode dianying mi" 我的電影迷
"Wode hua: Youbuwei zhai jie" 我的話：有不為齋解
woyou 臥遊
Wu Jichen 吳寄塵
Wu Shuangre 吳雙熱
"Wu Zhihui xiansheng shudu" 吳稚暉先生書牘
"Wu Zhihui xiejue zuoshou" 吳稚暉謝絕做壽
Wu Zhilao 吳稚老
"Wu Zhilao: kuairen, kuaiyu" 吳稚老：快人快語
wuji bifan 物極必反

"Wujing nüxue kai shizhou jinian youyihui" 務競女學開十週紀念游藝會
"Wuru sizhe de canren" 侮辱死者的殘忍
wutai xiaojiang 舞台笑匠
wuzu gonghe le 五族共和了
xi xiao 西笑
xi xiaohua 西笑話
Xi you bu 西游補
"Xiandai Zhongguo wenxue zhi langman de qushi" 現代中國文學之浪漫的趨勢
Xiangsan 祥三
xiangsheng 相聲
Xianqing ouji 閑情偶寄
Xianshi leyuan 先施樂園
xiao 笑
"Xiao" 笑
"Xiao bide" 小比得
Xiao de hao 笑得好
"Xiao de lishi" 笑的歷史
"Xiao niu xiao ma" 小牛小馬
xiao pengyou 小朋友
Xiao shijie 小世界
xiao shimin 小市民
Xiao wutai 笑舞臺
"Xiao yu xiju" 笑與喜劇
"*Xiaobao* fu" 《笑報》賦
xiaobing 笑枋
Xiaobing jun 小丙君
xiaodao 笑道
xiaodao 笑倒
Xiao dao 笑倒
xiaohua 笑話
xiaohua baichu 笑話百出
xiaohua xiaoshuo 笑話小說
xiaohua xietan 笑話諧談
xiaojiang 笑匠
xiaoju 笑劇

Xiaolin 笑林
xiaoma 笑罵
xiaoma you ta xiaoma, haoguan wo zi wei zhi 笑罵由他笑罵, 好官我自為之
xiaopinwen 小品文
Xiaoshi shi 笑史氏
"Xiaoshuo cailiao pifasuo" 小說材料批發所
"Xiaoshuo wuti lu" 小說無題錄
xiaotan 笑談
Xiaoxiao xiansheng 笑笑先生
"Xiazhai de shijie" 狹窄的世界
xibi 戲筆
Xidi 西諦
xie 諧
xiehouyu 歇後語
xiewen 諧文
xiexue 諧噱
"Xieyin" 諧隱
"Xieyin quyu" 諧音趣語
xiezhu 諧著
xiezi 楔子
xiezuo getihu 寫作個體戶
"Xiju" 喜劇
ximo 戲墨
Xin Fengshen zhuan 新封神傳
"Xin huiwenshi: hong yan fen fei" 新迴文詩：鴻燕分飛
Xin Guangling chao 新廣陵潮
Xin Jinghuayuan 新鏡花緣
Xin shijie 新世界
Xin Xiyou ji 新西游記
"Xin zhishi zhi zahuodian" 新知識之雜貨店
"Xin *Zishuo*" 新字說
Xing jiaoyu 性教育
xing leihui 行淚賄
xingshi 行事
xingshi 醒世

Xingyu yu xing'ai 性慾與性愛
xingzhi 性質
"Xingzuo" 星座
Xinjiu feiwu 新舊廢物
xinju 新劇
xinjuan 新鐫
Xinmin bao 新民報
xinong 戲弄
xinüe 戲謔
"Xinxian yuebing sheng zhuchong" 新鮮月餅生蛀蟲
xinyou 心遊
xiongfei 雄飛
Xiong Foxi 熊佛西
Xiong xifu 雄媳婦
Xiong Xiling 熊希齡
xiqing xiaoshuo 喜情小說
xishu 戲述
xiuxian 休閒
Xiuyuntian youxichang 繡雲天游戲場
xiwan zhi 細玩之
Xixiang ji 西廂記
xixiao numa 嬉笑怒罵
"Xiyang youmo zhuanhao" 西洋幽默專號
xu 續
Xu Jinfu 許廑父
Xu Maoyong 徐懋庸
Xu Shichang 徐世昌
Xu Tianneng 徐天能
Xu Wenchang de gushi 徐文長的故事
Xu Xiaolin 續笑林
Xu Yuehong 徐月虹
Xu Zheng 徐崢
Xu Zhongqi 徐仲蓁
Xuande 宣德
"Xue he lei de wenxue" 血和淚的文學

"Xuejiu bianxiang" 學究變相

xueshe 噱社

"Xujun xiaoshuo de fanmian" 徐君小說的反面

Xunling 勳齡

"Yaba lizan" 啞巴禮贊

Yan Duhe 嚴獨鶴

Yan Weisheng 燕尾生

yanbian jie de ren yan fei ruo shi, shuo shi ruo fei, yan luan yitong ye 言辯捷的人言非若是，說是若非，言亂異同也

Yang Chengyin 楊成因

Yang Lanwu 楊藍塢

yang lanwu 洋爛污

Yangjingbang tushuo 洋涇濱圖說

"Yangmi xiaoying" 洋迷小影

"Yangui nü kexue quancai" 煙鬼女科學全才

"Yangzhuang de chaoxijia" 洋裝的抄襲家

"Yangzhuang de xiaohua" 洋裝的笑話

Yao Hsin-nung 姚莘農

Yao Ke 姚克

"Yapo" 壓迫

Ye Xiaofeng 葉小鳳

Ye Yinquan 葉因泉

Yi 夷

"Yi fangmian de xin" 一方面的心

"Yi Liu Bannong jun" 憶劉半農君

Yi Peiji 易培基

"Yi xiao tu" 一笑圖

Yin Bansheng 寅半生

Yinbingshi zhuren 飲冰室主人

Yingbo 英伯

yingtui 英腿

yingxi 影戲

yishi 意識

yishi 軼事

Yishi bao—wenxue zhoukan 益世報—文學週刊

"Yishu de qiyuan yu youxi" 藝術的起源與遊戲
Yizhi 一知
"Yizhi mafeng" 一隻馬蜂
You Bankuang 憂半狂
"You ma ziji le" 又罵自己了
"You yu yi" 游於藝
"Youhua zhishuo, youpi zhifang" 有話直說, 有屁直放
youle chang 遊樂場
youma 優罵
youmiao 幽妙
youmo 幽默
youmo dashi 幽默大師
"Youmo de marenshu" 幽默的罵人術
"Youmo de weixian" 幽默的危險
youmo ti 幽默體
youmo wangguo 幽默王國
"Youmo wenxuan" 幽默文選
"*Youmo* yu *yumiao* zhi taolun" 「幽默」與「語妙」之討論
"Youmo zhendi" 幽默真諦
youmohua 幽默化
youmojia 幽默家
"Yousang: zhi *Guoyu zhoukan* jizhe" 友喪—致《國語週刊》記者
you ta yi mo 幽他一默
youxi 游戲
"Youxi chang: Hua shijie kaimu zhi suojian" 游戲場：花世界開幕之所見
"Youxi chang: Xin nian zhi Xin shijie" 游戲場：新年之新世界
youxi de shiye 游戲的事業
youxi renjian 游戲人間
"*Youxi shijie* fakanci" 游戲世界發刊詞
"Youxi wenzhang lun—fang Ouyang Xiu huanzhe zhuanlun" 游戲文章論—仿歐陽修宦者傳論
"Youxi wenzi zhi liufa siji" 游戲文字之六法四忌
"Youxi xinzhi" 游戲新誌
"Youxi zhi Zhongguo" 游戲之中國
youxichang 游戲場

youyi chang 游藝場
Yu 語
Yu Dezhu 余德珠
Yu Ling 禹玲
Yu Youren 于右任
Yu Tianfen 俞天憤
Yuan Muzhi 袁牧之
yuanquan shi 圓圈詩
yuanyang hudie pai 鴛鴦蝴蝶派
"Yuanzi zhi jieguo" 袁字之結果
Yulun shishi bao 輿論時事報
yumiao 語妙
Yunjian pai 雲間派
"Yuren jie" 愚人節
"Yuren tuiwei wenti de ceyan" 裕仁退位問題的測驗
Yutang 語堂
Yuwai xiaoshuo ji 域外小說集
Yuyan bao 寓言報
za 雜
"Zalun youmo" 裸論幽默
zan 贊
zang 臟
"Zatan youmo" 雜談幽默
zawen 雜文
zazu huixie 裸俎詼諧
Zeng Pu 曾樸
Zhang Chunfan 張春凡
Zhang Dai 張岱
"Zhang Mojun yu Xiong Xiling de xiaohua" 張默君與熊希齡的笑話
Zhang Shizhao 章士釗
Zhang Xianli 張獻勵
Zhang Yi'an 張亦庵
Zhang Yuehen 張月痕
Zhang Ziwei 張子韋
"Zhaozusi" 招租四

Zhe Lu 哲盧
zheng 正
Zheng Xiaoqiu 鄭小秋
Zheng Zhenduo 鄭振鐸
zhengjinghua 正經話
"Zhenglizhe de hua" 整理者的話
"Zhengyi sanwen bing tichang youmo" 徵譯散文並提倡幽默
"Zhenhua yu xiaohua" 真話與笑話
zhentan 偵探
Zhenwu zhaoxiangguan 真吾照相館
Zhenye 真耶
zhi hu zhe ye 之乎者也
"Zhi yatong" 治牙痛
Zhilao 稚老
zhishang kongyan 紙上空言
Zhitang 知堂
"Zhongguo de huaji wenxue" 中國的滑稽文學
"Zhongguo diyi? *Nanfu nanqi* yu tade 'jingdianhua'" 中國第一?《難夫難妻》與它的「經典話」
"Zhongguo juzuojia jiqi zuopin" 中國劇作家及其作品
"Zhongguo youmo zhuanhao" 中國幽默專號
Zhongguo zhentan an 中國偵探案
Zhongguo zuida youxi zhi chang 中國最大游戲之場
"Zhongyang meng" 中央夢
Zhou Gucheng 周谷城
Zhou Manhua 周曼華
Zhou Shoujuan 周瘦鵑
Zhu Zhanji 朱瞻基
Zhu Ziqing 朱自清
"Zhu Ziqing jun de 'Xiao de lishi'" 朱自清君的「笑的歷史」
zhuan 傳
zhuang 莊
Zhuang Binghai 莊病骸
"Zhufu" 祝福
Zhuo Bielin 卓別林 (also given as 卓別霖)

zhuo er bu qun 卓而不群
Zhuo Fuling 卓弗靈
"Zhuo hutuchong" 捉糊塗蟲
"Zhusheng gouyang zhi Zhongguoren" 豬生狗養之中國人
zi 字
Zijian nanzi 子見南子
Zishuo 字說
zixingche 自行車
"*Ziyou zazhi* zhushi" 自由雜誌祝詩
"Zizhiju yiyuan zhi jinqianzhuyi" 自治局議員之金錢主義
"Zuixin jinyanshu" 最新禁厭術
"Zuixin jinyanshu buyi" 最新禁厭術補遺
"Zuizao tichang youmo de liangpian wenzhang" 最早提倡幽默的兩篇文章
"Zujie malu fu" 租界馬路賦
zuo wenzhang 做文章
"Zuzhi neige" 組織內閣

BIBLIOGRAPHY

PERIODICALS

* Title translation appearing in original periodical.

Banjiao manhua 半角漫畫 (The Sketch)* (Guangzhou, 1929–35)
Banyue 半月 (The Half Moon Journal)* (Shanghai, 1921–25)
Beidou 北斗 (Big Dipper) (Shanghai, 1931–32)
Chahua 茶話 (Tea Talk) (Shanghai, 1946–49)
Chenbao 晨報 (Morning Post) (Beijing, 1916–36)
China Critic, The (*Zhongguo pinglun zhoubao* 中國評論週報)* (Shanghai, 1928–40, 1945)
Chinese Students' Monthly, The (*Zhongguo liu Mei xuesheng yuebao* 中國留美學生月報)* (New York, Ann Arbor, 1906–31)
Dazhong 大眾 (The Masses) (Shanghai, 1942–45)
Duli manhua 獨立漫畫 (Oriental Puck)* (Shanghai, 1935–36)
Haifeng 海風 (The Shanghai Gale)* (Shanghai, 1945–46)
Haiguang 海光 (The Hai Kwang Weekly)* (Shanghai, 1945–46)
Hong meigui 紅玫瑰 (Red Rose) (Shanghai, 1924–31)
Hong zazhi 紅雜誌 (The Scarlet Magazine)* (Shanghai, 1922–24)
Huaji huabao banyuekan 滑稽畫報半月刊 (Famous Funnies)* (Shanghai, 1936–37)
Huaji shibao 滑稽時報 (Comical Eastern Times) (Shanghai, 1914)
Huaji shijie 滑稽世界 (Funny World) (Shanghai, 1938–40)
Huaji zazhi 滑稽雜誌 (Funny Magazine) (Suzhou, 1913)
Jinri pinglun 今日評論 (Criticism Today) (Kunming, 1939–41)
Kaixin 開心 (The Happy Times)* (Singapore, 1929)
Kaixin tekan 開心特刊 (Happy Film Co. Fanzine) (Shanghai, ca. 1925–26)
Kōkkei shinbun 滑稽新聞 (Comical News) (Osaka, 1901–8)

Kuaihuo 快活 (The Merry Magazine)* (Shanghai, 1922)
Kuaihuo lin 快活林 (The Merry Voice)* (Shanghai, 1946–47)
Kuaihuo shijie 快活世界 (The Happy World)* (Shanghai, 1914)
Lianyi zhi you 聯益之友 (The Liengyi's Tri-Monthly; from 21 November 1930, The Liengyi's Friend)* (Shanghai, 1925–31)
Libailiu 禮拜六 (The Saturday)* (Shanghai, 1914–16, 1921–23)
Liming banyuekan 黎明半月刊 (The Aurora)* (Shanghai, ca. 1920s)
Lunyu banyuekan 論語半月刊 (The Analects Fortnightly) (Shanghai, 1932–37, 1946–49)
Mangyuan 莽原 (Wilderness) (Shanghai, 1926–27)
Manhua jie 漫畫界 (Modern Puck)* (Shanghai, 1936)
Meilibin bu aiguobao 美利賓埠愛國報 (The Chinese Times)* (Melbourne, 1902–14[?], 1917–22)
Minbao 民報 (The Minpao Magazine)* (Tokyo, 1905–10)
Minguo ribao 民國日報 (The Republican Daily News)* (Shanghai, 1916–32, 1945–47)
Minquan bao 民權報 (Civil Rights) (Shanghai, 1912–14)
Qingnian jie 青年界 (Youth World) (Shanghai, 1931–37)
Qingnian wenyou 青年文友 (Youth Literary Companion) (Hong Kong, 1952–ca. 1960s)
Qiri tan 七日談 (The Wednesday Post)* (Shanghai, 1945–46)
Rattle, The (Shanghai, 1896–97, 1900–1903)
Renjian shi 人間世 (This Human World) (Shanghai, 1934–35)
Renjian shi 人間世 (Chinese Humanist Monthly)* (Taipei, 1957–83)
Renmin ribao 人民日報 (People's Daily)* (Xibopo, 1946; Shijiazhuang, 1947–49; Beijing, 1949–)
Sanri huabao 三日畫報 (China Camera News)* (Shanghai, 1925–27)
Shanghai chenbao 上海晨報 (The Shanghai Morning Post)* (Shanghai, 1932–36)
Shanghai manhua 上海漫畫 (Shanghai Sketch)* (Shanghai, 1928–30)
Shanghai poke 上海潑克 (Shanghai Puck)* (Shanghai, 1918)
Shehui ribao 社會日報 (The Social Daily News)* (Shanghai, 1929–37)
Shenbao 申報 (The Shun Pao)* (Shanghai, 1872–1949)
Shenzhou ribao 神州日報 (The National Herald)* (Shanghai, 1907–47)
Shibao 時報 (The Eastern Times)* (Shanghai, 1904–39)
Shidai manhua 時代漫畫 (Modern Sketch)* (Shanghai, 1934–37)
Shishi xinbao 時事新報 (The China Times)* (Shanghai, 1907–11 [as: *Shishi bao* 時事報], 1911–49)
Shizi jietou 十字街頭 (Crossroads) (Shanghai, 1931–32)
Taibai 太白 (Shanghai, 1934–35)
Tanfeng youmo banyuekan 談風幽默半月刊 (Breezy Chats Humor Fortnightly) (Shanghai, 1936–37)
Thien Nam Sin Pao 天南新報 (Chinese Daily News)* (Singapore, 1898–1905)
T'ien Hsia Monthly (*Tianxia yuekan* 天下月刊)* (Shanghai, 1935–41)
Tonga Ilbo 東亞日報 (Tonga Daily) (Seoul, est. 1920)
Tuhua chenbao 圖畫晨報 (The Chen Pao Miscellany)* (Shanghai, 1932–36)
Tuhua ribao 圖畫日報 (Illustration Daily) (Shanghai, 1909–10)
Wanxiang 萬象 (Wan hsiang)* (Shanghai, 1941–44)

Wenxue xunkan 文學旬刊 (Literary Semi-Monthly) (Shanghai, 1921–25)
Wenxue yuebao 文學月報 (The Literary Monthly)* (Shanghai, 1932)
Wenxue zazhi 文學雜誌 (Literature) (Beiping [editorial], Shanghai [printing], 1937, 1947–48)
Wenyi zhendi 文藝陣地 (Literary Front) (Hankou, Chongqing, and Hong Kong, 1938–42)
Xiandai 現代 (Les Contemporains)* (Shanghai, 1932–35)
Xiandai pinglun 現代評論 (Beijing, 1924–27; Shanghai, 1927–28)
Xiao 笑 (Laughter) (Shanghai, 1935)
Xiao bao 笑報 (Laughter) (Shanghai, est. 1897)
Xiao hua 笑畫 (Illustrated Laughter) (Shanghai, 1923–24)
Xiaobao sanrikan 笑報三日刊 (The Ridicule Press)* (Shanghai, 1926–31)
Xiaolin bao 笑林報 (Forest of Laughs) (Shanghai, 1901–10)
Xiaolin zazhi 笑林雜誌 (Forest of Laughs Magazine) (Shanghai, 1915)
Xiaoshuo daguan 小說大觀 (The Grand Magazine)* (Shanghai, 1915–21)
Xiaoshuo huabao 小說畫報 (Illustrated Novel Magazine)* (Shanghai, est. 1917)
Xiaoshuo shijie 小說世界 (The Story World)* (Shanghai, 1923–29)
Xiaoshuo yuebao 小說月報 (Fiction Monthly) (Shanghai, 1910–31)
Xiju dianying 戲劇電影 (Stage and Screen) (Shanghai, 1926–)
Xin guomin ribao 新國民日報 (Sin Kok Min Jit Pao)* (Singapore, 1919–41; Kuala Lumpur, 1941)
Xin qingnian 新青年 (La Jeunesse)* (Beijing, 1915–26)
Xin Shanghai 新上海 (New Shanghai) (Shanghai, 1926–29)
Xin Shanghai 新上海 (New Shanghai) (Shanghai, 1946)
Xin shiji 新世紀 (La Novaj Tempoj, later Le Siècle Nouveau)* (Paris, 1907–10)
Xin shijie 新世界 (The New World) (Shanghai, 1916–27)
Xin xiaoshuo 新小說 (New Fiction) (Yokohama, 1902–3; Shanghai, 1903–6)
Xingdao ribao 星島日報 (Tsing Tao Daily)* (Hong Kong, est. ca. 1938)
Xingqi 星期 (The Sunday)* (Shanghai, 1922–23)
Xinmin congbao 新民叢報 (Sein Min Choong Bou)* (Yokohama, 1902–7)
Xinsheng wanbao 新生晚報 (New Life Evening News) (Hong Kong, 1945–76)
Xinwen bao 新聞報 (Sin Wan Pao)* (Shanghai, 1893–49)
Yican 一粲 (The Comical Weekly)* (Singapore, 1927–28)
Yijing wenshi banyuekan 逸經文史半月刊 (Yijing Literary and Historical Semi-Monthly) (Shanghai, 1936–37)
Yixiao bao 一笑報 (A Laugh) (Singapore, 1930)
Youxi bao 游戲報 (Play) (Shanghai, 1897–1910)
Youxi shijie 游戲世界 (World of Play) (Hangzhou, ca. 1907)
Youxi shijie 游戲世界 (The Recreation World)* (Shanghai, 1921–23)
Youxi zazhi 游戲雜誌 (The Pastime)* (Shanghai, 1913–15)
Yueyue xiaoshuo 月月小說 (The All-Story Monthly)* (Shanghai, 1906–9)
Yusi 語絲 (Threads of Discourse) (Beijing, 1924–27; Shanghai, 1927–30)
Yuxing 餘興 (Amusements) (Shanghai, 1914)
Yuzhou feng 宇宙風 (Cosmic Wind) (Shanghai, 1935–38; Guangzhou, 1938; Hong Kong, 1939; Guilin, 1944; Chongqing, 1945; Guangzhou, 1946–47)
Zazhi 雜誌 (Magazine) (Shanghai, 1938–39, 1942–45)

Zhenshanmei 真善美 (Truth, Goodness, Beauty) (Shanghai, 1927–31)
Zhenxiang huabao 真相畫報 (The True Record)* (Shanghai, 1912–13)
Zhongguo gonglun xibao 中國公論西報 (The National Review)* (Shanghai, 1907–16)
Zhongliu 中流 (The Current) (Shanghai, 1936–37)
Ziyou zazhi 自由雜誌 (Free Magazine) (Shanghai, 1913)

FILMS

Baimaonü 白毛女 (The White-Haired Girl) (Wang Bin 王濱 and Shui Hua 水華, dirs., 1950)
Guizi laile 鬼子來了 (Devils on the Doorstep) (Jiang Wen 姜文, dir., 2000)
Huo Yuanjia 霍元甲 (Fearless) (Ronny Yu 于仁泰, dir., 2006)
Laogong zhi aiqing 勞工之愛情 (Laborer's Love) (Zheng Zhengqiu 鄭正秋 and Zhang Shichuan 張石川, dirs., 1922)
Modern Times (Charles Chaplin, dir., 1936)
Perfect Understanding (Cyril Gardner, dir., 1933)
Taitai wansui 太太萬歲 (Long Live the Wives) (Sang Hu 桑弧, dir., 1947)
Tianming 天明 (Daybreak) (Sun Yu 孫瑜, dir., 1933)
Wutai jiemei 舞臺姐妹 (Stage Sisters) (Xie Jin 謝晉, dir., 1964)
Xiao wanyi 小玩藝 (Playthings) (Sun Yu 孫瑜, dir., 1933)
Xin nüxing 新女性 (New Women) (Cai Chusheng 蔡楚生, dir., 1934)

BOOKS AND ARTICLES

Notes:
1. *Chinese humor collections published between 1900-1937 are listed in appendix 1.*
2. *Editions of Which Classic? (He Dian) and related paratexts are listed in appendix 2.*

Adrian, Bonnie. *Framing the Bride: Globalizing Beauty and Romance in Taiwan's Bridal Industry.* Berkeley: University of California Press, 2003.
Altenburger, Roland. "Chains of Ghost Talk: Highlighting of Language, Distance, and Irony in *He Dian*." *Asiatica Venetiana* 6–7 (2001–2): 23–46.
Althusseur, Louis. *Lenin and Philosophy and Other Essays.* Translated by Ben Brewster. New York: Monthly Review Press, 1971.
Anderson, Marston. *The Limits of Realism: Chinese Fiction in the Revolutionary Period.* Berkeley: University of California Press, 1990.
Anonymous. *Courtesans and Opium: Romantic Illusions of the Fool of Yangzhou.* Translated by Patrick Hanan. New York: Columbia University Press, 2009.
Anonymous. *Mirage.* Translated by Patrick Hanan. Hong Kong: Chinese University Press, 2014.
Baccini, Giulia. "The Forest of Laughs (*Xiaolin*): Mapping the Offspring of Self-Aware Literature in Ancient China." PhD diss., Università Ca'Foscari Venezia, 2010.
Bakhtin, Mikhail. *Rabelais and His World.* Translated by Hélène Iswolsky. Bloomington: Indiana University Press, 1984.
Bao Lele 鮑樂樂, and Wang Yiming 王一明. *Huoshao doufudian* 火燒豆腐店 (Fire Burns the Tofu Shop). Shanghai: Shanghai wenhua chubanshe, 1958.

Baoweng laoren 抱甕老人, ed. *Jingu qiguan* 今古奇觀 (Remarkable Sights New and Old). Annotated by Gu Xuejie 顧學頡. 2 vols. Beijing: Renmin wenxue chubanshe, 1957.
Barmé, Geremie R. *An Artistic Exile: A Life of Feng Zikai (1898–1975)*. Berkeley: University of California Press, 2002.
———. *The Forbidden City*. Cambridge, MA: Harvard University Press, 2008.
Bayard, Pierre. *How to Talk about Books You Haven't Read*. Translated by Jeffrey Mehlman. New York: Bloomsbury, 2007.
Beijing tushuguan 北京圖書館, ed. *Minguo shiqi zong shumu* 民國時期總書目 (Comprehensive Bibliography of Books Published during the Republican Era, 1911–49). Vol. 2: Literary Theory, World Literature, Chinese Literature. Beijing: Shumu wenxian chubanshe, 1992.
Bender, Mark. *Plum and Bamboo: China's Suzhou Chantefable Tradition*. Urbana: University of Illinois Press, 2003.
Benjamin, Walter. *Illuminations: Essays and Reflections*. Edited by Hannah Arendt. New York: Harcourt, Brace & World, 1969.
Bergson, Henri. *Laughter: An Essay on the Meaning of the Comic*. Translated by Cloudesley Brereton and Fred Rothwell. London: Dodo Press, 2007.
———. *Xiao zhi yanjiu* 笑之研究 (A Study of Laughter; retranslation of *Le Rire* from Brereton and Rothwell's English translation). Translated by Zhang Wentian 張聞天. Shanghai: Shangwu yinshuguan, 1921 (preface date).
Berry, Michael. *A History of Pain: Trauma in Modern Chinese Literature and Film*. New York: Columbia University Press, 2008.
Bierce, Ambrose. *The Devil's Dictionary*. Project Gutenberg. www.gutenberg.org/9/7/972/.
Birrell, Anne. *Games Poets Play: Readings in Medieval Chinese Poetry*. Cambridge, UK: McGuinness China Monographs, 2004.
Bishop, John L. "Some Limitations of Chinese Fiction." *Far Eastern Quarterly* 15, no. 2 (February 1956): 239–47.
Brooks, Tim. *Lost Sounds: Blacks and the Birth of the Recording Industry, 1890–1919*. Champaign: University of Illinois Press, 2004.
Brooks, Van Wyck. *The Ordeal of Mark Twain*. New York: Dutton & Co., 1933.
Brosius, Christiane, and Roland Wenzlhuemer, eds. *Transcultural Turbulences: Towards a Multi-Sited Reading of Image Flows*. Berlin: Springer, 2011.
Brown, Jeremy, and Paul G. Pickowicz, eds. *Dilemmas of Victory: The Early Years of the People's Republic of China*. Cambridge, MA: Harvard University Press, 2008.
Cahill, James. *The Painter's Practice: How Artists Lived and Worked in Traditional China*. New York: Columbia University Press, 1994.
Cao Xueqin 曹雪芹, and Gao E 高鶚. *The Story of the Stone*. 5 vols. Translated by David Hawkes and John Minford. Harmondsworth: Penguin Books, 1973–86.
Certeau, Michel de. *The Practice of Everyday Life*. Translated by Steven Rendall. Berkeley: University of California Press, 1984.
Chan, Leo Tak-Hung. *The Discourse of Foxes and Ghosts*. Translated by Maria Galikowski and Lin Min. Honolulu: University of Hawai'i Press, 1998.
Chang, Eileen. *The Fall of the Pagoda*. Hong Kong: Hong Kong University Press, 2010 [1968].
Chen Bangjun 陳邦俊, ed. *Guang xieshi* 廣諧史 (Expanded History of Humor) (1579 preface). 10 vols. Taipei: Tianyi chubanshe, 1985.

Chen Diexian 陳蝶仙. *The Money Demon*. Translated by Patrick Hanan. Honolulu: University of Hawai'i Press, 1999.

Chen Geng 陳庚. *Xiao shi* 笑史 (A History of Laughter). Prefaces by Tong Hui of Changsha 長沙童翬 (1842), Li Wei of Huanxiangchuan 浣湘川李爲 (1841), Yin Xixian 殷熙賢 (1842), Xie Jinxian 謝金銜 (undated), Liu Rongchang 劉融昌 (undated), [author-editor] Juelaizi 覺來子 (1841). Commentaries by Juelaizi. Afterword by Lu Huang 路璜 (1844). Shanghai: Shenbaoguan, [1870s?].

Chen, Janet Y. *Guilty of Indigence: The Urban Poor in China, 1900–1953*. Princeton, NJ: Princeton University Press, 2012.

———. "The Sounds of 'Mandarin' in Gramophone Records and Film, 1922–1934." Unpublished paper presented at workshop "Language, Culture, and Power," Princeton University, 22–23 April 2012.

Ch'en, Jerome. *Yuan Shih-k'ai*. 2nd ed. Stanford: Stanford University Press, 1972.

Chen Jianhua 陳建華. *Cong geming dao gonghe: Qingmo zhi Minguo shiqi wenxue, dianying yu wenhua de zhuanxing* 從革命到共和：清末至民國時期文學、電影與文化的轉型 (From Revolution to Republic: Literary, Cinematic, and Cultural Transformations from the Late Qing to the Republican Period). Guilin: Guangxi shifan daxue chubanshe, 2009.

Chen Linghai 陳凌海, and Chen Hong 陳洪, eds. *Wu Zhihui xiansheng nianpu* 吳稚暉先生年譜 (Chronology of Mr. Wu Zhihui). Taipei: Xingtai yinshuachang, 1971.

Chen Mingyuan 陳明遠. *Wenhuaren de jingji shenghuo* 文化人的經濟生活 (The Financial Lives of Cultural Figures). Xi'an: Sha'anxi renmin chubanshe, 2013.

Chen, Peng-hsiang, and Whitney Crothers Dilley, eds. *Feminism/Femininity in Chinese Literature*. New York: Rodopi, 2002.

Chen Pingyuan 陳平原. *Zhongguo xiaoshuo xushi moshi de zhuanbian* 中國小說敘事模式的轉變 (Narrative Transformations of Chinese Fiction). Beijing: Beijing daxue chubanshe, 2003.

Chen Pingyuan 陳平原, Wang Dewei 王德威, and Gao Wei 高偉, eds. *Wan Ming yu wan Qing: Lishi chuancheng yu wenhua chuangxin* 晚明與晚清：歷史傳承與文化創新 (The Late Ming and the Late Qing: Historical Dynamics and Cultural Innovation). Wuhan: Hubei jiaoyu chubanshe, 2002.

Chen, Shih-Wen. "*Baozou manhua* (Rage Comics), Internet Humour and Everyday Life." *Continuum: Journal of Media & Cultural Studies* 28, no. 5 (September 2014): 690–708.

Chen Sihe 陳思和, and Wang Dewei 王德威, eds. *Jiangou Zhongguo xiandai wenxue duoyuan gongsheng tixi de xin sikao* 建構中國現代文學多元共生體系的新思考 (New Thoughts on the Construction of Pluralistic and Symbiotic Approaches to Modern Chinese Literature). Shanghai: Fudan daxue chubanshe, 2012.

Chen Weili 陳維禮, and Guo Junfeng 郭俊峰, eds. *Zhongguo lidai xiaohua jicheng* 中國歷代笑話集成 (Compendium of Jokes from Imperial China). 5 vols. Changchun: Shidai wenyi chubanshe, 1996.

Chen, Xiaomei, ed. *The Columbia Anthology of Modern Chinese Drama*. New York: Columbia University Press, 2010.

Chen Yingshi 陳英仕. *Qingdai guilei fengci xiaoshuo sanbuqu: "Zhan gui zhuan," "Tang Zhong Kui ping gui zhuan," "He Dian"* 清代鬼類諷刺小說三部曲—《斬鬼傳》、《唐鍾馗

平鬼傳》、《何典》 (A Trilogy of Satirical Qing Dynasty Ghost Novels: *Slaying the Demons, Zhong Kui of the Tang Dynasty Quells the Demons, Which Classic?*). Taipei: Showwe Information Co., 2005.

Cheng, Eileen J. *Literary Remains: Death, Trauma, and Lu Xun's Refusal to Mourn*. Honolulu: University of Hawai'i Press, 2013.

Chey, Jocelyn, and Jessica Milner Davis, eds. *Humour in Chinese Life and Letters: Classical and Traditional Approaches*. Hong Kong: Hong Kong University Press, 2011.

Cochran, Sherman. *Chinese Medicine Men: Consumer Culture in China and Southeast Asia*. Cambridge, MA: Harvard University Press, 2006.

Cohen, Paul A. *History in Three Keys: The Boxers as Event, Experience, and Myth*. New York: Columbia University Press, 1997.

Cohen, Ted. *Jokes: Philosophical Thoughts on Joking Matters*. Chicago: University of Chicago Press, 1999.

Confucius. *Analects, with Selections from Traditional Commentaries*. Translated by Edward Slingerland. Indianapolis: Hackett, 2003.

Crespi, John A. "China's *Modern Sketch*—1: The Golden Era of Cartoon Art, 1934–1937." MIT Visualizing Cultures. http://ocw.mit.edu/ans7870/21f/21f.027/modern_sketch/ms_essay01.html.

Daruvala, Susan. *Zhou Zuoren and an Alternative Chinese Response to Modernity*. Cambridge, MA: Harvard University Asia Center, 2000.

Davies, Christie. *Ethnic Humor around the World: A Comparative Analysis*. Bloomington: Indiana University Press, 1990.

———. *Jokes and Targets*. Bloomington: Indiana University Press, 2011.

Davies, Gloria. "The Problematic Modernity of Ah Q." *Chinese Literature: Essays, Articles, Reviews* 13 (December 1991): 57–76.

———. *Worrying about China: The Language of Chinese Critical Inquiry*. Cambridge, MA: Harvard University Press, 2007.

Davis, Jessica Milner. *Farce*. New Brunswick, NJ: Transaction Publishers, 2011.

Davis, Jessica Milner, and Jocelyn Chey, eds. *Humour in Chinese Life and Culture: Resistance and Control in Modern Times*. Hong Kong: Hong Kong University Press, 2013.

Davis, Mike Lee. *Reading the Text That Isn't There: Paranoia in the Nineteenth-Century American Novel*. New York: Routledge, 2005.

Dekobra, Maurice. *Confucius en pull-over, ou le beau voyage en Chine*. Paris: Baudinière, 1934.

———. *Confucius in a Tail-Coat: Ancient China in Modern Costume*. Translated by Metcalfe Wood. London: T. Werner Laurie, 1935.

———. *Le rire dans la steppe: l'humour russe*. Paris: Baudinière, 1927.

———. *Le rire dans le brouillard: anthologie des meilleurs humoristes anglais et américains*. Paris: Flammarion, 1926.

———. *The Crimson Smile*. Translated by Metcalfe Wood. London: T. Werner Laurie, 1929.

Deng Yu 鄧愚. "'Dongfang Zhuobielin' Xu Zhuodai" "東方卓別林" 徐卓呆 ("'Oriental Charlie Chaplin' Xu Zhuodai"). http://122.11.55.148/gate/big5/www.dfzb.suzhou.gov.cn/zsbl/1677127.htm.

Dentith, Simon. *Parody*. London: Routledge, 2000.

Denton, Kirk A., ed. *Modern Chinese Literary Thought: Writings on Literature, 1893–1945*. Stanford, CA: Stanford University Press, 1996.
Denton, Kirk A., and Michel Hockx, eds. *Literary Societies of Republican China*. Lantham, MD: Lexington, 2008.
Des Forges, Alexander. "From Source Texts to 'Reality Observed': The Creation of the 'Author' in Nineteenth-Century Chinese Vernacular Fiction." *Chinese Literature: Essays, Articles, and Reviews* 22 (December 2000): 67–84.
———. *Mediasphere Shanghai: The Aesthetics of Cultural Production*. Honolulu: University of Hawai'i Press, 2007.
Diegengsi, Que'ersi 迭更斯—卻而司 [Charles Dickens]. *Lüxing xiaoshi* 旅行笑史 (A Picaresque Comedy) [abridged translation of *The Pickwick Papers*]. Translated by Chang Jue 常覺 and Xiao Die 小蝶. Shanghai: Zhonghua shuju, 1918.
Dikötter, Frank. *The Age of Openness: China before Mao*. Hong Kong: University of Hong Kong Press, 2008.
———. *Sex, Culture, and Modernity in China: Medical Science and the Construction of Sexual Identities in the Early Republican Period*. Honolulu: University of Hawai'i Press, 1995.
Ding Xilin 丁西林. *Ding Xilin xiju ji 1: Xilin dumuju ji* 丁西林戲劇集1—西林獨幕劇集 (Plays of Ding Xilin 1: Xilin's One-Act Plays). Shanghai: Wenhua shenghuo chubanshe, 1947.
Dingqie quanxiang anjian Tang Zhong Kui quanzhuan 鼎鍥全像按鑑唐鍾馗全傳 (The Engraved and Completely Illustrated Complete Biography of Zhong Kui of the Tang). Emended by An Zhengtang 安正堂; printed by Liu Sousong 劉叟松. Series: *Guben xiaoshuo congkan* 古本小說叢刊 (2:5). Bejing: Zhonghua shuju, 1990.
Donne, John. *The Major Works*. Edited by John Carey. Oxford: Oxford University Press, 1990.
Dong, Xinyu. "China at Play: Republican Film Comedies and Chinese Cinematic Modernity." PhD diss., Harvard University, 2009.
———. "The Laborer at Play: *Laborer's Love*, the Operational Aesthetic, and the Comedy of Inventions." *Modern Chinese Literature and Culture* 20, no. 2 (Fall 2008): 1–39.
Dooling, Amy D. "In Search of Laughter: Yang Jiang's Feminist Comedy." *Modern Chinese Literature* 8, nos. 1–2 (Spring–Fall 1994): 41–67.
———. *Women's Literary Feminism in Twentieth Century China*. New York: Palgrave Macmillan, 2005.
Dorp, Rolf Harold von. "Wu Chih-hui and the Late Nineteenth Century Gentry: A Study of Major Intellectual Alternatives," Master's thesis, Brown University, 1969.
Du Fu 杜甫. *Du Shaoling xiangzhu* 杜少陵詳注 (Annotated Works of Du Fu). Commentary by Qiu Zhao'ao 仇兆鰲. 2 vols. Beijing: Beijing tushuguan chubanshe, 1999.
Eco, Umberto. *The Name of the Rose*. Translated by William Weaver. New York: Harcourt, 1983.
Elliott, Mark C. *The Manchu Way: The Eight Banners and Ethnic Identity in Late Imperial China*. Stanford, CA: Stanford University Press, 2001.
Elvin, Mark. *Changing Stories in the Chinese World*. Stanford, CA: Stanford University Press, 1997.
Fan Boqun 范伯群, and Kong Qingdong 孔慶東, eds. *Tongsu wenxue shiwu jiang* 通俗文學十五講 (Fifteen Lectures on Popular Literature). Beijing: Peking University Press, 2003.

Fan Huaqun 范華群, and Wei Shengying 韋聖英. "Huaji xi qiyuan yu xingcheng chutan" 滑稽戲起源與形成初探 (A Preliminary Investigation into the Origins and Formation of Huaji Drama). In *Zhongguo huaju shiliaoji* 中國話劇史料集 (Research Materials on the History of Chinese Spoken Drama), vol. 1. Edited by Zhongguo yishu yanjiuyuan huaju yanjiusuo 中國藝術研究院話劇研究所. Beijing: Wenhua yishu chubanshe, 1987, 309–40.

Feng Menglong 馮夢龍. *Feng Menglong quanji* 馮夢龍全集 (Complete Works of Feng Menglong). Edited by Wei Tongxian 魏同賢. 22 vols. Nanjing: Jiangsu guji chubanshe, 1993.

Feng Yuanjun 馮沅君. *Guyou jie* 古優解 (A Study of Ancient Jesters). [Shanghai?]: Shangwu yinshuguan, 1944.

Fernsebner, Susan R. "A People's Playthings: Toys, Childhood, and Chinese Identity, 1909–1933." *Postcolonial Studies* 6, no. 3 (2003): 269–93.

Fineman, Mia. *Faking It: Manipulated Photography before Photoshop*. New York: Metropolitan Museum of Art, 2012.

Foster, Paul B. *Ah Q Archaeology: Lu Xun, Ah Q, Ah Q Progeny and the National Character Discourse in Twentieth-Century China*. Oxford: Lexington Books, 2006.

Franke, Herbert. "Literary Parody in Traditional Chinese Literature: Descriptive Pseudo-Biographies." *Oriens Extremus* 21 (1974): 23–31.

Frankfurt, Harry G. *On Bullshit*. Princeton, NJ: Princeton University Press, 2005.

Freud, Sigmund. *The Standard Edition of the Complete Psychological Works of Sigmund Freud*. Translated and edited by James Strachey. 24 vols. London: Vintage; Hogarth Press, 2001.

Gatrell, Vic. *City of Laughter: Sex and Satire in Eighteenth-Century London*. New York: Walker & Company, 2006.

Genette, Gérard. *Paratexts: Thresholds of Interpretation*. Translated by Jane E. Lewin. Cambridge: Cambridge University Press, 1997.

Gerth, Karl. *China Made: Consumer Culture and the Creation of the Nation*. Cambridge, MA: Harvard University Press, 2003.

Giles, Herbert A., trans. *Quips from a Chinese Jest Book*. Shanghai: Kelly and Walsh, 1925.

Gimpel, Denise. *Lost Voices of Modernity: A Chinese Popular Fiction Magazine in Context*. Honolulu: University of Hawai'i Press, 2001.

Goh, Meow Hui. *Sound and Sight: Poetry and Courtier Culture in the Yongming Era (483–493)*. Stanford, CA: Stanford University Press, 2010.

Gunn, Edward M., Jr., ed. *Twentieth-Century Chinese Drama: An Anthology*. Bloomington: Indiana University Press, 1983.

Haifuding 海甫定 [Harald Höffding]. *Xinlixue gailun* 心理學概論 (Outlines of Psychology). 8th ed. English translation by Mary E. Lowndes. Chinese retranslation by Wang Guowei 王國維. Shanghai: Shangwu yinshuguan, 1926.

Hamm, John Christopher. *Paper Swordsmen: Jin Yong and the Modern Chinese Martial Arts Novel*. Honolulu: University of Hawai'i Press, 2006.

Han Bangqing 韓邦慶. *Haishang hua liezhuan* 海上花列傳 (Flowers of Shanghai). 3rd ed. 4 vols. Shanghai: Yadong tushuguan, 1935.

Han Xifeng 韓錫鋒, and Wang Qingyuan 王清原. *Xiaoshuo shufang lu* 小說書坊錄 (Register of Fiction Publishing Houses). Shenyang: Chunfeng wenyi, 1987.

Hanan, Patrick. *Chinese Fiction of the Nineteenth and Early Twentieth Centuries.* New York: Columbia University Press, 2004.
———. *The Chinese Vernacular Story.* Cambridge, MA: Harvard University Press, 1981.
———. *The Invention of Li Yu.* Cambridge, MA: Harvard University Press, 1988.
Harbsmeier, Christoph. "*Confucius Ridens*: Humor in the *Analects*." *Harvard Journal of Asiatic Studies* 50, no. 1 (June 1990): 131–61.
———. "Humor in Ancient Chinese Philosophy." *Philosophy East & West* 39, no. 3 (July 1989): 289–310.
Harder, Hans, and Barbara Mittler, eds. *Asian Punches: A Transcultural Affair.* Berlin: Springer, 2013.
Harris, Neil. *Humbug: The Art of P. T. Barnum.* Chicago: University of Chicago Press, 1975.
Hegel, Robert E. *Reading Illustrated Fiction in Late Imperial China.* Stanford, CA: Stanford University Press, 1998.
Heinrich, Larissa. *The Afterlife of Images: Translating the Pathological Body between China and the West.* Durham, NC: Duke University Press, 2008.
Hershatter, Gail. *Dangerous Pleasures: Prostitution and Modernity in Twentieth-Century Shanghai.* Berkeley: University of California Press, 1997.
Hill, Michael Gibbs. *Lin Shu, Inc.: Translation and the Making of Modern Chinese Culture.* New York: Oxford University Press, 2012.
———. "New Script (Sin Wenz) and a New 'Madman's Diary.'" Unpublished paper presented at "Language, Culture, and Power: The Linguistic Field in Early Twentieth-Century China," Princeton University, 20–21 April 2012.
Hinsch, Bret. *Passions of the Cut Sleeve: The Male Homosexual Tradition in China.* Berkeley: University of California Press, 1990.
Hockx, Michel. "Liu Bannong and the Forms of New Poetry." *Journal of Modern Literature in Chinese* 3, no. 2 (January 2000): 83–117.
———. *Questions of Style: Literary Societies and Literary Journals in Modern China, 1911–1937.* Leiden: Brill, 2003.
Höffding, Harald. *Outlines of Psychology.* Translated by Mary E. Lowndes. London: Macmillan, 1892.
Hou Xin 侯鑫, ed. *Hou Baolin jiucang zhenben Minguo xiaohua xuan* 侯寶林舊藏珍本民國笑話選 (Selections from Hou Baolin's Collection of Old and Rare Jokes of the Republican Era). Beijing: Zhonghua shuju, 2008.
Hsia, C. T. "The Chinese Sense of Humor." *Renditions* 9 (Spring 1978). www.cuhk.edu.hk/rct/renditions/sample/b09.html.
———. *C. T. Hsia on Chinese Literature.* New York: Columbia University Press, 2004.
———. *A History of Modern Chinese Fiction.* 3rd ed. Bloomington: Indiana University Press, 1999.
Hsu, Pi-Ching. "Feng Meng-lung's *Treasury of Laughs*: Humorous Satire on Seventeenth-Century Chinese Culture and Society." *Journal of Asian Studies* 57, no. 4 (November 1998): 1042–67.
Hu, Jubin. *Projecting a Nation: Chinese National Cinema before 1949.* Hong Kong: Hong Kong University Press, 2003.

Hu Ying. *Tales of Translation: Composing the New Woman in China, 1898–1918*. Stanford, CA: Stanford University Press, 2000.
Huang, Alexander C. Y. *Chinese Shakespeares: Two Centuries of Cultural Exchange*. New York: Columbia University Press, 2009.
Huang, Ching-sheng. "Jokes on the Four Books: Cultural Criticism in Early Modern China." PhD diss., University of Arizona, 1998.
Huang Ko-wu 黃克武, and Hsin-yi Lee 李心怡. "Ming-Qing xiaohua zhong de shenti yu qingyu: yi *Xiaolin guangji* wei zhongxin zhi fenxi" 明清笑話中的身體與情慾—以《笑林廣記》爲中心之分析 (Joking about Sex and the Body in Late Imperial China: An Analysis Based on the Jest Book *Xiaolin Guangji*). *Hanxue yanjiu* 漢學研究 (Sinological Research) 19:2 (December 2001), 343–74.
Huang Yanqing 黃言情. *Dasha xiaoshi* 大傻笑史 (The Hilarious Story of a Big Idiot). Hong Kong: Yanqing chubanbu, 1930.
Huang Zhongming 黃仲鳴. "Qintai keju: tantan 'youshi weizheng'" 琴台客聚：談談「有詩為証」 (Guests Gather on the Zither Stage: Thoughts on "A Poem Stands in Evidence"), *Wen Wei Po* 文匯報 (28 September 2008). http://paper.wenweipo.com/2008/09/28/OT0809280009.htm.
Huanqiushe bianjibu 環球社編輯部, ed. *Tuhua ribao* 圖畫日報 (Illustration Daily). 8 vols. Shanghai: Shanghai guji chubanshe, 1999.
Huizinga, Johan. *Homo Ludens: A Study of the Play-Element in Culture*. Boston: Beacon Press, 1955.
Humour in Literature East and West: Proceedings XXXVII International PEN Congress (June 18–July 3, 1970). Seoul: Korean PEN Center, 1970.
Huntington, Rania. *Alien Kind: Foxes and Late Imperial Chinese Narrative*. Cambridge, MA: Harvard University Asian Center, 2003.
Huters, Theodore. *Bringing the World Home: Appropriating the West in Late Qing and Early Republican China*. Honolulu: University of Hawai'i Press, 2006.
Huters, Theodore, R. Bin Wong, and Pauline Yu, eds. *Culture & State in Chinese History: Conventions, Accommodations, and Critiques*. Stanford, CA: Stanford University Press, 1997.
Hutt, Jonathan. "*Monstre Sacré*: The Decadent World of Sinmay Zau 邵洵美." *China Heritage Newsletter* 22 (June 2010). www.chinaheritagenewsletter.org/features.php?searchterm=22_monstre.inc&issue=022.
Hyde, Lewis. *Trickster Makes This World: Mischief, Myth, and Art*. New York: Farrar, Straus, and Giroux, 1998.
Idema, Wilt, trans. *Meng Jiangnü Brings Down the Great Wall: Ten Versions of a Chinese Legend*. Seattle: University of Washington Press, 2008.
Idema, Wilt L., and Lloyd Haft. *A Guide to Chinese Literature*. Ann Arbor: University of Michigan Center for Chinese Studies, 1997.
Ives, Maura C., ed. *George Meredith's Essay on Comedy and Other New Quarterly Magazine Publications: A Critical Edition*. Lewisburg, PA: Bucknell University Press, 1998.
Jenkins, Henry. *What Made Pistachio Nuts? Early Sound Comedy and the Vaudeville Aesthetic*. New York: Columbia University Press, 1992.

Jiang Jianguo 蔣建國. *Baojie jiuwen: Jiu Guangzhou de baozhi yu xinwen* 報界舊聞：舊廣州的報紙與新聞 (Old News: Newspapers and the News in Old Guangzhou). Guangzhou: Nanfang Daily Press, 2007.

Jiang Yasha 姜亞沙, Jing Li 經莉, Chen Zhanqi 陳湛綺, eds. *Minguo manhua qikan jicui* 民國漫畫期刊集粹 (Selected Cartoon Periodicals of Republican China). 10 vols. Beijing: Quanguo tushuguan wenxian weisuo fuzhi zhongxin, 2004.

Jiao Runming 焦潤明, and Su Xiaoxuan 蘇曉軒, eds. *Wan Qing shenghuo lüeying* 晚清生活掠影 (A Glimpse of Life in the Late Qing Dynasty). Shenyang: Shenyang chubanshe, 2002.

Jing Shisuo 荊詩索, and Ke Yanchu 柯岩初, eds. *Diguo bengkui qian de yingxiang* 帝國崩潰前的影像 (Portrait of an Empire on the Brink of Collapse). Taiyuan: Shanxi renmin chubanshe, 2011.

Joe Miller's Jests or, the Wits Vade-mecum. London: T. Read, 1739.

Jones, Andrew F. *Developmental Fairy Tales: Evolutionary Thinking and Modern Chinese Culture*. Cambridge, MA: Harvard University Press, 2011.

——. *Yellow Music: Media Culture and Colonial Modernity in the Chinese Jazz Age*. Durham, NC: Duke University Press, 2001.

Jordan, Donald A. *China's Trial by Fire: The Shanghai War of 1932*. Ann Arbor: University of Michigan Press, 2001.

Judge, Joan. *Print and Politics: "Shibao" and the Culture of Reform in Late Qing China*. Stanford, CA: Stanford University Press, 1996.

Kaikkonen, Marja. *Laughable Propaganda: Modern Xiangsheng as Didactic Entertainment*. Stockholm: Institute of Oriental Languages, Stockholm University, 1990.

Kancainu xiaoshi 看財奴笑史 (The Ridiculous History of a Miser). Shanghai: Zhenyuan xiaoshuoshe, [ca. 1920s].

Karnick, Kristine Brunovska, and Henry Jenkins, eds. *Classical Hollywood Comedy*. New York: Routledge, 1995.

Kao, George, ed. *Chinese Wit & Humor*. New York: Coward-McCann, 1946.

Kern, Edith. *The Absolute Comic*. New York: Columbia University Press, 1980.

Knight, Sabina. *Chinese Literature: A Very Short Introduction*. Oxford: Oxford University Press, 2012.

Kohn, Livia. *Laughing at the Dao: Debates among Buddhists and Daoists in Medieval China*. Magdalena, NM: Three Pines Press, 2008.

Kolatch, Jonathan. *Sports, Politics, and Ideology in China*. New York: Jonathan David Publishers, 1972.

Kowallis, John Eugene Von. *The Lyrical Lu Xun: A Study of His Classical-Style Verse*. Honolulu: University of Hawai'i Press, 1996.

——, trans. *Wit and Humor from Old Cathay*. Beijing: Panda Books, 1986.

Krishnan, Sanjay. *Looking at Culture*. Singapore: Artres Design & Communications, 1996.

La satire chinoise, politique et sociale, anné 1927. Pékin: La Politique de Pékin, 1927.

Labov, William. *Language in the Inner City: Studies in the Black English Vernacular*. Philadelphia: University of Pennsylvania Press, 1972.

Laing, Ellen Johnston. "*Shanghai Manhua*, the Neo-Sensationist School of Literature, and Scenes of Urban Life." *Modern Chinese Literature and Culture* (October 2010). http://mclc.osu.edu/rc/pubs/laing.htm.

Lao She 老舍. *Heavensent*. Translated by Xiong Deni. Hong Kong: Joint Publishing, 1986.

———. *Laoniu poche* 老牛破車 (An Old Ox Pulling a Rickety Cart). Shanghai: Chenguang chuban gongsi, 1948.

———. *Lao She lun chuangzuo* 老舍論創作 (Lao She on Literary Creation). Shanghai: Shanghai wenyi chubanshe, 1980.

———. *Lao She quanji* 老舍全集 (Complete Works of Lao She). 19 vols. Beijing: Renmin wenxue chubanshe, 1999.

———. *Lao She youmo ji* 老舍幽默集 (Lao She Humor Collection). Edited by Yin Xi 尹汐. Xinjing [Changchun]: Wenhua chubanbu, 1942 [Kangde 9].

———. *Lao Zhang de zhexue* 老張的哲學 (The Philosophy of Lao Zhang). Shanghai: Chenguang chuban gongsi, 1949.

———. *Teahouse/Chaguan* 茶館 (bilingual ed.). Translated by John Howard-Gibbon. Hong Kong: Chinese University Press, 2004.

———. *The Two Mas*. Translated by Kenny K. Huang and David Finkelstein. Hong Kong: Joint Publishing, 1984.

Larson, Wendy. *From Ah Q to Lei Feng: Freud and Revolutionary Spirit in 20th Century China*. Stanford, CA: Stanford University Press, 2009.

Lary, Diana. *The Chinese People at War: Human Suffering and Social Transformation, 1937–1945*. Cambridge: Cambridge University Press, 2010.

Laughlin, Charles A. *The Literature of Leisure and Chinese Modernity*. Honolulu: University of Hawai'i Press, 2008.

Lean, Eugenia. *Public Passions: The Trial of Shi Jianqiao and the Rise of Popular Sympathy in Republican China*. Berkeley: University of California Press, 2007.

Leary, Charles. "Sexual Modernism in China: Zhang Jingsheng and 1920s Urban Culture." PhD diss., Cornell University, 1994.

Lee, Hsinyi Tiffany. "One, and the Same: The Figure of the Double in Photographic Portraiture from the Early Republican Period." Unpublished paper prepared for Facing Asia Conference, The Australian National University, summer 2010.

Lee, Haiyan. "'A Dime Store of Words': *Liberty* Magazine and the Cultural Logic of the Popular Press." *Twentieth-Century China* 33, no. 3 (November 2007): 53–80.

———. *Revolution of the Heart: A Genealogy of Love in China, 1900–1950*. Stanford, CA: Stanford University Press, 2007.

Lee, Jen-der 李貞德. "'Xiaoji' kao: jianlun Zhongguo zhonggu yizhe dui xile de taidu" 「笑疾」考—兼論中國中古醫者對喜樂的態度 ("'Laughing Disorders' and Medical Discourse of Joy in Early Imperial China"). *Zhongyang yanjiuyuan lishi yuyan yanjiusuo jikan* 中央研究院歷史語言研究所集刊 (Journal of the Institute of History and Philology, Academia Sinica) 75, no. 1 (March 2004): 99–148.

Lee, Leo Ou-fan [Li Oufan 李歐梵]. *Shanghai Modern: The Flowering of a New Urban Culture in China, 1930–1945*. Cambridge, MA: Harvard University Press, 1999.

———. *Xiandaixing de zhuiqiu* 現代性的追求 (The Quest for Modernity). Beijing: Sanlian shudian, 2000.

Levy, Howard Seymour. *Chinese Sex Jokes in Traditional Times*. Taipei: The Orient Cultural Service, 1974.

Li Ao 李傲. *Fangpi, fangpi, zhen fangpi!* 放屁, 放屁, 真放屁! (Bullshit! Bullshit! Utter Bullshit!). Taipei: Tianyuan tushu youxian gongsi, 1984.

———. *Gou shi, gou pi, shi* 狗屎, 狗屁, 詩 (Dog Shit, Dog Farts, Poetry). Taipei: Guiguan tushu gongsi, 1984.

———. *Li Ao you maren le* 李敖又罵人了 (There Goes Li Ao, Cursing People Again!). Changchun: Shidai wenyi chubanshe, 1999.

———. *Nide, wode, tamade* 你的, 我的, 他媽的 (Yours, Mine, His Mother's). Taipei: Li Ao, 1984.

Li Boyuan 李伯元. *Li Boyuan quanji* 李伯元全集 (Complete Works of Li Boyuan). 5 vols. Edited by Xue Zhengxing 薛正興. Nanjing: Jiangsu guji chubanshe, 1997.

Li Jifeng 李繼鋒, Guo Bin 郭彬, and Chen Liping 陳立平. *Yuan Zhenying zhuan* 袁振英傳 (Biography of Yuan Zhenying). Beijing: Zhonggong dangshi chubanshe, 2009.

Li, Ju-chen [Li Ruzhen 李汝珍]. *Flowers in the Mirror*. Translated by Lin Tai-yi. Berkeley: University of California Press, 1965.

Li Nan 李楠. *Wan Qing, Minguo shiqi Shanghai xiaobao yanjiu: Yizhong zonghe de wenhua, wenxue kaocha* 晚清、民國時期上海小報研究：一種綜合的文化、文學考察 (Research on Shanghai Tabloids of the Late Qing and the Republican Era: An Integrated Cultural and Literary Investigation). Beijing: Renmin wenxue chubanshe, 2005.

Li Ruzhen 李汝珍. *Jinghua yuan* 鏡花緣 (Flowers in the Mirror). Shanghai: Shanghai guji chubanshe, 2006.

Li Yu 李漁. *Li Yu quanji* 李漁全集 (Complete Works of Li Yu). 10 vols. Hangzhou: Zhejiang guji chubanshe, 1992.

Li Zhao 黎照, ed. *Lu Xun Liang Shiqiu lunzhan shilu* 魯迅梁實秋論戰實錄 (True Record of Debates between Lu Xun and Liang Shiqiu). Beijing: Hualing chubanshe, 1997.

Liang Qichao 梁啟超. *Liang Qichao quanji* 梁啟超全集 (Complete Works of Liang Qichao). Edited by Yang Gang 楊鋼 and Wang Xiangyi 王相宜. 10 vols. Beijing: Beijing chubanshe, 1999.

Liang, Shen. "The Great World: Performance Supermarket." *TDR/The Drama Review* 50, no. 2 (Summer 2006): 97–116.

Liang Shiqiu 梁實秋. *Ma ren de yishu* 罵人的藝術 (The Fine Art of Reviling). Taipei: Yuandong tushu gongsi, 1994.

———. *The Fine Art of Reviling*. Translated by William B. Pettus. Los Angeles: Auk Press, 1936.

———. *Liang Shiqiu wenji* 梁實秋文集 (Collected Works of Liang Shiqiu). 15 vols. Xiamen: Lujiang chubanshe, 2002.

Liang Yuchun 梁遇春. *Liang Yuchun sanwenji* 梁遇春散文集 (Collected Essays of Liang Yuchun). Edited by Qin Xianci 秦賢次. Taipei: Hongfan shudian, 1979.

Lin Shu 林紓, and Wei Yi 魏易, trans. *Huaji waishi* 滑稽外史 (An Informal History of a Slippery Character). Shanghai: Shangwu yinshuguan, 1907.

Lin Yutang 林語堂. *Between Tears and Laughter*. New York: John Day, 1943.

———. *Confucius Saw Nancy, and Essays about Nothing*. Shanghai: Commercial Press, 1936.

———. *My Country and My People*. New York: Reynal & Hitchcock, 1935.

———. *The Gay Genius: The Life and Times of Su Tungpo*. New York: John Day, 1947.
———. *A History of the Press and Public Opinion in China*. Chicago: University of Chicago Press, 1936.
———. *The Importance of Living*. New York: Reynal & Hitchcock, 1937.
———. *The Little Critic: Essays, Satires and Sketches on China (First Series: 1930–1932)*. Shanghai: Commercial Press, 1935.
———. *The Little Critic: Essays, Satires and Sketches on China (Second Series: 1933–1935)*. Shanghai: Oriental Book, 1935.
———. *With Love and Irony*. Illustrated by Kurt Wiese. London: William Heinemann, 1941.
Link, E. Perry, Jr. *An Anatomy of Chinese: Rhythm, Metaphor, Politics*. Cambridge, MA: Harvard University Press, 2013.
———. "Does This Writer Deserve the Prize?" *New York Review of Books*, 6 December 2012. www.nybooks.com/articles/archives/2012/dec/06/mo-yan-nobel-prize/?pagination=false.
———. *Mandarin Ducks and Butterflies: Popular Fiction in Early Twentieth-Century Chinese Cities*. Berkeley: University of California Press, 1981.
———. "Politics and the Chinese Language: What Mo Yan's Defenders Get Wrong." www.chinafile.com/politics-and-chinese-language.
Liu Bannong 劉半農. *Bannong tan ying* 半農談影 (Bannong on Photography). Beijing: Zhongguo sheying chubanshe, 2000.
Liu, Chiung-yun Evelyn. "Scriptures and Bodies: Jest and Meaning in the Religious Journeys in *Xiyou Ji*." PhD diss., Harvard University, 2008.
Liu Guoying 劉國英, and Zhang Canhui 張燦輝, eds. *Xiu yuan zhi lu: Xianggang Zhongwen daxue zhexuexi liushi zhounian xiqing lunwenji—Tongyin juan* 修遠之路：香港中文大學哲學系六十周年系慶論文集—同寅卷 (The Long Road of Cultivation: Chinese University of Hong Kong Department of Philosophy Sixtieth Anniversary Essay Anthology, Tongyin volume). Hong Kong: Chinese University Press, 2009.
Liu Hsieh [Liu Xie 劉勰]. *The Literary Mind and the Carving of Dragons*. Translated by Vincent Yu-chung Shih. Hong Kong: Chinese University Press, 1983.
Liu I-Ching. *Shih-shuo hsin-yu: A New Account of Tales of the World*. Edited by Liu Chun. Translated by Richard B. Mather. Ann Arbor: Center for Chinese Studies, the University of Michigan, 2002.
Liu Jixing 劉繼興. "Mao Zedong weihe ai du qishu *Hedian*?" 毛澤東爲何愛讀奇書《何典》？ (Why Did Mao Zedong Enjoy Reading the Bizarre Book *Which Classic?*). *Yangcheng wanbao* 羊城晚報. Reposted on *Xinhuanet* (Guangdong) on 25 August 2010. www.gd.xinhuanet.com/newscenter/2010-08/25/content_20720766.htm.
Liu, Lydia H. *Translingual Practice: Literature, Culture, and Translated Modernity—China, 1900–1937*. Stanford, CA: Stanford University Press, 1995.
Liu Shaoming 劉紹銘 [Joseph S. M. Lau]. *Tilei jiaoling de xiandai Zhongguo wenxue* 涕淚交零的現代中國文學 (A Modern Chinese Literature of Tears and Sniveling). Taipei: Yuanjing chubanshe, 1979.
Liu T'ieh-yun [Liu E 劉鶚]. *The Travels of Lao Ts'an*. Translated by Harold Shadick. New York: Columbia University Press, 1990.

Liu Xiaobo. *No Enemies, No Hatred: Selected Essays and Poems.* Edited by Perry Link, Tienchi Martin-Liao, and Liu Xia. Cambridge, MA: Harvard University Press, 2012.
Lu Hsun [Lu Xun]. *A Brief History of Chinese Fiction.* Translated by Yang Hsien-yi and Gladys Yang. Peking: Foreign Languages Press, 1964.
———. *Old Tales Retold.* Translated by Yang Hsien-yi and Gladys Yang. Peking: Foreign Languages Press, 1961.
Lu Sifei 盧斯飛, and Yang Dongfu 楊東甫. *Zhongguo youmo wenxue shihua* 中國幽默文學史話 (A Historical Narrative of Chinese Humor Literature). Nanjing: Guangxi jiaoyu chubanshe, 1994.
Lu Xun 魯迅. *Lu Xun: Selected Works.* 4 vols. Translated by Yang Xianyi and Gladys Yang. Beijing: Foreign Languages Press, 1985.
———. *Lu Xun shuxin ji* 魯迅書信集 (Collected Letters of Lu Xun). 2 vols. Beijing: Renmin wenxue chubanshe, 1976.
———. "The True Story of Ah-Q." Translated by Yang Hsien-yi and Gladys Yang. www.marxists.org/archive/lu-xun/1921/12/ah-q/.
Lunyu 論語 (Analects of Confucius). Online at Scripta Sinica (Acacademia Sinica, Taipei): http://hanchi.ihp.sinica.edu.tw/ihp/hanji.htm.
Luo Zhufeng 羅竹風, ed. *Hanyu da cidian* 漢語大詞典 (Dictionary of Chinese). 13 vols. Shanghai: Hanyu da cidian chubanshe, 2001.
Ma Songbai 馬松柏. *Xianggang baotan huiyilu* 香港報壇回憶錄 (Memoirs of Hong Kong's Print Media Sphere). Hong Kong: Commercial Press, 2001.
Ma Yunzeng 馬運增, Chen Shen 陳申, Hu Zhichuan 胡志川, Qian Zhangbiao 錢章表, Peng Yongxiang 彭永祥. *Zhongguo sheying shi, 1840–1937* 中國攝影史, 1840–1937 (A History of Photography in China, 1840–1937). Beijing: Zhongguo sheying chubanshe, 1987.
Mair, Victor H., ed. *The Columbia History of Chinese Literature.* New York: Columbia University Press, 2010.
Makeham, John. *Transmitters and Creators: Chinese Commentators and Commentaries on the Analects.* Cambridge, MA: Harvard University Asia Center, 2004.
Mao Dun 茅盾, ed. *Zhongguo xin wenxue daxi—xiaoshuo juan* 中國新文學大系—小說卷 (Compendium of China's New Literature—Fiction), vol. 3. Hong Kong: Xianggang wenxue yanjiushe, 1986 [1935].
Marchetti, Gina. "*Two Stage Sisters*: The Blossoming of a Revolutionary Aesthetic." *Jump Cut* 34 (March 1989): 95–106. http://www.ejumpcut.org/archive/onlinessays/JC34folder/2stageSisters.html.
Martin, Brian G. *The Shanghai Green Gang: Politics and Organized Crime, 1919–1937.* Berkeley: University of California Press, 1996.
Mather, Jeffrey. "Laughter and the Cosmopolitan Aesthetic in Lao She's 二馬 (*Mr. Ma and Son*)." *CLCWeb: Comparative Literature and Culture* 16, no. 1 (March 2014). http://docs.lib.purdue.edu/clcweb/vol16/iss1/6.
McDougall, Bonnie S., trans. *Mao Zedong's "Talks at the Yan'an Conference on Literature and Art": A Translation of the 1943 Text with Commentary.* Ann Arbor: University of Michigan Center for Chinese Studies, 1980.
McKeown, Adam. *Chinese Migrant Networks and Cultural Change: Peru, Chicago, Hawaii, 1900–1936.* Chicago: University of Chicago Press, 2001.

McMahon, Keith. *The Fall of the God of Money: Opium Smoking in Nineteenth-Century China*. Lanham: Rowman & Littlefield, 2002.
Mellen, Joan. *Modern Times*. London: British Film Institute, 2006.
Meng Zhaochen 孟兆臣, ed. *Fangxing zhoubao* 方型週報 (Square-Shaped Weeklies). 11 vols. Beijing: Beijing chubanshe, 2009.
———, ed. *Lao Shanghai suyu tushuo daquan* 老上海俗語圖説大全 (Compendium of Old Shanghai Slang, Illustrated and Explained). Shanghai: Shanghai shehui kexue chubanshe, 2004.
Mittler, Barbara. *A Newspaper for China? Power, Identity, and Change in Shanghai's New Media, 1872–1912*. Cambridge, MA: Harvard University Asia Center, 2004.
Mo Yan 莫言. "Nobel Lecture: Storytellers." www.nobelprize.org/nobel_prizes/literature/laureates/2012/yan-lecture_en.pdf.
Morreall, John. *Taking Laughter Seriously*. Albany: State University of New York Press, 1983.
———, ed. *The Philosophy of Laughter and Humor*. Albany: State University of New York Press, 1987.
Morris, Andrew D. *Marrow of the Nation: A History of Sport and Physical Culture in Republican China*. Berkeley: University of California Press, 2004.
Moser, David. "Stifled Laughter: How the Communist Party Killed Chinese Humor." www.danwei.org/tv/stifled_laughter_how_the_commu.php.
Mostow, Joshua S., ed. *The Columbia Companion to Modern East Asian Literature*. New York: Columbia University Press, 2003.
Mullaney, Thomas S. "The Semi-Colonial Semi-Colon: The Discourse and Practice of Punctuation Reform, Horizontal Writing, and Stationary Reform in Republican China." Unpublished paper presented at workshop "Language, Culture, and Power," Princeton University, 22–23 April 2012.
Museum of Modern Art, Saitama, Hisako Okoshi, and Yuji Maeyama, eds. *Subtle Criticism: Caricature and Satire in Japan*. Saitama: Museum of Modern Art, Saitama, 1993.
Nappi, Carla. *The Monkey and the Inkpot: Natural History and Its Transformations in Early Modern China*. Cambridge, MA: Harvard University Press, 2009.
Ogawa, Isao. "History of Amusement Park Construction by Private Railway Companies in Japan." *Japan Railway & Transport Review* 15 (March 1998): 28–34.
Otto, Beatrice K. *Fools Are Everywhere: The Court Jester around the World*. Chicago: University of Chicago Press, 2001.
Owen, Stephen. *The End of the Chinese "Middle Ages": Essays in Mid-Tang Literary Culture*. Stanford, CA: Stanford University Press, 1996.
Pang, Laikwan. *The Distorting Mirror: Visual Modernity in China*. Honolulu: University of Hawai'i Press, 2007.
Parton, James. *Caricature and Other Comic Art in All Times and Many Lands*. New York: Harper & Bros., 1877.
Pollard, David E. *The True Story of Lu Xun*. Hong Kong: Chinese University Press, 2002.
Pope, Alexander. *An Essay on Man*. Springfield, MA: Timothy Ashley, 1802.
Postman, Neil. *Amusing Ourselves to Death: Public Discourse in the Age of Show Business*. New York: Penguin, 2006 [1985].

Pu Songling. *Strange Tales from a Chinese Studio*. Translated and edited by John Minford. New York: Penguin Books, 2006.

Qian Nairong 錢乃榮. *Shanghai yuyan fazhan shi* 上海語言發展史 (A History of the Development of Shanghai's Languages). Shanghai: Shanghai renmin chubanshe, 2003.

Qian, Suoqiao. *Liberal Cosmopolitan: Lin Yutang and Middling Chinese Modernity*. Leiden: Brill, 2011.

———, ed. *Selected Bilingual Essays of Lin Yutang* (*Lin Yutang shuangyu wenxuan* 林語堂雙語文選). Hong Kong: Chinese University Press, 2010.

———. "Translating 'Humor' into Chinese Culture." *HUMOR* 20, no. 3 (2007): 277–95.

Qian Xuantong 錢玄同. *Qian Xuantong wenji* 錢玄同文集 (Collected Writings of Qian Xuantong). 6 vols. Beijing: Zhongguo renmin daxue chubanshe, 2000.

Qian Zhongshu 錢鍾書. *Guanzhui bian* 管錐篇 (The Pipe and Awl Collection). 5 vols. Beijing: Zhonghua shuju, 1979.

———. *Humans, Beasts, and Ghosts: Stories and Essays*. Edited by Christopher G. Rea. New York: Columbia University Press, 2011.

———. *Limited Views: Essays on Ideas and Letters*. Translated by Ronald C. Egan. Cambridge, MA: Harvard University Press, 1998.

———. *Patchwork: Seven Essays on Art and Literature*. Translated by Duncan Campbell. Leiden: Brill, 2014.

———. *Qizhui ji* 七綴集 (Patchwork). Beijing: Sanlian shudian, 2003.

———. *Ren shou gui* 人獸鬼 (Human, Beast, Ghost). Shanghai: Kaiming shudian, 1946.

———. *Weicheng* 圍城 (Fortress Besieged). Shanghai: Chenguang chuban gongsi, 1949.

———. *Xie zai rensheng bianshang* 寫在人生邊上 (Written in the Margins of Life). Shanghai: Kaiming shudian, 1941.

Rao Shuguang 饒曙光. *Zhongguo xiju dianying shi* 中國喜劇電影史 (History of Chinese Cinema). Beijing: Zhongguo dianying chubanshe, 2005.

Rabinovitz, Lauren. *Electric Dreamland: Amusement Parks, Movies, and American Modernity*. New York: Columbia University Press, 2012.

Rea, Christopher, ed. *China's Literary Cosmopolitans: Qian Zhongshu, Yang Jiang, and the World of Letters*. Leiden: Brill, 2015.

———. "The Critic Eye 批眼." *China Heritage Quarterly* 30–31 (June–September 2012). www.chinaheritagequarterly.org/features.php?searchterm=030_rea.inc&issue=030.

Rea, Christopher, and Nicolai Volland, eds. *The Business of Culture: Cultural Entrepreneurs in China and Southeast Asia, 1900–65*. Vancouver: UBC Press, 2015.

Reed, Christopher A. *Gutenberg in Shanghai: Chinese Print Capitalism, 1876–1937*. Vancouver: UBC Press, 2004.

Rendiers, Eric Robert. *Borrowed Gods and Foreign Bodies: Christian Missionaries Imagine Chinese Religion*. Berkeley: University of California Press, 2004.

Renjian shi she 人間世, ed. *Ershi jinren zhi* 二十今人志 (Twenty Contemporary Personages). Shanghai: Shanghai Liangyou tushu youxian gongsi, 1935.

Rigby, Richard. "Sapajou's Shanghai." *China Heritage Quarterly* 22 (June 2010). www.chinaheritagequarterly.org/features.php?searchterm=022_sapajou.inc&issue=022.

Roberts, Claire. *Photography and China*. London: Reaktion Books, 2013.
Rocha, Leon Antonio. "Sex, Eugenics, Aesthetics, Utopia in the Life and Work of Zhang Jingsheng 張競生 (1888–1970)." PhD diss., Cambridge University, 2010.
Rohsenow, John S. *A Chinese-English Dictionary of Enigmatic Folk Similes (Hanyu xiehouyu cidian* 漢語歇後語詞典*)*. Tucson: University of Arizona Press, 1991.
Rojas, Carlos. *The Great Wall: A Cultural History*. Cambridge, MA: Harvard University Press, 2010.
———. *The Naked Gaze: Reflections on Chinese Modernity*. Cambridge, MA: Harvard University Asia Center, 2008.
Rolston, David L., ed. *How to Read the Chinese Novel*. Princeton, NJ: Princeton University Press, 1990.
———. *Traditional Chinese Fiction and Fiction Commentary: Reading and Writing between the Lines*. Stanford, CA: Stanford University Press, 1997.
Roy, David Tod, trans. *The Plum in the Golden Vase, or Chin P'ing Mei: Vol. 1, The Gathering*. Princeton, NJ: Princeton University Press, 1993.
Santangelo, Paolo, ed. *Laughing in Chinese*. Rome: ARACNE editrice S.r.l., 2012.
Santangelo, Paolo, and Yan Beiwen, eds. and trans. *Zibuyu, "What the Master Would Not Discuss," According to Yuan Mei (1716–1798): A Collection of Supernatural Stories*. 2 vols. Leiden: Brill, 2013.
Schonebaum, Andrew David. "Fictional Medicine: Diseases, Doctors, and the Curative Properties of Chinese Fiction." PhD diss., Columbia University, 2004.
Schor, Juliet, and Douglas Holt, eds. *The Consumer Society Reader*. New York: New Press, 2000.
Scott, A. C. *Actors Are Madmen: Notebook of a Theatregoer in China*. Madison: University of Wisconsin Press, 1982.
Shahar, Meir. *Crazy Ji: Chinese Religion and Popular Literature*. Cambridge, MA: Harvard University Press, 1998.
——— Shakespeare, William. *Love's Labour's Lost*. www.opensourceshakespeare.org/views/plays/playmenu.php?WorkID=loveslabours.
———. *The Tragedy of King Lear*. www.opensourceshakespeare.org/views/plays/playmenu.php?WorkID=kinglear.
Shanghai wenhua chubanshe 上海文化出版社, ed. *Huaji luncong* 滑稽論叢 (Essays on Huaji Comedy). Shanghai: Shanghai wenhua chubanshe, 1958.
Xiao Gan 蕭乾, ed. *Hubin lüeying* 滬濱掠影 (A Glimpse of Shanghai). Beijing: Zhonghua shuju, 2005.
Shen Congwen 沈從文. *Alisi Zhongguo youji* 阿麗思中國遊記 (Alice's Adventures in China). Shanghai: Xinyue shudian, 1928.
Shen, Shuang. *Cosmopolitan Publics: Anglophone Print Culture in Semi-Colonial Shanghai*. Piscataway, NJ: Rutgers University Press, 2009.
Shi Xisheng 時希聖, ed. *Wu Zhihui yanxing lu* 吳稚暉言行錄 (Words and Deeds of Wu Zhihui). Shanghai: Guangyi shuju, 1929.
Shi Yunyan 石雲艷. *Liang Qichao yu Riben* 梁啟超與日本 (Liang Qichao and Japan). Tianjin: Tianjin renmin chubanshe, 2005.

Shifman, Limor, and Mike Thewall. "Assessing Global Diffusion with Web Memetics: The Spread and Diffusion of a Popular Joke." *Journal of the American Society for Information Science and Technology* 60, no. 12 (2009): 2567–76.
Shu Yiqiao 舒亦樵, ed. *Zenyang shi maren yishuhua* 怎樣使罵人藝術化 (How to Curse Artistically). Shanghai: Zonghengshe, 1946 [1941].
Sima Qian 司馬遷. *Shiji* 史記 (Records of the Grand Historian). Online at Scripta Sinica (Academia Sinica, Taipei): http://hanchi.ihp.sinica.edu.tw/ihp/hanji.htm.
———. *Records of the Grand Historian: Qin Dynasty*. Translated by Burton Watson. New York: Columbia University Press, 1993.
Simon, Richard Keller. *The Labyrinth of the Comic: Theory and Practice from Fielding to Freud*. Tallahassee: University of Florida Press, 1985.
Sohigian, Diran John. "Confucius and the Lady in Question: Power Politics, Cultural Production and the Performance of *Confucius Saw Nanzi* in China in 1929." *Twentieth-Century China* 36, no. 1 (January 2011): 23–43.
———. "Contagion of Laughter: The Rise of the Humor Phenomenon in Shanghai in the 1930's." *positions: east asia cultures critique* 15, no. 1 (Spring 2007): 137–63.
———. "The Life and Times of Lin Yutang." PhD diss., Columbia University, 1991.
Song Mingwei. "Long Live Youth: National Rejuvenation and the Chinese Bildungsroman, 1900–1950." PhD diss., Columbia University, 2005.
Spielmann, M. H. *The History of "Punch."* New York: Cassell Publishing, 1895.
Stead, W. T. "Mark Twain," *Review of Reviews* 16 (August 1897), 123–33. Reprinted at the W. T. Stead Resource Site: www.attackingthedevil.co.uk/reviews/twain.php#sthash.YkWtSH4D.3JOWZKlb.dpbs.
Su Qing 蘇青. *Jiehun shinian* 結婚十年 (Ten Years of Marriage). Shanghai: Tiandi chubanshe, 1944.
Su Tong. *Binu and the Great Wall*. Translated by Howard Goldblatt. Edinburgh: Canongate Books, 2007.
Su Zhigang 宿志剛, Lin Li 林黎, Liu Ning 劉寧, and Zhou Jing 周靜, eds. *Zhongguo sheying shilüe* 中國攝影史略 (Outline History of Chinese Photography). Beijing: Zhongguo wenlian chubanshe, 2009.
Sun Juxian 孫菊儠. *Amulin xiaoshi* 阿木林笑史 (The Hilarious Story of a Moron). Shanghai: Zhenhuan xiaoshuoshe, 1923.
Sun Qingsheng 孫慶升, ed. *Ding Xilin yanjiu ziliao* 丁西林研究資料 (Research Materials on Ding Xilin). Beijing: Zhongguo xiju chubanshe, 1986.
T'ang, Leang-li, ed. *China's Own Critics: A Selection of Essays by Hu Shih and Lin Yu-tang, with Commentaries by Wang Ching-wei*. Tientsin: China United Press, 1931.
Tang, Xiaobing. *Global Space and the Nationalist Discourse of Modernity: The Historical Thinking of Liang Qichao*. Stanford, CA: Stanford University Press, 1996.
Tang Zhesheng 湯哲聲. *Zhongguo xiandai huaji wenxue shilüe* 中國現代滑稽文學史略 (Outline History of Modern Chinese Huaji Literature). Taipei: Wenjin chubanshe, 1992.
Terumoto Teruo 樽本照雄. *Xinbian zengbu Qingmo Minchu xiaoshuo mulu* 新編增補清末民初小説目錄 (Revised and Updated Bibliography of Late Qing and Early Republican Fiction). Jinan: Qilu shushe, 2002.

Thornber, Karen Laura. *Empire of Texts in Motion: Chinese, Korean, and Taiwanese Transculturations of Japanese Literature*. Cambridge, MA: Harvard University Asia Center, 2009.
Tian Bingxi 田炳锡 (Jun Byungsuk). "Xu Zhuodai yu Zhongguo xiandai dazhong wenhua" 徐卓呆與中國現代大眾文化 ("Xu Zhuodai and China's Modern Mass Culture"). PhD diss., Peking University, 2000.
Ting Hsi-lin [Ding Xilin 丁西林]. "Oppression." Translated by Joseph S. M. Lau. *Renditions* 3 (Autumn 1974): 117–24.
Ting, Lee-hsia Hsu. *Government Control of the Press in Modern China, 1900–1949*. Cambridge, MA: Harvard East Asian Research Center, 1974.
Trav S. D. *No Applause—Just Throw Money: The Book that Made Vaudeville Famous*. New York: Faber & Faber, 2005.
Trumble, Angus. *A Brief History of the Smile*. New York: Basic Books, 2004.
Tucker, Anne Wilkes, Dana Friis-Hansen, Kaneko Ryūichi, and Takeba Joe. *The History of Japanese Photography*. Edited and translated by John Junkerman. New Haven, CT: Yale University Press, 2003.
Twain, Mark. *A Double Barreled Detective Story* (1902). www.gutenberg.org/files/3180/3180-h/3180-h.htm.
VALDAR et al. *The History of China for 1912 in 52 Cartoons, with Explanatory Notes in English and Chinese*. Shanghai: National Review, 1913.
Volland, Nicolai. *Cold War Cosmopolitanism: China's Cultural Encounter with the Socialist World, 1949–1960*. Book manuscript.
Voogt, Alex de, and Irving Finkel, eds. *The Idea of Writing: Play and Complexity*. Leiden: Brill, 2010.
Wagner, Rudolf G. "China 'Asleep' and 'Awakening': A Study in Conceptualizing Asymmetry and Coping with It." *Transcultural Studies* 1 (2011): 1–139. http://archiv.ub.uni-heidelberg.de/ojs/index.php/transcultural/article/view/7315/2920.
——, ed. *Joining the Global Public: Word, Image, and City in Early Chinese Newspapers, 1870–1910*. Albany: State University of New York Press, 2007.
——. "The Shenbao in Crisis: The International Environment and the Conflict between Guo Songtao and the Shenbao." *Late Imperial China* 20, no. 1 (1999): 107–43.
Wakeman, Frederic, Jr. *Policing Shanghai, 1927–1937*. Berkeley: University of California Press, 1995.
Wang, Ban. *Illuminations from the Past: Trauma, Memory, and History in Modern China*. Stanford, CA: Stanford University Press, 2004.
Wang, David Der-wei. *Fictional Realism in Twentieth-Century China: Mao Dun, Lao She, Shen Congwen*. New York: Columbia University Press, 1992.
——. *Fin-de-siècle Splendor: Repressed Modernities of Late Qing Fiction*. Stanford, CA: Stanford University Press, 1997.
——. *The Monster That Is History: History, Violence, and Fictional Writing in Twentieth-Century China*. Berkeley: University of California Press, 2004.
Wang, David Der-wei, and Wei Shang, eds. *Dynastic Crisis and Cultural Innovation from the Late Ming to the Late Qing and Beyond*. Cambridge, MA: Harvard University Asia Center, 2005.

Wang Gungwu. *China and the Chinese Overseas*. Singapore: Eastern Universities Press, 1991.
Wang, Juan. *Merry Laughter and Angry Curses: The Shanghai Tabloid Press, 1879–1911*. Vancouver: UBC Press, 2013.
——. "Officialdom Unmasked: Shanghai Tabloid Press, 1897–1911." *Late Imperial China* 28, no. 2 (December 2007): 81–128.
——. "The Weight of Frivolous Matters: Shanghai Tabloid Culture, 1897–1911." PhD diss., Stanford University, 2004.
Wang Liqi 王利器, ed. *Lidai xiaohua ji* 歷代笑話集 (Jokes of the Dynastic Period). Shanghai: Gudian wenxue chubanshe, 1956.
Wang Min 王敏. *Subao an yanjiu* 蘇報案研究 (A Study of the *Subao* Case). Shanghai: Shanghai renmin chubanshe, 2010.
Wang, Y. C. *Chinese Intellectuals and the West, 1872–1949*. Chapel Hill: University of North Carolina Press, 1966.
Wang Yiqing. "Much Ado about TV Plagiarism." *China Daily*, 11 August 2012, 5. http://usa.chinadaily.com.cn/opinion/2012-08/11/content_15664859.htm.
Wang Zhongxian 汪仲賢, text; Xu Xiaoxia 許曉霞, illust. *Shanghai suyu tushuo* 上海俗語圖說 (Shanghai Slang Illustrated and Explained). Shanghai: Shanghai shehui chubanshe, 1935.
Wardroper, John. *Jest upon Jest*. London: Routledge and Kegan Paul, 1970.
Watson, Burton, trans. *Chuang Tzu: Basic Writings*. New York: Columbia University Press, 1996.
——. *Courtier and Commoner in Ancient China: Selections from the History of the Former Han*. New York: Columbia University Press, 1974.
Wei Shaochang 魏紹昌, ed. *Li Boyuan yanjiu ziliao* 李伯元研究資料 (Research Materials on Li Boyuan). Shanghai: Shanghai guji chubanshe, 1980.
——. *Wo kan yuanyang hudie pai* 我看鴛鴦蝴蝶派 (My Views on the Mandarin Ducks and Butterflies School). Hong Kong: Zhonghua shuju, 1990.
Wei Shaochang 魏紹昌, and Wu Chenghui 吳承惠, eds. *Yuanyang hudie pai yanjiu ziliao* 鴛鴦蝴蝶派研究資料 (Research Materials on the Mandarin Duck and Butterfly School). 2 vols. Shanghai: Shanghai wenyi chubanshe, 1984.
Weinbaum, Alys Eve, Lynn M. Thomas, Priti Ramamurthy, Uta G. Poiger, Madeleine Yue Dong, and Tani E. Barlow, eds. *The Modern Girl around the World: Consumption, Modernity, and Globalization*. Durham, NC: Duke University Press, 2008.
Weinstein, Jonathan Benjamin. "Directing Laughter: Modes of Modern Chinese Comedy, 1907–1997." PhD diss., Columbia University, 2002.
Wen Yüan-ning 溫源寧. *Imperfect Understanding*. Shanghai: Kelly and Walsh, 1935.
——. *Imperfect Understanding/Bugou zhiji* 不夠知己 (bilingual edition). Translated by Jiang Feng 江楓. Beijing: Waiyu jiaoxue yu yanjiu chubanshe, 2012.
White, E. B. *Essays of E.B. White*. New York: HarperPerennial, 1999.
White, E. B., and Katharine S. White, eds. *A Subtreasury of American Humor*. New York: Coward-McCann, 1941.
Widmer, Ellen, and David Der-wei Wang, eds. *From May Fourth to June Fourth: Fiction and Film in Twentieth-Century China*. Cambridge, MA: Harvard University Press, 1993.

Wilson, Christopher P. *Jokes: Form, Content, Use and Function.* London: Academic Press, 1979.
Wisse, Ruth R. *No Joke: Making Jewish Humor.* Princeton, NJ: Princeton University Press, 2013.
Witchard, Anne. *Lao She in London.* Hong Kong: Hong Kong University Press, 2012.
Wong Ain-ling 黃愛玲, ed. *Zhongguo dianying suyuan* 中國電影溯源 (Chinese Cinema: Tracing the Origins). Hong Kong: Hong Kong Film Archives, 2011.
Wong, Edward. "Kim Jong-un Seems to Get a New Title: Heartthrob." *New York Times*, 27 November 2012, A6. www.nytimes.com/2012/11/28/world/asia/chinese-news-site-cites-onion-piece-on-kim-jong-un.html?ref=asia&_r=1&.
Wong, Timothy C., ed. and trans. *Stories for Saturday: Twentieth-Century Chinese Popular Fiction.* Honolulu: University of Hawai'i Press, 2003.
Wong Yunn Chii, and Tan Kar Lin. "Emergence of a Cosmopolitan Space for Culture and Consumption: The New World Amusement Park-Singapore (1923–1970) in the Inter-War Years." *Inter-Asia Cultural Studies* 5, no. 2 (2004): 279–304.
Woodbury, Walter E., *Photographic Amusements, including a Description of a Number of Novel Effects Obtainable with the Camera.* Revised and enlarged by Frank R. Fraprie. 9th ed. Boston: American Photographic Publishing Co., 1922. www.gutenberg.org/files/39691/39691-h/39691-h.htm.
Wu Ching-tzu [Wu Jingzi 吳敬梓]. *The Scholars.* Translated by Yang Hsien-yi and Gladys Yang. New York: Columbia University Press, 1992.
Wu Jianren 吳趼人. *Ershi nian mudu zhi guai xianzhuang* 二十年目睹之怪現狀 (Strange Events Eyewitnessed over Twenty Years). 2 vols. Beijing: Remin wenxue chubanshe, 1985.
———. *Wu Jianren quanji* 吳趼人全集 (Complete Works of Wu Jianren). 7 vols. Harbin: Beifang wenyi chubanshe, 1998.
Wu Jiaqing 伍稼青. *Wu Zhihui xiansheng yishi* 吳稚暉先生軼事 (Anecdotes about Mr. Wu Zhihui). Taipei: Fenfang baodao zazhishe, 1977.
Wu Wo-yao 吳沃堯 [Wu Jianren 吳趼人]. *Vignettes from the Late Ch'ing: Bizarre Happenings Eyewitnessed over Two Decades.* Translated by Shih Shun-Liu. Hong Kong: Chinese University of Hong Kong, 1975.
Wu Zhihui 吳稚暉. *Wu Zhihui yanlun ji* 吳稚暉言論集 (Collected Speeches and Essays of Wu Zhihui). Edited by Qin Tongpei 秦同培. 2 vols. Shanghai: Zhongyang tushuju, 1927.
Xiaoshi daoren 小石道人. *Zhengxu Xitan lu* 正續嘻談錄 (Truly Delightful Chats, vols. 1 and 2). [publisher unknown], ca. 1882–84.
Xiaoshuo yuebao she 小説月報社, ed. *Xiao de lishi* 笑的歷史 (A History of Laughter). Shanghai: Shangwu yinshuguan, 1925.
Xiaoxiao xiansheng 笑笑先生, ed. *Shanzhong yixihua* 山中一夕話 (Chats from a Night in the Mountains) [alternative title: *Kaijuan yixiao* 開卷一笑 (Open the Book and Laugh)]. Edited by Haha daoshi 哈哈道士. Meishushi shuge [ca. 1621–44]. Copy held at the Harvard-Yenching Library.
Xu Banmei 徐半梅 [Xu Zhuodai 徐卓呆]. *Huaju chuangshiqi huiyilu* 話劇創始期回憶錄 (A Memoir of the Formative Period of Spoken Drama). Beijing: Zhonghua xiju chubanshe, 1957.

———. *Yingxi xue* 影戲學 (The Science of Shadowplay). Shanghai: Huaxian shangyeshe tushubu, 1924.
Xu Fulin 徐傅霖 [Xu Zhuodai 徐卓呆]. *Ticao shang zhi shengli* 體操上之生理 (Gymnastics Physiology). Shanghai: Zhongguo tushu gongsi, 1909.
Xu Xu 徐訏. *Xu Xu wenji* 徐訏文集 (Collected Writings of Xu Xu). 16 vols. Shanghai: Shanghai sanlian shudian, 2012.
Xu Yongchang 徐永昌. *Qiujizhai riji* 求己齋日記 (Journal of the Ask of Oneself Studio). 10 vols. Manuscript held at Library of the Insitute of Modern History, Academia Sinica.
Xu Zhuodai 徐卓呆. *Buzhi suoyun ji* 不知所云集 (The Unintelligible Collection). Shanghai: Shijie shuju, 1923.
———. "The Fiction Material Wholesaler." Translated by Christopher Rea. *Renditions* 67 (Spring 2007): 46–62.
———. *Huaji dashi Xu Zhuodai daibiao zuo* 滑稽大師徐卓呆代表作 (Representative Works of the Master of Comedy Xu Zhuodai). Edited by Fan Boqun 范伯群, and Fan Zijiang 范紫江. Nanjing: Jiangsu wenyi chubanshe, 1996.
———. *Qiyou cili zhi riji* 豈有此理之日記 (An Absurd Diary). Shanghai: Xiaoxing shuju, 1923.
———. *Riben roudao* 日本柔道 (Japanese Judo). Shanghai: Zhonghua shuju, 1935.
———. *Wuxiandian boyin* 無線電播音 (Wireless Broadcasting). Shanghai: Shangwu yinshuguan, [ca. 1920s–1930s].
———. *Yingxi xue* 影戲學 (The Science of Shadowplay). Shanghai: Huaxian shangyeshe tushubu, 1924.
———. *Zhuodai xiaoshuo ji* 卓呆小說集 (Zhuodai's Story Collection). Shanghai: Shijie shuju, 1926.
———. *Zuihou xiu pingguo* 醉後嗅蘋果 (Drunk and Sniffing Apple Blossoms). Shanghai: Shijie shuju, 1929.
Xuan Yongguang 宣永光. *Wangtan fenghua* 妄談瘋話 (Reckless Words and Crazy Talk). Harbin: Harbin Publishing House, 2012.
Xue Liyong 薛理勇. *Shanghai xianhua* 上海閑話 (Shanghai Gossip). Shanghai: Shanghai shehui kexue chubanshe, 2000.
Yan Fusun 嚴芙孫, ed. *Shanghai suyu da cidian* 上海俗語大辭典 (Dictionary of Shanghai Slang). Shanghai: Yunxuan chubanbu, 1924.
Yang Huasheng 楊華生, and Zhang Zhenguo 張振國, text; Li Shoubai 李守白, illust. *Shanghai lao huaji* 上海老滑稽 (An Old Comic Performer of Shanghai). Shanghai: Shanghai cishu chubanshe, 2006.
Yang Jialuo 楊家駱, ed. *Zhongguo xiaohua shu* 中國笑話書 (Chinese Joke Books). Taipei: Shijie shuju, 2002 [1961].
Yang, T. L., trans. *Officialdom Unmasked*. Hong Kong: Hong Kong University Press, 2001.
Ye Qianyu 葉淺予. *Wang xiansheng xinji* 王先生新集 (The New Mr. Wang Collection). 4 vols. Shanghai: Shanghai zazhi gongsi, 1936.
Ye Xiaoqing. *The Dianshizhai Pictorial: Shanghai Urban Life, 1884–1898*. Ann Arbor: University of Michigan Center for Chinese Studies, 2003.

Yeh, Catherine Vance. "Reinventing Ritual: Late Qing Handbooks for Proper Customer Behavior in Shanghai Courtesan Houses." *Late Imperial China* 19, no. 2 (1998): 1–63.

———. *Shanghai Love: Courtesans, Intellectuals, and Entertainment Culture, 1850–1910*. Seattle: University of Washington Press, 2006.

Yeh, Wen-hsin, ed. *Becoming Chinese: Passages to Modernity and Beyond*. Berkeley: University of California Press, 2000.

———. *Provincial Passages: Culture, Space, and the Origins of Chinese Communism*. Berkeley: University of California Press, 1996.

Young, Ernest P. *The Presidency of Yuan Shih-k'ai: Liberalism and Dictatorship in Early Republican China*. Ann Arbor: University of Michigan Press, 1977.

Youxi daguan 游戲大觀 (Panorama of Play). 6 vols. Shanghai: Guangwen shuju, 1919.

Yu Hua. *China in Ten Words*. Translated by Allan H. Barr. New York: Pantheon Books, 2011.

Yu Runqi 于潤琦, ed.; Zhou Chunhua 周春華, punct. *Qingmo Minchu xiaoshuo shuxi—huaji juan* 清末民初小說書系—滑稽卷 (Compendium of Stories from the Late Qing and Early Republican Periods—Comedy Volume). Beijing: Zhongguo wenlian chuban gongsi, 1997.

Yuan Jin 袁進, ed. *Huo zai weixiao zhong* 活在微笑中 (Living Amid Smiles). Shanghai: Dongfang chuban zhongxin, 1997.

Yuan Mei 袁枚. *Zi bu yu* 子不語 (What Confucius Didn't Talk About). Pan Jingyuan 潘敬元, punct. Shanghai: Dada tushu gongyingshe, 1935.

Yunjian diangong 雲間顛公. *Shanghai zhi pianshu shijie* 上海之騙術世界 (Shanghai's World of Swindlers). Shanghai: Saoye shanfang, 1924 [1914].

Zarrow, Peter Gue. *After Empire: The Conceptual Transformation of the Chinese State, 1885–1924*. Stanford, CA: Stanford University Press, 2012.

———. *Anarchism and Chinese Political Culture*. New York: Columbia University Press, 1990.

Zeitlin, Judith T. *Historian of the Strange: Pu Songling and the Chinese Classical Tale*. Stanford, CA: Stanford University Press, 1993.

———. *The Phantom Heroine: Ghosts and Gender in Seventeenth-Century Chinese Literature*. Honolulu: University of Hawai'i Press, 2007.

Zeng Jianglai 曾講來, ed. *Bengkui de diguo: Mingxinpian zhong de wan Qing* 崩潰的帝國：明信片中的晚清 (A Collapsing Empire: Postcards of the Late Qing). Beijing: Beijing daxue chubanshe, 2014.

Zhang Changhua 張昌華. "Zhengzhiquan wai de Wu Zhihui: 'Yige huaitou de haoren'" 政治圈外的吳稚暉："一個壞透的好人" ("Wu Zhihui outside the Political Sphere: 'A Thoroughly Rotten Good Man'"). http://news.sina.com.cn/c/2008-06-18/142215769784.shtml.

Zhang Henshui 張恨水. *Shanghai Express: A Thirties Novel*. Translated by William A. Lyell. Honolulu: University of Hawai'i Press, 1997.

———. *Tixiao yinyuan* 啼笑因緣 (Fate in Tears and Laughter). 2 vols. Shanghai: Sanyi shudian, 1931.

Zhang Jian 張健. *Zhongguo xiju guannian de xiandai shengcheng* 中國喜劇觀念的現代生成 (The Modern Formation of the Comic Idea in China). Beijing: Peking University Press, 2005.

Zhang Jingsheng 張競生. *Xing shi* 性史 (Sex Histories). Shanghai: Guanghua shuju, 1926.

———. *Xing shi* 性史 (Sex Histories). Beijing: Beixin shuju, 1926.

Zhang Kebiao 章克標. *Zhang Kebiao wenji* 章克標文集 (Collected Works of Zhang Kebiao). 2 vols. Edited by Chen Fukang 陳福康 and Jiang Shanqing 蔣山青. Shanghai: Shanghai shuhui kexue chubanshe, 2003.

Zhang Tianyi 張天翼. *Guitu riji* 鬼土日記 (Ghostland Diary). Shanghai: Zhengwu shuju, 1931.

———. *Zhang Tianyi wenji* 張天翼文集 (Works of Zhang Tianyi). 10 vols. Shanghai: Shanghai wenyi chubanshe, 1985–88.

———. *Zhang Tianyi xuanji* 張天翼選集 (Selected Works of Zhang Tianyi). Shanghai: Wanxiang shuwu, 1936.

Zhang Wenbo 張文伯. *Zhilao xianhua* 稚老閒話 (Shooting the Breeze with Old Wu Zhihui). Taipei: Zhongyang wenwu gongyingshe, 1952.

Zhang, Yingjin. *The City in Modern Chinese Literature and Film: Configurations of Space, Time, and Gender*. Stanford, CA: Stanford University Press, 1996.

Zhang Zhen. *An Amorous History of the Silver Screen: Shanghai Cinema, 1896–1937*. Chicago: University of Chicago Press, 2005.

Zhang Zhongli 張仲禮, ed. *Zhongguo jindai chengshi qiye, shehui, kongjian* 中國近代城市企業,社會,空間 (Urban Enterprise, Society, and Space in Late Qing and Republican China). Shanghai: Shanghai shehuikexue yuan, 1998.

Zhao Haiyan 趙海彥. *Zhongguo xiandai quwei zhuyi wenxue sichao* 中國現代趣味文學思潮 (The *Quwei*-ism Trend of Thought in Modern Chinese Literature). Beijing: Zhongguo shehui kexue chubanshe, 2005.

Zheng Yimei 鄭逸梅. *Qingmo Minchu wentan yishi* 清末民初文壇軼事 (Anecdotes from the Literary Field of the Late Qing and Early Republican Periods). Beijing: Zhonghua shuju, 2005.

———. *Shubao huajiu* 書報話舊 (Stories about Old Books and Periodicals). Beijing: Zhongshu shuju, 2005.

———. *Zheng Yimei xuanji* 鄭逸梅選集 (Selected Works of Zheng Yimei). 6 vols. Harbin: Heilongjiang renmin chubanshe, 1995.

Zheng Yimei 鄭逸梅, and Xu Zhuodai 徐卓呆. *Shanghai jiuhua* 上海舊話 (Tales of Old Shanghai). Shanghai: Shanghai wenhua chubanshe, 1986.

Zhongguo wenxue da cidian 中國文學大辭典 (Dictionary of Chinese Literature). 10 vols. Taipei: Baichuan shuju, 1994.

Zhou Yaoguang 周耀光. *Shiyong yingxiangxue* 實用映相學 (Practical Photography). Guangdong: Yuedong bianyi gongsi, 1911 [1907].

Zhou Zuoren 周作人. *Zhou Zuoren jingdian zupin xuan* 周作人經典作品選 (Selected Classic Works of Zhou Zuoren). Beijing: Dangdai shijie chubanshe, 2002.

———. *Zhou Zuoren: Selected Essays* (Chinese-English Bilingual Edition). Translated by David E. Pollard. Hong Kong: Chinese University Press, 2006.

———. *Zhou Zuoren yiwen quanji* 周作人譯文全集 (Complete Translations of Zhou Zuoren). Edited by Zhi An 止庵.11 vols. Shanghai: Shanghai renmin chubanshe, 2012.

Zhu Guangqian 朱光潛. *Zhu Guangqian quanji* 朱光潛全集 (Complete Works of Zhu Guangqian). 20 vols. Hefei: Anhui jiaoyu chubanshe, 1987.

Zhu Weigong 朱惟公 [Zhu Taimang 朱太忙], ed. *Xiandai wubai jia yuanquan shi ji* 現代五百家圓圈詩集 (Palindromic Poems by Five Hundred Poets). Shanghai: Guangyi shuju, 1933.

INDEX

Absolutely Bizarre and Hilarious Modern Jokes (Qianqi baiguai modeng da xiaohua), 189
Addison, Joseph, 202n14
"Address to the Crocodiles" (Han Yu), 41
advertising, 247n59; deceptive, 120, 248n72; parodies of, 53–54; for *Which Classic?*, 89, 93–95
age of irreverence: modern China's first, 159; reemergence of, 162–65
"Ah Guan from Shaoxing Rides the Train" (Jiang Xiaoxiao), 7
Ah Q (fictional character), 79–81, 84, 103, 131
"Ah Q zhengzhuan." *See* "True Story of Ah Q, The"
Alice's Adventures in China (Alisi Zhongguo youji) (Shen Congwen), 74
allegory: Chinese characters used for, 57–59, 60f, 61f, 62f; in cinema, 73, 75, 160; in jokes, 17, 34, 211n63; in illustration, 54–63, 55f, 57f, 58f, 62f, 72f, 76f, 219n50; in literature, 107, 109, 136; and play, 40, 42, 73; and photography, 70–73, 71f, 225n114; political and social, 75
All-Story Monthly, The (Yueyue xiaoshuo), 16, 206n3
Altenburger, Roland, 87–88, 230n37
Althusseur, Louis, 205n45
amusement halls, 63–65, 222nn81–84
amusement parks, 64, 223n86

Analects (Lunyu) (Confucius), 70, 89, 102, 147–48, 149f, 226n124
Analects Fortnightly, The (Lunyu banyuekan): ghost stories in, 139, 139f, 140–41f; humor in, 12, 104, 132–33, 136–42, 139f, 140–41f, 147–48, 151–57, 260n101; Lao She and, 136; launch of, 132, 138, 252n10; Lin Yutang and, 12, 104, 132, 142, 147, 151–52; *The China Critic (Zhongguo pinglun zhoubao)* and, 138, 142, 255n33, 255n41
Anderson, Marston, 97
anecdotes, jokes as, 22–28, 212n72
Anthology of New Humor (Shixie xinji) (Moyin zhuren), 168, 206n3
anthropomorphic Chinese characters, 59, 62f, 221n76
Anti-Japanese War *(kangzhan)*, 33, 78, 155, 159, 252n9
anti-Manchuism, 78, 99, 216n23
Aofeng laoren, 174
Applause! (Pai zhang ji) (Zhuoyin caotang), 182
Assorted Collection of Humorous Writings in Classical Chinese (Guwen huaji leichao) (Gu Yu), 173
Assorted Collection of Unofficial Sources on the Qing (Qing bai lei chao) (Xu Ke), 174
Aurora, The (Liming), 95–96

baihua (vernacular Chinese), 91–92
Bao Gengsheng, 185

INDEX

Bao Lele, 188, 245n37
Bao Tianxiao, 3
Basket of Fresh Jokes (Xinxian xiaohua louzi), 192
Berry, Michael, 3
Between Tears and Laughter (Tixiao jiefei) (Lin Yutang), 2
"Bird and the Shell-Fish, The," 218n43
Birrell, Anne, 214n6
Bizarre Tales (Guai hua) (Hu Jichen), 175
bizhan (wars of words), 82
Boxer Rebellion, 1, 18, 43
Brief History of Chinese Fiction, A (Zhongguo xiaoshuo shilüe) (Lu Xun), 84
"Brilliant Trick, A" (Lin Buqing), 36–37
Bugou zhiji. See *Imperfect Understanding*
bullshit, 39, 93, 101, 214n98; and ambiguous truth-claim of *xiaohua*, 39
Bust a Gut in Laughter (Xiao ci du) (Sanmen zhuren), 182

Cai Chusheng, 75
Cai Yuanpei, 91–92, 143
"Calf and Foal" (Wu Jianren), 17
Call to Arms, A (Nahan) (Lu Xun), 80
Can Xue, 165
Cao Xiujun, 183
Caricature and Other Comic Art in All Times and Many Lands (James Parton), 31
cartoons, 14, 36–37f, 37–38, 148, 149f, 204n29; play in, 54–61, 55f, 57f, 58f, 60f, 61f, 62f, 63f; political, 57, 75, 76f, 227n127. *See also* comic strips
censorship, 96, 143–44, 161, 163–64, 193–94, 229n16, 252n6
Certeau, Michel de, 123
chaizi. See glyphomancy
Chan Jia er xiansheng. See *Mr. Tangle & Mr. Between-the-Lines*
Chan, Shirley, 241n5
Chang, Eileen, 65, 156, 159–60, 165
Changqiu Shi, 171
Chao, Y. R. (Zhao Yuanren), 227n131
Chaplin, Charlie, 75; reception in China of, 10, 13, 68, 109, 111, 117, 137, 150, 242n15
Chenbao. See *Morning Post*
Chen Geng, 204n26
Cheng Shijue, 176, 186, 191
Cheng Zhanlu, 2, 110, 202n5
Chenhai Chixiaosheng, 178
Chen Jinghan (pseud. Lengxue), 3, 202n7
Chen Meigong, 208n32

Chen Pingyuan, 24, 210n47
Chen Yan, 175
Chen Zizhan, 132, 146, 148, 252n2, 257n60
China Critic, The (Zhongguo pinglun zhoubao), 32–34, 138, 156; and *The Analects Fortnightly (Lunyu banyuekan)*, 142, 255n33; and launch of humor trend, 142–45
Chinese characters, visual wordplay with, 5, 11, 57, 59
Chinese Characters Explained (Zishuo) (Wang Anshi), 5, 203n15
Chinese Communist Party, 3, 7, 144, 153, 156–57, 159–61, 264n28, 265n32; anti-communism, 100–102
Chinese constitution, 59, 60f, 221n71
Chinese Humanist Monthly (Renjian shi), 162, 263n20
Chinese Nationalist Party, 97, 100, 102, 150, 162, 238n110, 238n114, 260n95
Chinese Students' Monthly, The (Zhongguo liu Mei xuesheng yuebao), 32, 213n80
"Chinese Swine and Sons of Bitches" (Wu Zhihui), 78, 99
Chinese Times (Meilibin bu Aiguo bao), 57, 221n70
Chinese Wit and Humor (George Kao), 157, 262n121
Chuan, T. K. (Quan Zenggu), 34, 137–38, 150–51, 156, 255n29
City of Cats (Maocheng ji) (Lao She), 136
civilized play *(wenming xi)*, 73–74
Civil Rights (Minquan bao), 29, 50, 57, 59, 110, 221n68
Cohen, Ted, 21, 23
Cold-Blooded. *See* Chen Jinghan
Collection of Cold Laughs, A (Lengxiao congtan) (Qunxueshe tushu faxingsuo), 170
Collection of Humorous Writings, by Genre (Xiewenci leizuan) (Li Dingyi), 174
Collection of Taiwanese Jokes, with Parallel Translation (Duiyi Taiwan xiaohua ji) (Kawai Sanenaga), 33, 172
Comical Biography of an Opera Fan, The (Huaji ximi zhuan), 182
Comical News (Kōkkei shimbun), 109, 242n14
Comic Couplets (Huaji lianhua) (Dong Jianzhi), 190
comic fiction *(huaji xiaoshuo)*, 109–10, 209n45, 245n36
Comic Poems and Prose (Huaji shiwen ji) (Fan Zengxiang), 179

Comic Spirit, The (Huaji hun) (Li Dingyi), 28, 53, 107, 108f, 175, 207n13, 220nn57–58
comic strips, 57, 221n67
Comic Verse and Prose, Ancient and Modern (Gujin huaji shihua) (Fan Fan), 176
Compendium of China's New Literature (Zhongguo xin wenxue daxi), 5, 203n20, 234n71
Compendium of Funny Stories (Huaji gushi leibian) (Yang Ruquan), 184
Compendium of Funny Stories about Celebrities of the Qing Dynasty (Qingdai mingren xiaoshi daguan) (Xi Xutao), 177
Compendium of Jokes, Ancient and Modern (Gujin xiaohua daguan) (Li Xiaowu), 176
Compendium of Playful Literature (Youxi wenxue congkan) (Cao Xiujun), 183
Confucius, 24, 75, 88, 95, 102, 149f, 216n25; humor of, 147, 257nn54–55, 257n57; in literature, 45, 88, 90, 104, 145–48, 240n126, 252n4
Confucius Saw Nancy (Zijian nanzi) (Lin Yutang), 104, 147, 240n126, 257n55
constitution, Chinese, 59, 60f, 221n71
Les Contemporains (Xiandai), 136, 252n8, 254n19, 260n95
Crate of Fresh Jokes, A (Xinxian xiaohua yi da xiang) (Jin Zuxin), 190
Cui Bingleng, 183, 187
"Cure for Toothache," 53–54
cursing: China's "national oath," 81; and criticism, 81–82, 84; and cultural concern with genealogy and lineage, 81, 84, 97; *gui* (ghost/devil) as a curse, 85–87, 89; market appeal of, 93–94, 102–4; and mockery in literary and political discourse, 11, 78, 81, 83–84, 86–90, 94–95, 97, 100, 103–4, 150, 156, 162, 219n49, 228nn2–3, 228nn10–14, 229n15, 257nn59–60, 261n116; in *Which Classic? (He Dian)*, 84–87, 95, 235n77; by Wu Zhihui, 97–101, 237nn94–100

Daizi de xiaohua (Jokes on Simpletons), 170
"Damming the River" (Ma Xingchi), 54, 55f
Dao De Jing (The Way and Its Virtue), 39, 87, 230n32
Daruvala, Susan, 242n16
Dasha xiaoshi (Hilarious Tales of Idiocy) (Huang Yanqing), 183
Davies, Christie, 23, 206n12
Davies, Gloria, 228n3

Davis, Mike Lee, 128
Dazhong xiaohua (Jokes for All), 192
Dekobra, Maurice, 133, 150, 252n4
"Delightful Story of Blood and Tears, A" (Cheng Zhanlu), 2
Dentith, Simon, 219n52
Des Forges, Alexander, 241n7
devils. *See gui*
"Devil Farts" (Wu Zhihui), 100
"Devil Messenger, The" (Xu Zhuodai), 114–15, 246n45
Dianshizhai Pictorial (Dianshizhai huabao), 54
"Diary of a Madman" (Lu Xun), 4, 94, 129, 234n72
Di Baoxian, 45–47, 90, 216n31
Dickens, Charles, 110, 134–35, 155, 242n17
Ding Fubao, 205n41
Ding Xilin, 134–35, 153, 253nn14–15
Dong Jianzhi, 177, 190
Dong Zhenhua, 187
Dooling, Amy, 164
Double Barreled Detective Story, A (Mark Twain), 128
Double Over in Laughter (Xiao luan chang) (Sanmen zhuren), 182
Dream of the Red Chamber (Honglou meng), 2, 14, 20, 47–48, 69f, 127, 202n6. *See also New Story of the Stone*
dress-up photos, 67–68, 225n114, 264n23
Dudgeon, John, 224n97
Du Fu, 52
Du Heng, 153
Duiyi Taiwan xiaohua ji (Collection of Taiwanese Jokes, with Parallel Translation) (Kawai), 33, 172
Du Mu, 49, 217n41
Duyiwo tuishi (Happily Retired Cave-Dwelling Hermit), 34, 186

Eastern Times (Shibao), 47, 216n31, 242n19. *See also* Di Baoxian
Eat Your Tongue (Jiao she lu) (Li Jingzhong), 180
Eco, Umberto, 5
education reform, 216n25
Enlarged and Expanded Forest of Laughs, Featuring One Thousand New Elegant Jokes from Collections Ancient and Modern (Zengguang gujin xiaolin xinya yiqianzhong) (Chenhai Chixiaosheng), 29, 178

Ershi nian mudu zhi guai xianzhuang. See *Strange Events Eyewitnessed over Twenty Years*
erwo tu (two-mes photo). *See* split-self image
Esperanto, 98–99
"Essay on Man" (Alexander Pope), 44
Everyone Laughs (*Renren xiao*) (Zhao Tiaokuang), 178
Expanded Forest of Laughs (*Guang xiaolin*) (Li Dingyi), 28, 173
Expanded Forest of Laughs (*Xiaolin guangji*) (Youxi zhuren), 19–20, 22, 30, 104, 181, 208n31. See also *True Expanded Forest of Laughs* (Youxi zhuren)
Expanded Forest of Laughs (*Xiaolin guangji*) (Cheng Shijue), 176, 186, 191
Expanded History of Humor (*Guang xieshi*) (Chen Bangjun), 8, 204n31
Expanded Treasury of Laughs (*Guang Xiaofu*) (Feng Menglong), 187, 207n14, 208n30
"Exposing Plagiarism" (Xu Zhuodai), 127

fair play, 82, 229n15
Fan Boqun, 110
Fan Fan, 176
Fang Cheng, 188
Fan Zengxiang, 179
farce: as comic trend, 9–10, 12; defined, 107, 109, 241n5, 241n10; in fiction, 109–10, 119; hoaxes in, 123–24, 126, 128, 130; Lin Yutang and, 106–8, 117; plagiarism and, 124–28; practical jokes in, 12, 124–26, 128–30; reversal, 115, 245n44; in Shanghai, 7, 107, 112, 128, 130–31; Xu Zhuodai and, 106–7, 109, 110–31, 113f, 118f, 121f, 244n32, 247nn56–57, 250n89, 251nn92–93, 251n97. See also *huaji*; Shanghainese farce
Fashionable Jokes (*Shixing xiaohua*) (Chen Meigong), 208n32
Fate in Tears and Laughter (*Tixiao yinyuan*) (Zhang Henshui), 2
"Father's Duty, A" (Xu Zhuodai), 245n44
fengci. *See* satire
Feng Menglong, 21, 187, 204n26, 207n14, 208n30, 209n34, 212n72
Feng Yuanjun, 261n116
Feng Zikai, 75–77, 77f, 262n119
fenshen xiang. *See* split-self image
fiction genre (*xiaoshuo*), 20, 26–27, 109–10, 119; and Wu Jianren's promotion of "joke stories," 19–20

"Fiction Material Wholesaler, The" (Xu Zhuodai), 124–26
film, 162, 226n117, 242n15; trick cinematography in, 73, 117; Xu Zhuodai and, 117–18, 118f, 122, 248n67
Fine Art of Reviling, The (*Maren de yishu*) (Liang Shiqiu), 82–83, 229n17, 261n116
Flowers of Shanghai (*Haishang hua liezhuan*), 235n76
Flying Dragon Island (*Feilong dao*), 63–64, 222nn79–80
Forest of Laughs (*Xiaolin*), 21, 37–38, 108f, 172
Forest of Laughs: One Thousand Jokes (*Xiaolin yiqianzhong*) (Taicang Tang Zhenru), 183
Forest of Laughs: Ten Jokes (*Xiaolin shize*) (Handan Chun), 172
"For Rent" (Wu Jianren), 16
Fount of Laughter (*Xiao quan*) (Li Xinyan), 30, 188
Four Joke Books (*Xiaohua sizhong*) (Zhang Xiaochao), 181
Frankfurt, Harry G., 39, 214n98
Free Magazine (*Ziyou zazhi*), 51–52, 219n50. See also "Free Talk"; *Playful Magazine*
"Free Talk" ("Ziyou tan"), 51–52, 83, 133, 218n47. See also *Free Magazine*
Fresh Jokes and Remarkable Stories (*Xinxian xiaohua qitan*), 169
Fu Manchu (fictional character), 136, 253n17
Funny and Amusing Tale, A (*Huaji qushi*) (Zhao Zhongxiong), 180
Funny Chats, with New-Style Punctuation (*Xinshi biaodian huaji tan*) (Wu Jianren), 109, 180, 206n2
Funny Chats from the Garden of Literature (*Wenyuan huaji tan*) (Yunjian diangong), 172
Funny Shanghai, 107–8, 130
Funny Stories (*Huaji conghua*) (Chen Yan), 175
Funny Stories from the Ladies' Chambers (*Guifang xiaoshi*) (Zhao Tiaokuang), 29, 180, 212n65
Funny Stories from the Restoration of the Han and Extermination of the Manchus (*Xing Han mie Man huaji lu*), 169
funny words (*huaji zi*), 59, 221n72
Funny World (*Huaji shijie*) (Jiang Hangong), 23, 175
Funny World (*Huaji shijie*) (Zhao Tiaokuang), 177

Future of New China, The (Xin Zhongguo weilai ji) (Liang Qichao), 5, 44–49, 90, 215nn22–23, 216nn25–27
futuristic fantasy, 47, 216n28, 217n33

games: as play, 59, 61, 62f, 63f, 74–77, 77f, 214n6; political, 59, 61, 62f, 63f, 226n125
gaoxiao (making people laugh), 165, 265n36
ghosts. See *gui*
Ghostland Diary (Guitu riji) (Zhang Tianyi), 7–8, 239n122
glyphomancy *(chaizi)*, 59
Goh, Meow Hui, 227n131
Gongchandang. See Chinese Communist Party
(Gongheguo) Xin haha xiao (New Laughs (of the Republic)) (Li Jiezhai), 170
Great World, The (Da shijie), 63–65, 162, 263n19
guafen (carve like a melon), 50, 218n44
Guai hua (Bizarre Tales) (Hu Jichen), 175
Guanchang xianxing ji. See *Officialdom Unmasked*
Guang xiaofu. See *Expanded Treasury of Laughs*
Guang xiaolin (Expanded Forest of Laughs) (Li Dingyi), 28, 173
Guangyang Notes (Liu Jizhuang), 155
gui (ghost/devil), 103, 160, 231n40, 231n44; Ah Q as, 103; in *The Analects Fortnightly (Lunyu banyuekan)*, 139, 139f, 140–41f; Chinese cultural politics and, 100, 103–4; as epithet or curse, 88–89; history and definitions of term, 88–89; jokes and paradoxes involving, 86–90, 102; term used by Wu Zhihui, 100; in *Which Classic? (He Dian)*, 11, 86–88, 230n39
Guifang xiaoshi. See *Funny Stories from the Ladies' Chambers*
guji. See *huaji*
Gujin huaji shihua (Comic Verse and Prose, Ancient and Modern) (Fan Fan), 176
Gujin xiaohua daguan (Compendium of Jokes, Ancient and Modern) (Li Xiaowu), 176
Guoluren: Passerby, 90–91; variations on, 232n54
Guomindang. See Chinese Nationalist Party
Guo Yaochen, 174
Guwen huaji leichao (Assorted Collection of Humorous Writings in Classical Chinese) (Gu Yu), 173

Haft, Lloyd, 87
Ha! Ha! (Haha lu) (Yan Fusun), 177
haha jing. See ha-ha mirror
Haha lu. See *Ha! Ha!*
ha-ha mirror *(haha jing)*, 65–67, 66–67f, 162, 223nn94–95
Hanan, Patrick, 207n14, 212n72
Handan Chun, 172
Han Shiheng, 150–51, 259n79
Han Yu, 41, 214n7
Happily Retired Cave-Dwelling Hermit (Duyiwo tuishi), 34, 186
Happy Film Company *(Kaixin yingpian gongsi)*, 117, 118f, 122, 246n52
Happy Times (Kuaihuo lin) (Wu Gehan), 188
He Dian. See *Which Classic?*
"Heroic Boar-Slayer, The," 30
Hilarious Tales of Idiocy (Dasha xiaoshi) (Huang Yanqing), 183
Hill, Michael Gibbs, 46
history: as accumulation of jokes, 3–4; and *historia*, 8; loss of laughter in, 4–9, 202n10, 204n29; mockery influencing course of, 78–79; as used in titles of collections of stories and jokes, 8
"History of Laughter, A" (Zhu Ziqing), 5, 203n19
History of Pain, A (Michael Berry), 3
History of Pain, A (Tongshi) (Wu Jianren), 1, 201n1
hoaxes, 123–24, 126, 128, 160; and literary culture, 129–31. See also practical jokes
Hockx, Michel, 81
Hong zazhi. See *Scarlet Magazine, The*
Hou Baolin, 36
Hsia, C. T. (Xia Zhiqing): on humor, 152, 154–55, 202n7
Hu, Jubin, 225n116
huaji, belittlement and criticism of, 105, 131, 151, 165; cinema, 242n15; definitions of, 107, 109, 241n5, 241n10, 242n13; as general term for humor and comedy, 107, 241n5; *kōkkei* and, 242n14; literary market for, 109–10, 242nn18–19, 243n21; narrowing of meaning in modern age, 107; writers, 105, 107, 110, 243n21; *youmo* (humor) and, 107, 151, 241n5; *youxi* (play, games) and, 40, 107. See also farce; Shanghainese farce; *youmo*
Huaji conghua (Funny Stories) (Chen Yan), 175
Huaji congshu (Humor Anthology) (Hu Jichen), 170
Huaji gushi leibian (Compendium of Funny Stories) (Yang Ruquan), 184

Huaji hun (The Comic Spirit) (Li Dingyi), 28, 53, 107, 108f, 175, 207n13, 220nn57–58
Huaji lianhua (Comic Couplets) (Dong Jianzhi), 190
Huaji qushi (A Funny and Amusing Tale) (Zhao Zhongxiong), 180
Huaji shanren, 188, 258n78
Huaji shijie (Funny World) (Jiang Hangong), 23, 175
Huaji shijie (Funny World) (Zhao Tiaokuang), 177
Huaji shiwen ji (Comic Poems and Prose) (Fan Zengxiang), 179
Huaji wenji. See *Humor Collection*
Huaji wenxuan (Literary Humor Selections) (Huang Fuquan), 185
Huaji wenxuan (Literary Humor Selections) (Lei Jin), 173
huaji xi. See Shanghainese farce
huaji xiaoshuo (comic fiction), 109–10, 209n45, 245n36
Huaji ximi zhuan (The Comical Biography of an Opera Fan), 182
Huaji xinyu (New Funny Stories), 35f, 175
huaji zi. See funny words
Huang Chujiu, 65, 223n91, 248n72
Huang Fuquan, 185
Huang Tianshi, 78, 93
Huang Yanqing, 183
Huang Yao, 67f, 139, 140–41f
Huitu xuetang xiaohua, yiming xuetang xianxingji. See *Illustrated Amusing Stories from New-Style Schools; or, An Exposé of New-Style Schools*
Hu Jichen, 29, 111, 128, 170–71, 175, 188
humor: in *The Analects Fortnightly*, 12, 104, 132–33, 136–42, 139f, 140–41f, 147–48, 151–57, 260n101; classical, 146–50, 149f; as comic trend, 9–10, 12; communist, 156–58; criticism of, 152–55; definitions of, 134, 137, 150–52, 157–58, 253n12, 254n24; Ding Xilin and, 135–35, 253n15, humorists before *youmo*, 133–37; invention of, 117, 131, 133; Lao She and, 12, 137, 150–51, 154, 156, 185, 254n19, 254n24, 258n74, 260n105, 261n117, 262n13; Lin Yutang and, 12–13, 105, 132–34, 136–37, 142–44, 146–47, 149–54, 156–57, 159, 161–62, 253n11, 255n33, 259n79; Lu Xun and, 148–49, 151, 153, 157, 258n76; translation of, 137–46, 149; Western influences on, 133–36, 150, 155; Year of, 34, 132, 157, 165, 252n2;
Zhou Zuoren and, 146, 148, 151, 154. See also *huaji*; *youmo*
Humor Anthology (Huaji congshu) (Hu Jichen), 170
Humor Collection (Huaji wenji) (Yanyun jushi), 168
humorists, 133–37, 150, 154–55
Humorous Jokes (Youmo xiaohua) (Dong Zhenhua), 187
Humorous Jokes (Youmo xiaohua ji) (Guo Boliang), 190
Humorous Jottings (Youmo biji) (Hu Shanyuan), 148, 187
Humorous Poems and Prose by Lao She (Lao She youmo shiwen ji) (Lao She), 136, 185, 262n13
Hung, Kenneth, 163
Hu Shanyuan, 148, 187, 258n63
Hu Shi, 91–92, 102, 146, 233n60, 235n76, 237n92
Hutt, Jonathan, 250n91
Hyde, Lewis, 124, 249n75

Idema, Wilt, 87
Illustrated Amusing Stories from New-Style Schools; or, An Exposé of New-Style Schools (Huitu xuetang xiaohua, yiming xuetang xianxingji) (Lao Lin), 24, 169
Illustrated Jokes (Xiaohua xiaohua) (Xu Zhuodai), 28–29, 191
Imperfect Understanding (Wen Yüan-ning), 145–46; and Wen's column for *The China Critic*, 144, 256nn45–51, 257n52
Importance of Living, The (Lin Yutang), 73, 152, 156
"Inflamed" (pen name of Wu Zhihui), 78
In Praise of Jokes (Xiao zan) (Qingdu sanke and [Lu] Huiyin), 34, 184
"Insects in a Fresh Moon Cake," 50, 51f, 56
Instant Laughs (Yikan jiuxiao) (Cui Bingleng), 183
interpellation, 205n45
"Intimate Portraits" (Wen Yüan-ning), 144–46
irreverence, 9. See also age of irreverence

Japan, 33, 59, 74, 109, 112, 136; amusement halls of, 63, 223n86; in Chinese fiction, 45; Chinese humorists in, 13, 44, 99–101, 109–10, 243n24, 244n35; circulation of laughter between China and, 13, 21, 33–34, 149; humor of, 31, 59, 212n75; military conflicts with China, 1, 18, 33, 50, 59, 78, 143,

153, 155, 159, 189, 218n43, 246n49, 252n9, 254n18; photography of, 68, 224n103
Jenkins, Henry, 31, 153
Jia Baoyu (fictional character), 20, 47–49, 69f, 202n6, 217n36
Jia lao'er wenda (Q&A with the Folks) (Jia Lao'er), 190
Jiang Bao xiaoji (Laughs from Jiang and Bao) (Jiang Xiaoxiao and Bao Lele), 188, 245n37
Jiang Hangong, 23, 175
Jiang Xiaoxiao, 7, 188, 245n37
Jiao she lu (Eat Your Tongue) (Li Jingzhong), 180
Jiemen xiaochou lu (Relieving Boredom and Dispelling Worry) (Huaji shanren), 188, 258n79
Jie ren yi (Smile-Raisers) (Qian Decang), 185
Jie ren yi guangji (More Smile-Raisers) (Bao Gengsheng), 185
Jie yan (Smile-Raisers) (Zhonghua yingwen zhoubao she), 184
Jieyisheng, 190
Jingxuan yijian haha xiao (A Selection of Instant Laughs), 181
Jin Nong, 225n109
Jin Ping Mei (Lanling Xiaoxiaosheng), 14
Jin Zuxin, 190
Ji Zhizhong, 189
joke stories (*xiaohua xiaoshuo*), 10, 24–25
jokes (*xiaohua*): as anecdotes, 22–28, 212n72; authorship of, 18, 22, 30, 125, 206n12; as comic trend, 9–11; as concept used to interpret humor, 38; defined, 23, 209n38; difference between *xiaohua* and jokes, 23; in dynastic collections, 87, 208nn29–30, 208n32, 211n61; as folklore, 161, 263n18; as global phenomenon, 31–32; history as and of, 3–4, 20–1; and literary market, 10–11, 22, 28–38, 35f, 36–37f; plagiarism and spurious attribution of, 16, 18, 125, 163, 207n14; about politicians, 27–28, 27f; practical, 12, 124–26, 128–30; riddles as, 20; in Shanghai, 28; in storytelling, 86; seen as symptomatic of social and cultural problems, 38–40; and truth, 23–26, 38–39; types of, 210n47; used by writers to simulate social intimacy, 18, 26; Wu Jianren and, 16–28, 32, 38, 81, 109, 125, 201n1, 206nn2–3, 207n20, 210n49, 211n60
Jokes (*Xiaohua*) (Li Jinhui and Lu Yiyan), 180
Jokes (*Xiaohua*) (Mark Twain), 189

Jokes, vol. 3 (*Xiaohua - disan ce*) (Ji Zhizhong and Xu Banmei), 189
Jokes and Bizarre Sights (*Xiaohua qiguan*) (Li Dingyi), 28, 182
Jokes and New Stories (*Xiaohua xintan*) (Li Jiezhai), 170
Jokes and Remarkable Stories (*Xiaohua qitan*), 169
Jokes and Remarkable Stories (*Xiaohua qitan*) (Yiqingshizhu), 190
Jokes for All (*Dazhong xiaohua*), 192
Jokes on Simpletons (*Daizi de xiaohua*), 170
Jones, Andrew, 217n36
journalist-litterateurs, 23, 30
Journey to the West (*Xiyou ji*), 41, 123; sequels and parodies, 52, 61, 219n51

Kaikkonen, Marja, 161
Kaixin yingpian gongsi (Happy Film Company), 117, 118f, 122, 246n52
kangzhan. See Anti-Japanese War
Kao, George, 157, 262n121
Kawai Sanenaga, 33, 172
Kefa yixiao (Worth a Laugh) (Qinshi shanren), 29, 174
Kern, Edith, 130, 251n94
King of Fresh Jokes (*Xinxian xiaohua dawang*) (Zou Mengxia), 191
KMT. See Chinese Nationalist Party
Knight, Sabina, 202n6
Kōkkei shimbun (Comical News), 109, 242n14
Kolatch, Jonathan, 243n24
Kuaihuo (Merry Magazine), 61, 222n78
Kuaihuo lin (Happy Times) (Wu Gehan), 188
Kuomintang. See Chinese Nationalist Party
Kucha'an xiaohua xuan. See *Selected Jokes from the Bitter Tea Studio*

Laborer's Love (*Laogong zhi aiqing*) (Zheng Zhengqiu and Zhang Shichuan), 73, 250n89
Lanling Xiaoxiaosheng. See Scoffing Scholar of Lanling
Lao Can youji. See *Travels of Lao Can, The*
Lao She (Shu Qingchun): *The Analects Fortnightly* (*Lunyu banyuekan*) and, 136; humor and, 12, 135–37, 150–51, 154, 156, 185, 254n19, 254n24, 258n74, 260n105, 261n117
Lao She (Shu Qingchun), works of: *City of Cats* (*Maocheng ji*), 136; *Humorous Poems and Prose by Lao She* (*Lao She youmo shiwen ji*), 136, 185, 262n13; *The Philosophy of Old

Lao She (Shu Qingchun), works of *(continued)* *Zhang (Lao Zhang de zhexue)*, 135; *Teahouse (Chaguan)*, 161; *The Two Mas (Er Ma)*, 135–36, 253n17
Lao She youmo shiwen ji. See Humorous Poems and Prose by Lao She
Lary, Diana, 159
Laugh, A (Yi xiao tu) (Xuanzong), 5, 6f, 203n16
Laugh-Getters (Tiaoxiao lu) (Xu Zhuodai), 29, 179, 244n30
Laughing Through Tears (Po ti lu) (Li Jingzhong and Shen Ganruo), 3, 29, 171, 211n63
Laughlin, Charles, 205n45
Laughs for the Masses (Minzhong xiaolin) (Zhao Shuicheng), 184
Laughs for the Masses, vol. 2 (Minzhong xiaolin erji) (Liu Shiru et al.), 185
Laughs from Jiang and Bao (Jiang Bao xiaoji) (Jiang Xiaoxiao and Bao Lele), 188, 245n37
laughter: ambivalence about, 13; criticism of, 38–40, 131, 163–65; defined, 4; interpellation and, 205n45; loss of, 5, 7; as medical illness or disorder, 4, 7, 204n23, 204n27; mockery and ridicule and, 4, 80, 82, 83f, 104; selling, 2, 155; smile and, 4–5, 202n14; on societal scale, 39, 162, 164; tears and, 1–4; theories of, 228n7; trauma and, 202n10; women and, 5, 120, 121f, 159–60, 247n62, 248nn63–64. *See also* breaking into laughter; mockery; smile; *xiao*
Laughter Stage (Xiao wutai), 112, 117, 245n40
laugh to scorn *(xiaoma)*, 79–80, 83, 103–4
Laugh upon Laugh (Xiaoxiao lu) (Duyiwo tuishi), 34, 186
Lee, Haiyan, 219n50
Lee, H. Tiffany, 224n105, 224n107
Lei Jin (pseud. Mr. Tottering in the Clouds), 49–51, 211n62, 218n46; *Funny Chats from the Garden of Literature (Wenyuan huajitan)* by, 172; *Literary Humor Selections (Huaji wenxuan)* by, 173; *Shanghai's World of Swindlers (Shanghai zhi pianshu shijie)* by, 128
Lengxiao congtan (A Collection of Cold Laughs) (Qunxueshe tushu faxingsuo), 170
Lengxue. *See* Chen Jinghan
letter writing guides, 247n61
Li Ah Mao (fictional character), 120, 122–24, 128–29, 131, 248n66, 251n97
Li Amao waizhuan. See Unofficial Story of Li Ah Mao, The
Liang Qichao, 78, 99, 217n32; *The Future of New China (Xin Zhongguo weilai ji)* by, 5, 44–49,
90, 215nn22–23, 216nn25–27; *New Fiction (Xin xiaoshuo)* founded by, 19–20, 216n30
Liang Shiqiu, 80, 82–83, 144, 229n17, 261n116
Liang Yuchun, 146, 205n45, 241n5, 256n51
Li Ao, 162, 264n22
Li Baojia. *See* Li Boyuan
Li Boyuan (pseud. Youxi zhuren), 42, 142, 168, 207n19, 215n11, 215n14. *See also* Master of Play
Lidai huaji gushi xuanji (Selected Comical Stories from the Imperial Period) (Fang Cheng), 188
Li Dingyi, 128, 250n85; *Collection of Humorous Writings, by Genre (Xiewenci leizuan)* by, 174; *The Comic Spirit (Huaji hun)* by, 28, 53, 107, 108f, 175, 207n13, 220nn57–58; *Expanded Forest of Laughs (Guang Xiaolin)* by, 28, 173; *Jokes and Bizarre Sights (Xiaohua qiguan)* by, 28–29, 182; *Playful Writings (Youxi wenzhang)* by, 187, 192
Li Hanqiu, 222n78
Li Jiezhai, 170
Li Jinghan, 239n121
Li Jingzhong, 29, 171, 180, 211nn62–63
Li Jinhui, 180
Lim Boon Keng (Lin Wenqing), 145–46, 234n73, 256nn47–49
Lin Buqing, 35f, 36–37, 176, 213n93
Link, Perry, 163–64, 233n64, 241n7, 250n91, 251n93, 264n28
Lin Shu, 110, 242n17
Lin Wenqing. *See* Lim Boon Keng
Lin Yutang, 7, 38, 40, 264n21; *The Analects Fortnightly (Lunyu banyuekan)* and, 12, 104, 132, 142, 147, 151–52; farce and, 106–8, 117; humor and, 12–13, 105, 132–34, 136–37, 142–44, 146–47, 149–54, 156–57, 159, 161–62, 253n11, 255n33, 259n79; mockery and, 81–82, 104–5, 229n15, 240n127
Lin Yutang, works of: *Between Tears and Laughter*, 2; *Confucius Saw Nancy (Zijian Nanzi)*, 104, 147, 240n126, 257n55; *The Importance of Living*, 73, 152, 156; "The Little Critic" essays and Chinese translations of, 143–44; "On Humor," 137, 151–52
Li Qingya, 157, 254n24, 261n119
Li Shizhen, 4, 202n12
Literary Humor Selections (Huaji wenxuan) (Huang Fuquan), 185
Literary Humor Selections (Huaji wenxuan) (Lei Jin), 173

Lit-Man (fictional character), 124–26
"Little Critic, The," 143–44, 154, 156
little-taste essay *(xiaopinwen)*, 144, 154; criticized for triviality, 154–55
Liu, Chiung-yun, 214n3
Liu, Lydia, 207n20
Liu Bannong, 236n81, 236n85, 239n120, 251n92
Liu Dabai, 95–97, 102, 228n8
Liu E (Liu Tieyun), 1, 3, 163, 201n2, 202n7, 220n64. See also *Travels of Lao Can, The*
Liu Fu, 91–97, 130, 233nn57–58, 235n75. See also *Which Classic?*
Liu Jizhuang, 155
Liu Shiru, 185
Liu Tieyun. *See* Liu E
Liu Xiaobo, 164, 264n31
Liu Xie, 241n11
Liu Yuan, 149f
Li Xiaowu, 176
Li Xinyan, 30, 188
Li Yu, 12, 16, 38, 206n1, 208n30
Lloyd, Harold, 150
Long Live the Wives (Taitai wansui) (Sang Hu), 160
Love's Labour's Lost (Shakespeare), 3–4
Lu Huiyin, 34, 184
Lunyu. See Analects
Lunyu banyuekan. See Analects Fortnightly, The
Lu Xun (Zhou Shuren), 7, 19, 134, 160, 240n4, 265n34; humor and, 148–49, 151, 153, 157, 258n76; mockery and, 79–84, 92, 94–95, 97, 100–101, 103, 105, 229n15, 229n20, 234n72, 234n74, 235nn75–76, 239n120; on split-self photographs, 68, 70
Lu Xun (Zhou Shuren), works of: *A Brief History of Chinese Fiction (Zhongguo xiaoshuo shilüe)*, 84; *A Call to Arms (Nahan)*, 80; "Diary of a Madman," 4, 94, 129, 234n72; "My Lost Love," 74; "New-Year's Sacrifice," 3; "Ode to 'a Verbal Spat,'" 238n110; *Old Tales Retold (Gushi xinbian)*, 74, 131; "The Secret of Being a Joker," 38–39; *Stories from Abroad (Yuwai xiaoshuo ji)*, 128; "The True Story of Ah Q," 79–81, 84, 103, 107, 131
Lu Yiyan, 180

Ma Guoliang, 152
Manchus: anti-Manchuism, 78, 99, 216n23; lost privileges of, 25–26. See also Lao She; Puyi
manhua. See cartoons

Mao Zedong, 159–61
maren. See cursing; mockery
Maren de yishu. See *Fine Art of Reviling, The*
Master of Humor *(youmo dashi)*, 133
Master of Play *(Youxi zhuren)*, 20, 168; Li Boyuan as, 42, 207n19, 215n11; Shanghai Masters of Play, 42, 215n11
Ma Xingchi, 54–56, 55f, 57f
May 30th Movement, 80
May Fourth Movement, 2, 80, 91, 131
McKeown, Adam, 89, 231n44
"Meeting Li Guinian in the South" ("Jiangnan feng Li Guinian") (Du Fu), 52
Mencius, 148, 257n59
Meng Jiangnü, 1–2
Meredith, George, 151–53, 155
Merry Magazine (Kuaihuo), 61, 222n78
Miben Huaji wenfu daguan (Secret Vast Treasury of Comic Writing) (Zou Diguang), 176
Minguo xin haha xiao (New Laughs of the Republic) (Li Jiezhai), 170
Minzhong xiaolin (Laughs for the Masses) (Zhao Shuicheng), 184
Minzhong xiaolin erji (Laughs for the Masses, vol. 2) (Liu Shiru et al.), 185
mock-biographies, 53
mockery *(maren)*, 208n30; art of, 80–84, 83f; as comic trend, 9–11; and cursing, 11, 81, 83–84, 86–90, 94–95, 97, 100, 103–4, 229n15; influence on history, 78–79; and laughter, 80, 104; Lin Yutang and, 81–82, 104–5, 229n15, 240n127; Lu Xun and, 79–84, 92, 94–95, 97, 100–101, 103, 105, 229n15, 229n20, 234n72, 234n74, 235nn75–76, 239n120; as play, 78; politics and, 78–80; satire compared with, 81; scorn in, 79–80, 83, 103–4; *Which Classic?* and, 11, 84–97, 85f, 100–105, 234n72, 235n76, 236n81, 239n117; Zhou Zuoren and, 81–82, 95, 100. See also cursing
Mocking the Dao (Xiao Dao lun), 87, 230n32
Mocking Zen Buddhism (Xiao Chan lu) (Pan Youlong), 180
Modeng xiaohua. See Modern Jokes
modernization, 154
Modern Jokes (Modeng xiaohua) (Cui Bingleng), 187
More Smile-Raisers (Jie ren yi guangji) (Bao Gengsheng), 185
Morning Post (Chenbao), 79–80, 133, 253n11
Morreall, John, 228n7

Moser, David, 161
Mountain Lodge of Swept Leaves, The (Saoye shanfang), 50, 147, 218n45
Mo Yan, 163–65, 264n28, 265n32
Moyin zhuren, 168, 206n3
Mr. Foolish (Yugong), 30, 178
Mr. Tangle & Mr. Between-the-Lines (Chan Jia er xiansheng), 90
Mr. Tottering in the Clouds (Yunjian diangong). *See* Lei Jin
Mr. Wang (Ye Qianyu), 221n67, 248n67
Mullaney, Thomas, 227n131
"My Lost Love" (Lu Xun), 74

Name of the Rose, The (Umberto Eco), 5
Nannü xin xiaohua (New Jokes about Men and Women) (Lin Buqing and Qian Xiangsi), 35f, 36–37, 176, 213n93
National Herald, The (Shenzhou ribao), 54–56, 220n62
Nationalists, 79–80, 97–98, 101, 153
New Account of Tales of the World, A (Shishuo xinyu), A, 83
New Culture Movement, 80, 91
New Drama *(xinju)*, 112, 114, 119
Newest Humor Assortment (Zuixin huaji zazhi) (Yunjian diangong), 49, 172
"Newest Prohibition and Exorcism Methods" (Xu Zhuodai), 128
New Expanded Forest of Laughs, The (Xin Xiaolin guangji) (Wu Jianren), 19–20, 206n2
New Fiction (Xin xiaoshuo), 1, 19–20, 216n23, 216n30
New Forest of Laughs (Xin Xiaolin) (Xu Zhuodai), 29, 179, 244n30
New Funny Stories (Huaji xinyu), 35f, 175
New History of Laughter, A (Xin xiaoshi) (Wu Jianren), 1, 3, 8, 16
New History of Laughter, A (Xin xiaoshi) (Xu Zhuodai), 29, 179
New Investiture of the Gods (Xin fengshen zhuan) (Wu Jianren), 109–10, 242n17
New Jokes (Xin xiaohua) (Hu Jichen), 188
New Jokes about Men and Women (Nannü xin xiaohua) (Lin Buqing and Qian Xiangsi), 35f, 36–37, 176, 213n93
New Laughs (of the Republic) ((Gongheguo) Xin haha xiao) (Li Jiezhai), 170
New Laughs of the Republic (Minguo xin haha xiao) (Li Jiezhai), 170
New Literature *(xin wenxue)*, 84, 91, 93, 102, 130

New Story of the Stone (Xin Shitouji) (Wu Jianren), 47–49, 217n33. See also *Dream of the Red Chamber*
new woman, 120, 227n126
New Women (Xin nüxing) (Cai Chusheng), 75
New World (Xin shijie) amusement hall, 63–65, 223n89
"New-Year's Sacrifice" (Lu Xun), 3
Nicholas Nickleby (Charles Dickens), 110
Novaj Tempoj, La (Xin shiji), 99–100
novelistic mash-ups, 219n51

Ocean of Laughs (Xiao hai) (Zhang Jizu), 191
"Ode to 'a Verbal Spat'" (Lu Xun), 238n110
Officialdom Unmasked (Guanchang xianxing ji) (Li Boyuan), 26, 130; English translation of, 210n55
Old Society, 7
Old Tales Retold (Gushi xinbian) (Lu Xun), 74, 131
Oon Guan Neng. *See* Wen Yüan-ning
One Thousand Jokes (Qian xiao ji) (Yugong), 30, 178
"On Humor" ("Lun youmo"): by Lin Yutang, 137, 151–52; by Ramón Gómez de la Serna, 137
"On Laughter" ("Shuo xiao") (Qian Zhongshu), 155, 260n108
"Opening Day Advertisement" (Xu Zhuodai), 119–20, 124
operational aesthetic, 48–49, 117, 226n117
"Opium Addict as Master of the Sciences, The," 53
Oppression (Yapo) (Ding Xilin), 135, 253n15

Pai zhang ji (Applause!) (Zhuoyin caotang), 182
palindromic poems, 75–77, 77f, 227n131
Panorama of Humorous Prose (Xiewen daguan) (Aofeng laoren and Zhen Xiage), 174
Panorama of Jokes (Xiaohua daguan), 182
Panorama of Jokes (Xiaohua daguan) (Wu Gechang), 181
Panorama of Play (Youxi daguan), 40
Pan Youlong, 180
paratexts, 90–91, 231n49, 232n51
parody: definition of, 219n52; by serial parodists, 51–54
Passerby. *See* Guoluren
Pastime, The (Youxi zazhi). See *Playful Magazine*
"Peace and Quiet" (Feng Menglong), 21
Pengfu ji (Side-Splitters) (Guo Yaochen), 174

Pengfu tan (Side-Splitting Chats) (Hu Jichen), 29, 171
pen names, 3, 20, 42, 44–45, 50, 53, 90, 94, 135, 201n1, 202n7, 205n47, 206n2, 208n30, 224n101, 232n50, 237n89, 239n116; of Xu Zhuodai, 111, 244n32, 248n66, 251n97; of Zhou Shuren (Lu Xun), 74, 80, 83, 234n72
People's Daily (Renmin ribao), 156–57
"People's Humor, The," 156–57
petty urbanites *(xiao shimin)*, 107, 241n7
Philosophy of Old Zhang, The (Lao Zhang de zhexue) (Lao She), 135
photography: dress-up, 67–68, 225n114, 264n23; playful, 67–73, 69f, 70f, 71f, 72f, 224n97, 224n102, 224nn105–7, 225nn111–14, 264n23; self-beseeching *(qiuji tu)*, 70–73, 71f, 72f; split-self *(erwo tu, fenshen xiang)*, 68–73, 69f, 70f, 71f, 225n112, 225n114
pictorial supplements, 54
Pidgin Warrior, The (Yangjingbang qixia) (Zhang Tianyi), 74, 226n121
"Pig Tells of Nature's Law, A" (Wu Jianren), 17
Ping Jinya, 250n85
plagiarism, 22, 30, 124–28, 163, 225n114, 249n84, 250n85, 250n87, 264n27; and creativity, 126, 128; and spurious attribution of jokes, 16, 18, 125, 163, 207n14
"Plagiarist in Western Dress" (Xu Zhuodai), 126–27
Play (Youxi bao), 42, 207n19, 215n10, 215nn14–15
play: in cartoons, 54–61, 55f, 57f, 58f, 60f, 61f, 62f, 63f; as civilizing force, 73–77, 76f, 77f; as comic trend, 9–11; defined, 40–41; games as, 59, 61, 62f, 63f, 74–77, 77f, 214n6; ha-ha mirror and, 65–67, 66–67f; leisure amusements and, 49–51, 51f; mockery as, 78; parody and, 41–42, 47, 51–54, 74, 228n6; in photography, 67–73, 69f, 70f, 71f, 72f, 224n97, 224n102, 224nn105–7, 225nn111–14, 264n23; political agendas of, 44–49, 74; in Shanghai, 41–44, 49, 64, 222n81; in tabloids, 41–44, 43f, 52; venues, 63–65; Western influences on, 42–44, 43f, 57. See also *youxi*
playful pics *(youxi zhao)*, 68, 69f
Playful Magazine (Youxi zazhi), 52, 219n50. See also *Free Magazine*
Playful Writings (Youxi wenzhang) (Li Dingyi), 187, 192
Playthings (Xiao wanyi) (Sun Yu), 75
playthings *(wanyi)*, 40
play venues *(youxichang)*. *See* amusement halls

Political Jokes about Yuan Shikai (Yuan Xiangcheng zhengzhi xiaohua) (Changqiu Shi), 171
politics: cartoons about, 57, 75, 76f, 227n127; games and, 59, 61, 62f, 63f, 226n125; jokes about, 27–28, 27f; mockery and, 78–80
Pope, Alexander, 44
Po ti lu. See Laughing Through Tears
practical jokes, 12, 124–26, 128–30
Priceless Laughs (Qianjin yixiao lu), 176
"Promoted," 19–20
pseudonyms, 78, 90, 92, 99, 203n19, 213n93, 220n57, 232nn50–54, 238n110
publishing boom, 10, 107, 241n7
Puck, or the Shanghai Charivari, 31–32, 42–43
Punch, 13, 31, 212n67, 212n75
Puyi, Aisin-Gioro "Henry," 71, 136, 146
Pu Zhishui, 239n117

Q&A with the Folks (Jia lao'er wenda) (Jia Lao'er), 190
Qian Decang, 185
Qian Huafo, 139, 139f
Qianjin yixiao lu (Priceless Laughs), 176
Qianqi baiguai modeng da xiaohua. See Absolutely Bizarre and Hilarious Modern Jokes
Qian Suoqiao, 257n54, 262n120
Qian Xiangsi, 35f, 36–37, 176, 213n93
Qian xiao ji (One Thousand Jokes) (Yugong), 30, 178
Qian Xuantong, 92–94, 101, 130, 234n68, 237n92
Qian Zhongshu, 2, 154–56, 202n14, 260n108
Qiaopi hua. See Wisecracks
Qing bai lei chao. See Assorted Collection of Unofficial Sources on the Qing
Qingdai mingren xiaoshi daguan. See Compendium of Funny Stories about Celebrities of the Qing Dynasty
Qingdu sanke, 34, 184
Qinshi shanren, 29, 174
qiuji tu (self-beseeching photo), 70–73, 71f, 72f
Qiu Suwen (fictional character), 106–7, 120, 124, 160
Quan Zenggu. *See* Chuan, T. K.
Qunxueshe tushu faxingsuo, 170
quwei (taste), 109; multiple connotations of, 242n16

rage comics *(baozou manhua)*, 163
Rattle, The, 42–44, 43f

Records of the Grand Historian (Shiji) (Sima Qian), 8, 20, 109
Recreation World, The (Youxi shijie), 75, 226n124
Relieving Boredom and Dispelling Worry (Jiemen xiaochou lu) (Huaji shanren), 188, 258n79
Renjian shi (Chinese Humanist Monthly). See *Chinese Humanist Monthly*
Renjian shi (This Human World), 147, 263n20
Renren xiao (Everyone Laughs) (Zhao Tiaokuang), 178
Republican period: banquet allegory of, 49–50, 51f; jokes in, 28–38, 35f, 36f, 37f; openness of, 9–11
reversal farce, 115, 245n44
ridicule. *See* mockery
Ridicule Press, The (Xiaobao sanrikan), 82, 83f, 100
Roberts, Claire, 225n109
Roy, David Tod, 205n47
Russo-Japanese War, 50, 59

Sanmen zhuren, 182
Saoye shanfang. *See* Mountain Lodge of Swept Leaves, The
satire *(fengci)*, 29, 67, 81, 130, 152, 160; Lu Xun's reputation and, 84, 160; Mao Zedong's endorsement of, 159–61; *maren* (mockery) and, 84; *youmo* (humor) and, 151
Sayings of Jesters (You yu lu) (Wang Guowei), 33, 168
Scarlet Magazine, The (Hong zazhi), 128–29, 129f
Scholars, The (Rulin waishi) (Wu Jingzi), 20–21, 84
Science of Shadowplay, The (Yingxi xue) (Xu Zhuodai), 117, 226n116, 247n54
Scoffing Scholar of Lanling (Lanling xiaoxiaosheng), 14, 205n47
scorn, 79–80, 83, 103–4
Second Sino-Japanese War. *See* Anti-Japanese War
"Secret of Being a Joker, The" (Lu Xun), 38–39
Secret Vast Treasury of Comic Writing (Miben Huaji wenfu daguan) (Zou Diguang), 176
Selected Comical Stories from the Imperial Period (Lidai huaji gushi xuanji) (Fang Cheng), 188
Selected Jokes from the Bitter Tea Studio (Kucha'an xiaohua xuan) (Zhou Zuoren), 33–34, 148, 184, 213n86

Selection of Instant Laughs, A (Jingxuan yijian haha xiao), 181
self-beseeching photo *(qiuji tu)*, 70–73, 71f, 72f
serial parodists, 51–54
Serna, Ramón Gómez de la, 137, 254n26
sex: 149; in *Which Classic?*, 96–97; jokes, 19–21, 30, 103, 116, 150, 207n18, 208n22; public discourse about, 97, 236nn86–88
Sex Histories (Xing shi) (Zhang Jingsheng), 97, 236nn86–87
Shakespeare, William, 3–4, 112, 137, 154; *King Lear*, 239n116; *The Merchant of Venice*, 256n47
Shanghai: as center of joke writing, 28; farce in, 7, 107, 112, 128, 130–31; Funny, 107–8, 130–31; play in, 41–44, 49, 63, 222n81
Shanghainese farce *(huaji xi)*, 7, 65, 112–17, 131, 245nn36–37, 245n39. *See also huaji*; Xu Zhuodai; Yang Huasheng
Shanghai's World of Swindlers (Shanghai zhi pianshu shijie) (Yunjian diangong), 128
Shao Xunmei. *See* Zau, Sinmay
Shaw, George Bernard, 32, 81, 125, 132, 134, 137, 259n92
Shehui yuebao. *See Social News Monthly*
Shen Congwen, 74
Shen Ganruo, 3, 29, 171, 211n63
Shenzhou ribao. *See National Herald, The*
Shibao. *See Eastern Times*
Shiji. *See Records of the Grand Historian*
Shi Jiqun, 126–27, 244n30
Shishuo xinyu. *See New Account of Tales of the World, A*
Shitou ji. *See Dream of the Red Chamber*
shixiao (breaking into laughter): involuntary nature of, 7; irreverence and, 9–15; loss of laughter in history and, 4–9; multiple meanings of, 4–5
Shixie xinji (Anthology of New Humor) (Moyin zhuren), 168, 206n3
Shixing xiaohua (Fashionable Jokes) (Chen Meigong), 208n32
Shooting the Breeze (Xiasan huasi) (Dong Jianzhi), 177
Shun Pao (Shenbao), 8, 10, 54, 205n33. *See also* "Free Talk"; Shun Pao Publishing House
Shun Pao Publishing House (Shenbaoguan), 89, 231n46
Shu Qingchun. *See* Lao She
Side-Splitters (Pengfu ji) (Guo Yaochen), 174

Side-Splitting Chats (Pengfu tan) (Hu Jichen), 29, 171
Sima Zhen, 241n11
Simon, Richard Keller, 155
Sinographic puzzles, 5, 6f, 59, 61f. *See also* funny words
Sino-Japanese War, 18
Sin Wan Pao (Xinwen bao), 56
smile: laughter and, 4–5, 202n14; understanding, 151. *See also* laughter; *xiao*
Smile-Raisers (Jie ren yi) (Qian Decang), 185
Smile-Raisers (Jie yan) (Zhonghua yingwen zhoubao she), 184
"Smooth Path to the Peak of Officialdom" (Wu Jianren), 24
Social News Monthly (Shehui yuebao), 104, 240n124
Sohigian, Diran John, 152
"Source of New- and Old-Style People's Thinking, The" (Ma Xingchi), 56, 57f
split-self image *(erwo tu, fenshen xiang)*, 68–73, 69f, 70f, 71f, 72f, 225n112, 225n114
Stage Sisters (Wutai jiemei) (Xie Jin), 265n34
stand-up comedy. See *xiangsheng*
Stories from Abroad (Yuwai xiaoshuo ji) (Lu Xun and Zhou Zuoren), 128
storytelling, jokes in, 86
Strange Events Eyewitnessed over Twenty Years (Ershi nian mudu zhi guai xianzhuang) (Wu Jianren), 24–28, 130, 210n49; English translation of, 210n58
Sun Fuyuan, 74, 213n86
Sun Yat-sen, 80
Sun Yu, 75
Su Qing, 159, 262n4
Su Shi, 5, 203n15
Su Wen, 260n95

tabloids *(xiaobao)*: new wave of, 10; play in, 41–44, 43f, 52
Taicang Tang Zhenru, 183
Taiping Traveler (Taiping keren), 90, 232n52
Tao Qian (Tao Yuanming), 147
taste *(quwei)*, 109, 242n16
Teahouse (Chaguan) (Lao She), 161
tears: "debt of tears" in *Dream of the Red Chamber*, 2, 202n6; laughter and, 1–4; literary criticism and, 164–65; obligatory, 164
This Human World (Renjian shi), 147, 263n20
Thornber, Karen, 202n10
Threads of Discourse (Yusi), 74, 81–82, 93–97, 133

Three Thousand Jokes (Xiaohua sanqian) (Xu Zhuodai), 29, 111, 189
Tiaoxiao lu. See *Laugh-Getters*
Tibet, 49–50, 218n42
Tong Ailou, 219n50
Toulouse-Lautrec, Henri de, 70f
tragedy, 3, 33; history and, 164, 265n34; laughter and, 5; market for, 109, 160. *See also* tears; trauma
trauma, 3–4, 202n10
Travels of Lao Can, The (Lao Can youji) (Liu E), 1, 3, 54, 56, 163, 201n2, 220n64
Treasury of Laughs (Xiaofu) (Feng Menglong), 21, 209n34, 212n72
tricksters, 124, 128, 130–31, 161, 249n75. *See also* hoaxes; practical jokes
True Expanded Forest of Laughs, The (Zhenzheng Xiaolin guangji), 181
True Expanded Forest of Laughs, The (Zhenzheng Xiaolin guangji) (Youxi zhuren), 168, 207n19. See also *Expanded Forest of Laughs*.
True Record, The (Zhenxiang huabao), 56, 57f, 220n65
"True Story of Ah Q, The" ("Ah Q zhengzhuan") (Lu Xun), 79–81, 84, 103, 107, 131, 228nn5–6, 229n22, 240n4
Twain, Mark, 128, 156, 189, 249n83
"Two Couples" (Xu Zhuodai), 115–16, 131
Two Mas, The (Er Ma) (Lao She), 135–36

Unofficial Story of Li Ah Mao, The (Li Amao waizhuan) (Xu Zhuodai), 122–24, 246n49, 248n69

vernacular Chinese *(baihua)*, 91–92
visual wordplay, 5, 11, 57, 59

Wang, David Der-wei, 3, 48, 85–86, 88, 202n10, 265n35
Wang, Juan, 41
Wang Anshi, 5, 203n15
Wang Ban, 3
Wang Guowei, 33, 74, 109, 168, 226n119, 242n13
Wang Liqi, 22, 209n41
Wang Zhongxian, 117, 244n35
wanyi (playthings), 40. *See also* play; *youxi*
Warehouse of Jokes (Xiaohua ku) (Jieyisheng), 190
War of Resistance Against Japan. See Anti-Japanese War
wars of words *(bizhan)*, 82

Wasp, A (Yizhi mafeng) (Ding Xilin), 134; English translation of, 253n14
Way and Its Virtue, The (Dao De Jing), 39, 87, 230n32
"Weaving the Cabinet," 57, 58f
Wei Shaochang, 243n21
Wei Yi, 110, 242n17
Welcome Danger (Harold Lloyd), 150
wenming xi (civilized play), 73–74
Wenyuan huaji tan (Funny Chats from the Garden of Literature) (Yunjian diangong), 172
Wen Yüan-ning (Oon Guan Neng), 144–46, 256n45, 257n52
Western influences: on Chinese cartooning, 57; on Chinese laughter, 12–13; on humor in modern China, 133–36, 150, 155; on global circulation of jokes, 31–33; on late Qing tabloids, 42–44, 43f
What Confucius Didn't Talk About (Zi bu yu) (Yuan Mei), 88, 147, 231n41
Which Classic? (He Dian) (Zhang Nanzhuang): advertisements, 89, 93–95; commentaries, 233n56; devils and ghosts in, 11, 87–89, 230n39; Liu Fu's censoring of, 96–97; Mao Zedong requesting, 160; mockery and, 11, 84–97, 85f, 100–105, 234n72, 235n76, 236n81, 239n117; paratexts, 90–91; reception in the Republican era of, 91–97; sex in, 96–97; Wu Zhihui and, 97–99, 98f, 101–3, 238n107, 238n115, 239n120
White, E. B., 4, 7, 165
White-Haired Girl, The (Baimao nü) (Wang Bin and Shui Hua), 160
"Whore Revealed, The" (Wu Zhihui), 99
"Why John Wang Ordered His First Pair of Glasses," 209n46
Wisecracks (Qiaopi hua) (Wu Jianren), 16–17, 168, 206n3
Wofoshanren's Funny Chats (Wofoshanren Huaji tan) (Wu Jianren), 173
women: as humorists, 159–60, 262nn4–5; laughter and, 5, 120, 121f, 247n62, 248nn63–64; new, 120, 227n126
"Women's Playthings" (Xu Zhuodai), 106–7, 120–22, 124, 160
Woo, Tsin-Hang. See Wu Zhihui
World of Jokes (Xiaohua shijie) (Guohua shuju bianjisuo), 174
World of Laughs, vol. 1 (Xiao shijie chubian) (Shaoxing Xiao shijie bianjibu), 172

World of Play (Youxi shijie), 42
Worth a Laugh (Kefa yixiao) (Qinshi shanren), 29, 174
Wu dialect, 88, 95, 235n76
Wu Gechang, 181
Wu Gehan, 188
Wu Jianren, 211n62, 220n58; jokes and, 16–28, 32, 38, 81, 109, 125, 201n1, 206nn2–3, 207n20, 210n49, 211n60; productivity of, 207n15
Wu Jianren, works of: "Calf and Foal," 17; "Enjoying the Yellow Jacket," 17; "For Rent," 16; *Funny Chats, with New-Style Punctuation (Xinshi biaodian Huaji tan)*, 109, 180, 206n2; *A History of Pain (Tong shi)*, 1; *The New Expanded Forest of Laughs (Xin Xiaolin guangji)*, 19–20, 206n2; *A New History of Laughter (Xin Xiao shi)*, 1, 3, 8, 16; *New Investiture of the Gods (Xin Fengshen zhuan)*, 109–10, 242n17; *New Story of the Stone (Xin Shitou ji)*, 47–49, 217n33; "A Pig Tells of Nature's Law," 17; "Smooth Path to the Peak of Officialdom," 24; *Strange Events Eyewitnessed over Twenty Years (Ershi nian mudu zhi guai xianzhuang)*, 24–28, 131; *Wisecracks (Qiaopi hua)*, 16–17, 168, 206n3; *Wofoshanren's Funny Chats (Wofoshanren Huaji tan)*, 173
Wu Jingheng. See Wu Zhihui
Wutai jiemei. See *Stage Sisters*
Wu Woyao. See Wu Jianren
Wu Youru, 220n61
Wu Zhihui, 237nn92–93; "Chinese Swine and Sons of Bitches" by, 78, 99; cursing by, 97–101, 237nn94–100; "Devil Farts" by, 100; reputation as a "renowned reviler," 99; *Which Classic?* and, 97–99, 98f, 101–3, 238n107, 238n115, 239n120; "The Whore Revealed" by, 99

Xiandai. See *Les Contemporains*
xiangsheng (face and voice), 7, 36, 112, 161, 263n13
xiao: and death, 165; etymology and multiple meanings of, 4–5, 6f, 202n14, 203nn15–16; and mockery, 80, 104. See also *gaoxiao*; jokes; laughter; mockery; smile; *xiaoma*
xiaobao. See tabloids
Xiaobao sanrikan. See *Ridicule Press, The*
Xiao Chan lu (Mocking Zen Buddhism) (Pan Youlong), 180
Xiao ci du (Bust a Gut in Laughter) (Sanmen zhuren), 182

INDEX

Xiao Dao lun. See *Mocking the Dao*
Xiao hai (Ocean of Laughs) (Zhang Jizu), 191
xiaohua. See jokes
Xiaohua (Jokes) (Li Jinhui and Lu Yiyan), 180
Xiaohua (Jokes) (Mark Twain), 189
Xiaohua daguan (Panorama of Jokes), 182
Xiaohua daguan (Panorama of Jokes) (Wu Gechang), 181
Xiaohua - disan ce (Jokes, vol. 3) (Ji Zhizhong and Xu Banmei), 189
Xiaohua ku. See *Warehouse of Jokes*
Xiaohua qiguan (Jokes and Bizarre Sights) (Li Dingyi), 28–29, 182
Xiaohua qitan (Jokes and Remarkable Stories), 169
Xiaohua qitan (Jokes and Remarkable Stories) (Yiqingshizhu), 190
Xiaohua sanqian (Three Thousand Jokes) (Xu Zhuodai), 29, 111, 189
Xiaohua shijie (World of Jokes) (Guohua shuju bianjisuo), 174
Xiaohua sizhong (Four Joke Books) (Zhang Xiaochao), 181
Xiaohua xiaohua (Illustrated Jokes) (Xu Zhuodai), 29, 191
xiaohua xiaoshuo. See joke stories
Xiaohua xintan (Jokes and New Stories) (Li Jiezhai), 170
xiaojiang (artisan of laughter), 110–12
Xiaolin guangji (Expanded Forest of Laughs), 19–20, 22, 30, 104, 181, 208n31
Xiaolin guangji (Expanded Forest of Laughs) (Cheng Shijue), 176, 186, 191
Xiaolin shize (Forest of Laughs: Ten Jokes) (Handan Chun), 172
Xiaolin yiqianzhong (Forest of Laughs: One Thousand Jokes) (Taicang Tang Zhenru), 183
Xiao luan chang (Double Over in Laughter) (Sanmen zhuren), 182
xiaoma (laugh to scorn), 79–80, 83, 103–4
xiaopinwen. See little-taste essay
Xiao quan (Fount of Laughter) (Li Xinyan), 30, 188
Xiao shijie chubian. See *World of Laughs, vol. 1*
xiao shimin (petty urbanites), 107, 241n7
xiaosi, 165
Xiao wutai. See *Laughter Stage*
Xiaoxiao lu (Laugh upon Laugh) (Duyiwo tuishi), 34, 186
Xiao zan (In Praise of Jokes) (Qingdu sanke and Lu Huiyin), 34, 184

Xiasan huasi (Shooting the Breeze) (Dong Jianzhi), 177
Xia Zhiqing. See Hsia, C. T.
Xie Jin, 265n34
Xiewenci leizuan (Collection of Humorous Writings, by Genre) (Li Dingyi), 174
Xiewen daguan (Panorama of Humorous Prose) (Aofeng laoren and Zhen Xiage), 174
Xin fengshen zhuan (New Investiture of the Gods) (Wu Jianren), 109–10, 242n17
Xing Han mie Man huaji lu (Funny Stories from the Restoration of the Han and Extermination of the Manchus), 169
xinju (New Drama), 112, 114, 119
Xinshi biaodian Huaji tan (Funny Chats, with New-Style Punctuation) (Wu Jianren), 109, 180, 206n2
Xin shiji (La Novaj Tempoj, Le siècle nouveau), 99–100, 237n94
Xin Shitouji. See *New Story of the Stone*
Xinwen bao. See *Sin Wan Pao*
Xinxian xiaohua dawang (King of Fresh Jokes) (Zou Mengxia), 191
Xinxian xiaohua louzi (Basket of Fresh Jokes), 192
Xinxian xiaohua qitan (Fresh Jokes and Remarkable Stories), 169
Xinxian xiaohua yi da xiang (A Crate of Fresh Jokes) (Jin Zuxin), 190
Xin xiaohua (New Jokes) (Hu Jichen), 188
Xin Xiaolin (New Forest of Laughs) (Xu Zhuodai), 29, 179, 244n30
Xin xiaoshi (A New History of Laughter) (Xu Zhuodai), 29, 179
Xin Zhongguo weilai ji. See *Future of New China, The*
Xiong Xiling, 30
Xi Xutao, 177
Xiyou ji. See *Journey to the West*
X-ray, 27–28, 225n115
Xuanzong (emperor), 5, 6f, 203n16
Xu Banmei. See Xu Zhuodai
Xu Fulin, 244n31. *See also* Xu Zhuodai
Xu Ke, 174
Xu Maoyong, 151
Xu Wenchang, 34, 213n87
Xu Xu, 38, 152, 154, 214n97, 263n16, 263n20
Xu Zhuodai (a.k.a. Xu Banmei, Xu Fulin), 212n74, 243n25; as Artisan of Laughter, 110–12; comedic vision of, 128–31; death of, 161, 263n15; farce and, 106–7, 109, 110–31,

Xu Zhuodai *(continued)*
  113f, 118f, 121f, 244n32, 247nn56–57, 250n89, 251nn92–93, 251n97; film and, 117–18, 118f, 122, 248n67; hoaxes by, 123–24, 126, 128, 160; "Li Ah Mao" created by, 120, 122–24, 128–29, 131, 248n66, 251n97; names of, 111; schools founded by, 110, 243n24; theater and, 112–17, 113f, 118–19, 244n35, 245nn39–40; as Xu Banmei, 189, 225n116, 249n77
Xu Zhuodai (a.k.a. Xu Banmei, Xu Fulin), works of: "The Devil Messenger," 114–15, 246n45; "Exposing Plagiarism," 127; "A Father's Duty," 245n44; "The Fiction Material Wholesaler," 124–26; *Illustrated Jokes (Xiaohua xiaohua)*, 29, 191; *Laugh-Getters (Tiaoxiao lu)*, 29, 179, 244n30; "Newest Prohibition and Exorcism Methods," 128; *New Forest of Laughs (Xin Xiaolin)*, 29, 179, 244n30; *A New History of Laughter (Xin xiaoshi)*, 29, 179; "Opening Day Advertisement," 119–20, 124; "Plagiarist in Western Dress," 126–27; *The Science of Shadowplay (Yingxi xue)*, 117, 226n116, 247n54; *Three Thousand Jokes (Xiaohua sanqian)*, 29, 111, 189; "Two Couples," 115–16, 131; *The Unofficial Story of Li Ah Mao (Li Amao waizhuan)*, 122–24, 246n49, 248n69; "Woman's Playthings," 106–7, 120–22, 124, 159–60

Yan Fusun, 177, 211n62, 226n124
Yang Huasheng, 65, 222n82, 241n10
Yang Jiang, 159, 262n5
Yang Ruquan, 184
Yanyun jushi, 168
Year of Humor *(youmo nian)*, 34, 132, 157, 165, 252n2
Yeh, Catherine Vance, 41–42
Yeh, Wen-hsin, 228n7
Ye Qianyu, 36f, 37f, 37–38, 213n95, 221n67
Yikan jiuxiao (Instant Laughs) (Cui Bingleng), 183
Yingxi xue. See *Science of Shadowplay, The*
Yiqingshizhu, 190
youmo: in *The Analects Fortnightly (Lunyu banyuekan)*, 12, 104, 132–33, 136–42, 139f, 140f, 141f, 147–48, 151–57, 260n101; as comic trend, 9–10, 12; communist use of term, 156–58; criticism of, 152–55; defined, 132–33, 137, 150–52, 253n11, 254n24; Ding Xilin and, 253n15, dominance of term, 15, 157–58; *huaji* and, 107, 131, 151, 158, 165; humorists before, 133–37; Lin Yutang and, 12–13, 105, 132–34, 136–37, 142–44, 146–47, 149–54, 156–57, 159, 161–62, 253n11, 255n33, 259n79; Lu Xun and, 148–49, 151, 153, 157, 258n77; Mao Zedong and, 160–61; other transliterations of "humor" and, 137, 149; opposition to, 148; and rebranding of literary humor, 148, 151. See also humor
Youmo biji (Humorous Jottings) (Hu Shanyuan), 148, 187
youmo dashi. See Master of Humor
youmo nian. See Year of Humor
Youmo xiaohua (Humorous Jokes) (Dong Zhenhua), 187
Youmo xiaohua ji (Humorous Jokes) (Guo Boliang), 190
youle chang (amusement venues). See amusement halls
youxi. connotations and definitions of term, 41; and literature, 41, 52, 74–75, 226n125; as symbol of a culture of amusement, 40; term used in cinema and photography, 40, 68, 69f, 73, 75, 227n128; term used in illustration, 6f, 54, 55f, See also amusement halls; play
youxichang (play venues). See amusement halls
Youxi daguan (Panorama of Play), 40
Youxi shijie (The Recreation World), 75, 226n124
Youxi wenxue congkan (Compendium of Playful Literature) (Cao Xiujun), 183
Youxi wenzhang (Playful Writings) (Li Dingyi), 187, 192
Youxi zazhi. See *Playful Magazine*
youxi zhao (playful pics), 68, 69f
Youxi zhuren. See Li Boyuan; Master of Play
youyi chang (performing arts venues). See amusement halls
You yu lu. See *Sayings of Jesters*
Yuan Mei, 88, 231n41. See also *What Confucius Didn't Talk About*
Yuan Muzhi, 153
Yuan Shikai, 29, 56–59, 58f, 217n32, 220n62, 221n69
Yuan Xiangcheng zhengzhi xiaohua (Political Jokes about Yuan Shikai) (Changqiu Shi), 171
Yuan Zhenying, 97, 101–2
Yueyue xiaoshuo. See *All-Story Monthly, The*
Yugong (Mr. Foolish), 30, 178
Yu Hua, 164, 265n33

Yu Ling, 250n85
Yunjian diangong (Mr. Tottering in the Clouds). *See* Lei Jin
Yusi. See *Threads of Discourse*

Zau, Sinmay (Shao Xunmei), 130, 133, 151, 153, 156, 250n91, 252n7
Zeitlin, Judith, 8, 88, 230n35
Zengguang gujin xiaolin xinya yiqianzhong (Enlarged and Expanded Forest of Laughs, Featuring One Thousand New Elegant Jokes from Collections Ancient and Modern) (Chenhai Chixiaosheng), 29, 178
Zeng Pu, 130, 250n91
Zhang Dai, 18
Zhang Henshui, 2
Zhang Jian, 245n36
Zhang Jingsheng, 97, 236nn86–87. See also *Sex Histories*
Zhang Jizu, 191
Zhang Kebiao, 234n71, 239n120, 252n7
Zhang Mojun, 212n69
Zhang Nanzhuang, 102–3, 236n85. See also *Which Classic?*
Zhang Tianyi, 7–8, 74, 81, 226n121, 239n122, 254n19
Zhang Xiaochao, 181
Zhang Yingjin, 247n62
Zhang Zhen, 117, 225n112
Zhao Shuicheng, 184
Zhao Tiaokuang, 29, 111, 177–78, 180, 212n65
Zhao Zhongxiong, 180
Zheng Tianjian, 102
Zheng Zhenduo, 2

Zhen Xiage, 174
Zhenzheng Xiaolin guangji (The True Expanded Forest of Laughs), 181
Zhenzheng Xiaolin guangji (The True Expanded Forest of Laughs) (Youxi zhuren), 168, 207n19. See also *Expanded Forest of Laughs*
Zhongguo gongchandang. *See* Chinese Communist Party
Zhongguo xin wenxue daxi. See *Compendium of China's New Literature*
Zhonghua yingwen zhoubao she, 184
Zhou Shoujuan, 75, 218n47, 226n124, 247n59, 249n77
Zhou Shuren. *See* Lu Xun
Zhou Yaoguang, 224n102
Zhou Zuoren, 28, 184, 213n87, 238n105, 242n16, 250n85; humor and, 146, 148, 151, 154; on Mencius, 148, 257n59; mockery and, 81–82, 95, 100; *Selected Jokes from the Bitter Tea Studio (Kucha'an xiaohua xuan)* by, 33–34, 148, 184, 213n86; *Stories from Abroad (Yuwai xiaoshuo ji)* cotranslated by, 128
Zhuangzi, 147
Zhuoyin caotang, 182
Zhu Zhanji. *See* Xuanzong
Zhu Ziqing, 5, 203nn19–20
Zi bu yu. See *What Confucius Didn't Talk About*
Zijian nanzi. See *Confucius Saw Nancy*
"Ziyou tan." *See* "Free Talk"
Zou Diguang, 176
Zou Mengxia, 191
Zuixin huaji zazhi. See *Newest Humor Assortment*

STUDIES OF THE WEATHERHEAD EAST ASIAN INSTITUTE

Columbia University

Selected Titles
(Complete list at: http://www.columbia.edu/cu/weai/weatherhead-studies.html)

Chinese Law in Imperial Eyes: Sovereignty, Justice, and Transcultural Politics, by Li Chen. Columbia University Press, 2015.

The Age of Irreverence: A New History of Laughter in China, by Christopher Rea. University of California Press, 2015

The Nature of Knowledge and the Knowledge of Nature in Early Modern Japan, by Federico Marcon. University of Chicago Press, 2015

The Fascist Effect: Japan and Italy, 1915–1952, by Reto Hoffman. Cornell University Press, 2015

The International Minimum: Creativity and Contradiction in Japan's Global Engagement, 1933–1964, by Jessamyn R. Abel. University of Hawai'i Press, 2015

Empires of Coal: Fueling China's Entry into the Modern World Order, 1860–1920, by Shellen Xiao Wu. Stanford University Press, 2015

Casualties of History: Wounded Japanese Servicemen and the Second World War, by Lee K. Pennington. Cornell University Press, 2015

City of Virtues: Nanjing in an Age of Utopian Visions, by Chuck Wooldridge. University of Washington Press, 2015

The Proletarian Wave: Literature and Leftist Culture in Colonial Korea, 1910–1945, by Sunyoung Park. Harvard University Asia Center, 2015.

Neither Donkey Nor Horse: Medicine in the Struggle Over China's Modernity, by Sean Hsiang-lin Lei. University of Chicago Press, 2014.

When the Future Disappears: The Modernist Imagination in Late Colonial Korea, by Janet Poole. Columbia University Press, 2014.

Bad Water: Nature, Pollution, & Politics in Japan, 1870–1950, by Robert Stolz. Duke University Press, 2014.

Rise of a Japanese Chinatown: Yokohama, 1894–1972, by Eric C. Han. Harvard University Asia Center, 2014.

Beyond the Metropolis: Second Cities and Modern Life in Interwar Japan, by Louise Young. University of California Press, 2013.

From Cultures of War to Cultures of Peace: War and Peace Museums in Japan, China, and South Korea, by Takashi Yoshida. MerwinAsia, 2013.

Imperial Eclipse: Japan's Strategic Thinking about Continental Asia before August 1945, by Yukiko Koshiro. Cornell University Press, 2013.

The Nature of the Beasts: Empire and Exhibition at the Tokyo Imperial Zoo, by Ian J. Miller. University of California Press, 2013.

Public Properties: Museums in Imperial Japan, by Noriko Aso. Duke University Press, 2013.

Reconstructing Bodies: Biomedicine, Health, and Nation-Building in South Korea Since 1945, by John P. DiMoia. Stanford University Press, 2013.

Taming Tibet: Landscape Transformation and the Gift of Chinese Development, by Emily T. Yeh. Cornell University Press, 2013.

Tyranny of the Weak: North Korea and the World, 1950–1992, by Charles K. Armstrong. Cornell University Press, 2013.

The Art of Censorship in Postwar Japan, by Kirsten Cather. University of Hawai'i Press, 2012.

Asia for the Asians: China in the Lives of Five Meiji Japanese, by Paula Harrell. MerwinAsia, 2012.

Lin Shu, Inc.: Translation and the Making of Modern Chinese Culture, by Michael Gibbs Hill. Oxford University Press, 2012.

Occupying Power: Sex Workers and Servicemen in Postwar Japan, by Sarah Kovner. Stanford University Press, 2012.

Redacted: The Archives of Censorship in Postwar Japan, by Jonathan E. Abel. University of California Press, 2012.

Empire of Dogs: Canines, Japan, and the Making of the Modern Imperial World, by Aaron Herald Skabelund. Cornell University Press, 2011.

Planning for Empire: Reform Bureaucrats and the Japanese Wartime State, by Janis Mimura. Cornell University Press, 2011.

Realms of Literacy: Early Japan and the History of Writing, by David Lurie. Harvard University Asia Center, 2011.

Russo-Japanese Relations, 1905–17: From Enemies to Allies, by Peter Berton. Routledge, 2011.

Behind the Gate: Inventing Students in Beijing, by Fabio Lanza. Columbia University Press, 2010.

Imperial Japan at Its Zenith: The Wartime Celebration of the Empire's 2,600th Anniversary, by Kenneth J. Ruoff. Cornell University Press, 2010.

www.ingramcontent.com/pod-product-compliance
Lightning Source LLC
Chambersburg PA
CBHW030520230426
43665CB00010B/691